How to Cook *Everything*®
the basics

How to Cook *Everything*®
the basics
All You Need to Make Great Food
—WITH 1,000 PHOTOS—

Mark Bittman

PHOTOGRAPHY BY ROMULO YANES

Houghton Mifflin Harcourt
Boston · New York

This book is printed on acid-free paper. ♾

Copyright © 2012 Double B Publishing Inc. All rights reserved.

Photography copyright © 2012 Houghton Mifflin Harcourt Publishing Company

Published by Houghton Mifflin Harcourt Publishing Company

Published simultaneously in Canada

Photography by Romulo Yanes. Food styling by Susan Sugarman.

For information about permission to reproduce selections from this book,
write to trade.permissions@hmhco.com or to Permissions, Houghton Mifflin Harcourt
Publishing Company, 3 Park Avenue, 19th Floor, New York, New York 10016.

www.hmhco.com

Library of Congress Cataloging-in-Publication Data

Bittman, Mark.
    How to cook everything. The basics : all you need to make great food /
Mark Bittman.
        p. cm.
    Includes index.
        ISBN 978-0-470-52806-8 (hardback); 978-1-118-19852-0 (ebk);
    978-1-118-19920-6 (ebk); 978-1-118-19925-1 (ebk)
    1. Cooking. 2. Cookbooks. I. Title. II. Title: Basics : all you need to make
great food.
    TX714.B57316 2012
    641.5--dc23
                                2011048881
Printed in China

SCP 20 19 18 17 16 15 14

4500824202

With love, for Murray, Gert, Kate, and Emma

Acknowledgments

Most books are serious undertakings; this one was a mega-project, with many people working diligently for months or even years.

First and foremost is Kerri Conan, my longtime associate, who nearly killed herself on this, quite possibly the toughest and most rewarding project we've ever done together. Without her, there is no book.

The photos are amazing, no? Let's thank Romulo Yanes, who really may have changed the course of food photography with this one; Susan Sugarman, food stylist extraordinaire; and Kerri, who, along with those two, Adam Kowit, and Kelly Doe, kind of ran that show. Also Critter Knutsen; Adam McClure; Patrick Marinello; Greg Bogin; Rhoda Boon; Amy Wilson; Nina Lalli (who I knew when...); and Elizabeth Yoon.

At Wiley, my longtime and beloved publisher, who helped conceive and execute everything you're holding in your hands, there are Adam Kowit, my now-veteran editor, who really went beyond the call here; my old (maybe "long-term" is a better word?) colleagues Natalie Chapman, Linda Ingroia, Todd Fries, and Rob Garber; plus Heather Dabah, Meaghan McDonnell, Jeff Faust, Michael Olivo,

Abby Saul, Amy Zarkos, Brent Savage, Dean Karrel and his pals, Jessica Goodman, Michael Friedberg, and Gypsy "Welcome Back" Lovett. (There are about 200 others whose names I don't know, but I'm grateful to them anyway.) And Chris Benton, whose copy-editing, as usual, gave the manuscript a big boost.

A special shout-out to Sean Santoro and Wendy and Kim Marcus. You all know what you did.

I have lots of great friends and colleagues but want to thank especially Angela Miller, without whom this never would have happened. Also in that category: Doc "Let's Talk" Willoughby, Trish Hall, Chris Kimball, Slammin' Sam Sifton. Of immediate and immeasurable help were the wonderful Young Adults, Laura Virginia Anderson and Daniel Meyer; Suzanne Lenzer; and Meghan "The Rookie" Gourley.

The splendid design and much more are thanks to Kelly L. Doe.

Mark Bittman
NYC, Fall 2011

Contents

Why Cook?

It's too easy to eat without cooking in modern-day America, thanks to drive-through windows, take-out counters, vending machines, microwave meals, and other so-called conveniences. The problem is that no "convenience" food can compare to honest food, real ingredients prepared at home, no matter how simply or quickly you do it. My goal here is to make the case for the numerous and wonderful benefits of cooking: to make you a cook.

Cooking, at its heart, is simple and straightforward. Like most goal-oriented processes, you work through a few basic tasks to get from point A to point B; in cooking, the tasks include things like chopping, measuring, heating, and stirring. You use recipes instead of maps or instruction manuals. As with driving—or almost anything else—your basic skills provide the foundation. As you improve and gain confidence, you'll become more creative. In the meantime, even if you've never picked up a pot or pan in your life, you can—and should!—enjoy some time in the kitchen every day. I'm here to help both novices and experienced cooks do just that.

Why is home cooking so important?

▶ **Cooking is satisfying**. When you combine good ingredients with simple techniques, you create something more delicious than fast food and usually as good as "real" restaurant food. Not only that, you can customize the flavors and textures so that you eat exactly what you like, when you like.

▶ **Cooking saves money**. Once you make a few initial, generally inexpensive investments in basic cooking equipment and pantry ingredients, you can easily make all sorts of meals incredibly inexpensively.

▶ **Cooking produces truly nutritious food**. If you've ever read the small print on the packages of processed foods, you know they're almost always high in unhealthy fats, sugar, sodium, and strange ingredients. The first thing you learn from cooking is that fresh ingredients don't need much help to taste good. And when you take more control of what you eat and minimize the fake stuff, you'll improve your diet and your health.

▶ **Cooking is time well spent**. Here are some examples of what you can make in less than 30 minutes: a big vegetable salad, pasta with homemade tomato sauce and grated cheese, chili with rice, or chicken stir-fry. That's about as long as it takes to order a pizza or Chinese food and wait for it to be delivered, or to go to the nearest drive-through for a burger and fries, or to drive to the grocery store to pick up a frozen meal and then come home and pop it in the microwave. Think about it.

▶ **Cooking is rewarding**. Eating your own food—and sharing it with people you care about—is a crucial human activity. On a practical level, you're providing nourishment and sustenance. And on an emotional level, cooking can become relaxing, comforting, and downright pleasurable, as you pause from an otherwise hectic day and give yourself a chance to focus on something basic and essential and meaningful.

▶ **Cooking leads to family meals**. Family meals stimulate conversation, communication, and love. It's a fact.

Getting Started

Even if you're setting up your first kitchen, I'm guessing that your cupboards aren't entirely bare. You've probably got a few pots, pans, and gadgets, food in your fridge and pantry, maybe even a small appliance or two. Or maybe you already cook regularly and are fully stocked. Whatever your situation, I'll help you take inventory and evaluate what you need to make everyday meal preparation comfortable and enjoyable.

After that comes a visual guide to basic preparation, like rinsing and chopping, and cooking techniques—from boiling water (really) to roasting, braising, and grilling. These will become your go-to sections for quick reference as you start cooking.

There are a couple of different ways to use this book:

You can work straight through it. I've organized it so that both the chapters *and* the recipes and Basics information within them progress from easiest to most challenging. Since each element focuses on a lesson or set of lessons, you'll build knowledge and skills with each dish.

Or you can cherry-pick your way through the book and catch up on lessons by relying on the Learn More feature in the bottom right corner of each recipe. There you'll find cross-references to information taught elsewhere that's relevant to what you're cooking. And whenever you want instructions for a specific technique, just flip to the List of Lessons on page 460, where all the skills appear at a glance.

Setting up Your Pantry

Cooking is especially convenient if you don't have to run to the store every day. Stocking a few key foods in the cupboard and fridge will make it far easier for you to cook when you need to (and therefore more likely that you actually will!). Then when you pick up fresh produce, meat, poultry, or fish, you'll instantly have many options for what to do with it.

With these essentials, you'll be in good shape to cook everything in this book. You can fill your pantry all at once or gradually, so you have the option of making just one or two trips to the store with this list and finishing it off, or, if you're a bit more cautious (or if your kitchen is small), you can buy a few staples every time you hit the supermarket and accumulate staples on a need-to-cook basis.

One note: Often—not always—price reflects quality; good ingredients cost more than lousy ones. But just because something is expensive doesn't mean it's good. I'll tell you when I think it's worth spending extra money for an upgrade.

For the Cupboard

EXTRA VIRGIN OLIVE OIL Every time I refer to *olive oil* in this book, I mean extra virgin. It doesn't have to be expensive, but it should be full flavored. Once opened, it keeps for a month or two at room temperature, longer in the fridge.

VEGETABLE OIL You need a good neutral-flavored oil for frying and for those times you don't want the flavor of olive oil to dominate. My first choice is grapeseed, but other options include sunflower and safflower or even peanut oil (though its flavor is stronger). In general, stay away from the super-refined blends of the major brands. The good stuff—cold-pressed, rather than chemically extracted, is best—lasts only as long as olive oil.

VINEGAR Sherry vinegar is my favorite (and not terribly costly), but it can be hard to find; red and white wine vinegars are good alternatives. (When a recipe calls for *any wine vinegar*, you can use any of these three.) You might also want balsamic vinegar, which is sweet and mild. All of these keep for at least a year. (For more information on oils and vinegars, see page 112.)

SALT AND BLACK PEPPER Kosher salt (also commonly called coarse salt) and whole peppercorns, please. (See What Does *Taste and Adjust the Seasoning* Mean? on page 13.)

RICE AND OTHER GRAINS Invaluable and largely interchangeable. Freeze them if you don't think you'll use them within 6 months. (See Rice Basics, page 196, and Grain Basics, page 206.)

PASTA AND NOODLES The best Italian-style pasta is made in Italy. The best Asian-style noodles are also usually imported. Keep that in mind, and you'll be fine with whatever types you choose. (See Pasta Basics, page 172, and Asian Noodle Basics, page 190.)

BEANS Also known as *legumes*. Dried are cheap and utterly delicious. (See Bean Basics, page 250.) But canned and frozen are too convenient to ignore, so they're listed as options in many recipes. They'll keep for a year or longer.

CANNED TOMATOES Essential for tomato sauce as well as soups, stews, and other dishes. Diced are easier to handle than whole; steer clear of puréed or crushed tomatoes, which can be watery.

SPICES You don't need everything at all times, but you do want some at your fingertips. Blends like chili powder and curry powder are important, as are individual spices like cinnamon, cayenne, cumin, nutmeg, smoked paprika, and crushed red pepper. (See page 12 for more about using these and other seasonings.) Replace them every year or sooner if they lose potency.

Storage Containers

I try to avoid plastic: Not only is it environmentally unfriendly, but there are questions about its safety, especially if it's been heated or used for a while. Glass jars are an ideal alternative. If you're freezing in them, leave at least 1 inch at the top, because liquids expand as they freeze.

ONIONS AND GARLIC Long-lasting and essential to so many recipes. No powders, please.

DRIED HERBS Oregano, thyme, sage, rosemary, and tarragon are decent substitutes for fresh. (Dried parsley, basil, and mint are worthless.) They keep for about 6 months.

SOY SAUCE A must. Make sure it contains soy and wheat as primary ingredients and doesn't include caramel color or artificial flavorings. Keeps indefinitely.

FLOUR, CORNMEAL, BAKING POWDER, AND BAKING SODA Especially if you want to bake. Flour and cornmeal go bad after 3 months or so; store in the freezer for longer keeping. (See Bread-Baking Basics, page 394.)

SUGAR, HONEY, AND MAPLE SYRUP Essential for desserts and occasionally good in savory dishes too. (See pages 42 and 422 for more details.)

NUTS AND SEEDS Add crunch and flavor to salads, noodle dishes, and baked goods. If you don't think you'll use them up within a month or two, store in the freezer, where they'll keep indefinitely.

PEANUT BUTTER Grind your own if you can (the food processor works fine) and definitely avoid anything that contains more than peanuts and salt.

BREAD CRUMBS I urge you to make your own (see the recipe on page 386), but panko will do in a pinch.

COCONUT MILK Indispensable for Indian and Southeast Asian cooking. If you're worried about calories, use the reduced-fat kind.

For the Fridge

BUTTER Buy unsalted. Adds richness to just about anything. Store in the freezer if you don't use it that much.

EGGS For baking and eating scrambled, boiled, fried, and in omelets, frittatas, and fried rice. The basis of some super-fast meals. (See Egg Basics, page 50.)

FRESH HERBS They don't keep long, but they add incomparable flavor to all kinds of dishes. Just keep one or two on hand and store them like flowers—upright in a glass of water, in the fridge if possible.

OLIVES Instant flavor. If you don't think you like them, maybe you haven't found the right kind. There are hundreds, each with a slightly different taste and texture. Kalamata and Niçoise are two common ones to try. But you can always omit them from a recipe.

PARMESAN CHEESE Must be the real deal, from Italy, in a chunk.

TOFU If you're a vegetarian and/or like it. There are lots of types, but the firm regular kind (which should come packed in water and refrigerated) is versatile and works in all the recipes here.

LEMONS AND LIMES For their zest and juice; don't bother with citrus juice in a bottle.

FRESH CHILES Add heat to chili, stir-fries, pasta and noodle dishes, and salsa.

FRESH GINGER Not as widely used as onions and garlic, but still versatile and long-lasting.

CONDIMENTS Ketchup, Dijon-style mustard, mayonnaise, hot sauce, salsa (store-bought is okay, but for some easy recipes, see pages 80–83), and the like. Good for more than smearing on sandwiches.

APPLES, PEARS, ORANGES, GRAPEFRUIT, AND OTHER HARDY FRESH PRODUCE If you've got it, you'll eat it.

STOCK Homemade is best (see the recipes on pages 152–157); canned and packaged are not much better than water. Refrigerate stock for up to 5 days or freeze for up to 3 months.

The Meaning of Shelf Life
Different foods stay fresh longer than others. Raw fish stays fresh in the fridge for a day or two. Many vegetables keep for several days. You can prolong the "shelf life" of raw meat (for example) by freezing. Other ingredients, like fresh vegetables, can really be frozen only if they're cooked first—so why not eat them right away?

How long can you keep something in the freezer? Up to a year, I always say, though it won't be nearly as good as if you ate it within a month. Ditto pantry foods. So why wait? In short, eat what you buy as soon as possible.

All the Tools You Need

Granted, stocking your kitchen with equipment takes more time and money than buying food for the pantry and fridge. But it's a one-shot deal, and you don't need to break the bank or overstuff your cabinets. If you're on a budget, look for equipment at garage sales, thrift stores, flea markets, or online. Also consider visiting restaurant supply retailers, which charge much less than upscale boutiques.

The following lists include *all* of the equipment used in this book. The recipes specify which to use when, so you can develop efficient kitchen skills and minimize dish washing. I'm not including serving pieces in this book: If you're worried about appearances, simply dish up food in the kitchen; otherwise, take pots and pans to the table, as I usually do.

Two general rules about pots and pans: Avoid aluminum, which doesn't heat evenly and makes acidic foods taste and look funny, and make sure they're ovenproof—that is, no plastic handles.

The Absolute Minimum

1 STOCKPOT WITH A LID At least 2 gallons. Mostly for boiling pasta or vegetables. Stainless steel is best here.

2 LARGE POT WITH A LID 1 gallon is fine. For soups and stews; the heavier the better. Enameled cast iron or stainless steel is best.

3 SMALL OR MEDIUM SAUCEPAN WITH A LID 1 to 2 quarts. For salsas, sauces, boiled eggs, and so on.

4 LARGE SKILLET WITH A LID 12 inches. Your go-to pan, for everything from pancakes to stir-fries. Cast iron and stainless steel are my first choices. (You've got to "season" cast iron first: Wash and dry it well, then smear the inside with vegetable oil. Put the pan in a 350°F oven to heat for 1 hour; turn the oven off and let it cool; repeat whenever the pan looks dry.) Buy a second large skillet that's nonstick if you want to

try using less oil than called for in the recipes. (But you're limited in how you can use it since there is some concern about the safety of heating a dry nonstick pan to the smoking point.)

5 MEDIUM SKILLET WITH A LID 8 to 10 inches. Same deal as the big skillet; it's nice to have different kinds, so maybe this is your cast iron or nonstick. You'll use this one mostly for eggs and omelets or for cooking or reheating one or two portions.

6 KNIVES Invest in the best you can afford, preferably forged steel all the way through the handle. You really need only three; see page 8.

7 CUTTING BOARDS Wooden or plastic (the latter can go in the dishwasher; check out the thin, flexible ones, which are super-inexpensive and can be useful). To keep the board from sliding on the counter while you work, put a damp towel underneath it.

8 VEGETABLE PEELER Either vertical or U-shaped, your choice.

9 SMALL, MEDIUM, AND LARGE MIXING BOWLS Stainless steel is good, as is glass. If they nest, all the better.

10 WOODEN SPOONS OF VARIOUS SIZES AND SHAPES They're cheap, so get several. (They're critical if you have nonstick pans, since you can't use metal.)

11 SPATULA Preferably metal, for turning, stirring, and scraping. (You'll need one made from silicone if you've got nonstick cookware.) Start with a wide one and see if you want more.

12 POT HOLDERS Choose good thick thermal ones over silicone kinds, which are hard to use. Kitchen towels, folded several times, also work (they must be dry, or you may burn yourself). Whatever you use, keep it away from flames and heat sources.

13 KITCHEN TOWELS Cotton, please; and change them daily. Good for drying food, your hands, and equipment.

14 LARGE COLANDER Essential for rinsing produce and draining pasta.

15 MEASURING CUPS AND SPOONS One set of dry measuring cups (¼, ⅓, ½, and 1 cup), at least one 2-cup (or bigger) liquid measuring cup, and one set of measuring spoons (¼, ½, and 1 teaspoon, plus 1 tablespoon). Duplicates are convenient but not necessary.

16 TONGS Spring loaded, not the kind that look like scissors. They're crucial for grabbing and turning.

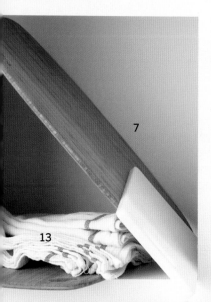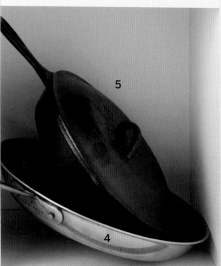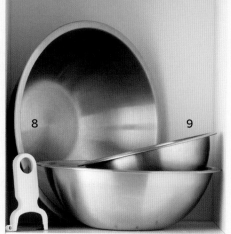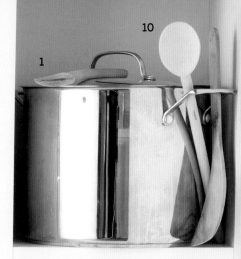

Other Handy Tools

1 MEDIUM WHISK This "balloon" kind is the ideal tool for quick hand beating.

2 LARGE METAL SPOONS For serving, tasting, and some stirring. You can use soupspoons if you'd like; otherwise get a good big one.

3 SLOTTED SPOON Essential for fishing food out of water and oil.

4 LADLE For soup and more.

5 BOX GRATER It should have several panels for different tasks—the larger the holes, the bigger the pieces. The side with fine holes—or a microplane grater, which is sharper—is ideal for Parmesan cheese and citrus rind.

6 KITCHEN TIMER The one on your microwave or oven is fine, of course.

7 STRAINER Any size is fine, though medium and large will be most useful. For draining grains and other fine foods or for straining solids out of liquids like stock.

8 SALAD SPINNER Get the kind that doesn't have holes in the bottom bowl so you can use it for storage as well as cleaning and drying; it keeps lettuce fresh in the fridge for several days.

9 KITCHEN SCISSORS Not just for opening packages. Get a sturdy pair so you can use them for snipping herbs and dried fruit as well as cutting up poultry.

10 QUICK-READ THERMOMETER Inexpensive, useful, and ideal for readings below 200°F; just stick it in and wait for the needle to stop moving. (For deep frying or candy making you'll need a thermometer that goes higher and clips onto a pot—see page 104.)

The 3 Knives You Need

SERRATED KNIFE A must for cutting bread and other baked goods, tomatoes, and melons. Look for at least an 8-inch blade.

CHEF'S KNIFE You'll use this for everything from chopping and mincing vegetables to slicing meat. Go with an 8- or 10-inch blade, depending on the size of your hand and your comfort level. Try to avoid getting a 6-inch blade unless you're quite nervous (or have very small hands); it won't be as versatile as a larger knife.

PARING KNIFE For peeling, trimming, and any precise cutting.

11 BRUSHES It's best to have one for meats and one for everything else. Silicone is nice, but you can save money by buying paintbrushes at a hardware store.

12 PEPPERMILL Even if you cook with ground pepper from a jar (make sure it smells potent), it's nice to have a peppermill on the table.

13 POTATO MASHER You can use a fork and a lot of elbow grease, but I bet that if you own a masher, you'll eat more mashed potatoes. (I prefer the kind with holes over the squiggly kind.)

14 SKEWERS Wooden are disposable and must be soaked in warm water for 20 to 30 minutes before you use them; metal are permanent and require no fuss; both are fine.

15 A RULER Until you feel comfortable eyeballing (and some people never do), essential for learning how to cut food into cubes or slices, rolling bread dough into shapes, or measuring the depth of water or oil in a pan. Metal is best, but plastic is okay as long as you don't put it near anything too hot.

16 A FOOD PROCESSOR OR A BLENDER The first is more versatile than the second, but an investment, to be sure. I use mine almost daily, and without one or the other, there are a handful of the recipes in the book you won't be able to make.

17 NUTCRACKER AND PICKS Handy to crack (and get inside of) all sorts of shells, from lobster and crab to, well, nuts.

CHIMNEY STARTER For starting lump charcoal without lighter fluid. (A wire grill brush is handy, too, for cleaning the grates, but in a pinch you can hold unsoaped steel wool or even aluminum foil in tongs.) Only if you have a grill, that is (see page 35).

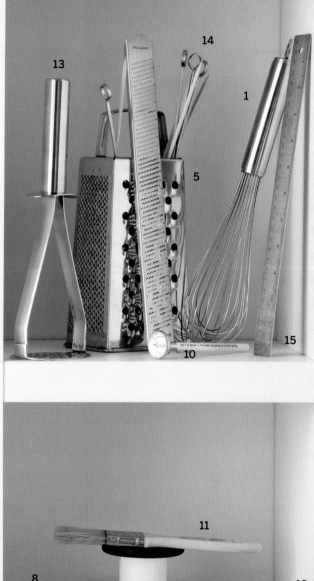

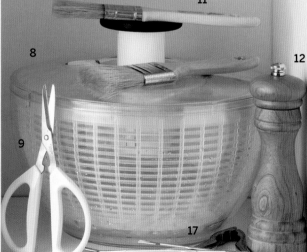

For Baking and Roasting

1 9 X 13-INCH ROASTING PAN OR RECT-ANGULAR BAKING PAN You might want two—one for roasting, one for baking (which can be glass)—but if you're going to have only one, it should be metal. If you're going to roast turkeys, large pieces of meat, or big batches of vegetables, you will need another, even larger rectangular pan; get the largest size that will fit in your oven.

2 LARGE RIMMED BAKING SHEET If you plan on baking cookies a lot, consider getting two rimless baking sheets also.

3 SQUARE BAKING PAN 8 or 9 inch. With the larger size, the food will spread out more and cook faster, so start checking at the minimum cooking time of the range named in the recipe.

4 WIRE RACKS One or more. For cooling baked goods and roasting. (If your roasting pan didn't come with a rack, make sure at least one of them fits inside your pan.)

5 LARGE GRATIN DISH 2-quart capacity. For casseroles, oven puddings, and baking. Oval or rectangular, take your pick.

6 A 9-INCH PIE PLATE Should be glass, though metal is okay; deep dish is unnecessary for the recipes here.

7 MUFFIN TIN 12 cup, preferably. Nonstick or steel is better than uncoated aluminum.

8 TWO 9-INCH ROUND CAKE PANS If you're going to make cakes, you'll need these. Nonstick is okay here.

9 ONE LOAF PAN The standard size is 8½ x 4½ x 2 inchs. Get metal—not glass—if you're going to have only one. This is really necessary only if you plan on making bread or loaf cake.

10 ROLLING PIN For pizza and pie dough in this book. I like the straight ones because you can feel the dough as you work. But some people like the kind with handles and ball bearings. Avoid tapered pins, which are less versatile and trickier to use.

11 RUBBER SPATULA The only way to remove every last drop of batter or dough from a mixing bowl.

12 COOKIE AND BISCUIT CUTTERS If you think you might be interested in rolling and cutting biscuit, scone, or cookie dough into fancy shapes. If you're fine with circles, you can also always use an inverted glass.

13 ELECTRIC MIXER Mostly for baking, as in mixing batters and doughs for cookies and breads. A handheld mixer is a fine place to start.

Building Flavor

All food has flavor, in varying degrees. Our palates recognize several different flavors—mainly sweet, salty, sour, and bitter—and we season things to enhance or emphasize these flavors or to create contrast among them.

We all have our own taste preferences (you might like sour food more than bitter) and thresholds (you might be sensitive to chiles, or not); part of learning to cook includes practicing how to use seasonings in the amounts, ratios, and combinations that work for you. Get in the habit of trying a bite of what you're cooking after every addition of salt or other seasoning to see if you want more. (There are a few exceptions to this rule—you probably don't want to taste raw poultry or eggs, for instance—but not many.) This single technique will turn you from a good cook into a great one.

FATS Generally, fats enhance and convey other flavors—a spoonful of oil doesn't taste great on its own, but many, many flavors are improved by cooking them with fat. In many cases you'll heat oil or butter and add other flavorful ingredients to infuse the fat with flavor before adding meat, poultry, vegetables, grains, or noodles. (For more about specific oils, see page 112; for butter, see page 423.)

AROMATICS By *aromatics* I mean onions, garlic, shallots, scallions, and ginger. You can count chiles, carrots, and celery in this group too. All of these highly fragrant ingredients are chopped or minced and cooked in fat—usually as the first step in a recipe—to soften them and maybe turn them a little golden (do not burn them, or anything else for that matter), with the ultimate goal of developing their flavor and aroma.

SALT I cook only with coarse salt, usually kosher or sea salt, and I rarely use measurements for salt in my recipes.

Instead I advise you to add a sprinkle at more than one point in the cooking process. Start by putting some salt in a small bowl on the counter, then grab a small amount between your thumb and two fingers—"a pinch." After you stir it in, taste and add more if you like. Remember you can always add, but it's a lot trickier to take it away.

PEPPER Whether freshly ground or from a jar, start with a good sprinkle—⅛ teaspoon or so—and go from there.

CHILES, FRESH OR DRIED The heat varies from chile to chile, so it's important to taste a little before using. Removing the seeds from fresh chiles helps reduce their heat; mincing helps distribute their flavor evenly (see page 276). Either add them to aromatic vegetables cooking in oil or use them to season a dish at the last minute. I generally figure a tablespoon per recipe is a good guess, but, again, it depends on the individual chile's heat; add more or less to suit your taste (and do taste!). You'll need

even less if using powdered or crushed dried chiles (often called *crushed red pepper*). If you're really into chiles, you'll want to buy them whole and either use them that way (and fish them out before serving) or grind them in a coffee grinder you designate for spices.

HERBS Fresh herbs provide fresh-tasting flavors that range from grassy to tart to peppery. To preserve their intensity, chop and add them toward the end of cooking or as a final garnish. In any given dish you can generally use up to ½ cup of chopped leaves from mild herbs like parsley, mint, cilantro, dill, basil, and chives; but start with no more than a tablespoon or so of leaves from stronger herbs like rosemary, oregano, sage, thyme, and tarragon. Again, taste and adjust as you go.

ACIDS A splash of vinegar or citrus juice can add a pleasant tartness as well as brighten and bring out the flavors of other ingredients. They're also crucial in salad dressings (see page 112). They're strong, so usually no more than a tablespoon or two is needed. (If you overdo it, add a little water or a pinch of sugar to dilute or balance the acidic flavor.)

SALTY AND/OR SMOKY INGREDIENTS Olives, capers, anchovies, bacon, soy sauce, and hard cheeses (like Parmesan) are salty and complex, with a flavor sometimes called *umami*, or *savoriness* (and found in other foods as well, from mushrooms to meat). All are simple ways to pump up the flavor in both hot and cold dishes.

SPICES These are flavorful dried pods, berries, seeds, barks, and roots. If you get serious about cooking, experiment beyond the several I recommend for the pantry and try buying whole spices and grinding them yourself; a coffee grinder does the trick. Toasting spices—in fat or in an empty dry pan—warms their essential oils and improves their flavor, so you will often add spices to aromatics and let them cook for a minute before adding other ingredients.

What Does *Taste and Adjust the Seasoning* Mean?

This is perhaps the most important instruction in the book. When I say "taste and adjust the seasoning," I mean add more salt and pepper, of course, plus more of anything else you might have used in the recipe, like spices, lemon juice, soy sauce, and so on. Add seasonings (especially salt) a little at a time, tasting frequently, so as not to overseason. If you overdo, adding a little water may help dilute the saltiness. You'll quickly get to a point where you can taste less frequently and eyeball the right amount of salt and other seasonings.

Bottom line: The key to seasoning any food is to add components in small increments and achieve the balance you like best.

Preparation

Here's a rundown of all the skills you need to get cooking.

Rinsing

It's usually best to rub fruit and vegetables gently under cool running water before using to get rid of grit, pesticides, and germs. (If you've got a lot to rinse, put everything in a colander first.) When something is extra-dirty—or has a thick skin—you might need to scrub stubborn bits off with a brush or sponge.

You should also rinse grains and beans, which can contain chaff, stones, other foreign matter, or just plain dirt. I don't rinse poultry and meat, but I do blot it with paper towels before cooking. All seafood should be rinsed, and clams, mussels, and oysters should always be scrubbed to remove sand. (Pat fish dry afterward.)

Holding a Knife

If you want to cut food safely and precisely—and you do—it's imperative to keep your knives sharp. The best way to do this is to buy a knife sharpener—it may be electric or manual, or it may even be an old-fashioned sharpening stone—or take them to your local hardware store to be sharpened every few months. Once you start cooking a lot, you'll also want to get a rod-looking tool called a *steel* to hone your knives between sharpenings.

Your grip should feel comfortable enough to make assertive movements. When cutting food, hold the knife by its handle fairly close to the blade. Rest your thumb on the inside of the hilt and wrap your fingers around the other side.

Trimming

This simply refers to removing any inedible or damaged parts before using a given ingredient, usually with a paring knife. When you become confident, you can hold the food in one hand and trim with the other hand. Until then, put the food on a cutting board and cut away from you to avoid hurting yourself.

For bigger pieces of fat you'll need a chef's knife.

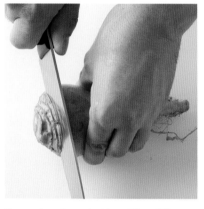

For most produce, start by cutting off the hard parts (like stems, cores, and blossom ends). Make several cuts if the fruit or vegetable is big.

Remove any blemished or bruised areas and any tough outer leaves.

For meat, fish, and poultry, cut off excess fat and gristle with a paring knife.

Peeling

A vegetable peeler and paring knife are usually all you need to remove unwanted or tough skins. (For the vegetable peeler, the kind with a ceramic blade is nice but not mandatory.) For big produce—like winter squash or pineapple—you'll need a chef's knife and a cutting board.

Peel away thin and medium skins by holding the fruit or vegetable in your nondominant hand and pulling a vegetable peeler toward you to scrape off the skin.

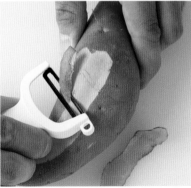

Or if it's more comfortable, pull the peeler away from you.

Try to follow the contours of the food and not remove too much flesh.

For thick-skinned vegetables and fruit, first cut a piece off one side so you have a flat, stable surface. Then use a paring or chef's knife to cut the peel off, trying to remove as little edible flesh as possible.

Cutting into Chunks

Unless you're grating or thinly slicing, you'll always start by cutting the food into large pieces—at least a couple inches or sometimes larger; the recipes will give more detail. I call these pieces *chunks* because I rarely fuss about making perfect shapes. Sometimes you stop here, and the recipe will specify the approximate size of the large pieces. But most often you'll want the food to be smaller, so you'll need to keep working.

The pieces need to be perfect shapes only if you care (I don't).

When cutting food into chunks, try to keep all the pieces around the same size and thickness so that they'll cook evenly, be easy to eat when raw, or be easy to cut into smaller pieces if that's what the recipe directs. You can tuck your fingers into your palm and use your knuckles to guide the knife or just make sure to keep everything away from the moving knife.

Chopping

The bulk of the directions in this book are for what I simply call *chopped* food. Sometimes this cut is referred to as *dice* or *cubes,* but I don't want you to strive for such perfect geometry unless you want to. As long as the food is cut into roughly the same size pieces, it will cook evenly.

Hold the sides of the food firmly with your other hand to steady it and carefully move your hand closer to—but still well out of the range of—the blade.

Scatter small, loose items on the board in a shallow pile as wide as your knife blade. Steady the tip with your free hand and use a rocking motion, pivoting as you chop through/up the food. Stop every now and then to gather the pieces.

For large items, first trim and peel the food as needed and cut it into manageable chunks so that there is a flat surface to put on the cutting board. Then use the knife tip to cut strips lengthwise. The space between these cuts will be the width of your pieces.

Now cut the strips crosswise to make small pieces. Put downward pressure on the knife as you work. (In cases where the food isn't so tall, it's handier to hold the tip of the knife against the cutting board for stability and lift the part closest to the handle up and down to chop.) Your goal is pieces about ¼ inch in size.

Mincing

Mincing is chopping until you get teeny pieces. Garlic, ginger, and chiles are really all I ever bother to mince. If you want herbs finer than chopped, you can certainly mince them, though I think most herbs taste better when cut in larger pieces since they tend to be less watery.

First chop the food. Then use a quick rocking motion—keeping the tip of the knife in contact with the cutting board—to cut the food into the tiniest pieces you can manage without driving yourself nuts. If it helps you stabilize the knife to hold the tip down with your free hand, go ahead. Using an open palm makes sure your fingers stay clear of the blade.

Slicing

You can cut food into slices before or after cooking. Usually vegetables are sliced before cooking and meat is sliced after, but there are exceptions, of course.

Slicing at a slight angle (as shown here) gives you more surface area and a nice presentation, but it's certainly fine to cut straight down. Thick slices are easier to

cut than thin ones, but with a little practice any size becomes easy. The recipes give specific directions, but here are some general guidelines.

For meat, draw a sharp chef's knife across the grain to get slices of fairly uniform width. For vegetables, set the blade in the food to steady it, then push assertively downward. (To determine which way the grain goes, look for lines or fibers like you would find in wood.) For cooked food you may need to pull and push the knife back and forth to work it all the way through. And for bread and other baked goods, use a serrated knife and a sawing motion. Raw meat for stir-fries and the like is easier to slice after it sits in the freezer for 30 minutes or so.

Measuring Dry Ingredients

For dry ingredients like flour, sugar, grains, dry beans, nuts, and cut vegetables or fruit, use flat-topped measuring cups designed for this purpose.

Use the measuring cup to scoop up the ingredient, letting it come a little bit above the rim. (You can fill the cup with a spoon, but I've never found the measurements are different.)

Then use the flat side of a butter knife to sweep the excess ingredient back into its container.

Same drill with measuring spoons.

Measuring Liquid Ingredients

You must use special measuring cups for liquids, since to get an accurate reading you'd end up overfilling a dry cup and making a mess.

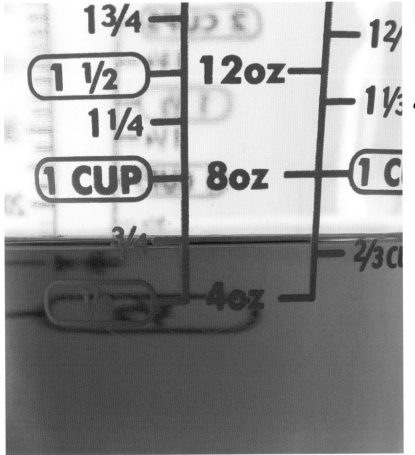

Fill the measuring cup to around the right marking, then squat down to eye level to check that the bottom line of liquid is even with the line on the cup—if not, add or pour off liquid until it's right.

You use the same set of measuring spoons for both dry and liquid ingredients.

Techniques

When classic kitchen vocabulary isn't simple, I sometimes opt for a more intuitive word.

Boiling

Boiling is straightforward and useful: Just fill a pot about two-thirds full with water, put over high heat, cover, and wait for bubbles to vigorously break the surface. Boiling is essential for cooking pasta, rice and other grains, beans, soup, and the most basic cooked vegetables. (See Boiled Greens on page 218.)

When large bubbles forcefully break the surface, the water has reached a rolling boil; now's the time to add whatever you're cooking.

Simmering or "Gently Bubbling"

Simmering is quieter boiling, at lower heat. Everyone's stove is a little different, but generally liquids simmer—or *bubble gently* or *bubble steadily* as I usually say—at the lowest setting if the pot is covered, somewhat higher if it's uncovered. This is the technique used most to develop flavor in soups and stews.

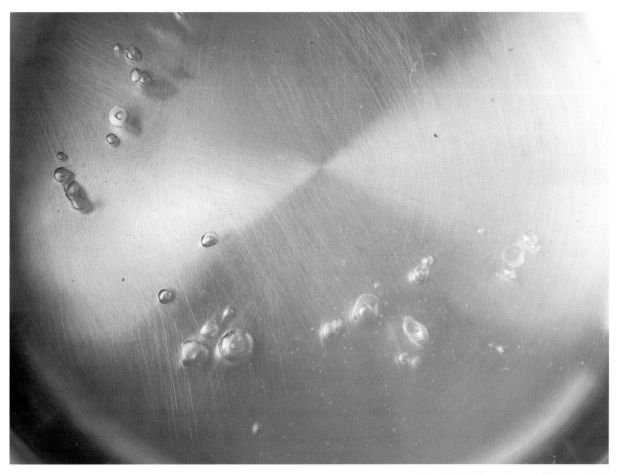

When liquid is simmering, small bubbles will occasionally burst through the surface.

STEAMED Tender but still crisp (crisp-tender) and ready for topping or tossing.

GRILLED Smoky, and as crisp or tender as you like.

BOILED Soft and watery. Good for puréeing.

ROASTED Gorgeous color, intensified flavors, and a slightly chewy texture.

STIR-FRIED Browned and flavorful from cooking in hot oil.

One Food, Five Cooking Methods

Understanding different ways to transfer heat helps you eat a nutritious, exciting, and richly varied diet.

Steaming

When you steam, instead of submerging food in a lot of boiling water you set it *above* a smaller amount of boiling water, usually in a large pot with a lid. Add water to just below the base of the steaming platform, put the food on there, cover, and turn the heat to high. Adjust the heat so the water bubbles vigorously but not violently. If you're going to be steaming something for more than a few minutes, be sure to check inside in case you need to add water or adjust the heat.

To rig your own steamer: Add about an inch of water to the pot, then put a heatproof plate upside down in the bottom.

Put another heatproof plate right side up on top of the first plate and use that to hold the food. The steam will circulate around the pot.

To use a collapsible steamer basket, just put it in the bottom of a pot and open it up.

Sautéing

Sautéing is cooking food in a skillet with some oil or butter (usually at least a couple of tablespoons) to brown it on the outside, while keeping it tender and moist on the inside. Many recipes in the book use this technique; a couple good examples are Pan-Cooked (Sautéed) Mushrooms on page 230 and Chicken Cutlets with Quick Pan Sauce on page 312. Since *saute* can sound intimidating, I use the word *cook* instead.

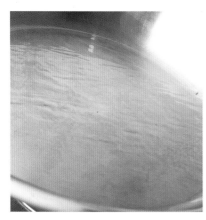

When oil is hot, it will shimmer and flow easily when you swirl it around in the pan. (You can use a pinch of flour or cornmeal to check; if it sizzles immediately, the oil is perfectly hot.) Oil usually takes a minute or two to get hot. If it starts smoking before you're ready to add food, remove it immediately from the heat. (Next time, try lower heat to begin with.)

A related term, sweating *is sautéing foods like vegetables at a low heat so they release water and don't brown. I just call this* softening.

Many recipes in this book instruct you to put butter (or oil) in a pan over medium to medium-high heat and wait for it to melt (or get hot) before you add other ingredients.

To cook in butter, swirl the pan when it starts to foam. Work quickly and add the food to the pan before the butter begins to turn brown.

Stir-Frying

Stir-frying is a lot like sautéing, but the heat is usually higher, and you keep the food moving as it cooks. (One of my favorite stir-fries is Stir-Fried Shrimp with Celery on page 364.) In Asian restaurants, stir-frying is done in a very hot wok with a special stove. Home cooks are better off using a large skillet over high heat. The large surface area helps keep food from becoming too crowded and creating steam.

Stir the food occasionally, allowing it to brown without burning. If you have a lot of food to stir-fry, work in batches so you don't overcrowd the pan. Test for doneness frequently, transfer one batch to a plate, and repeat. Then return everything to the pan right before serving.

Searing or Browning

When you cook food at high heat (usually but not exclusively in oil) in the oven or on the stove (or grill) without disturbing it, the outsides quickly get crisp and brown. With Pot Roast with Potatoes (page 280) the objective is to develop a nice crust that will keep the meat moist during long, slow cooking. With Grilled or Broiled Steak (page 266) you create a crust but limit cooking time so the inside stays on the rare side.

To sear, you'll need to turn the food to get all sides, but wait until it releases easily from the pan (or grill) before turning. That's how you know it's well browned.

Braising

This slow, high-moisture method of cooking results in rich flavor and super-tenderness. You can braise meat, poultry, fish, or vegetables. (A couple easy dishes to try are Curried Butternut Squash on page 242 and Braised Chicken, Mediterranean Style on page 324.)

Brown the ingredient in a little fat (if I'm feeling lazy, I skip this step; not quite as flavorful, but perfectly acceptable). Then add liquid to partially submerge the food. Cover and let the food cook at a gentle bubble—on the stove or in the oven—until it's tender enough to slide off a fork. This can take up to several hours, but with minimal attention.

Baking

The distinction between baking and roasting is subtle. The simplest (and most contemporary) way is to define baking as cooking batters or doughs in the oven. The moisture in the food essentially steams it in the oven from the inside out. That might sound like a mystery, but it's not a big deal. (And of course other foods—like chicken parts—are often referred to as *baked*.) A good place to start is with Blueberry Muffins on page 400.

It's true what everyone says about baking: You do need to measure carefully—more meticulously than with other sorts of dishes. But there's still a lot of room for substitutions and variations.

Roasting

Roasting is cooking dry food (or nearly so) in a fairly hot oven—anywhere between 350°F and 450°F. You might coat the ingredients in a little oil or butter before roasting to promote browning, but in any case it's cooked in a large, shallow pan so it remains dry. This method intensifies flavors and helps food develop a crisp exterior while maintaining a moist interior. You can roast any food you might expect to cook in a pan, like Rosemary-Roasted Potatoes (page 224).

Whenever you roast anything, it's a good idea to stir or turn the pieces occasionally so that they brown and crisp up evenly on all sides.

Broiling

Your broiler is located either inside or right below your oven; it provides direct and high heat from above that cooks and browns foods, much as grilling does—only upside down. Broiling works best with foods that cook to the desired doneness and become tender quickly. A good example: Grilled or Broiled Tomatoes (page 226). In the broiler, food can go from browned to burned very quickly, sometimes before the inside is cooked.

The heat in home broilers varies wildly. So check food frequently. If you need to, move the pan to a lower rack until the inside catches up with the outside, or if you have a low setting, use it.

Grilling

Grilling is cooking over hot coals or an open gas flame. With direct grilling, you put the food on a grate right over the heat source to promote quick cooking and browning; it's closely related to broiling. With indirect grilling—which is best for thick, slow-cooking foods—the ingredients are put to the side of the heat source and the lid is closed to promote slower, more even cooking. If you've got a grill, try a simple steak (page 266).

To light charcoal grills, put lump charcoal (much better than briquettes, which contain chemical additives) in a metal cylinder called a *chimney starter*, fill the bottom with paper, and light the paper.

When the edges of the charcoal turn white, distribute the coals across the bottom of the grill for direct cooking—or in a pile for indirect—and put the rack in place.

For direct cooking, put food over the coals.

For indirect cooking, put food on the cool side and cover.

If you have a gas grill (which isn't shown here), turn it on and let the grates heat up for a few minutes. To grill indirectly, turn on one or two of the burners and put the food on the cool side. When the coals are coated in ash and you can hold your hand over the grate for no more than 4 seconds, the grill is ready. When the grates are hot, scrub them with a wire brush before cooking. To grease the grill, douse a paper towel in oil and smear it around the grates with tongs.

Panfrying

When you cook food in about ½ inch of hot oil over medium-high heat, you're panfrying or shallow-frying. Since the food isn't totally submerged in the hot oil, you have to turn the pieces to cook each side. But since the idea of panfrying is to help food develop a brown crust, you must let it sit and cook, undisturbed, for a few minutes for it to become crisp. Adjust the heat during cooking so the fat sizzles without smoking.

Breading before panfrying helps keep the insides moist and the outsides crunchy, but it's not mandatory; you can pan-fry uncoated food, too. For a recipe with breading, check out Panfried Breaded Eggplant (page 244); without, see Zucchini Pancakes (page 248).

Deep Frying

Deep frying involves submerging food in 2 to 3 inches of oil, usually heated to 350–375°F. (A good place to start is Battered and Fried Squid on page 376.)

You can deep-fry in any large, heavy pot (you don't need a deep-fryer). Just make sure you use a vegetable oil that can stand high heat; peanut oil is my first choice. When you add the food to the oil, it should bubble, float to the surface of the oil, and turn golden within a minute.

Very important: Avoid letting the oil get so hot that it smokes (if it does, remove it from the heat right away), and don't fill the vessel so high that it overflows when you add the food.

The Basics in a Nutshell

To increase your odds of success, here are my five golden rules of the kitchen.

1. Anything you cook at home will be good.

Start with real ingredients and anything you make will taste better than anything from a box, bag, jar, or fast-food joint. And if you mess up, so what? Even the worst mistakes will probably still be edible. Chalk them up to experience and move on, knowing that you'll improve exponentially with just a little bit of practice. Really. You will.

2. Read the recipe through before starting.

Old-school advice, still valuable. Familiarizing yourself with a recipe before you start cooking allows you to gather all the equipment and ingredients you need ahead of time and prevents any unwelcome surprises. Until you get the hang of the pacing of cooking, it will also help if you prepare (chop, measure, etc.) all your ingredients before you start to cook—this will, initially at least, help you relax at the stove and be able to focus on the task at hand.

3. It's okay to serve dishes warm or at room temp.

No rush. No pressure. Keep this in mind when you're trying to serve more than one dish at a time; it's virtually impossible to serve a large, complicated meal if you want everything piping hot, but it's very easy to do it if you accept that some dishes will be closer to room temperature. Only soup, eggs, and some pasta dishes really *must* be served hot. That said, you don't want to leave food sitting out at room temperature for a total of more than 2 hours—including serving time—without refrigerating (if it's over 90°F out, make that 1 hour). Other than that, give yourself a break, slow down, and enjoy the process.

4. Trust your senses.

The recipes in this book are designed to hone your powers of observation. If something isn't cooking as fast as the recipe says it will, the heat under the pan is too low; if you smell something burning, it is (quickly move your pot off the stove). Your eyes, ears, nose, fingers, and tongue will tell you if something's wrong—and they'll become more sensitive as you cook more—so don't ignore them. Even if you think you don't know anything about cooking, your intuition and senses can guide you through a recipe. And your intuition will be sharpened and improved by experience, so making judgment calls will become second nature and soon you'll be able to recognize how something smells *before* it burns.

5. Be safe—but not insane—about cleanliness.

Wash your hands before you handle any food, keep your equipment and work surfaces clean, and don't let cooked food touch anything that previously touched raw food. You should keep your refrigerator at 40°F and your freezer at 0°F or colder. Things get a little trickier when we talk about eating rare or raw meat, poultry, fish, or eggs. If you want to minimize the risk of bacteria, you must cook everything thoroughly. But since that's not always the tastiest way to eat some foods, well, use your judgment, but at least buy high-quality products from sources you trust, refrigerate them immediately, and handle them as discussed here.

Breakfast

By happy coincidence, the first meal of the day is also the easiest to cook, even on the busiest, most stressful mornings. In the time it takes to unwrap and heat a Pop-Tart, you can fry an egg, pour a bowl of granola, slice fruit, or toast some bread. And in the time it takes to stand in line for a latte, you can whip up a smoothie *and* a cup of coffee and take them wherever you need to go.

Making breakfast will instantly improve your cooking skills and your eating habits. A simple scrambled egg teaches you how to control the heat under a skillet and anticipate and recognize doneness. Every time you cut up a piece of fruit you practice knife handling by peeling, trimming, and slicing. Learn to measure and mix simple batters with an easy batch of pancakes. These are confidence-building recipes you can cook for yourself or for others, without the pressure of getting a lot of food on the table at the same time.

If you're a more advanced cook, you can use this chapter to vary breakfast and brunch dishes and sharpen techniques you already know or to learn new tricks: Experiment filling and folding an omelet, try novel ingredients and toppings for hot cereal, and include perfectly cooked eggs in other dishes throughout the book.

The most important thing about cooking breakfast might be that you begin your day in the kitchen, and that's my idea of getting the best possible start.

Making Breakfast

Dairy—and Not

So many choices:

Milk Comes in nonfat (skim), 1 percent milk fat, 2 percent, and whole (usually 3.25 percent). Fat has flavor, so whole milk is my first choice for cooking (and for everything really). But you can use reduced-fat (not nonfat) for most of the recipes in this book (unless the recipe says otherwise). Avoid skim milk, which is watery in both taste and texture.

Cream With more fat, richer and thicker than milk. Heavy and whipping cream (which run 30 to 36 percent fat) can be whipped. Light cream contains less fat, and half-and-half—half milk and half cream—still less. Both make soups, sauces, and baked foods, well, creamy. Sour cream is thicker and tangier. Warm all creams gently; boiling causes them to curdle.

Yogurt Milk that's been cultured with bacteria, which thickens it and sours it, sometimes slightly and sometimes greatly. Check the label for "live, active cultures"—or similar wording—and skip the stuff with gelatins, gums, stabilizers, or sugar and flavors. It comes in whole, low-fat, and nonfat versions, in both regular and super-creamy Greek and Mediterranean styles. My rules for choosing milk apply to yogurt: Full-fat is best.

Other Milks For people who have trouble digesting cow's milk (or for those who object to it), these can be a real boon on cereal or in coffee. You can use them in recipes too, as long as you don't expect the results to be the same. Soy, rice, nut (usually almond), coconut, oat, and goat milks are the most common. Rice and oat milks are the most neutral tasting; soy and goat the strongest. Full-fat coconut milk is super-rich but also comes in a reduced-fat choice. Many of these are sweetened.

Maple Syrup

Like real olive oil, real maple syrup is the only option in its class; everything else is essentially water laced with sugar, corn syrup, and artificial color. Look for "Real Maple Syrup"; when in doubt, check the ingredients (they should not include artificial maple flavor!). Yes, it's more expensive; it's also incomparably delicious, a gift from nature, with flavor way beyond mere sweetness. I prefer Grade B maple syrup: It's cheaper, darker, and stronger tasting than Grade A. Stored in the fridge, maple syrup will keep for months. When you want some, warm a little gently in the microwave or in a small pot on the stove before using or let it come to room temperature on the counter while you're cooking.

GRADE A   GRADE B

Breakfast Meats

Yum. Bacon. Sausage. Ham. Here's what to do with them:

On the stove: Put the bacon or sausage in a skillet over medium-low heat. Bacon pieces can touch and even overlap a little; sausage should have a little space for ideal browning. Check every couple of minutes, but don't fuss: You'll hear and smell either cooking as it begins to brown. If parts start to brown too fast, lower the heat; if they're not sizzling, raise it a bit. If the fat in the pan starts to smoke, move it off the heat for a few seconds. Turn pieces as they brown on the bottom. Sausage is done when the interior is no longer pink (you can peek inside by cutting in with a sharp knife); bacon is done *before* it looks the way you want to eat it—it gets crisper as it cools. Draining on paper towels before eating is always a good idea.

To cook ham: Put a thin film of olive oil in a skillet over medium heat. When it's hot, add the ham and cook gently, stirring (if it's chopped) or turning (if it's in slices or steaks) as necessary to heat it through and brown it a bit. Remove it from the pan before it gets too dry; really you're just browning and warming it up (it's already cooked when you start).

Big-Batch Bacon or Sausage: Heat the oven to 450°F and spread the meat in a single layer in a roasting pan. Roast, checking every 5 minutes or so and turning occasionally. As the meat cooks, take out the extra fat by tipping the pan a little and spooning or pouring it into a heatproof bowl. Turn the pieces as they brown and release from the pan. Total cooking time will be 20 to 30 minutes, depending on how much you cook and how you like it.

Oatmeal or Other Hot Cereal

You cook all hot cereals the same, adjusting the water so they're creamy, thick, or in between.

TIME **15 minutes**
MAKES **2 servings**

Pinch salt

1 cup rolled oats (not instant)

1 tablespoon butter, optional

Maple syrup, sugar, or honey, to taste

Milk, cream, or half-and-half, optional

½ cup raisins or any chopped dried fruit or fresh fruit, optional

¼ teaspoon ground cinnamon, optional

1 Put 2¼ cups water in a medium saucepan with the salt and the oats and turn the heat to high. When the water boils, turn the heat to low and cook, stirring frequently, until the water is just absorbed and big bubbles are popping on the surface, about 5 minutes. Stir in the butter if you're using it, cover the pan, and remove it from the heat.

2 Five minutes later, uncover the pan and stir. Drizzle or sprinkle on a little sweetener, pour in a splash of milk, and sprinkle on the fruit and cinnamon, as you like. Stir, taste, add more sweetener if necessary, and serve.

I like my oatmeal relatively creamy. For thicker oatmeal, use ¼ cup less water; for really thick, use ½ cup less.

SALTING THE WATER Start with cold water and add a little salt, even if you plan to sweeten it later.

COOKING AND THICKENING As soon as the water comes to a boil, lower the heat so the mixture bubbles gently.

RESTING TIME When the mixture is cloudy and thick, add the butter, cover, and remove the pot from the heat to develop creaminess.

Tips

▶ Do not—I repeat—do not use instant oatmeal here or anywhere else. It has almost no flavor and saves very little time.

▶ You can cook steel-cut oats and other grains—like bulgur, quinoa, or cornmeal—using the same recipe; just allow extra time. Keep cooking, stirring, and tasting, adding water if the mixture becomes too thick, until the grains become tender.

▶ To make sure you have hot cereal on hand whenever you want it, triple this recipe; keep whatever is left in the fridge for up to a week. Then just warm some in the microwave.

Variations

▶ **Grits:** This southern favorite is made with ground dried hominy, a kind of cornmeal with a tortillalike taste. You can find it—called simply *grits*—in most supermarkets; again, don't buy the instant kind. In Step 1, use grits instead of the oatmeal and increase the water to 2½ cups. Before turning on the heat, whisk the mixture until it's smooth and free of lumps. Turn the heat to medium-high, whisking frequently, until it barely comes to a boil. Lower the heat so that the mixture bubbles gently and cook, whisking frequently, until it gets thick, with big, plopping bubbles, 10 to 15 minutes. (You want it to stay soupy as it cooks, so add water—2 tablespoons at a time—as necessary.) Then add the butter, cover, and let rest as described in the recipe. You can sweeten grits or add a handful of grated cheddar cheese.

Learn More

▶ Maple Syrup (page 42), Grain Basics (page 206), Preparing Fruit (page 430)

Granola and Muesli

Granola is baked. Muesli isn't. And both are completely customizable.

TIME   **10 to 45 minutes,
plus time to cool**

MAKES   **about 8 cups**

---

6 cups rolled oats

**2 cups chopped nuts
(walnuts, pecans, almonds,
cashews, etc.)**

**1 cup shredded
unsweetened coconut**

**1 teaspoon ground
cinnamon, or to taste**

Pinch salt

**½ cup packed brown sugar,
honey, or maple syrup, or
more to taste**

**1 cup raisins or chopped
dried fruit**

1 If you're making granola, heat the oven to 350°F.

2 In a large bowl, combine the oats, nuts, coconut, cinnamon, and salt. For muesli, sprinkle the oat mixture with the brown sugar; for granola, drizzle it with honey or syrup. Toss well to thoroughly distribute the sweetener. Taste and stir in a little more to make the cereal sweeter if you like. If you're making muesli, add the raisins and you're done.

3 If you're making granola, spread the mixture evenly on a rimmed baking sheet and put in the oven. Bake for 30 to 35 minutes, stirring occasionally to make sure the granola is toasting evenly. The browner it gets without burning, the crunchier the granola will be.

4 Remove the pan from the oven and add the raisins. Cool on a rack. The pan will still be quite hot, so stir the granola once in a while until it cools to keep it from burning in spots. Spoon the granola—or muesli—into a sealed container and store in the refrigerator; it will stay fresh for a couple months.

*Call it muesli: Add the
raisins and stop here.*

TOSSING TO COMBINE
The idea is to distribute the brown sugar among the oats and other ingredients.

SWEETENING ALTERNATIVES
For granola, instead of brown sugar, toss the mixture with honey or syrup.

Granola

Muesli

Tips

▶ *Any* cereal you make yourself will be better (and mostly cheaper) than anything that comes in a box or a bag. (It's shocking how good raw oats are.) And you'll never get bored of granola and muesli, since by switching up the nuts, fruit, and sweeteners, they never come out the same way twice.

▶ Don't worry if the granola is slightly chewy when it comes out of the oven; it will crisp up as it cools in the pan.

Variations

▶ **3 Ways to Vary Granola or Muesli:**

1 Use different nuts or dried fruit. I don't combine more than one type of nut or fruit at a time because I like the flavors to be distinct, but you certainly can. Some dried fruit to try: cranberries, apricots, blueberries, pineapple, or figs.

2 Instead of the cinnamon, try ¼ teaspoon freshly grated nutmeg or ground allspice or ½ teaspoon ground cardamom or ginger.

3 Replace the coconut with more oats, nuts, or fruit.

Learn More

▶ Chopping nuts (page 19), Maple Syrup (page 42)

TURNING MUESLI INTO GRANOLA Make sure the cereal is spread evenly on the baking sheet and not too thin or it might burn.

TOASTING EVENLY Keep an eye on the granola and toss it every few minutes. Remove the pan when the cereal is a little lighter than you want it and toss it a couple times as it cools.

Vanilla-Peach Smoothie

Why not make a different flavor every day?

TIME   5 minutes

MAKES   2 large or
4 small servings

2 cups yogurt

½ cup orange juice, or
more as needed

½ teaspoon vanilla extract

½ frozen banana, optional

2 cups unsweetened frozen
sliced or chopped peaches

1 Put the yogurt, juice, vanilla, and the banana if you're using it in the blender first, followed by the peaches.

2 Start by pulsing the machine, then turn it on and whiz until smooth. If the mixture is not moving much, add a splash more orange juice. Serve right away, ideally in chilled glasses or over ice (though if you've used the frozen banana, it'll be plenty cold).

You can make really rich, dairy-free smoothies by using a whole frozen banana and skipping the yogurt.

LAYERING THE INGREDIENTS The blender will work best if you put the liquids and the banana in first, then add the remaining fruit (and ice if the fruit isn't frozen).

PURÉEING Add a little more liquid if necessary to get the mixture moving, then put the lid back on and let the smoothie get smooth.

Tips

▶ No frozen fruit handy? No problem. Wait until after blending to add the juice (you might not need it) and start with fresh fruit; add a few ice cubes to the blender after the fruit. (Don't put the ice cubes into the container first, or the machine will have a hard time getting moving.)

Variations

▶ **Mango-Ginger Smoothie:** 2 cups mango, 1 frozen banana, 1 cup white grape juice, and toss 2 thin slices of peeled fresh ginger into the blender.

▶ **Orange Cream Smoothie:** 2 cups orange juice, 1 cup Greek yogurt, 1 cup ice, and 1 frozen banana.

▶ **Cherry-Melon Smoothie:** 1 cup pitted cherries, 1 cup honeydew or cantaloupe chunks (frozen or fresh), 1 frozen banana, and 1 cup orange juice.

▶ **Piña Colada Smoothie:** 2 cups pineapple chunks (frozen or fresh), 1 frozen banana, and ½ cup coconut milk and ½ cup water or pineapple juice.

▶ **Strawberry-Vanilla Smoothie:** 4 cups strawberries (frozen or fresh), 1 cup yogurt, ½ teaspoon vanilla extract, and white grape juice or water as needed.

▶ **Blueberry-Lemon Smoothie:** 2 cups blueberries (frozen or fresh), 1 frozen banana, and 2 tablespoons fresh lemon juice mixed into ½ cup orange juice with a little honey or sugar.

Learn More

▶ Dairy—and Not (page 42), Preparing Fruit (page 430)

Egg Basics

Buying Eggs

▶ You want to use the freshest eggs possible, but that's easier said than done, thanks to a confusing and meaningless labeling system. (For more information, see Chicken Lingo, page 307.) Try to find locally raised eggs if you can. Whichever you choose, look for the sell-by date; it should be at least a couple weeks in the future.

▶ Buy only large or extra-large eggs, since the recipes in this book (and most others) work best with those sizes. Once you get eggs home, leave them in the carton and put them in the coolest part of the fridge—usually the bottom, in the back. (Don't store them in those cute little cups in the door.) You can tell how good they are when you crack one open: A really fresh egg will have a firm yolk that sits high on a mound of whites. If it's runny and thin, with a flat yolk, it's a little on the old side; you can still eat it, though, unless it smells bad.

▶ To keep bits of shell from getting into the part you eat, open an egg by smacking the side definitively—but not aggressively—on a flat, hard surface, stopping your hand when you hear a crack.

▶ Most of what's inside an egg is the white, which contains more than half of the egg's protein and none of its fat. The yolk has the majority of the vitamins and the remaining protein and minerals. Don't freak out if you see a small blood spot in the yolk; you'll never notice it once the egg is cooked. If it bugs you, remove it with the tip of a sharp knife.

Soft- or Medium-Boiled Eggs

LOWER THE EGGS INTO THE WATER
Choose a pot that will comfortably hold all the eggs you want to cook and still have room to cover them with 2 inches of water. Bring the water to a boil and adjust the heat so the water bubbles gently. Lower the egg (or eggs) into the water with a spoon and let them fall off gently so they don't crack against the sides or bottom.

MAINTAIN A GENTLE BUBBLE Adjust the heat so the water never returns to a rolling boil. Then cook the eggs for 3 to 7 minutes, depending on how runny you like them. A timer is handy, since the texture inside the shell changes pretty fast. (The photos on the facing page will give you an idea of what to expect.)

COOL THEM DOWN When the desired time is up, run cold water into the pot just until you can handle the eggs. Once you remove one, crack the shell and scoop the insides into a small bowl (or eat straight from the shell), or if the white is firm enough, just peel the egg. Sprinkle with salt and pepper and serve.

Hard-Boiled Eggs

PUT THE EGGS IN A POT WITH COLD WATER
The process is slightly different than for soft-cooked eggs. Choose a pot that will comfortably hold all the eggs you want to cook, add the eggs, and then add enough cold water to cover them by 2 inches. Put the pot over medium-high heat and bring it to a gentle boil; turn off the heat and cover. The average large to extra-large egg will be ready 9 minutes later.

GET AN ICE BATH READY Cooling the eggs quickly after cooking helps prevent the yolk from developing a harmless (but not too pretty) green ring. Fill a medium bowl with lots of ice and some water. After the eggs steep for 9 minutes, transfer them to the ice bath and let sit for a minute or so. Then eat right away or refrigerate for up to a week or two. To serve, crack the shell gently on all sides, peel, and sprinkle with salt and pepper.

IS IT DONE YET?
Eggs cook in a flash. Check out the difference a minute makes.

For what I would consider the perfect egg, shoot for 6 minutes.

3-MINUTE SOFT-BOILED EGG The yolk is completely runny and barely warm and the white still slightly liquid. If you want the white very soft but no longer liquid, let it go to 4 minutes.

5-MINUTE SOFT-BOILED EGG You'll get a cooked but runny yolk with some soft white.

7-MINUTE MEDIUM-BOILED EGG The white will be fully cooked and almost solid, but some of the yolk may have hardened.

9-MINUTE HARD-BOILED EGG Firm, but not quite dry, yolk and white.

11-MINUTE HARD-BOILED EGG Still edible, but a little chalky—best for chopping into salads.

Scrambled Eggs

The foolproof way to make sure the texture is exactly how you like it.

TIME **10 minutes**

MAKES **2 to 4 servings**

4 eggs

Salt and freshly ground black pepper

2 tablespoons butter or olive oil

1 Crack the eggs on a flat, hard surface and open them into a bowl. Sprinkle with some salt and pepper and whisk until the yolks and whites are just combined.

2 Put the butter or oil in a medium skillet, preferably nonstick, over medium-high heat. When the butter has melted or the oil is hot, pour the eggs into the pan. Let the eggs cook for just a few seconds to heat up, then begin stirring frequently and scraping the sides of the pan.

3 As the eggs begin to curdle, some parts may look like they're drying out; whenever you see that, remove the pan from the heat and continue stirring until the cooking slows down a bit. Then return the pan to the heat and continue cooking. The eggs are done when they're creamy, soft, and still a bit runny; do not overcook or the eggs will become tough. (If you like them that way, go ahead.) Serve right away.

You can also use a fork. Watch for a uniform color.

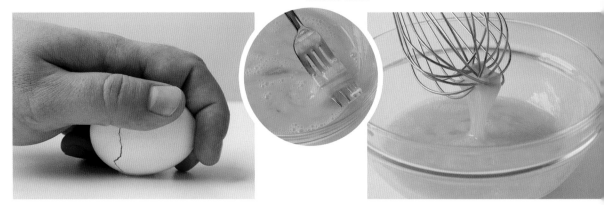

CRACKING AN EGG Smack the side of the egg definitively—but not too aggressively—on a flat, hard surface, stopping your hand when you hear the shell crack.

This way you keep egg shell chips from getting into the part you want to eat.

BEATING EGGS Whisk the eggs until they're just combined; over-beating will make their texture thin and runny.

If you're going to add anything—like chopped herbs or grated cheese—wait until the eggs just start to set.

Tips

▶ You can add a little milk or cream to make the scrambled eggs silkier and less eggy tasting. But don't add too much or they might get watery; figure 1 tablespoon for every 2 eggs.

▶ A wooden spoon or heat-proof rubber spatula is ideal for gently scraping the pan as the eggs cook.

Variations

▶ **11 Things to Add to Scrambled Eggs:**

1 1 teaspoon chopped fresh stronger herbs, like oregano, tarragon, or thyme

2 1 tablespoon chopped fresh milder herbs, like parsley, chives, chervil, basil, or mint

3 Tabasco, Worcestershire, or other prepared sauce, to taste

4 ¼ cup grated or crumbled cheddar, goat, or other melting cheese

5 2 tablespoons grated Parmesan cheese

6 2 tablespoons chopped scallions

7 ½ cup chopped cooked mushrooms, onion, spinach, or other vegetables

8 ½ cup chopped smoked salmon or other smoked fish

9 ½ cup chopped cooked shrimp, crab, lobster, or oysters

10 1 or 2 chopped tomatoes

11 Any cooked salsa, drained if it's watery

Learn More

▶ Egg Basics (page 50), Grating Cheese (page 176), Chopping Herbs (page 78)

HEATING THE FAT Add the eggs when the butter is foaming but not yet changing color or the oil thins a bit and just begins to shimmer.

ADJUSTING THE TEXTURE The more you stir—and the lower the heat—the silkier the eggs. Moving the pan on and off the burner is the fastest way to control the temperature.

Fried Eggs

Almost as delicate as poached eggs—minus the fuss—and perfect in all the same dishes.

TIME **10 minutes**
MAKES **1 or 2 servings**

1 tablespoon butter or olive oil

2 eggs

Salt and freshly ground black pepper

1 Put the butter or oil in a medium skillet, preferably nonstick, over medium heat. When the butter has melted or the oil is hot, swirl it around the pan until the bottom is coated.

2 After about a minute, when the foam from the butter subsides or the oil shimmers, crack the eggs into the skillet. As soon as the whites lose their translucence—this takes only a minute—turn the heat to low and sprinkle the eggs with salt and pepper.

3 The eggs are done when the whites are completely firm and opaque, even around the yolk. (If you like them less runny, cook them for 1 or 2 minutes longer so the yolks aren't so jiggly.) Gently lift them out of the pan with a spatula, being careful not to break the yolks, and eat them right away.

The lower the heat, the more tender the eggs.

CRACKING EGGS INTO THE PAN Open the egg when it's 1 or 2 inches above the pan. The closer it is, the less chance the yolk will break on impact.

ENCOURAGING EGGS TO COOK EVENLY Cut the thickest part of the whites (next to the yolks) so the uncooked whites will run down to the surface of the pan.

Tips

▶ Fat matters when you cook eggs: Butter will be rich and luxurious, while olive oil gives you a more complex, earthy flavor.

▶ You can fry as many eggs at a time as will fit comfortably in the pan. Just be sure to increase the amount of fat too. If the whites run together, separate them with a spatula as they harden. They won't be as attractive, but this way everyone can eat at the same time.

Variations

▶ **Eggs in the Hole.** Eggs and toast all together: For each egg, use a small glass or other round object to cut a circle in the center of a slice of bread. In Step 1, double the amount of butter or oil; when it's ready, put the bread slices and the rounds in the pan and cook for a minute or so. Turn, then crack the eggs into the holes in the bread. When the eggs begin to firm up, carefully flip the slices with a spatula. Cook on the second side for a few more seconds, sprinkle with salt and pepper, and serve with the rounds.

Learn More

▶ Egg Basics (page 50), Cracking an Egg (page 52), 7 Things to Put Under Poached (or Fried) Eggs (page 57)

To remove fried or over-easy eggs, slide a spatula under each, gently lift it out of the pan, and let it slide onto a plate.

FOR OVER-EASY EGGS When the whites begin to get firm but are still not fully set, slip a spatula underneath each egg and gently flip it.

Poached Eggs

Restaurant-style fare at home and easy to master.

TIME **10 minutes**
MAKES **1 or 2 servings**

2 eggs

Salt and freshly ground
black pepper

1 Put about 1 inch of water in a small saucepan and bring to a boil. Lower the heat so the water barely bubbles.

2 Crack one of the eggs on a flat, hard surface and open it into a shallow bowl, being careful not to break the yolk. Gently slip it into the water. Repeat with the other egg.

3 Cook the eggs undisturbed for 3 to 5 minutes, just until the white is set and the yolk has filmed over. The longer you cook them, the thicker the yolks become. Lift the eggs out of the pan with a slotted spoon, letting as much water as possible drain off. (If you want to make them look really nice, trim off the raggedy bits with kitchen shears.) Serve right away, sprinkled with salt and pepper.

Keep an eye on the water and adjust the heat as necessary.

The more the egg jiggles when you shake the spoon, the runnier the yolk is.

MAINTAINING A GENTLE BOIL If the water isn't hot enough, the whites will spread out and won't set; furious bubbling will break the yolks.

SLIDING THE EGGS INTO THE WATER Easy does it so you avoid breaking the yolk. Lower the bowl's edge into the water so the egg slips out smoothly.

REMOVING THE EGGS FROM THE PAN Let each one drain in the slotted spoon for a few seconds before serving.

For a change from toast, try serving poached eggs on rice, noodles, or potatoes.

Tips

▶ If you boil an egg in its shell for 6 minutes, you have a perfect substitute for a poached egg. Run under cold water, crack the shell, and peel—gently—as you would a hard-boiled egg.

▶ You can poach as many eggs as will fit comfortably in the water, so use as large a pan as you need. To keep the eggs from clumping together, let each set a bit before adding the next. Try to keep track of which went in first and take them out in the same order.

▶ To poach eggs for a large group, poach them ahead of time, but take them out of the water about 30 seconds earlier than you normally would and transfer them to bowl of ice water. Before serving, reheat them in gently bubbling water.

Variations

▶ **7 Things to Put Under Poached (or Fried) Eggs:**
1 Toasted bread, English muffins, or split chunks of Corn Bread (page 396)
2 Tossed Green Salad (page 110)
3 Tomato sauce (pages 178–181)
4 A bowl of beans (page 250)
5 Pasta with Garlic and Oil (page 174)
6 Plain (or fancy) rice (pages 196–199)
7 A cooked hamburger patty (page 268)

Learn More

▶ Egg Basics (page 50), Cracking an Egg (page 52)

Cheese Omelet

The filling and folding are easy, and in 15 minutes you've got a whole meal.

TIME **15 minutes**
MAKES **2 servings**

4 eggs

2 tablespoons milk or cream, optional

Salt and freshly ground black pepper

2 tablespoons plus 1 teaspoon butter

½ cup grated cheddar cheese

1 Crack the eggs on a flat, hard surface and open them into a medium bowl. Add the milk if you're using it, whisk until the yolks and whites are just combined, and sprinkle with some salt and pepper.

2 Put the 2 tablespoons butter into a medium skillet, preferably nonstick, over medium-high heat. When it has melted, swirl it around the pan until the bottom is coated and the foaming stops.

3 Pour the egg mixture into the pan and cook, undisturbed, for about 30 seconds, then use a wooden spoon or rubber spatula to gently push the outer edges of the eggs toward the center. As you do this, tip the pan to allow the uncooked eggs in the center to spread into the gaps and cook. Continue this process until the omelet is mostly set around the edges but still quite runny in the center, a total of about 3 minutes (if you like well-done eggs, cook until the center firms up, another 1 or 2 minutes).

4 Lower the heat to medium and sprinkle the cheese over the eggs, mostly toward the center. To fold the omelet, see the photos. If the eggs still look too wet inside after folding, continue to cook just until the eggs are no longer runny. Slide the omelet out of the pan and onto a plate, smear the remaining 1 teaspoon butter over the top (it will melt), cut in half crosswise, and serve.

The top will be uneven and full of folds, but that's okay.

FORMING THE OMELET As the eggs cook, push the sides of the omelet toward the center, tipping the pan so the uncooked parts stream to the edges.

FOLDING AN OMELET Slip a spatula halfway under one side and fold the omelet in half. Hold it in place for a moment, until the eggs and filling set.

REMOVING THE OMELET FROM THE PAN When the eggs have just set, gently slide the omelet from the pan, using a spatula to help.

Tips

▶ A nonstick (or well-seasoned cast-iron) pan prevents the eggs from sticking.

▶ To make an omelet for one, use half of each ingredient and cook in a small (6- to 8-inch) skillet. For a thinner omelet, use a large (12-inch) skillet.

▶ You don't want to brown the eggs, but they need to set up quickly, so make sure the pan is good and hot when they go in. If the fat starts to "spit," lower the heat a bit.

▶ Resist the temptation to overstuff the omelet or you'll have trouble folding and get-ting it out of the pan. For 4 eggs, use no more than 1 cup of filling.

Variations

▶ **8 Other Fillings:**

1 Any cheese that will soften a bit, about ½ cup

2 Cooked and chopped mush-rooms, onion, spinach, or sim-ply cooked leftover vegetables, ½ to 1 cup

3 Diced ripe tomatoes, drained dry, about ½ cup

4 Cottage or goat cheese (mixed with chopped fresh herbs if you like), about ½ cup

5 Chopped ham, crisp-cooked bacon, sausage meat, or other chopped meat, about ½ cup

6 Herbs: 1 teaspoon chopped fresh stronger herbs like oreg-ano, tarragon, or thyme or 1 ta-blespoon milder ones like pars-ley, chervil, basil, or mint

7 Cooked seafood, like shrimp, scallops, lobster, or crabmeat, shredded or chopped, 1 cup

8 Chopped red bell pepper, about ½ cup

Learn More

▶ Egg Basics (page 50), cheese for cooking (page 389), Grating Cheese (page 176)

Spinach Frittata

When you leave an omelet flat in the pan, the "extras" become more important than the eggs.

TIME **30 minutes**

MAKES **4 servings**

6 eggs

½ cup freshly grated Parmesan cheese

Salt and freshly ground black pepper

3 tablespoons olive oil

½ small red onion, chopped

1 pound fresh spinach, chopped

1 Position the rack under a broiler about 4 inches from the heat source and turn it to high. Crack the eggs on a flat, hard surface and open them into a bowl. Add the cheese, sprinkle with some salt and pepper, and whisk until the yolks and whites are just combined.

2 Put the olive oil in a medium oven-proof skillet, preferably nonstick, over medium-high heat. When it's hot, add the onion, sprinkle with salt and pepper, and cook until soft, 3 to 5 minutes.

3 Add the spinach and cook, stirring and tossing frequently, until the leaves wilt and release their liquid; lower the heat if necessary to keep everything from burning. Once the spinach starts to dry and stick to the pan, after 3 to 5 minutes, turn the heat to low. Cook,

stirring occasionally, until there is no water left in the pan and the spinach is coated in oil, another minute or so, then spread out the spinach in the pan.

4 Pour the egg mixture over the spinach and onions, evenly distributing the vegetables if necessary. Cook, undisturbed, until the eggs are firm at the bottom and the top is still runny, 8 to 10 minutes.

5 Put the pan under the broiler until the eggs finish setting and brown lightly, 2 to 4 minutes, watching to make sure the frittata doesn't burn. (Be careful removing the pan from the oven since the handle will be hot.) Cut the frittata into wedges and serve right away, or warm, or at room temperature.

It's also fine to add the spinach to the pan in a couple batches, as the leaves wilt and make some room.

WILTING THE VEGETABLES The spinach will be a tad unruly in the pan until it wilts. Keep tossing and stirring until it softens and releases its water.

DRYING OUT THE VEGETA-BLES There should be no water left in the pan and the spinach should be glossy with oil before you add the eggs.

Tips

▶ For a thicker frittata, use a smaller pan, keep the heat low, and extend the cooking time. You still want the eggs to barely set; don't brown the bottom by turning up the heat.

▶ Frittatas are ideal for entertaining since you can make them ahead and serve them warm or at room temperature. Cut them into wedges for plated appetizers (a little tomato sauce is a lovely addition) or into bite-sized squares to serve with toothpicks.

Variations

▶ **Any-Vegetable Frittata:** Try asparagus, zucchini, tomatoes, red bell pepper, peas, or carrots, for example. As with the spinach, figure a pound or so and chop them up a bit if they're big. Some will take longer to cook than others, but follow the directions in Steps 2 and 3 and figure a range of 5 to 15 minutes. Add the eggs when the vegetables are completely dry and tender.

▶ **Using Other Cheeses in Frittatas:** Crumbly or soft cheeses—feta, goat, or ricotta—are all fine replacements for the Parmesan.

Learn More

▶ Egg Basics (page 50), Grating Cheese (page 176), Salad Greens (page 108), Chopping Onions (page 19)

ADDING THE EGGS If the vegetables bunch up—and they will—spread them out again, without actually stirring the eggs. Lower the heat if you hear too much sizzling.

JUDGING DONENESS The frittata is ready for the broiler when the top is beginning to set around the edges but still a bit loose in the center.

Baked Eggs with Onions and Cheese

One of the best egg dishes for a small crowd—you can cook a lot at one time.

TIME **45 minutes**
MAKES **4 to 8 servings**

---

4 tablespoons (½ stick) butter or olive oil

4 onions (about 1 pound), sliced

1 cup bread crumbs, preferably fresh

2 cups grated Gruyère, fontina, or other melting cheese

8 eggs

Salt and freshly ground black pepper

Toasted bread or English muffins for serving

1 Heat the oven to 350°F. Put the butter or oil in a large skillet over medium heat. When the butter has melted or the oil is hot, add the onions. Cook them, stirring occasionally, until they are very soft and tender but not browned, at least 15 minutes. (Adjust the heat as necessary to keep them sizzling gently without darkening.)

2 Spread the onions over the bottom of a 9 x 13-inch baking pan. Sprinkle half the bread crumbs over the onions, then sprinkle on half the cheese. Use the back of a spoon to make 8 nests in the mixture. Crack the eggs on a flat, hard surface and open them into each indentation. Top with a sprinkle of salt and pepper and the remaining bread crumbs and cheese.

3 Bake for 15 to 20 minutes, or until the cheese is melted and the egg whites are opaque. The yolks should be a little more jiggly than you want them, since they'll keep cooking after you take the pan out of the oven. Serve with toasted bread.

It's not a big deal if a yolk breaks, but if it bothers you, scoop the egg out with a big spoon and try another.

CREATING THE BASE Use your hands or a large spoon to sprinkle the bread crumbs and cheese evenly over the onions.

MAKING ROOM FOR THE EGGS The "nests" need not all be the same size as long as each is deep enough to hold an egg.

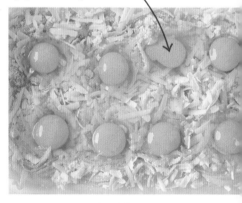

PLACING THE EGGS Carefully open each egg above an indentation and drop it gently into the nest so that as much of the white stays with the yolk as possible.

Tips

▶ Any cooked vegetable works as a bed for baked eggs: roasted or mashed potatoes, spinach or other greens, summer or winter squash, chopped asparagus, or even grated carrots. Just make sure they're already tender and you have enough to fill the bottom of the baking dish and make the indentations.

▶ To make a smaller batch, cook half the amount of onions in an ovenproof skillet and make indentations for 4 eggs. Depending on the size of the skillet, the eggs might take less time to cook, so start checking them after 10 minutes.

Variations

▶ **Baked Eggs with Tomato:** Use 8 large tomatoes (about 2 pounds) instead of the onions. Chop them into big chunks and cook them as described in Step 1, until they release their water and the pan becomes fairly dry. (This should still take about 15 minutes.) Then just follow the recipe the same way. When the pan comes out of the oven, garnish with ¼ cup chopped fresh herbs—like parsley, chives, or cilantro—if you've got them.

Learn More

▶ Egg Basics (page 50), Fresh Bread Crumbs (page 386), cheese for cooking (page 389), Grating Cheese (page 176), slicing onions (page 232)

French Toast

A fancy breakfast that's easy and never fussy.

TIME **20 to 30 minutes**
MAKES **4 servings**

---

8 slices or ½ loaf
good-quality bread

2 eggs

1 cup milk

Salt

1 tablespoon sugar,
optional

1 teaspoon vanilla extract,
optional

2 tablespoons butter,
or probably more

1 Put a large skillet, preferably non-stick, over medium-low heat while you prepare the egg mixture for soaking the bread. Heat the oven to 200°F.

2 If the bread is whole, cut it into 8 slices no more than 1 inch thick. Crack the eggs on a flat, hard surface and open them into a wide, shallow bowl large enough to hold a few slices of the bread. Add the milk and whisk until the mixture is smooth. Then whisk in a small pinch of salt and the sugar and vanilla if you're using them.

3 Put 2 or 3 slices of bread in the bowl. Use a fork to turn the slices, pressing on the crusts a little if needed to help them soak up the liquid.

4 Sprinkle a couple drops of water into the pan; if the drops skid across the surface before evaporating, it's hot enough. If not, turn up the heat a bit. Put a pat of the butter in the skillet. When it stops foaming, lift a piece of bread from the egg mixture and let it drip off, then transfer it to the pan. Repeat soaking and transferring the bread until the skillet is comfortably full; don't overcrowd or the toast will be hard to maneuver and won't brown properly.

5 Cook each piece until nicely browned underneath, 3 to 5 minutes, adjusting the heat if necessary to keep the bread from burning. You might need to move the slices around in the pan to help them cook evenly. When the bottom turns golden brown, turn and cook on the other side, another 3 to 5 minutes. Serve right from the pan and keep cooking the remaining batches. Or transfer them as they finish cooking to an oven-proof plate and put them in the oven to stay warm for up to 20 minutes.

Either a whisk or a fork works fine here.

MAKING THE CUSTARD It doesn't take long to whisk the eggs and milk into a smooth, creamy mixture.

Tips

▶ Buttery, eggy breads like challah or brioche make soft, custardy French toast with crisp outsides. For something heartier, try a whole grain loaf. Airy loaves with big holes work only if you cut them 1 to 2 inches thick.

▶ Slightly dry stale bread is ideal here, because it soaks up the egg mixture like a sponge. Fresh bread is okay too, but dry the slices on a baking sheet in a 200°F oven for a few minutes if you have time.

▶ Topping ideas: fresh berries, yogurt, maple syrup, jam, a sprinkle of powdered sugar, or a drizzle of molasses.

Variations

▶ **3 Ways to Vary French Toast:**

1 Instead of vanilla, flavor the custard with a pinch of ground cinnamon, cardamom, cloves, ginger, or nutmeg.

2 Press sliced almonds or unsweetened grated coconut onto the top of the bread before transferring it to the skillet.

3 While the toast is staying warm in the oven, melt a little more butter in the skillet and cook some sliced apples or bananas for 2 to 3 minutes and serve them on top of the toast.

Learn More

▶ Bread and Sandwich Basics (page 382), Judging the Pan's Heat (page 66), Maple Syrup (page 42)

AVOIDING SOGGINESS Press down gently with a fork to help saturate the bread evenly. Thick-crusted slices will require a little bit more soaking time.

RECOGNIZING DONENESS Leave plenty of elbow room in the pan. They're ready to flip when they smell like toast and get brown on the bottom. Then turn them over like pancakes.

Pancakes

A simple and forgiving batter that works with lots of different add-ins.

TIME   20 to 30 minutes
MAKES   4 to 6 servings

2 cups all-purpose flour

2 teaspoons baking powder

½ teaspoon salt

1 tablespoon sugar

2 eggs

1½ to 2 cups milk

2 tablespoons melted and cooled butter, plus more (unmelted) butter for cooking

1 Put a large skillet, preferably non-stick, over medium-low heat while you make the batter.

2 Combine the flour, baking powder, salt, and sugar in a large bowl and stir to mix well. In a smaller bowl, beat the eggs with 1½ cups of the milk, then stir in the 2 tablespoons cooled melted butter.

3 Add the egg mixture to the dry ingredients, stirring only enough to moisten the flour and distribute the liquid evenly; don't worry about a few lumps. If the batter seems thick, add a little more milk—the thinner the batter, the thinner the pancakes and the more they'll spread out in the pan.

4 Sprinkle a couple drops of water into the pan; if the drops skid across the surface before evaporating, it's hot enough. If not, turn up the heat a bit. Put a pat of butter in the skillet. When it stops foaming, ladle small amounts of batter onto the skillet, making any size pancakes you like. Cook, undisturbed, until the edges are set and bubbles appear in the center of the pancakes, 2 to 4 minutes. If the pancakes are cooking too fast or too slowly, adjust the heat a little bit at a time.

5 Carefully slip a spatula under a pancake to peek and see if it's brown on the bottom. If so, lift it from the pan and turn it over. Cook the second side until it's lightly browned, another 2 or 3 minutes, and serve right away.

Lumps.

MIXING JUST TO COMBINE Don't overstir the batter; better for it to be a little lumpy than for you to stir it too much, which will make the pancakes tough and rubbery.

JUDGING THE PAN'S HEAT If the water drops just sit there, the pan isn't hot enough. If they evaporate in a flash, it's too hot.

LEAVING ROOM You need space to flip the pancakes. Small ones are easier to handle, so until you get the hang of it, use no more than ¼ cup batter for each.

Tips

▶ The first batch of pancakes—which are never quite as good as those that follow—usually require higher heat than the following batches, since the skillet builds up and retains heat.

▶ Pancakes are best eaten immediately, but you can keep them warm on an ovenproof plate in a 200°F oven for about 15 minutes.

▶ To cook pancakes on an electric griddle, set the temperature to 350°F and adjust it as necessary to keep the batter sizzling gently without burning. Or use a stovetop griddle just like a skillet.

Variations

▶ **Partially Whole Grain Pancakes:** Replace ½ cup of the flour with cornmeal or whole wheat flour.

▶ **Spiced Pancakes:** Spike the batter with a pinch of ground cinnamon or ginger or 1 tablespoon grated lemon or orange zest.

▶ **Loaded Pancakes:** Right after you pour the batter into the pan, sprinkle with blueberries, banana slices, chopped nuts, chocolate chunks, or granola.

Learn More

▶ Melting Butter (page 70), Combining Dry Ingredients (page 396), Combining Wet Ingredients (page 396), Maple Syrup (page 42), Preparing Fruit (page 430)

Peek under the pancake to see if it's golden brown underneath. If it is, flip it.

WAITING FOR BUBBLES Pancakes are ready when the edges set and they smell like sweet toast, not burned. Don't rush to turn them or they won't hold together.

Appetizers and Snacks

The old-school word *appetizers* may no longer be hip, but at least it's descriptive: This broad category of recipes comprises full-flavored nibbles that prime your appetite. I like my starters and snacks to be all that for sure, but I want them quick and casual too. That's what makes these recipes perfect for a basic cookbook.

Of course you can buy much of the food in this chapter at any supermarket—jarred, bagged, boxed, or frozen. But once you dive in you'll quickly discover that home-cooked dishes blow the processed stuff away. Your version will be fresher, tastier, and free of chemicals and additives. And in many cases, preparing it won't take any longer than heating a tray of what-have-you taken out of the freezer.

We start with two of the best snacks imaginable: popcorn and roasted nuts. Utterly simple? Yes. But also beloved, and invaluable for the important cooking skills they teach. From there we tackle classic dips and spreads, along with their accompaniments, and then move on to several dishes good for passing around at parties, serving at the start of a sit-down dinner, or eating as the main component of a casual supper or lunch. Along the way you'll pick up tips for assembling easy appetizer trays and learn what you can and can't prepare ahead of time.

The only other thing I can say is: Be prepared for a flood of compliments. You're about to surprise your friends and family—and probably even yourself.

Real Buttered Popcorn

The perfect fast food and a great place to experiment with your stove and your spice rack.

TIME **10 minutes**

MAKES **4 to 6 servings (12 to 14 cups)**

---

2 tablespoons vegetable oil

½ cup popping corn

4 tablespoons (½ stick) butter

Salt

1 Put the vegetable oil in a large pot over medium-high heat. Add 3 kernels of popcorn and cover the pot. Put the butter in a small saucepan over low heat; when the butter melts, remove the pot from the heat.

2 When the 3 kernels pop, remove the lid from the pot and add the remaining corn. Cover and shake the pot once or twice, holding the lid on. Cook, shaking occasionally, as the corn begins to pop vigorously. Adjust the heat—and remove the pot from the burner briefly if needed—to keep the corn popping steadily without burning. When you can count to 3 between pops, 3 to 5 minutes after adding the corn, remove the pot from the heat.

3 Pour the popcorn into a large bowl, drizzle with the butter, and sprinkle with a big pinch of salt. Toss, taste and add more salt if you like, and serve.

You don't want the oil to get so hot it smokes or the popcorn will have a scorched taste.

Olive oil is another option: Put it in the pot instead of the butter and warm it up a bit.

Just quickly slide the pan back and forth.

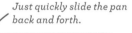

HEATING THE OIL Listen carefully for the popping of the test kernels—your signal that the oil is the right temperature to add the remaining corn.

MELTING BUTTER Adjust the heat so it slowly turns to liquid and gets hot but doesn't burn or smoke. If it's ready before the popcorn is, that's okay.

POPPING PROPERLY Carefully hold the lid on tight while shaking the pan. If you smell burning, remove the pot from the heat and turn it down a bit before continuing.

Tips

▶ Use your ears: When the popping slows down, and a couple of seconds go by between pops, it's time to turn off the heat.

▶ It's unlikely that every single kernel will pop. If a few kernels are left at the bottom of the pan when the popping sounds stop, just leave them there (or eat them if you like). It's better to sacrifice a few kernels than to burn your popcorn.

▶ For lighter popcorn, leave out the extra drizzle of fat altogether.

▶ Eat the popcorn while it's hot if you can.

Variations

▶ **7 Quick Seasonings for Popcorn.** In Step 3, sprinkle the popcorn with any of the following instead of, or in addition to, the salt:

1 1 teaspoon freshly ground black pepper

2 ½ teaspoon crushed red pepper, or to taste

3 1 teaspoon chili powder, curry powder, or cayenne

4 2 to 4 tablespoons freshly grated Parmesan cheese

5 ¼ cup chopped nuts

6 ¼ cup chopped dried fruit

7 ¼ cup shredded unsweetened coconut

Learn More

▶ Spices (page 2), Grating Cheese (page 176)

Roasted Nuts

Bye-bye, Mr. Peanut. Hello, homemade party nuts.

TIME   **15 minutes**
MAKES   **4 to 6 servings
(2 cups)**

**2 cups any unsalted nuts
(like peanuts, almonds,
cashews, or a mixture)**

**2 tablespoons vegetable oil
or melted butter**

**Salt and freshly ground
black pepper**

1 Heat the oven to 450°F. Toss the nuts
in a bowl with the oil and a sprinkle of
salt and pepper.

2 Spread the nuts in an even layer on a
rimmed baking sheet and roast, shaking occasionally, until lightly browned,
5 to 10 minutes. Let the nuts cool for a
few minutes, then serve while they're
still a little warm.

*Watch them, because they can
start to burn quickly. They'll
become crisper as they cool.*

*You need to use a rimmed
baking sheet whenever
the food will be sliding
around in the pan, or if
there are juices, oil, or
pan drippings to contain.*

SPREADING NUTS IN PAN If they
don't fit in one layer, use a second
baking sheet or work in batches.

ROASTING EVENLY Shaking the
pan helps roll the nuts around
and cook evenly. When they're
done, the nuts will be medium
brown and smell toasty; they
won't be completely crisp, though.

Tips

▶ You can use any shelled nuts that you have on hand, but I especially like any combination using pecans, walnuts, almonds, pistachios, and cashews.

▶ Use your nose: At about the same time that the nuts begin to turn light brown, your kitchen will start smelling nutty. That intoxicating smell means they're done, so get them out of the oven before they scorch.

Variations

▶ **Toasted Nuts:** When recipes call for "toasted nuts," use this same method, only don't toss them in oil or butter and skip the salt. To make them in a dry skillet—which takes a little longer than the oven but is easier to watch and great for lesser amounts—work in single-layer batches, keep the heat at medium-low, and shake the skillet frequently to promote even browning.

▶ **Roasted Herbed Nuts:** Toss the nuts with 1 tablespoon chopped fresh rosemary or thyme leaves along with the salt and pepper.

▶ **Sweet-Hot Nuts:** Toss the nuts with ¼ cup packed brown sugar and ½ teaspoon cayenne (more or less) along with the salt and pepper.

▶ **Honey-Roasted Nuts:** Drizzle ¼ cup honey over the nuts along with the salt and pepper and toss.

Learn More

▶ Roasting (page 33), Melting Butter (page 70), Building Flavor (page 12)

Crudités with Warm Olive Oil Dip

Warm, flavored olive oil brings a platter of raw vegetables to life.

TIME **30 to 60 minutes**

MAKES **8 servings**

---

3 to 4 pounds assorted raw vegetables, like carrots, cucumbers, radishes, bell peppers, and celery

1 cup olive oil

1 tablespoon minced garlic

Salt and freshly ground black pepper

1 Prepare the vegetables by trimming, coring, peeling, or removing seeds as necessary. Cut them lengthwise into sticks or crosswise into coins or slices; you want pieces you can easily pick up with your hands and use for dipping.

2 Put the vegetables in small bowls or on a platter. If you're serving right away, refrigerate them until everything is ready. If you're preparing them in advance, cover the vegetables with clean damp towels and refrigerate them for up to a few hours.

3 Put the oil, garlic, and a sprinkle of salt and pepper in a small saucepan over low heat. Cook, stirring frequently, until the oil is warm and fragrant and the garlic puffs and turns golden but not brown, 5 to 10 minutes. Serve the oil warm alongside the vegetables.

Avoid using precut carrots; they don't have much flavor.

If you want to add other flavors to the oil—see the Variations for ideas— put the ingredients in the pot now.

CUTTING INTO STICKS (OR SPEARS) The ideal size for dipping is 2 to 3 inches long and about ½ inch wide. But anywhere near that range is fine.

CUTTING OTHER SHAPES Cut ovals (on the diagonal) and crescents (as with bell peppers) to make a more interesting presentation.

FLAVORING THE OIL Heat the oil as gently as possible. Burnt garlic (dark brown, with bits of black) will make the oil taste bitter.

Tips

▶ Some other vegetables for crudités: zucchini, jícama (peeled), cherry tomatoes (served with toothpicks), scallions (trimmed but left whole), button mushrooms (whole or halved), daikon or kohlrabi (both peeled), and fennel (trimmed and sliced).

▶ To prepare crudités up to a day in advance, refrigerate the cut raw vegetables in ice water to keep them crisp and the parboiled vegetables (see the Variations) in airtight containers. Before serving, drain the raw vegetables and pat them dry with towels.

Variations

▶ Other vegetables work in a crudité spread, even if you can't (or don't want to) eat them raw. You can cook small waxy potatoes (red or white; peel on; halved or sliced), green or other long beans (trimmed but left whole), and rutabagas or sweet potatoes (peeled and sliced). Boiling or steaming is easiest since you can nab them from the heat while they're still crisp and immediately "shock" them in a bowl of ice water to stop the cooking. Grilled and roasted vegetables can also work, again provided they've still got

a little crunch when you try to pick them up.

▶ A few vegetables work either cooked or raw: asparagus, broccoli or cauliflower (cut into florets), beets or turnips (peeled and sliced), and sugar snap peas (trimmed but whole).

▶ To add more flavor to the oil: When you warm the olive oil in Step 3, add 1 tablespoon chopped fresh rosemary, oregano, or thyme leaves or 1 teaspoon dried, or a mashed anchovy or two. (The flavored oil is also perfect for dipping bread and brushing on sandwiches.)

Learn More

▶ Vegetable Basics (page 216), Trimming (page 16), Peeling (page 17), Preparing Bell Peppers (page 117), Shocking Vegetables (page 238)

How to Throw a Party

Appetizers on the Fly

Here are three classic appetizer platters, perennial hits that give you the chance to mix and match store-bought and homemade foods in any proportions you like:

Antipasto, Your Way If you have access to an Italian market or well-stocked deli case, start with prosciutto (or another dry-cured ham), salami, bresaola (air-dried beef), capicola (seasoned pork sausage), or mortadella (the most delicious bologna ever); get a little of each if you can. This stuff is all rich and flavorful, so make sure it's thinly sliced. Then to serve, fold each slice over a few times, or bunch it together, so that it's easy to grab. It's nice to add one or two Italian cheeses, like sliced provolone or fresh mozzarella, or chunks of Parmesan or Gorgonzola. And then you've got to have some vegetables (either homemade or store-bought): olives, dried tomatoes, roasted red peppers, marinated artichokes or onions, pickles, cherry tomatoes, or shaved fennel. Serve the assortment on one large platter or several small plates and bowls, along with sliced fresh or toasted bread and a cruet of olive oil for drizzling.

The Cheese Tray Cheese is much like wine: You decide how much of an enthusiast you want to be, but in the meantime, just keep tasting. To put together a basic cheese platter, zero in on three or four different styles or textures of cheese, and get one kind in each category. For example, a hard cheese (like Parmesan or manchego), a medium-firm cheese (like cheddar or Gruyère), and a soft cheese (like Camembert, or a blue or fresh goat cheese). Another way to go: Try assembling one cow's milk cheese, one goat's milk cheese, and one sheep's milk cheese; or all aged cheeses. (If you don't live near a specialty cheese store, head for the best supermarket you know; many have decent selections now.) I like to serve whole wedges—each with its own knife—so guests can cut their own pieces. Good accompaniments include something crunchy—crackers, crusty bread, or crostini—and something fruity—grapes, orange segments, sliced apples or pears. For something more unusual, try olives, toasted nuts, and a small jar of really good fruit preserves. It's easiest for guests to navigate the platter if cheese is on a flat surface or board, with little bowls and plates for the sides.

Not-Your-Usual Nachos Definitely more thought-out than chips and salsa, but not much more work. The setup is done in advance: For 6 to 8 people, figure a large bag of tortilla chips. Then make (or purchase) one or two different salsas (pages 82–83); chop some scallions, cilantro, and black olives; cook some black or refried beans (see page 390 or open a can). About an hour beforehand, make some guacamole (page 84) and grate some cheddar, Jack, or, better still, Mexican melting cheese like Oaxaca or cotija. Alternate the cheese with layers of tortilla chips on a rimmed baking sheet. Twenty minutes before guests are due, heat the oven to 350°F, put the beans on the chips, and put all the trimmings out on the table. Then all you have to do is pop the nachos in the oven while you greet and serve drinks; they're ready when the cheese starts to bubble, 10 to 15 minutes later. Sprinkle the top of the nachos with scallions, cilantro, and olives and serve.

Roasted Peppers
(page 98)

Shaved Fennel
Salad (page 128)

6 Easy Ways to Keep the Life in Your Party

1 Treat Your Friends and Family Like Guinea Pigs It's perfectly acceptable, and lots of fun, to practice on your guests—I've done it for years. You need to try new things in the kitchen, and they need to eat.

2 Don't Bite Off More than You Can Chew Plan to prepare only as many dishes as you can actually envision yourself cooking. (Or get help!)

3 Make the Right Amount of Food If you're having 12 people for appetizers and dinner, make three times one recipe that serves 4, or 2 dishes that each serve 6 to 8—you get the idea.

4 Do Whatever You Can Way Ahead of Time Your job at the last minute is to greet guests and pour drinks. Do most of the cooking and setup in advance.

5 Serve Whatever You Can at Room Temperature This strategy removes the pressure to time a meal so that dishes all get to the table hot, which isn't really a big deal.

6 Focus on Finger Food Eating hand to mouth—with a napkin running interference—is the epitome of casual entertaining and sparks lively mingling and conversation.

Herb Dip

With little more work, you can do way better than soup mix stirred into sour cream.

TIME **10 minutes**

MAKES **6 to 8 servings**

1 small bunch fresh parsley or dill or a combination

2 cups sour cream or yogurt

2 scallions, chopped

1 tablespoon fresh lemon juice

Salt and freshly ground black pepper

About 6 cups food for dipping, like cut-up raw or cooked vegetables or crackers, chips, or breadsticks

1 Strip the herb leaves from their thickest stems by pulling with your fingers or snipping them free with scissors. Chop the leaves; the finer you go, the more smooth and refined the dip will be. You want at least ½ cup chopped herbs; use more for a stronger flavor if you'd like. Save the rest for another use.

2 Whisk together the sour cream, scallions, lemon juice, herbs, and a sprinkle of salt and pepper in a medium bowl. Taste and adjust the seasoning. Serve right away with vegetables, crackers, chips, or breadsticks, or cover and refrigerate for up to a day.

Keep chopping until the herbs are as small as you want them.

STRIPPING LEAVES FROM SOFT HERB STEMS Gather the leaves and twist, or pluck them individually to free from the stem. These techniques work for herbs like parsley, cilantro, basil, and dill.

To snip herbs, cut just below where leaves meet stem. Use whichever way you find easier.

CHOPPING HERBS Lift the handle of the knife to rock the blade up and down, while your other hand steadies it and keeps the tip in contact with the cutting board.

Tips

▶ Diligence in cutting the herbs into teeny bits gets you to a smoother dip but isn't mandatory. If you've got a food processor, by all means use it here for a super-smooth, bright green dip. Remove the herb leaves as described in Step 1, then combine all the ingredients in the work bowl and give 'er a whirl.

Variations

▶ **To use other fresh herbs:** You can substitute mild ones like cilantro, mint, or chives for the parsley and dill. Try different combinations and see what you like best. If you want the stronger taste of the more aromatic herbs like oregano, sage, rosemary, or thyme, combine 1 tablespoon with ¼ cup parsley; you can always add more. You can use basil too (up to ½ cup), but the dip will start to discolor after a couple of hours.
▶ **Herb Spread:** Substitute cream cheese or goat cheese for the sour cream. The first will be rich and milky tasting; the second will be tangy and grassy. If your spread is too thick, stir in milk or cream, 1 tablespoon at a time.

Learn More

▶ Dairy—and Not (page 42), Preparing Scallions (page 295), Vegetable Basics (page 216), preparing vegetables for dipping (page 74)

Mashing as you whisk will help the herbs release even more flavor.

ADDING THE HERBS The flavor will disperse quickly into the dip. Start with ½ cup herbs and a little salt and pepper before mixing; then taste and add more if you need it.

Fresh Tomato Salsa

Utterly useful. Turn the page for more ways to vary ingredients and flavors.

TIME **30 to 45 minutes**
MAKES **6 to 8 servings
(about 4 cups)**

**4 large tomatoes (about
1½ pounds)**

**1 medium white onion,
chopped, or 4 scallions,
chopped**

**1 or 2 fresh hot green chiles
(like jalapeño), seeded and
minced**

2 teaspoons minced garlic

**1 cup chopped fresh
cilantro or parsley leaves
(about 1 large bunch)**

**3 tablespoons fresh lime
juice, or more to taste**

**Salt and freshly ground
black pepper**

1 Remove the core from a tomato with a paring knife, then quarter them and chop the wedges into small chunks. Scrape the pieces and all the juice on the cutting board into a large bowl. Repeat with the remaining tomatoes.

2 Add the onion, chile, garlic, cilantro, and lime juice to the tomatoes. Sprinkle with salt and pepper, then taste and adjust the seasoning, adding more lime juice if you like. If you have time, let the salsa sit at room temperature for 15 minutes for the flavors to blend; then serve. (You can make the salsa ahead and refrigerate it for up to 2 hours; bring it back to room temperature before serving.)

*By all means, add another
tomato to this recipe if
you'd like.*

CORING TOMATOES Cut around the tomato core without going too deep; use your thumb for stability and hold the knife at a slight angle so you cut a cone that lifts right out.

CUTTING TOMATOES Roughly chopping the tomatoes breaks them up for more varied textures.

Tips

▶ Salsa is best made with fresh ingredients in season. And with the variations that follow on the next two pages, you can do just that—year-round—with all sorts of fruits, vegetables, and seasoning.

▶ Salsa is good with crudités or as a sauce for simply cooked vegetables. I also like it tossed with grains, beans, or rice. And a spoonful or two on top of grilled or broiled fish, chicken, or meat is a game changer.

▶ If you're out of fresh herbs or chiles, just skip them and add 1 teaspoon ground cumin and a pinch of cayenne or crushed red pepper instead.

▶ If you don't like spicy food, just leave out the chile; you might want to add more garlic.

Learn More
▶ Chopping onions (page 19), Preparing Chiles (page 276), mincing garlic (page 20), Chopping Herbs (page 78), Salsa Variations (page 82)

I always use every drop of a good fresh tomato.

CAPTURING THE JUICE Use the back side of a knife to scrape the fruit, seeds, and juice off the cutting board into the bowl.

Salsa Variations

Change Is Good

And easy. The chunky fresh salsa on the previous page is essentially a classic Mexican concoction known as *pico de gallo*. The basic formula works with lots of fruits and vegetables. To try any of these ideas: Follow the directions for Fresh Tomato Salsa. Instead of the tomatoes, use about 1½ pounds of the main ingredient listed in the variation and chop it as described; the rest of the stuff remains the same unless otherwise mentioned. To learn more about preparing different fruits and vegetables, see The List of Lessons beginning on page 458.

Citrus Salsa Peel oranges, tangerines, or grapefruits or a combination. Divide the fruit into segments and chop, removing the seeds as you work.

Pepper Salsa Red, orange, or yellow bell pepper, cored, seeded, and chopped.

Apple Salsa Any green or red apple works, the crisper the better. Don't bother to peel them; just core and chop. Instead of the white onion, use red onion or 2 large shallots. Parsley is a nice switch from cilantro.

Peach or Plum Salsa Sweet and juicy. No need to peel. Cut the fruit in half and remove the pit before chopping. Substitute basil or mint for the cilantro.

Radish or Jícama Salsa You'll need to peel jícama but not radishes. Try minced ginger instead of the garlic and mint instead of the cilantro or parsley.

Cucumber Salsa Peel and seed 2 large or 3 medium cucumbers. Substitute red onion for the white and lemon juice for the lime.

Pineapple Salsa This is a bit of a pain, but it's really worth it: Use 1 firm medium fruit without much green on the outside. Cut crosswise to remove the top and bottom. Then stand the fruit upright and cut downward around all sides to remove the peel. Cut the fruit into manageable pieces and chop the fruit into small pieces, leaving behind the tough core that runs through the center. (See page 430 for photos)

Melon Salsa Works with cantaloupe, honeydew, watermelon, whatever; figure about 2 pounds before peeling. Cut the fruit in half or into manageable pieces, remove the seeds, and cut the flesh free of the rind before chopping.

Fresh Tomatillo (Green) Salsa Remove the papery skin from the tomatillos and core them as you would tomatoes; then chop. Use 2 chopped fresh mild green chiles (like poblano) instead of the hot chile.

Pineapple Salsa

Jícama Salsa

Fresh Tomatillo Salsa

Guacamole and Chips

The real deal is made from simply seasoned, lightly mashed avocados and little else.

TIME **30 minutes**
MAKES **6 to 8 servings
(about 4 cups)**

2 large or 3 medium
avocados (about 2 pounds)

1 small onion, chopped

1 medium fresh hot green
chile (like jalapeño), seeded
and minced

½ teaspoon minced garlic

1 teaspoon chili powder

1 tablespoon fresh lime
juice, or more to taste

Salt and freshly ground
black pepper

2 tablespoons chopped
fresh cilantro leaves for
garnish

6 to 8 cups tortilla chips
(1 large bag)

1 Cut each avocado in half lengthwise and remove the pit. Scoop out the flesh from both halves with a large spoon and put it in a medium bowl.

2 Add the onion, chile, garlic, chili powder, lime juice, and a sprinkle of salt and pepper. Mash the mixture with a fork or potato masher until it's as smooth or as chunky as you like. Taste and adjust the seasoning.

3 Garnish with the cilantro and serve immediately with a bowl of tortilla chips. (You can also wait to add the herb; cover the guacamole tightly with plastic wrap, pressing down so the wrap is touching the top; and refrigerate for up to 2 hours before garnishing and serving.)

*To dislodge the pit safely
from the blade, hit the knife
handle against the corner
of the counter or grab it
with a towel.*

*The pit always
stays with one half.*

HALVING AN AVOCADO Remove the nubby stem, then cut through the fruit lengthwise to reach the pit. Rotate the avocado against the knife to cut all the way around it. Then twist the halves apart.

REMOVING THE PIT Carefully strike the pit with a sharp knife in one swift but not too aggressive stroke. It will stick inside the pit. Turn and lift the knife to remove the pit.

Tips

▸ Avocados begin to turn brown quickly once the flesh is exposed to air. So if you're not going to eat it immediately, be sure to cover the guacamole soon after making. This will buy you a little time, but not more than an hour or two.

▸ I won't deny that handling avocados can be intimidating at first. Your priority should be to work the knife safely; don't worry about whether the flesh gets a little mangled in the process. You'll get better with practice.

Variations

▸ **5 Fast Guacamole Stir-Ins.** Right before serving, try adding up to 1 cup of any of these:
1 Fresh or frozen corn kernels
2 Salsa (any kind)
3 Chopped tomato
4 Firm mild cheese, like crumbled queso fresco or grated cheddar
5 Chopped cooked shrimp or crab

Learn More

▸ Chopping onions (page 19), Preparing Chiles (page 276), mincing garlic (page 20), Chopping Herbs (page 78)

SCOOPING OUT THE FLESH
Insert a spoon underneath the flesh, against the skin, and run the spoon all the way around to separate and lift the flesh from the skin.

MASHING Not too thoroughly: You want some chunks of avocado remaining.

Hummus with Pita

A Middle Eastern classic for dipping, spreading, or smearing on sandwiches.

TIME **15 minutes with cooked chickpeas**

MAKES **6 to 8 servings (about 3 cups)**

2 medium garlic cloves, or more to taste

2 cups cooked or drained canned chickpeas (liquid reserved if you cooked them yourself)

½ cup tahini, or to taste

¼ cup olive oil, or more as needed

2 tablespoons fresh lemon juice, or more to taste

1 tablespoon paprika or cumin, plus more for garnish

Salt and freshly ground black pepper

1 tablespoon chopped fresh parsley leaves for garnish

8 small or 4 large pitas, cut into triangles or torn into large pieces

1 Put the garlic in a food processor or blender and pulse the machine until the cloves are chopped up a bit.

2 Add the chickpeas, tahini, oil, lemon juice, and paprika and sprinkle with salt and pepper. Turn on the machine and let it run, adding the chickpea cooking liquid or more oil—1 tablespoon at a time—until you get a smooth purée.

3 Taste and adjust the seasoning and pulse the machine a few times to combine. Serve, drizzled with another tablespoon of oil if you like, and sprinkled with a pinch of paprika and the parsley. Serve with the pita.

If you don't have a food processor or blender, mince the garlic first, then mash the remaining ingredients with a potato masher. Use a little more olive oil to keep the hummus from becoming too thick; some chunks are fine.

USING THE FOOD PROCESSOR OR BLENDER If your machine can't handle everything at once, purée half or a third of the ingredients, transfer the mixture to a bowl, and repeat.

ADDING LIQUID Pour in the liquid a tablespoon at a time, purée a bit, then check the consistency before adding more. Once it's in, you can't take it out.

Tips

▶ If you're cooking the chick-peas, make sure they're fully tender—quite soft—for this recipe.

▶ Tahini is a paste made by grinding sesame seeds; it's much like peanut butter. You'll find it in some supermarkets and any Greek or Middle Eastern market or health food store.

▶ When you adjust for seasoning in Step 3, here's your chance to emphasize different flavors. For nuttiness add tahini, for brightness more lemon, and for bite a little minced garlic.

▶ If you want to serve this with crisp pita, toast the pitas whole on a baking sheet in a 450°F oven for 5 to 10 minutes, turning once or twice. Let them cool a bit, then cut or tear them.

Variations

▶ **White Bean Spread with Lemon and Rosemary:** Skip the tahini and increase the olive oil to ½ cup. Use white beans instead of chickpeas, and 1 tablespoon chopped fresh rosemary leaves (or 1 teaspoon dried) instead of the cumin. Serve, drizzled with the table-spoon of olive oil and sprinkled with the parsley if you like.

Learn More

▶ Bean Basics (page 250), Crushing and Peeling Garlic (page 247), Chopping Herbs (page 78)

Use a blender for an even smoother hummus.

ADJUSTING THE TEXTURE Purée as little or as much as you like. A blender will give you smoother texture but probably require more liquid to keep the blades moving.

Quick Pickle Spears

A tangy marinated cucumber that doesn't take days to get that way.

TIME **45 minutes, plus time to chill**

MAKES **24 pickle spears**

½ cup white wine vinegar or sherry vinegar

2 tablespoons olive oil

1 tablespoon minced garlic

1 teaspoon salt

1 bay leaf

2 large or 3 medium cucumbers (about 1½ pounds)

1 Put the vinegar, oil, garlic, salt, bay leaf, and 2 cups water in a large pot and bring the mixture to a boil.

2 Meanwhile, trim the tops and bottoms from the cucumbers and peel them if you like. First cut them in half crosswise, then in half lengthwise. Then cut each piece lengthwise into 3 spears.

3 Once the liquid reaches a boil, add the cucumbers and remove from the heat. Let the cucumbers sit in the brine for 30 minutes; stir a few times to make sure all the cucumbers are submerged at least part of the time.

4 To chill quickly, transfer the pickles and brine to the freezer and cool, stirring occasionally, until the cucumbers crisp a bit and are cold throughout, 5 to 10 minutes. Or transfer them to the refrigerator to chill overnight. Serve the pickles in their brine or remove them as you need them (they'll keep in the brine for at least a week).

Since these were thin-skinned, uncoated cucumbers, I didn't bother to peel them.

PREPARING CUCUMBERS I often don't remove cukes' seeds, but I do cut off the bitter ends.

CUTTING PICKLE SPEARS Cut the cucumber pieces into thirds at an angle to make spears.

▶ Pickling is a chemical process that draws water out of food with a brine—any mixture that contains salt—to flavor and preserve it. Many pickling brines also contain vinegar (especially for quick pickles like this one). The salt draws out the moisture, producing a crisper vegetable, while the vinegar adds flavor.

▶ To peel or not to peel? If the skin is thick or treated with a waxy or oily coating (you'll be able to see and feel it), peel. Sometimes even thin, unwaxed skins can be bitter, so when in doubt, take a taste.

▶ If you ever see small pickling cucumbers (which are no more than about 4 inches long), grab 'em. Just trim the ends and cut them lengthwise into spears for this recipe.

Variations

▶ **7 Other Vegetables That You Can Pickle This Way.** Figure about 2 pounds before trimming and cut each into florets, slices, or spears:

1 Cauliflower
2 Broccoli
3 Onions
4 Celery
5 Zucchini
6 Carrots
7 Bell peppers

Learn More

▶ Vinegar (page 112), Trimming (page 16), Peeling (page 17), mincing garlic (page 20)

You can't substitute just any vinegar here because it needs to have a high percentage of acidity to preserve and crisp the pickles.

"PICKLING" The warm brine will pickle the cucumbers faster than if they marinated at room temperature.

Bruschetta

Pronounced *brew-sketta*: Italian for toasted, seasoned, and topped bread.

TIME   15 to 20 minutes
MAKES   4 to 8 servings

1 medium loaf any rustic bread (about 1 pound)

Olive oil as needed

1 to 4 garlic cloves, halved

Salt and freshly ground black pepper

1   Prepare a grill or turn on the broiler; the heat should be medium-high and the rack about 4 inches from the heat source.

2   Trim and slice the bread into at least 8 pieces, each about 1 inch thick. Brush both sides lightly with oil, then grill or broil them, turning once, until browned on both sides, 3 to 5 minutes.

3   While the bread is still hot, rub one or both sides with the garlic. Put the bread on a plate, then drizzle it with olive oil (a teaspoon or so per slice is not too much); sprinkle with salt and pepper and serve warm. (Or you can top the bruschetta with any of the ideas on the next pages.)

Whole grain, sourdough, even corn bread—all fair game in my book.

I like my bread on the dark side, but cook it however you like.

Think of the bread as "grating" the garlic.

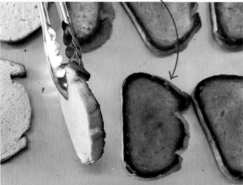

SLICING THE BREAD No matter what shape loaf you start with, you want the slices to be 1 inch thick and no bigger than your hand.

TOASTING BRUSCHETTA The bread should be slightly charred, but not totally black, which means you should keep an eye on it all the time.

TOPPING BRUSCHETTA The warm bread absorbs some of the flavor of the garlic as you rub, so the taste stays mild.

Use a full-flavored, fresh olive oil for drizzling since that's the predominant seasoning.

Tips

▶ You can use almost any good bread for bruschetta: Pick a loaf that's crusty on the outside and tender, not too chewy, on the inside. (Just ask for help at the bakery if you don't know.) You want the center to be moist, without any gaping holes. It can be made of white flour, whole grain, or a mix. Don't buy pre-sliced bread; it'll be too thin, and you'll end up with breakfast toast (which isn't bad; it's just not bruschetta).

▶ If you just want a scent of garlic, use one clove to rub all eight slices of bread; if you're a garlic fiend, use four.

Variations

▶ **Crostini:** Essentially large croutons. Use a baguette instead of a rustic loaf. In Step 2, cut the bread crosswise into slices no more than ½ inch thick so you have between 16 and 24 pieces. Brush with the oil and grill or broil or bake them in a 400°F oven, turning once, until they are golden brown on both sides (they will take about half the time of the thicker bruschetta). Rub with garlic if you like (skip the dousing of oil) and top them however you like; see the next page.

Learn More

▶ Bread and Sandwich Basics (page 382), Grilling (page 35), Broiling (page 34), Bruschetta Toppings (page 92)

Bruschetta Toppings

The World's Best Toast

Even at its simplest—seasoned with garlic and olive oil as on the preceding pages—bruschetta is a sublime convergence of textures and flavors. Quite simply the best toast you'll ever eat.

And as with toast, you can put whatever you like on top. The additions can be as simple as a piece of cheese or as complicated as braised meat. (Juicier toppings or extra olive oil make for softer bread.) All of which makes bruschetta perfect for bringing leftovers back to life. The result is casual to be sure, but take both the bread and the topping seriously and you end up with something that is exponentially better than the sum of its parts.

A Dozen Simple Ways to Top Bruschetta

Get your ingredients ready, then make the basic recipe on page 90. After adding the garlic and oil in Step 3, top with anything from this list. Try them alone or in combination, adjusting the quantities to taste:

1 Chopped ripe tomatoes (about 4 cups)
2 Chopped fresh basil leaves (1 cup packed)
3 Shaved or grated Parmesan cheese (about ½ cup)
4 Sliced fresh mozzarella (1 pound)
5 Ricotta cheese (about ½ cup)
6 Chopped olives or capers (½ or ¼ cup respectively)
7 Grated lemon or orange zest (2 tablespoons)
8 Sliced apples, pears, or plums (about 1 pound)
9 Chopped toasted nuts (½ cup)
10 Anchovies (1 or 2 per slice, with chopped parsley)
11 Sliced salami, prosciutto, or other smoked or cured meat (4 to 8 ounces)
12 Cooked crumbled sausage or bacon (4 to 8 ounces)

10 Recipes to Use on Bruschetta

Each of the recipes below from elsewhere in the book will be enough to top 8 to 12 slices of bread. Prepare the dish, before beginning to put the Bruschetta together (page 90)—skip the garlic and oil in Step 3 and, when the bruschetta comes out of the oven, spoon or spread on the topping, using any pan juices to drizzle over all just before serving.

1 Fresh Tomato Salsa (page 80), or any of the Salsa Variations (page 82)
2 Tomato Sauce (page 178)
3 Pesto (page 184)
4 Pan-Cooked (Sautéed) Mushrooms (page 230)
5 Caramelized Onions (page 232)
6 Quick Skillet Beans with Tomatoes (page 252)
7 Spanish-Style Lentils with Spinach (page 256)
8 Shrimp Scampi (page 362)
9 Braised Beef with Red Wine (page 278)
10 Sausage and Peppers (page 288)

Ricotta and Chopped Olives

Grated Lemon Zest and Anchovies

Quick Skillet Beans with Tomatoes

Deviled Eggs

An old-school nibble that never goes out of style and is easy to update.

TIME **15 minutes with precooked eggs**

MAKES **4 servings**

---

4 hard-boiled eggs

Salt

2 tablespoons mayonnaise

1 teaspoon Dijon-style mustard, or more to taste

¼ teaspoon cayenne, or more to taste

1 teaspoon paprika or chopped fresh parsley leaves for garnish

1 When you're ready to make the deviled eggs, crack the shells gently on all sides and peel; cut the eggs in half lengthwise and carefully remove the yolks.

2 Combine the yolks with a sprinkle of salt, the mayonnaise, mustard, and cayenne in a small bowl and mash the mixture with a fork until smooth. Taste and adjust the seasoning, adding more mustard and cayenne if you like.

3 Carefully spoon the filling back into the whites. Sprinkle the tops with paprika and serve or cover tightly with plastic wrap and refrigerate for up to a day. (They're best when not too cold, so remove them from the fridge about 15 minutes before serving.)

You can use your fingers to remove yolks or fill the egg whites—it'll make things easier.

REMOVING THE YOLK Scoop the yolk out gently so the white stays in one piece.

MASHING THE FILLING The classic texture is quite smooth, but you can make it chunky if you prefer.

Variations

▶ For a lighter, tangier version of Deviled Eggs, use yogurt instead of mayonnaise (half of each is good too).

▶ **Herbed Deviled Eggs:** In Step 2, add 2 tablespoons chopped fresh chives and 1 teaspoon chopped fresh tarragon leaves.

▶ **Curried Deviled Eggs:** In Step 2, use yogurt instead of the mayonnaise if you like and 1 teaspoon curry powder instead of the mustard. Add 1 tablespoon chopped pistachios or cashews. Garnish with chopped fresh cilantro leaves.

▶ **Crabby Deviled Eggs:** In Step 2, add ½ cup lump crabmeat. (You'll have lots of filling, so pile it high.)

▶ **Tangy Deviled Eggs:** In Step 2, add 2 tablespoons chopped capers or pickles.

Learn More

▶ Egg Basics (page 50), Hard-Boiled Eggs (page 51), Chopping Herbs (page 78)

STUFFING THE EGGS Don't be stingy with the filling; it's what makes deviled eggs so great.

USING A PLASTIC BAG TO FILL SOMETHING Another option: Put the yolk mixture in a resealable plastic bag, cut off a corner, and squeeze gently into the whites.

Quesadillas

Lightning quick for the perfect midnight snack, quick supper, or simple finger food.

TIME 20 to 25 minutes
MAKES 4 servings

¼ cup vegetable oil

4 flour tortillas (about 7 inches across)

1 cup grated cheddar or Jack cheese

2 scallions, chopped

1 or 2 fresh jalapeño chiles, thinly sliced, optional

1 cup fresh tomato (or any other) salsa for serving

1 Heat the oven to 200°F. Put a wire rack on a rimmed baking sheet and set it in the middle of the oven.

2 Put 1 tablespoon of the oil in a large skillet over medium heat. When the oil is hot, put a tortilla in the skillet. Top with a quarter of the cheese, scallions, and chiles if you're using them.

3 Cook until the cheese begins to soften a bit and the tortilla turns golden, 3 to 5 minutes; then fold the tortilla in half with a spatula. Flip with a spatula and cook until the cheese is just melted and both sides are toasted, another minute or two. Transfer the quesadilla to the prepared baking sheet to keep warm.

4 Repeat the process with the remaining tortillas and fillings, starting with heating the oil. (The quesadillas will keep in the oven for up to 30 minutes.) Cut into wedges and serve with the salsa.

You don't even have to cut them. Simply fold in half and eat out of hand.

FILLING Sprinkle the toppings evenly over half of the tortilla instead of in a pile; the quesadillas will cook more evenly and hold together better.

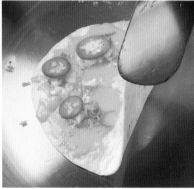

FOLDING Once you fold the quesadilla, flatten it a bit with the spatula.

CUTTING INTO WEDGES Cut downward firmly through all the layers into wedges—or just in half.

Tips

▶ Use any flour—or even corn—tortillas in the recipe. I'm not crazy about the flavored kinds, but whole wheat has a wonderfully nutty taste.

▶ You can cook the quesadillas without oil; a dry skillet will give you a slightly chewier, charred crust. Both ways are delicious.

Variations

▶ **5 Possible Additions to Quesadillas.** You don't want to overstuff the tortillas, but little bits of this or that adds extra flavor and texture. Figure up to ½ cup total—alone or combined—from this list:

1 Chopped black olives

2 Sautéed mushrooms

3 Cooked or canned black beans

4 Chopped or shredded cooked chicken, beef, or pork

5 Lump crabmeat or cooked shrimp

Learn More

▶ Cheese for cooking (page 389), Grating Cheese (page 176), Preparing Chiles (page 276), Fresh Tomato Salsa (page 80), Salsa Variations (page 82)

Roasted Peppers

Incomparably fresh and sweet—perhaps the best thing you can do with bell peppers.

TIME **20 to 90 minutes,
    depending on the method**
MAKES **4 to 8 servings**

**8 large bell peppers
(any color)**

Salt

2 to 4 tablespoons olive oil

1 Heat the oven to 450°F or position the rack under the broiler about 4 inches from the heat source and turn it to high. Put the peppers on a rimmed baking sheet lined with foil. Roast or broil, turning the peppers as each side browns, until they have darkened and collapsed, 15 to 20 minutes under the broiler, 50 to 60 minutes if roasting.

2 Gather up the corners of the foil from the pan and tightly wrap the peppers (use a kitchen towel to help if the foil is too hot). Cool until you can handle them, about 15 minutes, then remove the skin, seeds, and stems. (You can do this under running water to make it a little easier.) Don't worry if the peppers fall apart.

3 Serve the peppers within an hour or so, sprinkled with a pinch of salt and drizzled with 2 tablespoons olive oil, or more if you like. (Or drizzle them with 1 or 2 tablespoons of olive oil and store them in the refrigerator for up to a few days; bring them back to room temperature before serving.)

If you want them really charred and smoky-tasting, you've got to use the broiler— and check frequently.

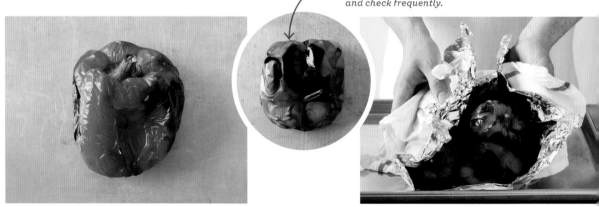

PROPER DONENESS The skin should be darkened, even blackened a bit, and blistered. Roasting gives you a little more control than broiling.

WRAPPING IN FOIL The foil will be hot, so be careful. But try to seal the package tightly so the peppers steam a bit as they cool.

This is my favorite way to eat them—alone with lots of olive oil.

PEELING ROASTED PEPPERS Do the best you can with cleaning the peppers. Water helps remove the skin quickly, but if bits of skin adhere stubbornly, don't worry about it.

Tips

▶ Any pepper can be roasted, but red, yellow, and orange are sweeter than green. If you like the sharp flavor of green peppers, you'll love them roasted. You can also roast poblano chiles, though the skins are more difficult to remove.

▶ To roast peppers on a grill: Prepare a grill; the heat should be medium-high and the rack about 4 inches from the fire. When the fire is hot, put the peppers directly over the heat. Grill, turning as each side blackens, until they collapse, 15 to 20 minutes. Then continue with Step 2, using a piece of foil to wrap them after they come off the fire.

Variations

▶ **6 Ways to Eat Roasted Peppers:**
1 With a fork
2 On a green salad
3 On a sandwich or bruschetta
4 Tossed with pasta
5 Puréed in a blender or food processor with 1 cup cream cheese or sour cream to make a spread
6 Puréed in a blender with another ¼ cup (or more) olive oil and salt to make a condiment that's good for anything from burgers to steamed fish

Learn More

▶ Grilling (page 35), Broiling (page 34)

Stuffed Mushrooms

Gorgeous appetizers, much simpler to make than you might think.

TIME   30 to 35 minutes
MAKES   4 to 6 servings

¼ cup olive oil

1 pound button mushrooms

1 egg

½ cup bread crumbs, preferably fresh

½ cup freshly grated Parmesan cheese

½ cup chopped fresh parsley leaves

1 tablespoon minced garlic

Salt and freshly ground black pepper

1 Heat the oven to 400°F. Grease a baking sheet with 2 tablespoons of the oil. Trim off the bottoms of the mushroom stems. Then pull on the stems to separate them, being careful to leave the caps intact. Chop the stems and combine them in a bowl with the egg, bread crumbs, cheese, parsley, garlic, and a sprinkle of salt and pepper.

2 Stir the remaining oil into the mixture and fluff with a fork. Stuff the mushroom caps with the bread crumb mixture, then put them stuffed side up on the baking sheet.

3 Bake until the stuffing is browned and crisp on top, 15 to 20 minutes. Let cool a little, then serve, warm or at room temperature, on toothpicks or with napkins.

If you don't want to use your fingers, try filling the caps using two teaspoons.

REMOVING MUSHROOM STEMS After trimming, gently rock the stems so they loosen enough to pull out; be careful to leave the cap intact.

CHOPPING MUSHROOM STEMS Rock the knife back and forth over the uneven pieces to chop them roughly.

FILLING THE MUSHROOMS Don't overstuff the caps or cram the filling in; the mushrooms will shrink as they bake.

Tips

▶ Mushrooms are notoriously dirty, but they're easy enough to clean: Rinse them under cold running water or in a salad spinner. (Despite what you may have heard, this doesn't make them soggy.)

▶ Mushrooms are also a strange shape. To trim them, slice off cracked, dried ends and any scarred or discolored patches that you definitely wouldn't want to eat.

▶ Make your own bread crumbs if you can. If not, use panko, which is larger, airier, and crisper than other store-bought crumbs.

Variations

▶ **Nutty Stuffed Mushrooms:** Use chopped walnuts, pecans, or pistachios instead of bread crumbs and 2 tablespoons melted butter in the stuffing instead of the olive oil.

▶ **Stuffed Mushrooms with Bacon Bread Crumbs:** Omit the cheese. Put 4 bacon slices in a medium skillet over medium-low heat, and cook until crisp, but not too brown. After draining, chop the bacon and add to the stuffing along with the oil in Step 2.

Learn More

▶ Types of mushrooms (page 231), Fresh Bread Crumbs (page 386), Grating Cheese (page 176), Chopping Herbs (page 78), mincing garlic (page 20)

Crab Cakes

For the best crab cakes: more crab, less filler. Simple as that.

TIME **20 to 30 minutes, plus time to chill**
MAKES **4 to 8 servings**

---

1 pound fresh lump crabmeat

1 egg

¼ cup mayonnaise

1 tablespoon Dijon-style mustard

Salt and freshly ground black pepper

2 tablespoons bread crumbs, preferably fresh, or more as needed

1 cup all-purpose flour for dredging, or more as needed

4 tablespoons olive oil

2 lemons, quartered, for serving

1 Pick over the crabmeat with your hands to remove any cartilage or shell. Combine the crab, egg, mayonnaise, mustard, and a sprinkle of salt and pepper in a large bowl. Add just enough bread crumbs to hold the mixture together and form cakes; start with 2 tablespoons and use more if necessary. (Or refrigerate the mixture without the crumbs for up to a few hours until you're ready to cook and then add the crumbs to form the mixture into cakes.)

2 When you're ready to cook, put the flour on a plate, sprinkle with salt and pepper, and stir to combine. Shape the crab mixture into 8 cakes (no more than 1 inch thick and about 2 inches across).

3 Put the oil in a medium or large skillet over medium-high heat and heat until the oil is hot. Dredge both sides of each cake in the flour and gently lay them into the skillet, being careful not to overcrowd the pan. (Work in batches if necessary and keep the first cakes warm in a 200°F oven.)

4 Cook, carefully turning once with a spatula and adjusting the heat as necessary so they don't burn, until browned and crisp on both sides, 3 to 5 minutes per side depending on their thickness. Serve right away with the lemon wedges.

This mixture is too loose to form cakes; stir in more bread crumbs 1 tablespoon at a time and then test again to make sure the cakes don't become too dense.

MIXING CRAB CAKES This is the density you need to form cakes. To make sure, try pressing a small amount together before adding more bread crumbs.

Tips

▶ Try to find lump or jumbo lump crabmeat; the pieces of crab are bigger (better for the texture) and usually higher quality.

▶ The recipe offers a guide for making eight cakes, but the overall size is up to you. Four larger cakes are fine for a main course, while mini versions are always a hit at parties.

Variations

▶ **Even Richer Crab Cakes:** Use butter instead of olive oil for cooking. In Step 3, wait for it to melt and foam before adding the crab cakes to the pan and be ready to adjust the heat so the butter doesn't burn.

▶ **Crab Cakes with Vegetables:** For more color and crunch. Try chopped red bell peppers, scallions, or celery or grated carrots or celery root. Add no more than 1 cup total.

▶ **Shrimp or Salmon Cakes:** Pulse 1 pound peeled raw shrimp or salmon fillet in a food processor until chopped but not puréed. Use this instead of the crab in Step 1 and continue with the recipe.

Learn More

▶ Fresh Bread Crumbs (page 386), Shellfish Basics (page 360)

FORMING CAKES Use a light touch; the more you handle them, the tougher they get. You can make several at a time, but don't dredge them in the flour until you're ready to cook.

SIZZLING, NOT BURNING Adjust the heat as they cook to keep the oil hot and bubbly without smoking and darkening.

Sweet Potato Fritters

This will get you over "fear of frying" and reward you with beautiful, delicious fritters.

TIME   **30 to 40 minutes**
MAKES   **4 to 8 servings**

About 1 pound sweet potatoes

⅓ cup all-purpose flour, or more as needed

⅓ cup cornmeal

¼ cup chopped red onion

1 egg, lightly beaten

Salt and freshly ground black pepper

Vegetable oil for deep frying

1 Heat the oven to 200°F. Line an oven-proof plate or baking sheet with paper towels. Peel and grate the sweet potatoes and squeeze or press them dry if necessary; you want 3 packed cups; save the rest for later.

2 Combine the grated sweet potato, flour, cornmeal, onion, egg, and a sprinkle of salt and pepper and mix well with a fork. If the mixture looks too liquid, add more flour, 1 tablespoon at a time. (You can make the batter ahead of time and refrigerate for up to a couple of hours before cooking.)

3 Put 2 inches of oil in a large pot over medium heat. When the oil is hot, carefully drop spoonfuls of the sweet potato mixture into the pot. (Work in batches to avoid crowding the pot.)

4 Cook, turning them with tongs or a slotted spoon as necessary so they brown on all sides, until they're cooked through, 5 to 7 minutes. Transfer the finished fritters to the paper towel–lined plate and put it in the oven to keep warm while you make the rest. Serve hot or at room temperature, with more salt and pepper if you like.

If you don't have a thermometer, use a pinch of cornmeal or flour to test when the oil is ready for frying: It should sizzle immediately but not burn.

DRYING GRATED VEGETABLES Press them into a strainer over a bowl or just squeeze them between your hands.

HEATING OIL FOR DEEP FRYING To use a thermometer for deep frying, clip it on the side of the pot and make sure the tiny hole that registers the temperature isn't touching the pot.

PUTTING THE FRITTERS IN THE OIL To minimize splattering, hold one spoon close to the oil and scrape the batter into the oil with another spoon.

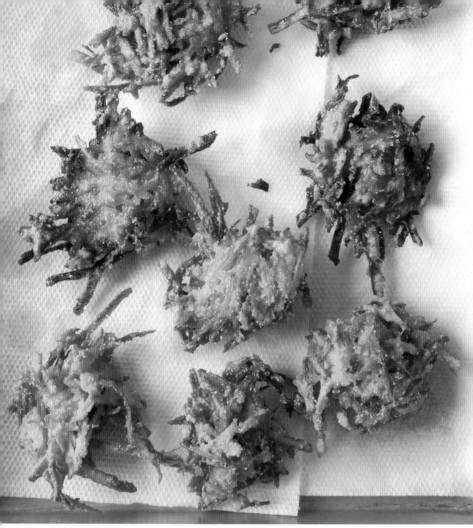

Tips

▶ Even if you like to deep-fry a lot, there's no need to invest in an expensive appliance. Just buy a thermometer designed to clip to the side of your pot and register up to 400°F. Adjust the heat to keep the oil steady at about 365°F, even as you add and remove food from the pot.

Variations

▶ **7 More Fritter Ideas.** These are just some of the other vegetables and fruits that work well in this recipe:
1 Starchy potatoes (like russets or baking potatoes)
2 Zucchini (really squeeze them dry)
3 Carrots
4 Celery root
5 Beets
6 Butternut squash
7 Apples

Learn More

▶ Deep Frying (page 37), peeling sweet potatoes (page 17), Grating Sweet Potatoes (page 240), chopping onions (page 19), shredding vegetables in a food processor (page 121)

RECOGNIZING DONENESS The fritters should be golden on the outside and soft but not wet in the middle.

Check inside: You should still be able to tell the sweet potatoes were grated.

Salads

Salad wants to be a part of your life, and there are many reasons to let it in. When you're short on time, few main dishes come together more quickly. When you're trying to eat better, salad is the easiest way to get vegetables into your diet. And when you want a side dish, salad goes with almost everything.

Salad also helps you learn and practice the most basic kitchen skills—rinsing, draining, chopping, slicing, whisking, and tossing—without much risk of messing anything up. It doesn't matter if you tear lettuce into 1-inch or 2-inch pieces or if you slice tomatoes thickly or thinly—the results will be fine in any case.

What does matter, of course, is the quality of your ingredients. When the focus is on mostly raw vegetables, seasoned only with olive oil, lemon juice or vinegar, and salt and pepper, every component has to pull its weight. Eating salads will teach you to recognize great produce, superior oil, flavorful vinegar, and excellent add-ons.

This chapter covers how to choose greens and use them to quickly and easily produce a classic tossed salad—and much more: You'll discover that your own salad dressing is not only cheaper and better than bottled dressing but almost as easy. You'll explore how to turn salads into meals by adding sturdier vegetables, beans, grains, cheese, and even fish, poultry, or meat. And in the process you'll learn that salads are endlessly variable additions to your daily table.

Salad Greens

Heads and Leaves

Salad greens fall into two categories: Head and loose-leaf—a distinction that matters only in how you trim them; they all toss, dress, and cook the same way. The leaves of head lettuces and some other greens grow from a core, which must be removed along with the outer leaves. Loose-leaf greens grow in small bunches as opposed to tight, round heads. Their stems usually require trimming. Here are the most common for both worlds:

HEAD   *LOOSE LEAF*

Romaine Lettuce Lots of crunch, more flavor than iceberg. A must for Caesars.

Iceberg Lettuce The tightly packed head that looks like a bowling ball. Crisp and watery; best mixed with other greens or served shredded as a garnish or cut into big wedges.

Boston Lettuce Small, loose heads with a soft, buttery texture; best dressed at the last moment.

Radicchio Gorgeous white and purple leaves curled around small, tight heads. Crunchy like cabbage but way more bitter.

Belgian Endive Long narrow heads with firm, crunchy, and elegant ivory leaves that are perfect for dipping.

Napa Cabbage A long-leafed cabbage with mild, tender leaves to use as lettuce or in stir-fries.

Spinach Delicious both raw and cooked. But be prepared: It shrinks a lot when heated.

Escarole Sturdy, jagged, full-flavored leaves that go from white at the center to dark green at the edges; fine raw but more delicate when cooked.

Arugula Crunchy-chewy; spicy, mustardy, and lovable.

Watercress Soft but peppery; use like spinach.

Frisée Wispy, jagged leaves; crisp and sharply bitter.

Dandelion Greens Dark green, long, narrow, jagged leaves that can be tough and bitter; best when young.

Mesclun A popular mixture of assorted delicate head and loose-leaf greens that may include some listed here along with varieties like mizuna, beet greens, and oak leaf, as well as herbs and flowers.

Buying, Preparing, and Storing Salad Greens

Look for firm, brightly colored leaves that show no signs of wilting. Browning or yellowing is a bad sign, as are greens that look limp, soggy, or (ugh) slimy. And if you're buying packaged greens (I can't stop you, though it's not my first choice), peer into the container from every angle to get a good look.

Since virtually all greens are interchangeable, buy what's in season and looks best. Locally grown greens should be your first choice whenever possible. In the dead of winter, when lettuce looks a little beaten up, I make salads with cabbage, kale, or other hearty, longer-keeping greens.

To calculate quantities: Figure about 1½ pounds of greens will yield 6 to 8 cups of torn pieces, after trimming. That's the amount used in most of the recipes that follow.

The window of freshness for most salad greens is short—a few days at most. If you can't get to them right away, trim and rinse them in advance. A salad spinner makes this process incredibly easy, but owning one isn't essential.

TRIM For heads, start by trimming off the tough core with a knife. Then remove the rough outer leaves and any hard, brown, or discolored parts with your hands. For loose-leaf greens, discard anything nasty, then trim off tough or damaged stems.

CUT Break the head apart and tear (or cut) the remaining leaves into bite-sized pieces so they're 1 to 2 inches on all sides. The exception is if you're drizzling dressing over a pile of leaves or a wedge instead of serving tossed salad; then leave them whole.

RINSE If you have a salad spinner, put the greens in the insert and fill the bowl with water. If not, use a stockpot with a colander or strainer set inside. Or just put the greens right in the pot of water and transfer them later to the colander to drain.

SWIRL AND REPEAT Loosen dirt and sand from the leaves with your hand. Then lift out the insert, pour out the water, and repeat once or twice. When this water looks clear and contains no trace of dirt, the greens are ready.

DRY To remove as much water as possible from the greens, you can give them a whirl in the salad spinner or gently pat, shake, and toss them with a clean towel. They should be fluffy, with only small drops of water visible.

STORE Put the dried greens in the fridge in the covered salad spinner; or wrap them loosely in towels, transfer the bundle to a plastic bag, and seal it loosely. Greens prepared these ways should keep in the refrigerator for 2 to 4 days.

Tossed Green Salad

Lettuce tossed with dressing you make in the same bowl.

TIME **10 minutes**
MAKES **4 servings**

---

6 to 8 cups torn greens, one type or an assortment

⅓ cup olive oil, or more as needed

2 tablespoons wine vinegar, balsamic vinegar, or sherry vinegar, or more as needed

Salt and freshly ground black pepper

1 Put the greens in a large bowl. Pour the oil and vinegar over them and sprinkle with pinch of salt and a grinding of pepper.

2 Toss the greens quickly and lightly; taste and adjust the seasoning and serve right away.

If the leaves are still wet, toss them gently in the bowl while holding a clean towel between your hands.

Salt and pepper are also key.

STARTING WITH DRY GREENS
Add the greens with your hands to feel whether they're dry enough; if they're too damp, the salad will get soggy.

MAKING A SIMPLE DRESSING
Start with no more than ⅓ cup oil and 2 tablespoons vinegar—you can always taste and add more of either or both after tossing.

Tips
▶ Want to make this salad ahead of time? Put the oil, vinegar, salt, and pepper in the bottom of the salad bowl, then put the lettuce on top. Cover loosely with a clean damp towel and put in the fridge for up to 3 hours. Toss just before serving.
▶ Instead of the vinegar, try fresh lemon or lime juice.

Variations
▶ **Tossed Green Salad with Asian Flavors:** Instead of the olive oil, use vegetable or peanut oil; substitute rice vinegar or lemon or lime juice for the wine vinegar. (A few drops each of sesame oil and soy sauce are nice touches if you've got 'em.)
▶ **Tossed Salad with Fruit, Cheese, and Nuts:** Add 1 or 2 pieces sliced fruit (like apples), ½ cup grated or crumbled cheese (like Parmesan or blue), and ½ cup toasted nuts (like walnuts or almonds).
▶ **Tossed Greek Salad:** Use romaine for the lettuce if you like and add 1 small sliced cucumber, ⅓ cup crumbled feta cheese, ¼ cup pitted and chopped black olives, and ½ cup fresh mint leaves.

Learn More
▶ Salad Greens (page 108), Oil and Vinegar (page 112), Vinaigrette in a Jar (page 114)

Overdressed greens are neither pretty nor tasty.

TOSSING ISN'T STIRRING To coat the leaves evenly without damaging them, work from the bottom of the bowl upward and lift gently with your hands, a large fork and spoon, or salad tongs.

Oil and Vinegar

Oils

Oils vary more in flavor than you might imagine, especially if you choose those that are minimally processed or unfiltered, which I recommend. Start with small bottles: You'll get to know their different characteristics without too big an investment.

Olive Oil High in healthy fats, delicious, wonderfully assertive flavor; indispensable for cooking and drizzling. Buy only extra virgin; other kinds are too bland.

Vegetable Oils When a recipe calls for vegetable oil, a neutral or light flavor is the goal, for times you want other ingredients to shine through. But try to avoid buying blends labeled *vegetable oil*. Choose high-quality individual oils like grapeseed, peanut (which is not from tree nuts), sunflower, or safflower, preferably cold pressed or minimally processed. (If they're a little cloudy, that usually means they're unfiltered.) These are good for pan- and deep frying too.

Sesame Oil Be sure to buy the dark kind, made from toasted sesame seeds. Strong in both flavor and aroma; a must for finishing many stir-fries and other Asian dishes. In dressings I usually combine just a little bit with peanut or a neutral oil like grapeseed. Generally not used for high-heat cooking.

Nut Oil Almond, hazelnut, walnut, and other nut oils are distinctive and delicious in dressings. You'll usually use them in small amounts, combined with vegetable or olive oil, because they can be overwhelming (and they're expensive). Generally not used for cooking.

Vinegars

Vinegars vary in acidity, a percentage indicated on the label. Sherry vinegar (the strongest) has a little more than twice as much acidity as rice vinegar and citrus juices. Red and white wine, balsamic, and cider vinegars fall somewhere in between.

Red Wine Vinegar Classic and when of high quality quite delicious.

White Wine Vinegar Lighter, less strong than red (just like the wines), equally useful.

Balsamic Vinegar Deeply colored, sweet, this has become an American standard. The best is aged (and expensive) and is labeled *aceto balsamico tradizionale di Modena*.

Sherry Vinegar My favorite vinegar, but not always easy to find. Look for the word *Jerez* on the label; it should come from that region in Spain.

Rice Vinegar Mild, light-colored Asian-style vinegar good for cooking, dressings, and sauces.

Cider Vinegar Made from apple cider or juice. Fruity and—at its best—complex.

White Vinegar An industrial product, best used for pickling or when you want acidity with no flavor. Great for cleaning too.

OIL

VINEGAR

The Components of Dressing—and More

Oil and vinegar are the most versatile ingredients in your pantry. Oil is crucial for its richness and ability to amplify and distribute flavors; vinegar is a mild acid made by fermenting fruit, seeds, or grains. We immediately associate these ingredients with salad, but they're used for both cooking and seasoning a wide variety of sweet and savory dishes.

Both oil and vinegar should be kept in airtight glass or ceramic bottles in

a cabinet or other cool, dark place. I store all the oil except what I'm going to use within a few days in the refrigerator—it turns cloudy when chilled but goes back to its normal color at room temperature. Always smell and taste oil before using it—a sour, musty flavor means that it's rancid and should be thrown out. Vinegar will get cloudy as it ages and develop a thick sediment. This won't hurt you but indicates that the flavor is probably past its prime—time for a new bottle.

Vinaigrette—my go-to salad dressing—is, at its most basic, a sauce made by combining fat (usually oil), acid (usually vinegar), and flavoring. This is the classic dressing for a salad of raw greens, also fantastic served on cooked vegetables, fish, poultry, or meat. In this chapter the previous recipe shows you how to mix it in a bowl as you toss the salad, and the following recipe describes how to make a batch of vinaigrette in a jar.

Vinaigrette in a Jar

The only dressing recipe you'll ever need: It's easy, delicious, and totally customizable.

TIME **5 minutes**

MAKES **About 1½ cups (10 to 12 servings)**

1 cup olive oil

⅓ cup any wine vinegar or balsamic vinegar, or more to taste

2 teaspoons Dijon-style mustard

Salt and freshly ground black pepper

1 Put the oil, vinegar, and mustard in a small glass jar along with a pinch each of salt and pepper. (If you want to add any extra ingredients, now is the time; see the Variations.)

2 Screw on the top of the jar and shake until the dressing becomes thick and creamy. Taste and adjust the seasoning, adding small sprinkles of salt and pepper if you like. If you want more vinegar, add it 1 teaspoon at a time until the balance tastes right to you.

3 Shake the jar again and serve right away or refrigerate for up to 3 days; shake well before every use.

The consistency doesn't look so different in the blender, but it won't separate as fast—if that matters to you.

SEEING THE PROPORTIONS The ratio of vinegar to oil should be between 1 to 3 and 1 to 4. Eventually you'll be able to eyeball the proportion without measuring.

BRINGING THE INGREDIENTS TOGETHER A quick shake holds the oil and vinegar together long enough to pour. If you want a dressing that remains emulsified for days, use a blender.

Tips

▶ A vinaigrette is an emulsion, a blend of oil droplets suspended in liquid, in this case vinegar, with flavorings. Using a jar is the easiest way to make a creamy, smooth, emulsified dressing: Shaking the jar just before serving pulls everything together, at least temporarily. (If the oil starts to float to the top, you just shake again.) A blender is easy and more efficient: It creates an emulsion that lasts for days.

Either method delivers a fresher, more flavorful, smoother, altogether better dressing than anything out of a bottle.

▶ If the flavor seems too acidic, add more oil; too oily, add more vinegar. (Sometimes a few drops of water is all you need.) Just taste and adjust as you go. In the end, the tartness of the acidic component is the dominant taste, while the fats provide body and background flavor. The possible combinations are virtually endless.

Variations

▶ **10 Possible Additions.**
Include any of these along with the oil and vinegar—alone or in combination:

1 1 minced garlic clove or small chopped onion or shallot
2 ¼ cup chopped fresh parsley, basil, or dill leaves or 1 tablespoon rosemary, tarragon, or thyme leaves
3 1 inch fresh ginger, peeled and minced
4 1 tablespoon honey or maple syrup
5 1 pinch crushed red pepper or 1 minced fresh chile
6 ¼ cup freshly grated Parmesan cheese
7 ½ cup crumbled blue or feta cheese
8 ¼ cup chopped dried tomatoes
9 ¼ cup pitted and chopped olives (green or black)
10 2 tablespoons sour cream or yogurt

Learn More

▶ Oil and Vinegar (page 112)

Chopped Salad

With as much vegetables as lettuce, this is perfect as a hearty side or starter or light meal.

TIME **30 minutes**
MAKES **4 to 6 servings**

1 small head romaine lettuce

2 medium carrots, chopped

2 small celery stalks, chopped

1 small red onion, chopped

1 cucumber, peeled, seeded, and chopped

1 bell pepper, cored, seeded, and chopped

3 tablespoons olive oil

1 tablespoon any wine vinegar, or more to taste

Salt and freshly ground black pepper

1 Trim and core the lettuce and tear it into bite-sized pieces. You should have about 4 cups; save any extra for later.

2 Combine the carrots, celery, onion, cucumber, bell pepper, and lettuce in a large bowl.

3 Pour the olive oil and vinegar over all and sprinkle lightly with salt and pepper. Toss the ingredients quickly and lightly, then taste and adjust the seasoning; serve right away.

With large carrots, a lengthwise cut makes chopping quick work.

CHOPPING CARROTS INTO SMALL PIECES I don't worry about the shape, but they should all be similar size.

CHOPPING OR SLICING CELERY
You want all the vegetables roughly the same size: about ½ inch. Or you can skip the lengthwise cuts and just slice the stalks into thin crescents.

Variations

▶ **Changing Chopped Salad:** Figure each of the chopped vegetables in the main recipe measures between 1 and 1½ cups. Then you can replace any or all of them with equal quantities of raw sliced or chopped fennel, avocadoes, radishes, tomatoes, or cabbage or chopped chilled cooked vegetables, like green beans, asparagus, snow peas, or broccoli.

▶ For a fancier presentation, put the lettuce on plates, top with the vegetables, and drizzle with vinaigrette.

▶ **8 Possible Additions to Chopped Salad.** Use up to 1 cup, alone or in combination:

1 Oil-packed canned tuna or sardines, drained

2 Chopped ham, prosciutto, or other cured meat

3 Crumbled cooked bacon

4 Grated, crumbled, or cubed cheese, like cheddar, Swiss, blue, or feta

5 Shredded cooked chicken or turkey

6 Chopped hard-boiled eggs (3 or 4)

7 Cooked or canned chickpeas or white beans

8 Cooked shrimp, lump crabmeat, or other cooked fish

Learn More

▶ Salad Greens (page 108), Oil and Vinegar (page 112), chopping onion (page 19)

SEEDING AND CHOPPING CUCUMBERS Peel the cucumber, cut it in half lengthwise, and scrape the seeds out with a spoon. Make lengthwise cuts then chop crosswise.

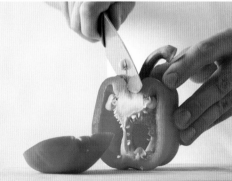

PREPARING BELL PEPPERS Put the pepper upright or on its side, then cut downward around the core and seeds to remove them. Then cut out the white pith with a paring knife.

Caesar Salad

The restaurant classic is easy to make and utterly fantastic.

TIME **20 minutes**
MAKES **4 servings**

1 medium garlic clove, halved

2 eggs

2 tablespoons fresh lemon juice

6 tablespoons olive oil

2 or 3 oil-packed anchovies

Dash Worcestershire sauce, or more as needed

2 medium heads romaine lettuce, torn into pieces (about 8 cups)

Salt and freshly ground black pepper

1 cup croutons

½ cup freshly grated Parmesan cheese

1 Rub the inside of a large bowl with the cut sides of the garlic clove, then throw the halves away.

2 Bring a small saucepan of water to a boil and adjust the heat so it bubbles gently. Use a spoon to lower the eggs into the pot and cook for 60 to 90 seconds. Remove the eggs with a slotted spoon, let cool just enough to handle, then crack them into the bowl and scoop out the white that clings to the shell if necessary to remove all of the egg.

3 Beat the eggs with a fork. Gradually drizzle in the lemon juice and then the oil, beating all the while. Stir in the anchovies and Worcestershire sauce, using the fork to mash the anchovies into bits and incorporate them into the dressing.

4 Add the lettuce and toss well. Taste a piece, then sprinkle with salt, lots of pepper, and a little more Worcestershire sauce if you like; toss again. Top with the croutons and Parmesan, then toss one last time at the table. Serve right away.

Eggs too hot to handle? Run them under cold water before cracking.

RUBBING GARLIC AROUND THE BOWL This technique—using a garlic clove cut in half—gives the dressing just a suspicion of garlic flavor.

CRACKING CODDLED EGGS The egg will be unevenly cooked, so scrape along the inside shell to make sure you get all of it into the bowl.

Tips

▶ The croutons are crucial here, so be sure to make your own; they're as easy as toast.
▶ This dressing is one that doesn't keep after you make it. But it's easy enough to whip up a batch on the spot.
▶ If you're concerned about eating raw eggs, skip Step 2 and substitute ⅓ cup silken tofu for the eggs—just put it in the bowl at the beginning of Step 3.
▶ A "dash" of Worcestershire sauce means a few drops— shake the bottle over the dressing a couple of times, stir to incorporate, then taste to determine whether it needs more.

Variations

▶ **How to Turn Caesar Salad into a Main Course:** Super-easy, especially if you have leftovers around. Some ideas: Toss a small can of drained tuna into the dressing in Step 3. Or top the tossed salad with 8 to 12 ounces of sliced grilled or broiled chicken breast, shredded roast chicken, cooked shrimp, or lump crabmeat. For a lighter version, try adding a medium chopped zucchini and 1 cup drained cooked or canned white beans.

Learn More

▶ Salad Greens (page 108), Egg Basics (page 50), Croutons (page 384), Grating Cheese (page 176), Tossing Isn't Stirring (page 111)

This process of warming but not fully cooking the eggs is called coddling.

BEATING THE EGGS TO MAKE DRESSING Keep stirring while adding the lemon juice and oil and you'll get a smooth, creamy, mayonnaiselike dressing.

Spicy Coleslaw

I like my coleslaw mayo free and with a kick. For a creamy version, see the variations.

TIME **1½ hours,**
  mostly unattended
MAKES **8 servings**

2 tablespoons Dijon-style mustard, or more to taste

2 tablespoons fresh lemon juice, or more to taste

1 teaspoon minced garlic

1 tablespoon minced fresh chile (like jalapeño), or more to taste, optional

¼ cup vegetable oil

1 medium Napa cabbage (about 1½ pounds)

1 large red bell pepper, cored, seeded, and chopped

4 medium scallions, chopped

Salt and freshly ground black pepper

¼ cup chopped fresh parsley leaves for garnish

1 Whisk together the mustard, lemon juice, garlic, and chile if you're using it in a large bowl. Drizzle in the oil a little at a time, whisking constantly, so that the mixture comes together and emulsifies. (Or purée the dressing ingredients in a blender, and transfer to a large bowl.)

2 Trim or pull the outer leaves from the cabbage and then remove the core with a paring knife. Switch to a chef's knife and cut the cabbage into halves or quarters, then thinly slice each piece; the slices will naturally fall into shreds. (You can also use a food processor to shred or grate the cabbage.)

3 Add the cabbage, bell pepper, and scallions to the bowl and toss to combine. Sprinkle with salt and pepper and refrigerate for at least 1 hour to let the flavors mellow and the cabbage soften and exude some juice. (You can refrigerate it longer, up to 24 hours, if you like; cover with plastic wrap first and expect some extra water to pool at the bottom of the bowl.) Just before serving, toss the coleslaw with the parsley. Taste, and adjust the seasoning with additional mustard, chile, lemon, salt, or pepper. Serve with a slotted spoon.

This method is easiest for any kind of cabbage and fine if you're going to chop up the leaves anyway.

CORING WHOLE CABBAGE To remove the core with leaves intact, cut a cone around the stem with a paring knife and pull it out, using your knife for leverage.

CORING HALVED CABBAGE Cut the head in half with a chef's knife first, then remove the core by cutting downward on both sides.

Tips

▶ Napa cabbage is almost as tender as lettuce but stays crisp. For more crunch, try Savoy or regular green or red cabbage; all work well, and each gives a different texture.

▶ Fresh herbs wilt (some even turn black) soon after you chop them, especially if you combine them with any liquid—which is why it's always a good idea to wait until right before serving to add herbs to salads.

Variations

▶ **Creamier Slaw:** Substitute mayonnaise or sour cream for some or all of the oil.

▶ **Mexican-Style Slaw:** Substitute lime juice for the lemon juice, 2 grated medium carrots for the bell pepper, and cilantro for the parsley.

▶ **Apple Slaw:** For a fruity, crunchy fall salad, substitute 2 grated medium tart apples for the bell pepper.

Learn More

▶ Mincing garlic (page 20), Preparing Chiles (page 276), Preparing Bell Peppers (page 117), Preparing Scallions (page 295), Chopping Herbs (page 78)

SHREDDING CABBAGE Cut the cabbage into halves or quarters depending on how long you want the shreds. Then start cutting crosswise.

SHREDDING CABBAGE IN A FOOD PROCESSOR It's fast to shred cabbage and other vegetables using a food processor fitted with the shredding disk. For a finer texture, use the grating disk.

Curried Chickpea Salad

A wildly popular salad with Indian flavors that keeps well in the fridge to enjoy anytime.

TIME **45 minutes,
  mostly unattended**
MAKES **6 to 8 servings**

**1 tablespoon fresh lime
juice, or more to taste**

**1½ teaspoons curry
powder, or more to taste**

2 scallions, chopped

**Salt and freshly ground
black pepper**

**¼ cup coconut milk, or
more to taste**

**4 cups cooked or drained
canned chickpeas**

**1 large red bell pepper,
cored, seeded, and
chopped**

**½ cup fresh or thawed
frozen peas**

**½ cup chopped fresh
cilantro leaves**

1 Combine the lime juice, curry powder, scallions, and a sprinkle of salt and pepper in a large bowl. Stir in the coconut milk.

2 Add the chickpeas, bell pepper, and peas to the bowl and toss gently until everything is coated with dressing, adding more coconut milk 1 tablespoon at a time if the salad seems dry.

3 Let the salad sit for at least 30 minutes, stirring once or twice to distribute the dressing. (Or refrigerate for up to 5 days.) When you're ready to eat, stir in the cilantro. Taste and adjust the seasoning and moisture, adding more lime juice, coconut milk, or curry powder if you like. Serve cold or at room temperature.

MAKING THE DRESSING Mix the juice, seasonings, and coconut milk right in the bowl before adding everything else. That's one less dish to wash.

SUBSTITUTING FATS IN DRESSINGS Coconut milk makes a super-rich and slightly sweet replacement for oil. You can use the "light" kind, but the dressing won't be as thick or creamy.

Tips

▶ This salad is good with canned beans but superior with cooked dried chickpeas, which have a more intense flavor. You can also control the texture so the chickpeas are as firm or tender as you like them.

Variations

▶ **Curried Chickpea Salad with Rice or Grains:** Add up to 1 cup cooked rice or other grain in Step 2.
▶ **Curried Chickpea Salad with Greens:** Toss the chickpeas with 1 to 2 cups lettuce, arugula, or spinach just before serving.
▶ **Southwestern Black Bean Salad:** Some easy switches yield a totally different result: Substitute chili powder for the curry powder, olive oil for the coconut milk, black beans for the chickpeas, and corn kernels for the peas.

Learn More

▶ Bean Basics (page 250), Preparing Scallions (page 295), Preparing Bell Peppers (page 117), Chopping Herbs (page 78)

The difference in texture between canned chickpeas (on the right) and beans you cook yourself is obvious when you put them side by side and smash them.

TESTING CHICKPEA DONENESS
For salads, don't cook them so long that they get mushy or start to fall apart. Test by mashing a couple with a fork; they should look about like this.

Tabbouleh

The Middle Eastern classic done right: with lots of herbs and just enough bulgur.

TIME **40 minutes**
MAKES **4 servings**

½ cup medium- or coarse-grind bulgur

Salt

1¼ cups boiling water

⅓ cup olive oil, or more as needed

¼ cup fresh lemon juice, or more to taste

Freshly ground black pepper

2 cups chopped fresh parsley leaves and small stems

1 cup chopped fresh mint leaves

½ cup chopped scallions

4 medium tomatoes, cored, seeded, and chopped

1 Put the bulgur in a large bowl with a pinch of salt, add the boiling water, and stir once. Let sit until tender but not mushy, 10 to 20 minutes depending on the grind. If any water remains, put the bulgur in a strainer and press down on the grains with the back of a large spoon to remove as much of the water as possible.

2 Return the bulgur to the bowl and add the oil, lemon juice, and a sprinkle of pepper. (You can make the salad ahead to this point: Cover and refrigerate for up to 24 hours; bring it back to room temperature before continuing.)

3 When you're ready to serve, add the parsley, mint, scallions, and tomatoes and toss gently with a fork. Taste, adjust the seasoning, adding more olive oil or lemon juice if you'd like, and serve.

The bulgur swells and softens as it steeps.

SOFTENING BULGUR Put the bulgur in a large heatproof bowl—some plastic bowls will melt in the heat of boiling water, which you don't want.

JUDGING DONENESS The bulgur will be fluffy and have absorbed most of the liquid when it's ready—but taste to make sure it's tender but still a bit chewy.

The drier the bulgur, the fluffier it will be (and the more dressing it will absorb).

DRAINING BULGUR If any water remains in the bowl after soaking, transfer it to a strainer and press down on the bulgur to get it as dry as possible without pushing it through the holes.

Tips
▶ Fresh herbs are the heart of good tabbouleh—so make sure the parsley and mint are fresh and sprightly, not yellow, dried out, or wilted. This is a rare case when it's fine to use some stems in addition to parsley leaves for added crunch and flavor; but use only the small ones attached directly to leaves, not the thick ones that hold entire sprigs together.

Variations
▶ Couscous makes an excellent substitute for bulgur in this salad; follow the same directions, checking for doneness after 5 minutes (10 minutes for whole wheat couscous).
▶ **5 Possible Additions to Tabbouleh.** Add any of these along with the herbs in Step 3; you will need to add a little more olive oil and lemon juice:
1 1 cup chopped cucumber (peeled and seeded first)
2 1 cup cooked or canned chickpeas or white beans
3 ½ cup chopped almonds
4 ½ cup crumbled feta cheese
5 ¼ cup chopped pitted black olives

Learn More
▶ Grain Basics (page 206), identifying bulgur grinds (page 210), Chopping Herbs (page 78), Preparing Scallions (page 295), preparing tomatoes (page 80)

Tomato, Mozzarella, and Bread Salad

Bread salad (*panzanella*) meets the tomato-and-cheese combo known as *caprese*.

TIME **45 minutes**

MAKES **4 servings**

½ pound Italian or French bread (about ½ loaf)

4 medium tomatoes

4 ounces fresh mozzarella cheese, cut into ½-inch cubes

⅓ cup olive oil

2 tablespoons balsamic vinegar

Salt and freshly ground black pepper

½ cup chopped fresh basil leaves

1 Heat the oven to 350°F. Cut the bread crosswise into slices about 1 inch thick. Put them on a baking sheet and toast in the oven, turning once or twice, until they are crisp and golden, about 15 minutes. Let cool and store if you like, tightly covered, for up to 2 days.

2 While the bread is toasting, core and roughly chop the tomatoes and put them and their juices in a large bowl. Add the mozzarella, oil, and vinegar; sprinkle with salt and lots of pepper and toss several times to combine well.

3 Fill a medium bowl with water, add the toasted bread, and soak until the pieces start to absorb some water and soften, 2 to 3 minutes. Gently squeeze the water out of the croutons and crumble them into the salad.

4 Toss well to combine the ingredients and let the salad sit for 15 to 20 minutes. Toss with the basil, taste and adjust the seasoning, and serve.

Like wringing out a sponge—but gently.

PROPERLY TOASTED BREAD For this salad the pieces should be lightly golden and crisp—the idea is to get it as dry as possible but not too brown.

SOAKING AND SQUEEZING THE TOAST When the bread has absorbed enough water to make it moist but not soggy, start fishing out slices—a couple at a time—and squeeze them dry.

BREAKING BREAD Rub your fingers together to crumble the squeezed bread into bite-sized pieces over the salad bowl. It's okay if you get some smaller crumbs; they'll add texture.

Tips

▶ Fresh mozzarella is usually made into balls, not bricks or strings. It's creamier and whiter than aged mozzarella, with a superior milky flavor. You can find packages of it in most supermarkets now, but if you have an Italian deli or grocery nearby, you may find super-fresh mozzarella that's stored in water, like good feta cheese (itself a possible substitute in this salad).

▶ For a heartier version, use whole grain bread.

▶ For a crunchier salad, cut the bread slices into cubes before toasting and add them to the salad without soaking. After the resting time in Step 4, you might decide you need more oil.

▶ For a hint of garlic, cut a clove in half and rub the cut side on the bread before toasting.

Variations

▶ **Lebanese Bread Salad (*Fattoush*):** Skip the mozzarella. Substitute four 6-inch pitas for the bread and cut each into 8 wedges. Add 1 chopped medium cucumber (peeled and seeded first if you like) and 1 cored, seeded, and chopped red bell pepper at the beginning of Step 2. Finish with chopped fresh parsley leaves instead of the basil in Step 4.

Learn More

▶ Bread and Sandwich Basics (page 382), preparing tomatoes (page 80), cheese for cooking (page 389), Chopping Herbs (page 78)

Shaved Fennel Salad

Slicing vegetables super-thin makes for awesome texture.

TIME   **20 minutes**
MAKES   **4 servings**

1 large piece Parmesan cheese (you won't use it all)

2 large or 3 medium fennel bulbs (about 1½ pounds)

3 tablespoons olive oil, or more as needed

1 tablespoon fresh lemon juice, or more as needed

Salt and freshly ground black pepper

1 Take the cheese out of the fridge so it comes to room temperature, which will make it easier to shave. Trim the bottom, stalks, and feathery leaves off the fennel bulbs; save some of the leaves for garnish and discard the rest. Cut the bulbs in half top to bottom.

2 Working with one half at a time, put the flat side against the cutting board and slice crosswise into slices as thin as you can manage. Put the fennel slices in a large bowl. Chop the reserved leaves, but don't add them to the bowl yet.

3 Hold the cheese firmly in one hand and shave ribbons off with a vegetable peeler. It's okay if they break up a bit. Stop when you have about ½ cup shavings. Save the remaining cheese for another use.

4 Drizzle the fennel with the olive oil, lemon juice, and a sprinkle of salt and pepper. Toss with your hands or utensils to break up the slices a bit. Taste and adjust the seasoning, adding more olive oil or lemon juice if you like. Leave the salad in the bowl or transfer to a platter or plates; top with the Parmesan shavings and fennel leaves and serve right away.

This takes practice: Don't worry if they're not perfect slices.

TRIMMING FENNEL Remove and discard the stalks and hard bottom, but save the feathery leaves to chop and use as you would an herb, for garnish.

SHAVING VEGETABLES Hold the fennel firmly with curled fingers, but keep your hand away from the blade. Work slowly, using assertive downward strokes with a sharp chef's knife to make slices as thin as you can manage.

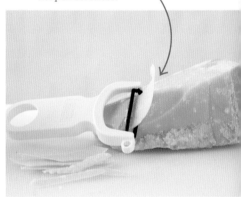

SHAVING HARD CHEESE Use the same motion as you would for peeling potatoes.

Tips

▶ Look for mostly white, clean, taut, unblemished fennel bulbs. They will keep wrapped loosely in plastic for up to a week in the refrigerator.

▶ Shaving vegetables is much easier with a mandoline. You can get effective but inexpensive models made of plastic fitted with a ceramic or metal blade; they work just like a box grater. It's a good investment if you like eating raw vegetables, because you'll wind up making even more salads like this one.

Variations

▶ If you can't find (or don't like) fennel, use celery. Cut it crosswise at a 45-degree angle so you get long, thin slices. Crumbled feta cheese is nice with celery instead of Parmesan.

▶ Other vegetables that make nice shaved salads: button mushrooms, radishes, zucchini, or parsnips; use any instead of the fennel here. (Combinations are good too.) Trim and peel as necessary, and if they're large, cut them in half as you would the fennel before slicing thinly.

Learn More

▶ Trimming (page 16), Parmesan cheese (page 4)

Mediterranean Potato Salad

I prefer mine with a mustardy vinaigrette and classic *salade Niçoise* ingredients.

TIME **45 minutes, with pre-cooked eggs**

MAKES **4 servings**

---

1 pound waxy or all-purpose potatoes, peeled and cut into 1-inch chunks

Salt

½ pound green beans, trimmed and cut into 1-inch pieces

2 tablespoons any wine vinegar, or more as needed

½ cup olive oil, or more as needed

1 teaspoon minced garlic

1 small shallot, minced

1 teaspoon Dijon-style mustard

Freshly ground black pepper

2 hard-boiled eggs, sliced or chopped

½ cup pitted black olives, chopped

1 pint cherry or grape tomatoes, halved

1 Put the potatoes in a large pot with enough water to cover them by 1 inch or so; add a large pinch of salt. Bring to a boil, then lower the heat so the water bubbles gently. Cook the potatoes until they are just beginning to get tender, 5 to 7 minutes, then add the green beans.

2 Cook until the potatoes are tender but still firm and not at all mushy and the green beans are brightly colored and crisp-tender, another 3 to 5 minutes. Drain in a colander, rinse in cold water for 1 minute, and drain again.

3 While the potatoes are cooking, put the vinegar, oil, garlic, shallot, mustard, and a sprinkle of salt and pepper in a large bowl and stir to combine. Add the potatoes and green beans along with the eggs, olives, and tomatoes and toss gently to combine. Taste and adjust the seasoning and serve.

Keep the water at a gentle bubble and test the potatoes frequently.

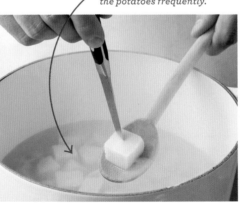

KNOWING WHEN TO ADD THE BEANS As soon as you can insert a knife easily into the potatoes but they're not quite ready to eat, it's time to add the beans.

Wait until the potatoes are tender, even if the beans are getting a little soft—crunchy potatoes are no fun to eat.

READY TO DRAIN The potatoes should be just tender but no longer crunchy, and the green beans crisp-tender and bright green—all at the same time.

Tips

▸ Waxy potatoes—the kind with thin red or white skin—are ideal for salad (and boiling in general), because they keep their shape better than higher-starch potatoes. (All-purpose potatoes like Yukon Gold are a good second choice.) Use starchy baking potatoes if you must, but be prepared for them to disintegrate a bit.

▸ For a drier texture, return the drained potatoes and beans to the empty hot cooking pot for a few minutes to dry.

Variations

▸ **American-Style Potato Salad:** Pare all the ingredients down to just the potatoes and salt and pepper. (And increase the quantity of the potatoes to about 1½ pounds.) Prepare and cook the potatoes as described in Steps 1 and 2 (without the beans). While the potatoes cook, whisk together ½ cup mayonnaise, 3 tablespoons any wine vinegar, and some salt and pepper in a large bowl. Toss the warm drained potatoes in the dressing, adding 2 chopped celery stalks and ¼ cup chopped scallions. Garnish with chopped fresh parsley leaves if you like and serve right away or refrigerate for up to a day.

▸ **Traditional** *Salade Niçoise*: Make the recipe through Step 2. In Step 3, use a small bowl or blender to prepare the dressing. Divide 6 cups torn assorted lettuces among 4 plates and put the potatoes, green beans, eggs, olives, tomatoes, and one 7-ounce can tuna (preferably packed in olive oil) on top of the lettuce. Drizzle with the dressing and serve.

Learn More

▸ Types of potatoes (page 235), preparing potatoes (page 224), mincing garlic (page 20), Egg Basics (page 50)

Warm Spinach Salad with Bacon

Meaty, rich, and delicious, especially since the dressing cooks the spinach a bit.

TIME **30 to 40 minutes**

MAKES **4 servings**

---

2 tablespoons olive oil

½ pound slab or thick-cut bacon, cut into 1-inch pieces

1 large shallot or small red onion, chopped

8 cups torn spinach leaves

¼ cup any wine vinegar, or more to taste

1 teaspoon Dijon-style mustard, or more to taste

Salt and freshly ground black pepper

1 Put the oil in a medium skillet over medium heat; when it's hot, add the bacon and cook, stirring occasionally, until it's crisp and lightly browned, 8 to 12 minutes. Add the shallot and cook until it begins to soften, 1 to 2 minutes more. Turn the heat to low to keep the mixture warm without further cooking.

2 Meanwhile, fill a large bowl with hot tap water and let it sit for 1 minute to warm the bowl. Pour out the water, dry the inside of the bowl, and put the greens in the bowl.

3 Add the vinegar and mustard to the skillet, turn the heat to medium-high, and bring the mixture just to a boil, stirring. Taste the dressing and add salt (it won't need much), lots of pepper, and a little more vinegar or mustard if you like. If the dressing looks too thick, add a few drops of water.

4 Pour the piping-hot dressing over the greens, toss to wilt the spinach a bit, and serve right away.

Adjust the heat and stir frequently to keep the bacon and shallots from burning.

If you don't want the spinach to wilt, let the dressing cool a little, but not so much that the fat hardens.

![Cooking bacon for the dressing]

COOKING BACON FOR THE DRESSING Cutting the bacon up and cooking it in oil helps the pieces get crisp and flavor the dressing with the fat, which melts into the olive oil.

ADDING THE SHALLOT The bacon should be almost as crisp as you want it when you add the shallot. Add it 1 to 2 minutes earlier for chewier bacon.

FINISHING THE DRESSING The rendered bacon fat becomes part of the dressing when you add the vinegar and mustard to the skillet. It should still be hot so that it wilts the spinach.

Tips

▶ Choose the best bacon you can afford, preferably naturally smoked without a lot of chemicals. *Slab* just means that it's not presliced and that is has a rind. If all you can find is sliced bacon, that's okay too; choose the thickest cut available.

Variations

▶ **BLT Salad:** Substitute torn lettuce for the spinach and skip warming the bowl in Step 2. Let the dressing cool before pouring it over the salad and add 2 cored, seeded, and chopped large ripe tomatoes at the last minute.

▶ **5 Other Ideas:**

1 Use arugula, escarole, frisée, or sliced Napa cabbage instead of the spinach.

2 Top each serving with a poached or fried egg.

3 Cook sausage instead of bacon: Squeeze it out of the casing into the pan of hot oil or cut it into chunks.

4 Cook ham or prosciutto instead of bacon: Cut either into ½-inch pieces.

5 Add 2 cups cherry tomatoes to the dressing in Step 3 when you add the vinegar. Omit the mustard and reduce the vinegar to 3 tablespoons.

Learn More

▶ Chopping onions (page 19), Salad Greens (page 108)

Soups and Stews

The original one-pot meals, easy, beloved, healthful, and inexpensive—what could be better? The ingredients are easy to vary, the preparation is minimal, and once things get rolling, you're free to go do something else for a while.

Since the techniques for making both soups and stews are so similar, I make the distinction simply by the ratio of liquid to solids: Soups are more watery than stews. With both you want fresh ingredients—this isn't an excuse to cook with rejects—but since you're concerned only with the results of cooking everything together, they need not be as pristine as if you were serving them raw or featuring them on a plate. (Nor do they need to be perfectly chopped.) No time to make stock? Don't sweat it: Water is a fine base for many recipes. (Stock, however, is great and valuable stuff, and of course I've included a section on it here.) And since there's rarely pressure to capture food at some optimal point of doneness, these dishes are almost impossible to overcook. How easy is that?

Soup always refrigerates and often freezes perfectly, so if you really love your efforts (and you will), consider cooking double batches and setting some aside in convenient serving sizes. Even straight from the freezer, it reheats quickly in the microwave or on top of the stove. And leftovers often taste better than the first bowl.

With all of this going for homemade soup, there's no reason to buy packaged or canned soup ever again.

Soup Basics

The Three Bs

Whether you're following a recipe or improvising, the steps remain the same. This basic formula will yield about 6 cups soup—enough for 4 bowl-sized servings.

Scraping the bottom of the pan to loosen the flavorful browned bits disperses them in the broth.

BROWN For a meaty soup, heat 2 tablespoons butter or oil over medium heat and cook up to 1 pound of bacon, sausage, or cubes of pork shoulder or beef chuck until the meat begins to brown and crisp, 5 to 10 minutes.

Add aromatic vegetables and cook until they start to color and soften (for vegetarian soup, start here): Cook at least 2 cups chopped aromatics—like onions, shallots, celery, carrots, garlic, and/or ginger—in the butter or oil until they're soft and golden, 5 to 10 minutes. Remember to sprinkle with lots of salt and pepper. Once everything is sizzling and browned, add herbs or spices, tomato paste, or citrus zest. Start with small quantities (say a teaspoon or two); you can always add more when finishing the soup.

BROTH Broth is the result of cooking liquid with the flavor base you created in the Brown step. You can use water, stock, juice, wine, beer, or a combination. Go easy on juice or wine, since they have a strong flavor, but a splash mixed with water or stock can be wonderful. Chopped tomatoes—fresh or canned—are another option to replace some of the liquid. They become saucy and add a brightness that complements many other ingredients. Start with 4 cups liquid, and as the soup cooks, be prepared to add up to 2 cups more, depending on how much other stuff you end up adding to the pot. The goal is about 1½ cups of soup for each serving.

BOIL Bring the soup to a boil, then lower the heat so that the mixture bubbles steadily but not vigorously. You can now add other ingredients, starting with those that take the longest time to cook and working to the fastest-cooking items. Precooked additions (like noodles and leftover vegetables, meat, or poultry) need just a minute to warm up in the hot soup just before serving. It's almost impossible to overcook soup; even if the vegetables are mushy, it will be good. So relax, check it once in a while to see if you need to add more liquid, and let it do its thing until it looks, well, soupy and the textures please you. Taste and adjust the seasonings, then grab the ladle and bowls.

Puréeing Soup

Puréeing quickly turns everyday soup into a rich, smooth, impressive treat. You probably don't want to purée anything with more than a couple of primary ingredients to keep the flavors and color distinct.

USE A POTATO MASHER The easiest way to smooth out soup is with a potato masher—just stick it in the pot and press down and swirl around to break things up a bit. You won't get a purée, but the lack of hassle is unbeatable. And I like the contrasting textures.

OR USE A MACHINE Ultra-smooth soup requires a blender: Let the soup cool slightly first. Then carefully fill the container a little more than halfway, put the lid on, and start at low or medium speed until the liquid is moving. If you go full blast right away, the hot soup may splatter out the top and burn you, so build up to a higher speed. (Holding a towel over the blender lid helps keep you safe.) If you have more soup left to purée, scrape the puréed soup into a large bowl or another pot and repeat the process.

FINISH PURÉED SOUP Put the mixture back in the pot over medium heat to make it hot again. If it's too thick, add some cream, milk, stock, or water to thin it out. Start with a splash and go from there. (When adding dairy, make sure the soup is just barely bubbling and never comes to a rolling boil, which can cause the soup to curdle.) Just before serving, taste and adjust the seasoning as usual.

Smarter Water

I won't kid you: Soup made with stock will always taste richer and have a more luxurious texture than soup made with water. But this is important: It's better to make soup with water than not to make soup at all. The water will obviously assume the flavors of whatever else goes in the pot, so, in effect, it becomes stock as you cook.

Here are a few ways to improve water-based soups:

1 Be patient with the aromatic vegetables as they brown and soften in the fat and add more of them for extra oomph.
2 Use good-quality vegetables and meats.
3 Don't skimp on herbs, spices, salt, or pepper.
4 Add a splash of wine, juice, or soy sauce with the water.
5 Finish the soup with a drizzle of olive oil or a pat of butter.

Gazpacho

The savory smoothie from Spain is almost too easy.

TIME **20 minutes**
MAKES **4 servings**

2 pounds tomatoes, cored, or one 28-ounce can diced tomatoes, including the juice

1 medium cucumber, peeled, seeded, and cut into chunks

2 or 3 thick bread slices (a day or two old is best), crusts removed, torn into small pieces

¼ cup olive oil, plus more for garnish

2 tablespoons any wine vinegar, or more to taste

1 medium garlic clove, cut in half

Salt and freshly ground black pepper

½ red or yellow bell pepper, cored, seeded, and chopped, for garnish

2 scallions, chopped, for garnish

1 Cut the tomatoes into chunks if they're large and put them in a blender or food processor with the cucumber, bread, oil, vinegar, garlic, and 1 cup water; sprinkle with salt and pepper and pulse the machine on and off until smooth. If the mixture seems too thick, thin it by gradually adding water, 1 tablespoon at a time.

2 Taste, adjust the seasoning with salt, pepper, or vinegar, and serve right away or refrigerate and eat within a couple of hours. Garnish each serving with the bell pepper, scallions, and a drizzle of olive oil.

Don't forget the tomato juices—they add a lot of flavor.

ADDING CHOPPED VEGETABLES
There's no need to fuss over how the vegetables are chopped when they're going into a machine. Rough chunks are fine.

BLENDING COMPLETELY Stop the machine to scrape down the sides, then continue blending until the gazpacho is as chunky or smooth as you want it.

Tips

▶ Use flavorless tomatoes and you'll get flavorless gazpacho. So when tomatoes aren't in season, use good-quality canned.

▶ I like sherry vinegar in gazpacho (they're both Spanish, after all), but since it's quite tart, start with just 1 teaspoon and taste. If you don't have sherry vinegar, any good red or white wine vinegar is fine.

Variations

▶ **Fruit Gazpacho:** Try fresh peaches, melon, or mangoes instead of tomatoes, only figure 2½ pounds. Trim and peel as necessary.

▶ **Spicy Gazpacho:** Seed and mince ½ fresh hot chile (like jalapeño) and add it to the other garnishes.

Learn More

▶ Soup Basics (page 136), preparing tomatoes (page 80), preparing cucumbers (page 117), Preparing Bell Peppers (page 117), Preparing Scallions (page 295)

JUDGING CONSISTENCY I like mine fairly smooth. If you don't have a blender, chop the ingredients by hand as much or as little as you like, combine them in a bowl, and mash a bit.

Some folks prefer chunky gazpacho, which requires some elbow grease. Half puréed, half chopped is a nice compromise.

Tomato Soup

Not only way better than canned, but one of the best (and fastest) soups you can make.

TIME **35 to 40 minutes**
MAKES **4 servings**

---

2 tablespoons olive oil

1 large or 2 medium onions, halved and thinly sliced

1 carrot, chopped

Salt and freshly ground black pepper

2 tablespoons tomato paste

1 sprig fresh thyme or ½ teaspoon dried

2 pounds tomatoes, cored and chopped, or one 28-ounce can diced tomatoes, including the juice

2 to 3 cups water or tomato juice

1 teaspoon sugar, optional

¼ cup chopped fresh basil leaves for garnish, optional

1 Put the oil in a large pot over medium heat. When it's hot, add the onion and carrot, sprinkle with salt and pepper, and cook, stirring, until the vegetables begin to soften, 3 to 5 minutes. Add the tomato paste, lower the heat a bit, and continue to cook, stirring to coat the vegetables with the paste, until the paste begins to darken (don't let it burn), 1 to 2 minutes.

2 Strip the thyme leaves from the stem and add them to the pot along with the tomatoes. Cook, stirring occasionally, until the tomatoes break down, 10 to 15 minutes. Add 2 cups of the water and bring to a boil, then adjust the heat so that the mixture bubbles gently. Let the soup cook until the flavors meld, 5 more minutes.

3 Taste and adjust the seasoning; if the soup tastes flat (but salty enough), stir in the sugar. If the soup is too thick, add more water, ¼ cup at a time. If it's too thin, continue to cook until it thickens and reduces slightly (this will also intensify the flavors). Garnish with the basil if you're using it and serve.

The tomato paste is ready when it smells sweet and fragrant.

ADDING THE TOMATO PASTE It's okay if the vegetables are lightly colored when you add the tomato paste, but don't let them get too dark, because they have more cooking to do.

COOKING THE TOMATO PASTE This step gives the paste time to brown and lose any bitter flavor, so don't rush. Lower the heat if the mixture is darkening too fast.

It makes sense to strip the leaves over the pot so they fall right in.

STRIPPING LEAVES FROM HARD HERB STEMS Hold the sprig by the thick end and pull downward so the leaves come free.

Tips

▶ There's no need to peel the tomatoes; in fact, tomato skins intensify the flavor of the soup. If you don't want big pieces of skin in your bowl, cut the tomatoes into small pieces.

▶ Tomato paste comes in cans and tubes: Grab a tube when you see it; use what you need and keep the rest handy in the fridge.

Variations

▶ **Cream of Tomato Soup:** Before tasting in Step 3, stir in up to 1 cup cream and cook the soup long enough to heat it up, but don't let it boil.

▶ **Hearty Tomato Soup:** Add ½ cup white rice, bulgur, or couscous with the water in Step 2, along with 1 more cup liquid. Cook until the grain is tender, 5 to 15 minutes, and be prepared to add a little more water if the soup gets too thick.

▶ **Spiced Tomato Soup:** Instead of the fresh thyme and basil, try adding 1 tablespoon curry or chili powder or 1 teaspoon smoked paprika (pimentón) along with the tomato paste in Step 1.

Learn More

▶ Soup Basics (page 136), Vegetable Basics (page 216), slicing onions (page 232), preparing carrots (page 116), preparing tomatoes (page 80), Chopping Herbs (page 78)

Minestrone

Learn the basic formula of this Italian classic, then vary the vegetables at will.

TIME   **About 1 hour**
MAKES   **4 to 6 servings**

¼ cup olive oil, plus more for garnish

1 medium onion, chopped

1 medium carrot, chopped

1 medium celery stalk, chopped

Salt and freshly ground black pepper

2 large potatoes or turnips, peeled if you like and cut into small chunks

1 cup chopped tomatoes (canned are fine; don't bother to drain)

1 medium zucchini, cut into small chunks

1 bunch sturdy leafy greens like kale or escarole, chopped

½ cup freshly grated Parmesan cheese for garnish

1   Put the oil in a large pot over medium heat. When it's hot, add the onion, carrot, and celery; sprinkle with salt and pepper. Cook, stirring frequently, until the vegetables soften and begin to darken around the edges, 10 to 15 minutes.

2   Add the potatoes and sprinkle with a little more salt and pepper. Cook, stirring occasionally, until the vegetables are all brown in spots, 5 to 10 minutes. Add 6 cups water, stirring to scrape up any brown bits from the bottom of the pan. Add the tomatoes, bring the mixture to a boil, and then lower the heat so the mixture bubbles steadily. Cook, stirring every now and then, until the tomatoes break down a bit, about 15 minutes.

3   Add the zucchini and greens and raise the heat if necessary to keep the mixture at a steady bubble. Cook until all the vegetables are very tender, another 10 to 15 minutes. Taste and adjust the seasoning and serve topped with the cheese and a drizzle of olive oil.

By small chunks I mean about ½ inch, or the size of your thumbnail.

CARAMELIZING THE AROMATICS
They will go through stages as they cook and color. After a few minutes they'll begin to soften; adjust the heat and keep cooking until they begin to color.

ADDING THE HARD VEGETABLES
The idea is to build flavor layer by layer: As different ingredients cook, they add multiple dimensions of texture too.

ADDING THE LIQUID When the vegetables begin to brown in spots, add the liquid and scrape up the bits stuck on the bottom. This is called *deglazing*.

ADDING GREENS AND TENDER VEGETABLES The greens and zucchini add a final touch of freshness. You could use herbs here too, like a handful of chopped basil.

Tips

▶ This easily varied vegetable soup helps you start thinking of vegetables in groups: aromatics (garlic, onions, celery, and carrots); hard (or sturdy); tender (like zucchini or green beans); and greens. So if you look at the ingredient list that way, you can mix and match vegetables depending on what you have in the fridge or what looks best in the store.

▶ To give the soup even more flavor, cut the rind from a piece of Parmesan cheese and add it along with the water. (Or cut a piece of rind into small chunks; it will soften enough to eat and is a real treat.)

Variations

▶ **Hearty Minestrone:** For a meal in a bowl, cook up to 1 pound sausage or bacon with the aromatics in Step 1. Or add 1 cup any small pasta and an extra cup of water about 5 minutes after adding the greens in Step 3. Or simply stir in 1 cup cooked (or canned) chickpeas or cannellini beans a few minutes before serving.

Learn More

▶ Soup Basics (page 136), Vegetable Basics (page 216), chopping onions (page 19), preparing carrots (page 116), preparing celery (page 116) , preparing potatoes (page 224), preparing tomatoes (page 80), Grating Cheese (page 176)

Miso Soup

The best "instant" soup you'll ever have.

TIME **About 15 minutes**
MAKES **4 servings**

⅓ cup any miso

½ pound any tofu, cut into small cubes, optional

4 scallions, chopped

1 Put 6 cups water in a large pot over medium heat. When steam rises from the surface of the liquid and small bubbles appear along the edges of the pot, ladle ½ cup of the water into a small bowl with the miso and whisk until smooth.

2 Lower the heat under the pot to medium-low and add the miso slurry; stir once or twice, then add the tofu if you're using it. Do not let the mixture boil; let it sit for a minute or two to heat the tofu through. Stir in the scallions and serve.

For some chew, use firm tofu; for a more custardy texture, use silken tofu. Or you can skip the tofu altogether.

MAKING A SLURRY When you mix miso (or any pasty or powdery ingredient) into hot or cold water, it becomes a *slurry* that will disperse evenly in liquids without clumping.

ADDING THE MISO SLURRY Just stir the mixture to combine and heat the miso and water—but don't bring the soup to a boil.

ADDING MORE INGREDIENTS After the miso dissolves in the water, you can add tofu or quick-cooking vegetables to warm and soften in the soup.

Tips

▶ Miso is a paste made from soybeans (or other beans) and grain (usually rice or barley) fermented with salt. Look for naturally made, unpasteurized miso, found refrigerated in plastic tubs or in jars. Second choice is the shelf-stable miso sealed in plastic pouches; avoid the powdered stuff altogether. The names and types can be confusing, so just remember: The darker the miso, the deeper the flavor—and the packages are usually identified by color, ranging from white to yellow, red, and brown. Since you use them all the same way, try different kinds—perhaps starting with white or yellow—and see which you like best.

▶ Once opened, store all miso in the refrigerator in a tightly sealed container, where it will keep for months. To avoid spoiling, always use a clean spoon when you scoop it out of the container.

▶ Dissolve miso in water that's just below a boil. Overheating it destroys a lot of the flavor and some nutritional benefit.

▶ To make miso soup more substantial, right before serving stir in cooked or soaked Asian noodles, chopped leftover cooked meat or seafood, or a couple cooked scrambled eggs.

Learn More

▶ Soup Basics (page 136), tofu (page 4), Preparing Scallions (page 295)

Lentil Soup

One of my all-time favorite weekend lunches, ready in less than an hour.

TIME **About 45 minutes**
MAKES **4 servings**

2 tablespoons olive oil

1 medium onion, chopped

1 medium carrot, chopped

1 medium celery stalk, chopped, any leaves reserved for garnish

1 cup dried lentils, rinsed and picked over

3 bay leaves

Salt and freshly ground black pepper

1 Put the oil in a large pot over medium heat. When it's hot, add the onion and cook, stirring frequently, until soft, 2 to 3 minutes. Add the carrot and celery and keep cooking and stirring until the carrot turns bright orange, about 2 more minutes.

2 Add the lentils, bay leaves, and 6 cups water; sprinkle with salt and pepper. Bring to a boil, then lower the heat so the soup bubbles steadily and cook, stirring occasionally, until the lentils are tender, 25 to 35 minutes. If the soup gets too thick, add more water, about ¼ cup at a time.

3 Just before serving, fish out the bay leaves. Taste and adjust the seasoning, garnish with any reserved celery leaves, and serve.

I don't like my soup too thick, but if you do, add ¼ cup extra lentils.

If the soup seems too thin, raise the heat to boil some of the liquid off—but make sure to stir it frequently.

RINSING BEANS Put the lentils in a mesh sieve and run them under cool water for a minute or two, sorting through the beans with your fingers and looking for pebbles or other foreign matter.

SOFTENING THE VEGETABLES Cook the celery and carrot with the onion until the carrot turns bright orange and the onions soften and develop flavor.

ADJUSTING THE TEXTURE As the soup bubbles, it will thicken; if it starts to get too thick or stick to the bottom of the pot, add more water.

Tips

▶ It's rare, but occasionally there are pebbles or other foreign matter in lentils and other dried beans. So it's a good idea to pick over them to pull out any pebbles or foreign matter during rinsing.

Variations

▶ **Lentil Soup with Root Vegetables:** Cut whatever you like—potatoes, turnips, rutabagas, or celery root—into ½-inch chunks and add them to the pot when you add the lentils; they'll help thicken the soup too.

▶ **Meaty Lentil Soup:** Reduce the olive oil to 1 tablespoon and use it to cook up to ½ pound raw sausage chunks, ground meat, or chopped bacon in Step 1 before adding the vegetables (these will take 5 to 10 extra minutes to cook). Then continue with the recipe.

▶ **Split Pea Soup:** Substitute green split peas for lentils; cook them in Step 2 until they disintegrate, 45 to 60 minutes.

▶ **Luxurious Lentil Soup:** Purée all or half of the soup. Remember to fish out the bay leaves before puréeing.

Learn More

▶ Soup Basics (page 136), Bean Basics (page 250), chopping onions (page 19), preparing carrots (page 116), preparing celery (page 116)

Garlicky White Bean Soup

Quite possibly the most delicious and simplest of all the bean soups.

TIME **1¼ to 1¾ hours, mostly unattended**

MAKES **4 servings**

1½ cups any dried white beans, rinsed and picked over

1 medium garlic bulb, cloves peeled

1 tablespoon chopped fresh rosemary leaves or 1 teaspoon dried

Salt and freshly ground black pepper

Olive oil for garnish

1 Put the beans, garlic, and rosemary in a large pot with 6 cups water over medium-high heat. Bring to a boil, then lower the heat so the mixture bubbles steadily.

2 Cook, stirring every 20 minutes or so and adding more water if the mixture gets too thick or dry, until the beans are tender and falling apart, 45 to 90 minutes depending on the bean and whether or not you soaked them first.

3 Sprinkle with salt and pepper and stir vigorously to break them up even more. If you like, you can mash or purée some or all of the soup at this point. Taste, adjust the seasoning with more salt or pepper, and serve with a drizzle of olive oil on top of each bowl.

The blender whips up the smoothest texture; food processor–puréed bean soup will still be a little gritty.

CHECKING THE THICKNESS Stir the beans every 20 minutes or so to make sure they have enough liquid; add water ½ cup at a time if the beans look too dry or are starting to stick to the pot.

PURÉEING BEAN SOUP When the beans are tender and creamy, you can semipurée the soup with a potato masher or purée everything until smooth in a blender or food processor.

Tips

▶ The most common white beans are navy, cannellini, and Great Northern, any of which will work in this soup.

▶ The creaminess of this soup depends on cooking the beans until they're quite soft, almost mushy. If you soak the beans before making the soup, you can shave 30 minutes or so off the cooking time.

▶ To use canned beans: Figure about 2 cans (about 15 ounces each); drain and rinse them well. Chop the garlic and consider using stock instead of water; you'll gain some intensity of flavor. Put everything in the pot in Step 1 and cook until the vegetables are tender, 15 to 20 minutes.

Variations

▶ **White Bean Soup with Lots of Vegetables:** In Step 2, during the last 5 minutes of cooking, add 1 to 2 cups of chopped greens such as spinach, kale, escarole, or collards and cook until the greens have wilted, 3 to 10 minutes.

▶ **White Bean Soup with Shrimp:** In Step 2, during the last 5 minutes of cooking, add 1 pound peeled shrimp to the soup and cook, stirring occasionally, until it turns pink and opaque, 3 to 5 minutes.

Learn More

▶ Soup Basics (page 136), Bean Basics (page 250), Stripping Leaves from Hard Herb Stems (page 141)

Smoky Red Bean Soup

The smokiness comes from ham hocks. And all you do is get the pot bubbling, then walk away.

TIME 1¼ to 2 hours,
    mostly unattended
MAKES 6 to 8 servings

1½ cups any dried red
beans, rinsed and picked
over

2 or 3 smoked ham hocks
or 1 ham bone

1 medium onion, chopped

1 medium to large carrot,
chopped

1 medium celery stalk,
chopped

2 bay leaves

1 teaspoon fresh thyme
leaves or a pinch dried

Salt and freshly ground
black pepper

1 Put the beans and 8 cups water in a stockpot over medium-high heat. Add the ham, onion, carrot, celery, bay leaves, and thyme. Bring to a boil, then turn the heat down so the mixture bubbles gently but steadily.

2 Cook, stirring once in a while, until the beans are very tender and just starting to break apart and the meat is falling from the bone, 60 to 90 minutes depending on the bean and whether or not you soaked them. Add more water as needed, ½ cup at a time, to keep the mixture soupy during cooking.

3 Sprinkle with some salt and pepper, stir, and turn off the heat. Remove the hocks (or bone) from the pot. For a smoother, creamier texture, press down on the soup in the pot with a potato masher to break up some of the beans.

4 When the meat is cool enough to handle, pull it from the bone, chop it, and return it to the soup. Bring the soup to a boil, stirring frequently and adding a little more water if it seems too thick. (Or refrigerate, covered, for up to 2 days; reheat before continuing.) Taste and adjust the seasoning and serve.

If you just happen to have a ham bone handy (and you might if you just ate roast ham), that would be perfect in this soup.

CHOOSING THE MEAT Ham hocks are easy to find and have a smoky taste. Use a few bacon slices in a pinch.

SEASONING SOUP WITH HAM Put the meat in at the very beginning so it has plenty of time to flavor the soup.

REMOVING MEAT FROM BONES
The meat is ready when it's quite soft and tender. Pull what meat you can away from the fat and bone, then chop it up a bit before stirring it back in.

Most of the fat from the pork has melted, which makes the soup super-creamy.

Tips

▶ Kidney and pinto beans are the most widely available red beans, but you can make this soup with almost any bean: Try pink, black, or white beans or even chickpeas. Many soups are even better the next day, and that's especially true for this one. To reheat, put the pot over medium heat and stir frequently until the soup is bubbling hot. Or warm individual bowls in the microwave on high; just be sure to stop and stir once or twice.

▶ If you can't find either ham hocks or a ham bone, substitute ½ pound chopped bacon or pancetta; neither will need to be removed.

Variations

▶ **Beefy Bean Soup:** No smokiness, but even meatier. Instead of the ham, use about 1½ pounds bone-in chuck steak or 1 pound beef stew meat.

▶ **Vegetarian Smoky Red Bean Soup:** Skip the ham and add 1 tablespoon smoked paprika (pimentón) with the vegetables in Step 1. If you like, add 2 cups chopped peeled or unpeeled potatoes or turnips for the last 20 minutes of cooking.

Learn More

▶ Soup Basics (page 136), Bean Basics (page 250), Stripping Leaves from Soft Herb Stems (page 78), Puréeing Soup (page 137)

Full-Flavored Vegetable Stock

It's almost too simple: Just throw everything in a pot and go do something else.

TIME **1 to 2½ hours,**
mostly unattended
MAKES **About 3 quarts**

¼ cup soy sauce

2 large onions (don't bother
to peel), cut in half

4 large carrots (don't
bother to peel), cut into
large pieces

4 large celery stalks, cut
into large pieces

1 large potato, cut into
chunks

6 garlic cloves (don't bother
to peel)

15 button mushrooms

2 large tomatoes, roughly
chopped (or use one
28-ounce can; don't bother
to drain)

2 bay leaves

6 sprigs fresh parsley,
optional

Salt and freshly ground
black pepper

1 Put the soy sauce and all of the vegetables, the bay leaves, and the parsley if you're using it in a stockpot with a good sprinkle of salt and pepper. Add 1 gallon (16 cups) water and turn the heat to high. Bring just to a boil and then lower the heat so that the mixture bubbles steadily.

2 Cook, undisturbed, until the all the vegetables are very tender, at least 30 minutes. To develop more intense flavors, let the stock cook for up to 2 hours; check on it once in a while to make sure it's still bubbling gently.

3 When the stock is done, turn off the heat and let it cool slightly, then put a strainer or colander over a large pot and carefully pour in the stock; press down on the vegetables to extract as much liquid as possible from them. Sprinkle the stock with a little salt and pepper and discard the vegetables. Use the stock immediately or refrigerate it for up to 5 days or freeze it for up to 3 months.

The whole house will smell delicious while the stock is cooking.

PREPARING VEGETABLES FOR STOCK Only cut up those that don't fit into the pot whole and the onions, which you'll want to halve so their insides are exposed to the water.

ADJUSTING THE BOIL If you adjust the heat so the stock bubbles steadily but not too violently, you won't have to fuss over it for at least an hour.

Tips

▶ Once you have vegetable stock, you can use it instead of water in any of the soups or stews in this chapter, and you won't believe how much flavor it adds. Even a 15-minute vegetable stock—an onion, a carrot, a stalk of celery, and a bay leaf, simmered together—is better than the packaged stuff.

▶ Onion, garlic, and potato skins contribute to the flavor of the stock, so leave them on; you'll strain them out later. Rinse or scrub them to remove dirt first—that's all.

▶ Other vegetables you can add to the pot: sweet potatoes, peeled and seeded winter squash, zucchini, parsnips, and ½ cup dried tomatoes or mushrooms.

▶ Vegetables you *shouldn't* add to the pot: Eggplant and bell peppers will make the stock bitter. Add strong-tasting vegetables like asparagus, broccoli, cauliflower, turnips, cabbage, greens, beets (which will also color the stock), or rutabagas only if you want the soup to taste like them.

Learn More
▶ Stock Options (page 156)

Pressing on the vegetables makes the stock a little cloudy, but I'll take flavor over appearance any day.

STRAINING AND PRESSING The juice extracted by using the back of a spoon to press down on the solids in the strainer is the most flavorful.

Chicken Stock and Chicken Noodle Soup

Yes, from scratch. Yes, you can do it. Yes, it will be worth the work.

TIME   1½ to 2½ hours, mostly unattended

MAKES   4 servings (plus extra chicken)

One 3- to 4-pound chicken, whole or in parts

1 large onion (don't bother to peel), cut in half

4 large garlic cloves (don't bother to peel)

3 large carrots, 1 whole, 2 chopped

3 large celery stalks, 1 whole, 2 chopped; leaves reserved for garnish

2 bay leaves

6 sprigs fresh parsley, optional

Salt and freshly ground black pepper

½ pound small pasta like shells, orzo, or broken angel hair

1 Combine the chicken, onion, garlic, whole carrot, whole celery stalk, bay leaves, and parsley if you're using it in a stockpot. Add 8 cups water. Bring to a boil, then lower the heat so that the liquid bubbles gently but steadily.

2 Cover and cook, stirring gently every 15 minutes or so, until the chicken is fully cooked, 30 to 40 minutes for parts, 50 to 60 minutes for a whole one. If necessary, add water to keep the chicken submerged. To check for doneness, use a slotted spoon or tongs to carefully lift out some chicken and pierce it with a thin-bladed knife. You should meet no resistance, and the meat should be white all the way to the bone and maybe starting to fall off in places.

3 Carefully transfer the chicken from the pot to a shallow bowl with tongs. When it's cool enough to handle, pull off and discard the skin; pull the meat off the bones and cut it into bite-sized pieces. Reserve 2 cups for the soup and refrigerate the rest for another use. If you have time, return the bones to the pot and let the stock simmer for another 15 to 30 minutes.

4 Put a strainer or colander over a large pot and carefully pour in the stock; press down on the vegetables to extract as much liquid as possible, then dis-

card them. Skim the fat off the top. You should have about 7 cups; if not, add some water. Sprinkle the stock with a little salt and pepper. (If you just want to make chicken stock, stop here.)

5 Put the pot over medium-high heat. Bring it just to a boil, then lower the heat so that the liquid bubbles steadily. Add the chopped carrots and celery and cook, stirring occasionally, until the vegetables are as crisp or tender as you like them, anywhere from 10 to 30 minutes.

6 Stir in the pasta and the reserved 2 cups chicken; adjust the heat so the mixture bubbles steadily and keep cooking until the pasta is tender but not mushy, another 5 to 10 minutes. Taste and adjust the seasoning, garnish with the reserved celery leaves, and serve.

SEPARATING THE MEAT FROM THE BONES Wait until the chicken is fairly cool. Breaking the carcass apart is a messy but easy job, and it's the only way to get the good stuff.

Tips

▶ Making a big batch of stock is only marginally more difficult than making a small one: Double the recipe—or make as much as you can, in the largest pot you have—then divide the stock among small containers to keep in the freezer.

▶ If you have leftover cooked pasta, noodles, rice, or even more vegetables, you can stir them into the soup in Step 6 and cook the soup just long enough for them to heat through (a minute or two) and serve right away.

Variations

▶ **More Flavorful Chicken Stock:** Put all the vegetables into the pot with the chicken (don't bother to chop the extra celery and carrot) and let it cook for 90 minutes in Step 2. Strain and skim the fat off the top as described in Step 4. (The chicken that's left won't be very flavorful chicken, but you can still remove the meat from the bones as in Step 3 and use it elsewhere if you like.)

Learn More

▶ Stock Options (page 156), Pasta Basics (page 172), Chicken Basics (page 306), Chicken (or Turkey) Salad (page 336)

CHOPPING COOKED CHICKEN INTO BITE-SIZED PIECES You'll need about 2 cups for the soup. The leftovers are good for making chicken salad or whatever else you like.

STRAINING CHICKEN SOUP Press every bit of juice from the vegetables and anything else in the strainer. The stock will become a little cloudy, but it'll also be more flavorful.

SKIMMING FAT FROM SOUP OR STOCK Tilt a large spoon into the liquid to get the fat but not the stock. If you have time, put it in the fridge for several hours and remove the fat when it hardens.

Stock Options

Pick a Bone

After learning how to make the stocks on the preceding pages—the concept should be fairly obvious: Cook fresh ingredients in bubbling water long enough and they will flavor the water.

Now that real butchers and fishmongers are making a comeback, it's a little easier to get your hands on bones, which add both flavor and viscosity to many stocks. Lucky you if you can find them for free, but be prepared to pay. As you become more experienced and start to cut up your own fish and meat, store bones and trimmings in a zipper bag in the freezer and use them for stock.

▶ Meat stock is best made with raw, meaty beef, veal, lamb, or pork bones, which you can augment with inexpensive cuts of meat like neck and shin.

▶ Fish stock is best made with scraps: heads and bones from white fish. The fastest—and some of the best—seafood stock comes from shrimp shells (or lobster shells if you have access to them). Avoid using fish gills and innards; they'll turn the stock bitter.

▶ With poultry you have a couple options. The only surefire way to get the most flavorful poultry stock is to start with whole raw chicken (or chicken or turkey parts). You can also use the leftovers from a carved roasted chicken to make a small amount of stock (say about 1 quart); a turkey carcass (which is larger and more flavorful) will yield at least 2 quarts. But whenever you can, enhance stock made from carcasses with raw bones or trimmings, like wing tips and backbones or a couple of (relatively inexpensive) legs.

▶ Whatever bones you choose, figure about three times the volume of water to bones: If you have 2 cups shrimp shells, put them in a pot with 6 cups water. Then start adding other ingredients. For every 4 cups water, add at least 1 onion, halved, 2 large celery stalks, and 2 large carrots to the pot, along with a few bay leaves or sprigs of thyme or parsley if you have them. Any of these will add some fresh-tasting flavors and balance the richness of the bones (or shells). Now just follow the recipe for making stock as described in Chicken Stock and Chicken Noodle Soup recipe on page 154. For an even more full-flavored stock, try the technique on the facing page.

Making stock should be inspirational, not intimidating.

Change the Seasonings

Infusions Spices and other intensely flavored foods will infuse the water with flavor during cooking. Try adding a few tablespoons of tomato paste or several dried mushrooms, for example. A cup or so of red or white wine is an always elegant choice, as are other herbs besides parsley, like thyme, rosemary, or sage. Love garlic? A whole unpeeled bulb of it will not be too much. Want a smoky flavor? Throw in a ham hock or a couple slices of raw bacon along with the other ingredients.

Asian Flavorings If you'll be using the stock in Asian dishes (like noodle soups or stir-fries), consider adding a sliced (unpeeled) 2-inch piece of fresh ginger, a bunch of trimmed scallions, a tablespoon of sesame oil, or whole spices like a cinnamon stick, several cloves, or 1 or 2 star anise. For a Thai twist, throw in 1 whole stalk of lemongrass and use cilantro sprigs instead of parsley. For Indian-style stock—wonderful in curries and spiced soups—add sliced unpeeled ginger and 1 tablespoon of curry powder and substitute cilantro for the parsley.

Salt It's crucial too, but wait to add it until you actually cook with the stock or you may wind up oversalting it.

Stock from Roasted Ingredients

INTENSIFY ANY STOCK Heat the oven to 400°F. Put the meat, fish, or poultry scraps and bones—with or without any vegetables—in a roasting pan. Figure about 6 pounds of ingredients total for 12 cups of stock. Drizzle with ¼ cup olive oil and toss everything to coat; sprinkle with salt and pepper.

ROAST Stir or turn the ingredients every 20 minutes or so, until the pieces are deeply browned on all sides, for 40 to 60 minutes. Don't worry about cooking everything perfectly, since eventually everything's going to be submerged in water anyway; but be careful not to burn anything.

Roasting intensifies the color of the stock, too.

DEGLAZE THE PAN After transferring the roasted ingredients to the stockpot, set the pan over one or two burners and turn the heat to medium-high. Add 2 cups water and scrape up any browned bits from the bottom of the pan as the water starts to bubble away; pour the water into the stockpot along with whatever herbs or spices you want to use. Then cover with about 1 gallon more water and follow the recipe for Chicken Stock as described on page 154.

Egg Drop Soup

The Chinese-restaurant favorite, made sublime with homemade stock.

TIME **15 minutes**

MAKES **4 servings**

---

6 cups chicken stock

1 tablespoon soy sauce, or more to taste

4 eggs

Salt and freshly ground black pepper

2 scallions, chopped

1 teaspoon sesame oil, or more to taste

¼ cup chopped fresh cilantro leaves, optional

1 Put the stock and soy sauce in a large pot over medium-high heat and bring to a boil. Meanwhile, beat the eggs with a sprinkle of salt and pepper until well combined.

2 When the stock is boiling, adjust the heat so that it bubbles gently, not furiously. Pour the eggs into the stock in a slow stream, stirring constantly. You want them to scramble softly but not clump, so it's important to keep stirring until the eggs are cooked, 1 to 2 minutes.

3 Stir in the scallions and sesame oil, then taste and adjust the seasoning with more salt, pepper, soy sauce, or sesame oil. Serve, garnished with the cilantro if you like.

Just keep stirring and everything will be fine.

SIMMERING THE STOCK This is what the bubbling stock should look like. Too hot, and the eggs will cook too fast and break up into big curds; too low, and the eggs will dissolve into the soup.

ADDING THE EGGS Once the stock is the right temperature, pour in the eggs in a slow, steady stream.

This soup's other name is "egg flower soup."

Tips

▶ This is one soup where water really doesn't cut it. If you are a vegetarian or don't have chicken stock handy, make Full-Flavored Vegetable Stock (page 152). Or, if you must, use the best store-bought stock you can find.

Variations

▶ **Straciatella:** Italy's version of egg drop soup. Skip the soy sauce, scallions, sesame oil, and cilantro. In Step 1, beat the eggs with ¼ cup freshly grated Parmesan cheese. Garnish with additional cheese and a bit of chopped fresh parsley leaves if you like.

▶ **Egg Drop Soup or Straciatella with Greens:** Whether you make the main recipe or the preceding variation, just before stirring in the eggs in Step 2, add 2 cups chopped spinach or watercress to the bubbling stock.

▶ **Egg Drop Soup or Straciatella with Noodles:** With Egg Drop Soup, serve over ½ pound cooked Chinese egg noodles. With Straciatella, serve over ½ pound of any cooked pasta.

Learn More

▶ Soup Basics (page 136), Chicken Stock (page 154), Egg Basics (page 50), Beating Eggs (page 52), Preparing Scallions (page 295), Chopping Herbs (page 78)

Corn Chowder with Cheddar

Wonderfully gooey and flavorful, with crunch.

TIME   **About 1¼ hours**
MAKES   **4 servings**

6 ears fresh corn

Salt and freshly ground black pepper

4 tablespoons (½ stick) butter

2 scallions, white and green parts separated and chopped

½ teaspoon sugar

¼ cup all-purpose flour

1 cup grated cheddar cheese

3 cups whole milk, or more as needed

1 Shuck the corn, remove the silk, and cut off the stem end so the cob has a flat surface. Then stand each ear up on a cutting board and scrape off the kernels with a chef's knife. Transfer the kernels to a bowl as you work.

2 Put the corncobs and 4 cups water in a large pot over medium-high heat. Sprinkle with salt and pepper. Bring to a boil, then lower the heat so the water bubbles gently. Cover and cook, checking to make sure the cobs are always covered with water, until the liquid is quite cloudy, about 30 minutes. Discard the corncobs and transfer 3 cups of the broth to a medium bowl or saucepan. (Save the rest if you like; no need to wipe out the pot.)

3 Return the pot to medium-high heat and add the butter. When it melts and foams, add the white parts of the scallions and the sugar and cook, stirring occasionally, until soft, about 1 minute. Lower the heat to medium and stir in the flour. Cook, stirring constantly with a wooden spoon, until the mixture starts to turn golden and the flour no longer smells raw, just a couple of minutes. Then add the cheese and stir until it just starts to melt, less than a minute.

4 Add the reserved corncob broth and milk and raise the heat to medium-high. Stir or whisk constantly until the flour is dissolved and the soup starts to thicken, about 2 minutes. Add the corn kernels and bring to a boil, then lower the heat so the soup bubbles gently. Cook, stirring occasionally, until the corn is tender and the soup has thickened, 10 to 15 minutes. Add a little more milk if you like a thinner soup. Taste, adjust the seasoning, garnish with the scallion greens, and serve.

It's crucial that the cob be stable on the cutting board.

REMOVING CORN FROM THE COB Work slowly and carefully and keep your fingers out from under the knife. Turn and rotate the cob to get everything off.

Tips

▶ The kernels tend to fly everywhere unless you use deliberate knife strokes. You have two choices: Use a downward scraping motion with a chef's knife or try a sawing motion with a serrated knife—neither way is better; it all depends on what feels comfortable to you.

▶ Corncobs add a sweetness to the soup and intensify the corn flavor. You can make this soup with frozen corn kernels (figure about 4 cups), but use 3 cups chicken or vegetable stock instead of the water or the soup will be bland.

Variations

▶ **Other cheeses to try:** Semi-soft cow's cheese like Gruyère or Emmental melts beautifully and adds a nutty creaminess. Parmesan or manchego gives you some sharp and pleasant grittiness. A hard or soft goat cheese will add tang. Or go in a totally different direction and use a cheese that doesn't melt, like feta or queso fresco. Instead of cooking it with the flour in Step 3, wait until the soup is ready and stir it into the pot right before serving. In all cases, use the same amount: grated if hard, crumbled if soft.

Learn More

▶ Soup Basics (page 136), Preparing Scallions (page 295), Shucking Corn (page 236), cheese for cooking (page 389), Grating Cheese (page 176)

COOKING FLOUR WITH BUTTER
Stir constantly, pressing to break up lumps, until the mixture turns golden and smells like toast. Then add the cheese.

ADDING THE CORN BROTH At first the soup will look like a watery, lumpy mess. Don't worry; it all comes together after cooking for a couple minutes.

Creamy Potato and Leek Soup

You can use this recipe as a model for just about any creamy vegetable soup.

TIME **About 1 hour**
MAKES **4 servings**

---

2 tablespoons butter

3 medium potatoes, any type, peeled and cut into 1-inch cubes

3 large leeks, white and light green parts only, well rinsed and thinly sliced crosswise

Salt and freshly ground black pepper

6 cups chicken, beef, or vegetable stock or water

½ cup cream

2 tablespoons chopped fresh chives for garnish

1 Put the butter in a large pot over medium heat. When the butter melts, add the potatoes and leeks. Sprinkle with salt and pepper and cook, stirring, until the leeks start to soften, 3 to 5 minutes.

2 Add the stock, bring to a boil, then lower the heat so the liquid bubbles gently. Cook, stirring occasionally, until the vegetables are very tender, 20 to 30 minutes. Cool the mixture slightly, then carefully transfer it to a blender or food processor; work in batches if necessary to avoid filling the container more than two-thirds full. Start the machine at low or pulse to get the soup moving, then increase the speed. Purée the mixture until it's as lumpy or smooth as you like.

3 Return the soup to the pot, turn the heat to medium-low, and stir in the cream. Adjust the heat so the mixture barely bubbles but doesn't come to a full boil. Cook, stirring, just to heat everything through, 2 to 3 minutes. (Or refrigerate the soup, covered, for up to 2 days; reheat before continuing.) Taste and adjust the seasoning and serve, garnished with the chives.

Transfer the first batch of puréed soup to a big bowl or pot and then repeat with more soup. Or just use a potato masher right in the pot.

Adjust the heat so the vegetables cook gently without coloring.

"SWEATING" THE VEGETABLES
Cook the vegetables until they release some of their moisture and glisten but are not yet golden.

BLENDING IN BATCHES If you overfill the blender or food processor, it may splatter up; work in batches and you won't get burned.

Tips

▶ Leeks are often sandy, so rinse them in a colander after chopping, as you would greens.

▶ This soup is best made with stock, but it's still really good if you don't have any handy and need to use water. To make it a bit more decadent and flavorful, reduce the water to 5 cups and increase the cream to 1 cup.

Variations

▶ **Vichyssoise:** A French-American classic that's delicious and fortifying in summer. Simply serve this soup chilled. You can make it up to a day ahead of time; remember that cold soups usually need a bit more salt.

▶ **Creamy Onion and Potato Soup:** For a slightly different flavor, substitute 3 medium onions for the leeks. Cut them in half, then slice into thin crescents.

▶ **Other vegetables to try:** Broccoli, peas, carrots, winter squash, sweet potatoes, mushrooms, or asparagus. Trim, peel, and chop them as necessary. The cooking time may vary a bit in Step 2, so just keep an eye on them and taste frequently. Purée the soup whenever the vegetables become super-tender.

Learn More

▶ Soup Basics (page 136), Stock Options (page 156), preparing potatoes (page 224)

Barley Soup with Hearty Greens

Bites of chewiness combined with bites of silkiness make for perfect texture.

TIME **45 to 55 minutes**

MAKES **4 servings**

---

2 tablespoons olive oil, plus more for serving

1 medium onion, chopped

1 tablespoon minced garlic

Salt and freshly ground black pepper

1 cup pearled barley

7 cups chicken, beef, or vegetable stock or water

About 2 pounds hearty greens (like kale, collards, or chard)

1 Put the oil in a large pot over medium-high heat. When it's hot, add the onion and cook, stirring occasionally, until it's soft, 3 to 5 minutes. Stir in the garlic, sprinkle with salt and pepper, and cook until fragrant, about 1 minute more.

2 Add the barley and cook, stirring constantly to coat every grain in the fat, until it starts to toast and stick to the pot, 3 to 5 minutes. Add the stock and bring to a boil, then lower the heat so the liquid bubbles steadily. Cover the pot and cook, stirring occasionally, until the barley is almost tender but still with a tiny bit of crunch, 20 to 25 minutes. Add up to 1 cup water if the soup looks too dry.

3 Meanwhile, separate the leaves of the greens from the stems using a knife or shears. Keep the leaves and stems separate and roughly chop both.

4 When the barley is just tender, turn the heat to medium-high, uncover the pot, and add the stems. Bring the soup to a boil, add the leaves, then lower the heat so the mixture bubbles steadily again. Cover and cook until the barley is fully tender but not mushy and the greens are bright colored and tender, another 5 to 10 minutes. Taste, adjust the seasoning, add another 1 or 2 tablespoons olive oil if you like, and serve.

Scissors are a handy tool for this job.

TOASTING BARLEY This step adds a lot of flavor and gives the kernels a chewy texture.

The barley should glisten and turn golden; if it starts to get too brown, turn down the heat.

SEPARATING LEAVES AND STEMS Cut down either side of the rib in the center of each leaf to separate the two leaf halves from the stem.

▶ Water works fine here, but as always you'll get deeper flavor with stock. You can cheat by adding a couple bay leaves or a chopped-up medium celery stalk and carrot along with the barley. (Remember to fish out the bay leaves before serving.)

▶ The stems of hearty greens are predictably tougher than the leaves, but they have great flavor and texture, so instead of throwing them away, add them to the pot a few minutes before the leaves to give them ample time to get tender. You can also use spinach, beet greens, or mustard greens, treated in the same manner if they have thick stems.

Variations

▶ **Mushroom-Barley Soup:** Skip the greens and add 1 pound cleaned and roughly chopped mushrooms along with the onion in Step 1. Cook until they're tender before adding the garlic and continuing with the recipe.

Learn More

▶ Soup Basics (page 136), Chicken Stock (page 154), Stock Options (page 156), Grain Basics (page 206)

If all you have are tender greens, go ahead and use them here. There's no need to separate the stems and leaves; just chop them up a bit.

GIVING THE STEMS A HEAD START Cut both parts into bite-sized pieces, but keep them in two separate piles. Then add the stems to the soup first and bring it to a boil.

Hot and Sour Soup

Lots of black pepper and rice vinegar give this popular soup its signature kick.

TIME **40 minutes**
MAKES **4 servings**

1 tablespoon sesame oil

3 tablespoons soy sauce, or more to taste

3 tablespoons cornstarch

½ pound boneless pork loin

6 cups chicken or vegetable stock or water

1 tablespoon minced garlic

1 tablespoon grated or minced fresh ginger

½ pound shiitake mushrooms, stems removed and caps sliced

½ pound extra-firm tofu, cut into ½-inch cubes

2 celery stalks, roughly chopped

¼ cup rice vinegar, or more to taste

Freshly ground black pepper

Salt

¼ cup chopped fresh cilantro leaves for garnish

½ cup chopped scallions for garnish

1 Whisk together 1 teaspoon of the sesame oil with 1 tablespoon of the soy sauce and 1 tablespoon of the cornstarch in a medium bowl. Cut the pork crosswise into thin slices, then cut each slice into sticks no more than ½ inch wide. Add the meat to the bowl; toss to coat it in the soy mixture and let it sit.

2 Meanwhile, put the stock, garlic, and ginger in a large pot over medium-high heat and bring to a boil. Add the mushrooms, reduce the heat to low so that the liquid bubbles steadily, and cook until the mushrooms are softened and the broth is darkened a bit, 3 to 5 minutes.

3 Bring the soup back to a boil over medium heat and add the meat. Stir to make sure the pieces do not stick together and cook until the meat is no longer pink, 1 to 3 minutes. Then add the tofu, celery, vinegar, a generous sprinkle of black pepper, and the remaining 2 tablespoons soy sauce. Lower the heat so the soup bubbles gently and cook until the flavors meld a bit, just a minute or two.

4 Whisk the remaining 2 tablespoons cornstarch with ¼ cup water in a small bowl to make a slurry. Stir the cornstarch mixture into the soup and cook, stirring, until it just begins to thicken, about 1 minute. Turn off the heat and stir in the remaining 2 teaspoons sesame oil; taste and adjust the seasoning with salt, pepper, soy sauce, or vinegar. Garnish with the cilantro and scallions and serve.

MARINATING THE MEAT Adding cornstarch to the marinade gives the soup a silky, soft texture. Be sure to break up any lumps as you stir to keep the soup smooth.

MAKING A CORNSTARCH SLURRY After the ingredients begin to cook and flavor the soup, whisk together the slurry ingredients until smooth.

Tips

▶ The "hot" comes from black pepper; the "sour" comes from the rice vinegar. Adjust the quantities of both up or down to suit your taste. If you do accidentally overseason with either, don't panic; just dilute the soup with a little more stock or water.

Variations

▶ **Hot and Sour Soup with Chicken, Beef, Seafood, or Tofu:** Try substituting boneless, skinless chicken breast or thighs, flank steak, or chopped peeled shrimp or crab instead of the pork. (If you use seafood, add it in Step 4 about 1 minute before you stir in the cornstarch slurry.) Or skip the meat altogether and use twice as much tofu in Step 3.

▶ **Hot and Sour Soup with Eggs:** For more body and contrasting textures, stir in eggs as you would for Egg Drop Soup (page 158): After you add the cornstarch in Step 4, beat two eggs and pour them into the soup slowly, whisking all the while, until they form nearly translucent ribbons.

Learn More

▶ Soup Basics (page 136), Pork Basics (page 284), Chicken Stock (page 154), Full-Flavored Vegetable Stock (page 152), preparing ginger (page 222), types of mushrooms (page 231), tofu (page 4)

STIRRING IN THE SLURRY Keep stirring after adding the slurry so the soup keeps moving and the cornstarch dissolves.

FINISHING THE SOUP Keep the soup at a gentle bubble, but don't let it boil. As soon as you see it start to thicken, it's time to add the remaining ingredients and eat.

Clam Chowder

The real deal from New England, with fresh clams of course.

TIME **About 1 hour**
MAKES **4 servings**

About 3 pounds littleneck or other hard-shell clams, well scrubbed, those with broken shells discarded

4 slices bacon (about 4 ounces), chopped

1 large onion, chopped

½ pound all-purpose potatoes, like Yukon Gold, peeled if you like

4 cups fish, chicken, or vegetable stock or water

1 teaspoon fresh thyme leaves or ½ teaspoon dried

Salt and freshly ground black pepper

1 cup milk

1 cup cream or half-and-half

1 tablespoon butter, optional

¼ cup chopped fresh parsley leaves for garnish

1 Put 2 cups water in a large pot over high heat, add the clams, cover, and bring to a boil. Cook until most of the clams open, 3 to 5 minutes after the water starts boiling, then remove them from the pot, reserving the cooking water. Let the clams cool.

2 Remove the meat from the clams (if any are still closed, open them with a dull knife) and discard the shells. Cut them into bite-sized pieces. Carefully pour the liquid—but not the grit—into a small bowl. Rinse and dry the pot.

3 Put the bacon in the pot over medium-high heat and cook, stirring occasionally, until it renders fat and gets a little crisp, 3 to 5 minutes. Add the onion and cook, stirring frequently, until it softens a little, a minute or two.

4 Meanwhile, cut the potatoes into about ½-inch cubes. Add the stock, reserved clam-cooking liquid, potatoes, and thyme to the pot and cook, stirring occasionally, until the potatoes are tender, 10 to 15 minutes. If you want a thicker soup, roughly mash the potatoes with a potato masher.

5 Sprinkle the soup with salt and pepper, then add the milk and cream. Reduce the heat to low, add the clams, and bring just to a gentle bubble. Turn off the heat, add the butter if you're using it, and stir until it melts. Taste and adjust the seasoning with salt or pepper, then garnish with the parsley and serve.

CHECKING THE CLAMS About 3 minutes after you hear the water start boiling, peek to see if any have opened. Stop cooking whenever most of the shells have opened.

GETTING AT CLAM MEAT Your hands are the best tool here, so let the shells cool a bit before digging in. And be sure to work over the pot to capture the juice.

Tips

▶ Hard-shell clams—which include littlenecks, cherrystones, and quahogs—often have some sandy residue on the outside of their shells (their insides are almost always sand-free), so they need a bit of rinsing—sometimes even scrubbing with a stiff brush—under running water before you use them. Always discard any clams that aren't tightly closed or have broken shells when you go to use them (this goes for mussels and oysters too).

▶ Call me a purist, but I don't like to thicken clam chowder with flour—it buries the subtle flavor of the clams.

Variations

▶ **Manhattan-Style Clam Chowder:** Skip the potatoes, milk, and cream. Add 1 cup chopped carrot, 1 cup chopped celery, and 3 cups chopped tomatoes (canned are fine; don't bother to drain) along with the stock and clam liquid in Step 4.

▶ **Fish Chowder:** Skip the clams and cook 2 cups chopped sturdy white fish (like cod or halibut) in the water in Step 1. Then just continue with the recipe.

Learn More

▶ Soup Basics (page 136), Stock Options (page 156), Shellfish Basics (page 360), types of potatoes (page 235), preparing potatoes (page 224), Dairy—and Not (page 42)

LEAVING SEDIMENT BEHIND
There will probably be some grit at the bottom of the pot; pour carefully to leave it there.

THICKENING WITH POTATOES
The starch in potatoes is just perfect in soups. Mash them a bit right in the pot before you add the cream and clams.

Pasta and Grains

I've yet to meet anyone who doesn't love starchy, comforting dishes based on pasta, noodles, rice, and grains. Even during the low-carb craze, when the country seemed to go bonkers for meat, eggs, and cheese, did anyone give up these staples cheerfully? No, which is why that fad didn't last—life without carbohydrates is decidedly unfun.

Nor is it smart. Whole grain starches (which include whole wheat pasta and noodles and brown rice) are packed with fiber, vitamins, and minerals. Even the less nutrient-dense carbohydrates like refined wheat and rice can be a sound part of a sane diet.

Anyway: We love them. And cooking pasta and grains is almost as easy as boiling water. The only trick is learning how to recognize—and anticipate—the different stages of doneness.

(And observing how these foods change color while cooking in water will help you with other, more complicated skills and recipes.)

This chapter starts with pasta and sauces that come together in less than 30 minutes and beat anything out of a jar. Then come easy techniques and flavorful stir-ins for traditional and not-so-traditional rice and grain dishes. You'll learn how to throw together quick, easy Asian noodles and simple one-dish meals that are as good as those served in most restaurants and rival the speed of takeout.

In fact, once you start making pasta and grains at home, you will probably think twice about going out to eat this kind of food, and I can almost guarantee you won't need to spend another dime on boxed or frozen processed stuff.

Pasta Basics

How to Cook Pasta

BRING A STOCKPOT OF WATER TO A BOIL AND SALT IT
Figure at least 1 gallon (16 cups; but you don't need to measure; just use a lot!) per pound of pasta; less than that and the noodles may stick together. Your 2-gallon stockpot is perfect; fill it about two-thirds to the top and turn the heat to high. To flavor the pasta and help prevent sticking, add several large pinches of salt (about 2 tablespoons) for every gallon of water. And don't add oil to the cooking water; the sauce will never properly cling to the pasta and become creamy.

WHEN THE WATER BOILS, ADD THE PASTA AND STIR To keep the noodles from sticking together when they first go in the water, toss long pasta strands with tongs or a wooden spoon as they soften or stir cut pasta with a slotted wooden spoon. When the water starts boiling again, adjust the heat so it bubbles enthusiastically without overflowing and continue to stir occasionally as the pasta cooks.

AFTER 5 MINUTES, START TASTING Carefully fish out a piece with a slotted spoon or tongs, blow on it to cool, take a bite, and look inside. Taste another piece every minute or so. When the noodle still has a little resistance but isn't hard and chalky inside, the pasta is ready to drain; it will continue to cook in the sauce.

PULL THE DISH TOGETHER Ladle out at least 1 cup of the cooking water, then drain the pasta. The pasta needs to rest in the colander for only a few seconds; you want it still slightly moist (don't rinse it!). The noodles are ready to toss with the heated sauce, adding some of the reserved water for creaminess. Tongs work well for strands; use a spoon for cut noodles.

Saucing and Tossing

The best—and most authentic—way to cook pasta is to combine the sauce and the pasta with a little of the cooking water. The idea is to coat and flavor the noodles and release their starch to add creaminess. If you like more sauce, double all the ingredients except the pasta.

Pasta cooking times vary depending on their shape, manufacturer, and storage conditions. So the only way to know when pasta is ready is to taste it. Here's what's going on inside at different stages.

Undercooked pasta—which is still hard and chalky inside—needs to boil for a couple more minutes before tossing but is perfect for baked pastas.

When you bite down, pasta should offer resistance and have a teeny bit of the tough interior still remaining. The Italians call this texture *al dente* or "to the teeth." I call it "with bite"— barely tender but not at all mushy.

This is overcooked: plump and beginng to lose its shape. Even if the pasta isn't mushy yet, it will be by the time you drain, sauce it, and get it to the table.

What About Fresh Pasta?

Making your own fresh pasta isn't difficult, but it requires more patience than most beginning cooks have. You can buy it, though, preferably from a store or restaurant that makes it fresh (stay away from the supermarket stuff). Use it in place of dried pasta in any of these recipes. Start tasting after 1 minute.

Pasta with Garlic and Oil

An absolute classic, destined to be one of your favorites.

TIME   **20 to 30 minutes**
MAKES   **4 servings**

Salt

⅓ cup olive oil, or more as needed

2 tablespoons minced garlic

Crushed red pepper, to taste, optional

1 pound long thin pasta, like spaghetti or linguine, or any other pasta

½ cup chopped fresh parsley, optional

1 Bring a stockpot of water to a boil and salt it. Put the oil, garlic, red pepper if you're using it, and a pinch of salt in a large skillet or saucepan over medium-low heat. Cook until the garlic just turns golden but not brown, 2 to 4 minutes. Turn off the heat and let the mixture sit.

2 When the water boils, cook the pasta until it is tender but not mushy; start tasting after 5 minutes. When it's done, scoop out and reserve at least 1 cup of the cooking water, then drain the pasta.

3 Return the sauce to medium heat and stir once in a while until it's hot again. Add the pasta to the sauce in the skillet along with a splash of the cooking water and toss to coat, adding a little more oil or cooking water if necessary to create a slightly creamy sauce. Taste and adjust the seasoning with more salt or red pepper, then toss with the parsley if you're using it and serve.

Taste a strand, add more salt or red pepper if you want, and taste again.

Listen for the garlic to sizzle and watch for it to puff up a bit.

COOKING GARLIC To keep the garlic from burning and turning bitter, keep the heat low and occasionally shake the pan and stir. Adjust the heat if necessary.

USING PASTA WATER As you toss everything together, the starch in the cooking water combines with the pasta to thicken the sauce. Add more oil or water if it looks dry as you toss.

Tips

▶ Linguine, spaghetti, or other long pastas are classic for this Roman dish, but it's still delicious with cut pasta.

▶ Don't freak out about the amount of oil in the recipe; it will combine with the pasta water to create a simple and delicious sauce. (Plus, it's just a bit over a tablespoon per serving.)

▶ Grated cheese is not traditional in this dish and tends to dry the sauce out too much.

Variations

▶ **Pasta with Capers, Olives, or Anchovies:** While the garlic is cooking in the oil, stir in 2 tablespoons capers or chopped olives or a couple of oil-packed anchovies—but not all three or the pasta will be too salty.

▶ **Pasta with Bread Crumbs:** In Step 1, add another tablespoon of oil to the pan with the garlic. When you toss the pasta for the last time before serving, add some toasted or fried fresh bread crumbs.

Learn More

▶ Pasta Basics (page 172), mincing garlic (page 20), Chopping Herbs (page 78), Fresh Bread Crumbs (page 386)

Pasta with Eggs and Cheese

Think of this as Italian comfort food; add bacon and you get classic carbonara.

TIME **20 to 30 minutes**
MAKES **4 servings**

Salt

3 eggs

½ cup freshly grated pecorino Romano or Parmesan cheese, or more to taste

1 pound linguine or other long pasta

Freshly ground black pepper

1 Bring a stockpot of water to a boil and salt it. Heat the oven to 200°F and put a large ovenproof bowl in it for about 5 minutes. When the bowl is warm—handle it with oven mitts to avoid burning yourself—crack the eggs on a flat surface and open them into it. Beat them with a fork or whisk until uniformly colored. Then stir in the cheese.

2 When the water boils, cook the pasta until it is tender but not mushy; start tasting after 5 minutes. When it's done, scoop out and reserve at least 1 cup of the cooking water, then drain the pasta.

3 Immediately toss the pasta with the eggs in the bowl; if it's too dry (unlikely), add a little of the pasta-cooking water. Taste and add more salt or cheese if you want, then add black pepper—I suggest a lot—and serve.

Adjust your hands so your fingers and thumb stay far away from the grater!

Don't dawdle between draining the pasta and tossing it with the sauce or the cheese won't melt.

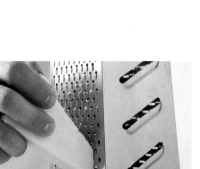

GRATING CHEESE Each side of the box grater yields a different texture. Press the hunk of cheese against the side you want and run it up and down over the holes repeatedly.

USING A MICROPLANE This kind of grater is razor-sharp, and the results are fluffy—perfect for hard cheeses like pecorino or Parmesan. (It doesn't work well with anything softer.)

TOSSING PASTA WITH EGGS Add the hot pasta immediately to the eggs and toss. The eggs will cook and form a thick, creamy sauce in the residual heat.

Tips

▸ It sounds strange to make a sauce from raw eggs, but the warm bowl and hot pasta cook the eggs perfectly.

▸ Pecorino is a sharp, salty Italian cheese made from sheep's milk (*pecora* means "sheep"); use more or less depending on your taste. If you find the flavor is too strong, use Parmesan instead.

▸ Long pasta is traditional with smooth sauces like this, but cut pasta is easier to toss; use whichever you like.

Variations

▸ Toss in 1 cup fresh or thawed frozen peas just before serving.

▸ Toss ½ cup chopped ham or prosciutto with the pasta and eggs just before serving.

▸ **Richer Pasta with Eggs and Cheese:** Add up to ¼ cup cream to the eggs and cheese in Step 1.

▸ **Carbonara:** You can buy pancetta—salted, cured, and rolled pork belly— at the deli counter of most supermarkets. If you can't find it, use regular bacon. Just chop 4 ounces of meat up and cook it as described on page 43. Toss the crisped pancetta or bacon (as well as the pan drippings if you like) with the pasta and egg mixture just before serving.

Learn More

▸ Pasta Basics (page 172), Egg Basics (page 50)

Pasta with Tomato Sauce

You will see: There's no reason to buy pasta sauce in jars.

TIME **25 to 30 minutes**
MAKE **4 servings**

Salt

3 tablespoons olive oil, or more as needed

1 medium onion, chopped

One 28-ounce can diced tomatoes, including the juice

Freshly ground black pepper

1 pound any dried pasta

½ cup freshly grated Parmesan cheese, plus more for serving

½ cup chopped fresh basil leaves for garnish, optional

1 Bring a stockpot of water to a boil and salt it. Put the oil in a large skillet over medium-high heat. When it's hot, add the onion. Cook, stirring occasionally, until soft, 2 to 3 minutes. Add the tomatoes and sprinkle with salt and pepper.

2 Adjust the heat so the sauce bubbles enthusiastically and cook, stirring occasionally, until the tomatoes break down and the mixture begins to thicken and appear more uniform in texture, 10 to 15 minutes. Taste, adjust the seasoning, and adjust the heat so the tomato sauce stays hot but doesn't boil.

3 When the water boils, cook the pasta until it is tender but not mushy; start tasting after 5 minutes. When it's done, scoop out and reserve at least 1 cup of the cooking water, then drain the pasta.

4 Add the pasta and a splash of the cooking water to the sauce in the skillet and toss to coat, adding a little more oil or cooking water if necessary to create a slightly creamy sauce. Taste and adjust the seasoning and add more oil if you'd like; then toss with the cheese and the basil if you're using it. Serve, passing more cheese at the table.

Watch the heat and stir every now and then to make sure the sauce doesn't start to stick and burn.

BUILDING THE SAUCE Once the onion has softened, add the tomatoes to the pan.

BEGINNING TO THICKEN After about 5 minutes, the tomatoes will start to break down and thicken the sauce.

FULLY THICKENED The sauce is done when the tomatoes break down and the sauce isn't at all watery. You want a relatively uniform consistency, but some chunks of tomato will remain.

Tips

▶ You can whip up a batch of tomato sauce from scratch in the time it takes to boil water and cook pasta.

▶ Diced tomatoes are super-convenient whether in cans, cartons, or jars. Just don't buy crushed tomatoes or tomato purée, which are both much too watery.

▶ Canned whole tomatoes will give you an even meatier sauce and are easy enough to deal with: First drain off the liquid from the can and save it; you may need it to thin the sauce (or drink!). Don't bother to core them, but do use a knife to hack away at the tomatoes right in the can to break them up a bit.

▶ Here's how to make extra sauce for the freezer: Complete the sauce through Step 2, doubling the amounts of oil, onions, tomatoes, and salt and pepper. Let half of the sauce cool and pack it in sealed containers and freeze. Eat within 6 months or so. To defrost, heat it slowly in a pan over low heat, let it sit overnight in the fridge, or microwave it.

Learn More

▶ Pasta Basics (page 172), chopping onions (page 19), Grating Cheese (page 176), Chopping Herbs (page 78), Tomato Sauce Variations (page 180)

Tomato Sauce Variations

Tomato Sauce with Fresh or Dried Herbs Stir any of the following herbs into the sauce just before serving: ¼ to ½ cup chopped fresh basil, parsley, dill, or mint; 10 fresh sage leaves; 1 tablespoon chopped fresh rosemary, oregano, or marjoram (or 1 teaspoon dried); 2 teaspoons chopped fresh thyme (or ½ teaspoon dried); or ½ teaspoon chopped fresh tarragon (or ¼ teaspoon dried).

Vegetable-Tomato Sauce Chop up whatever leftover vegetables you have (grilled anything is especially nice) and warm them up in the sauce just before serving. If you don't have anything handy, chop 2 cups raw eggplant, zucchini, cauliflower, broccoli, or bell peppers. In Step 1, cook them alone in the oil until the vegetables are soft and tender, 10 to 15 minutes; add more oil to the pan if it starts to look too dry. Remove the vegetables with a slotted spoon, then add the onion to the pan and continue with the recipe. When the sauce is almost done, stir the vegetable back in just long enough to heat through.

Spicy Tomato Sauce Known as *arrabbiata*. Skip the onion and in Step 1 put 1 tablespoon chopped garlic in the oil along with 1, or 3, or 5 (or up to 10 if you like things really hot) small dried red chiles or a big pinch of crushed red pepper. Cook, stirring, until the garlic is brown—deeply colored (but *not* burned)—then turn off the heat for a minute, add the tomatoes, and proceed. Remove the whole chiles before serving.

Tomato Sauce with Fresh Mushrooms Cook 1 pound sliced trimmed mushrooms (any kind) along with the onion until they shrink and all their liquid evaporates, 5 to 10 minutes (see page 230); then add the tomatoes and proceed with the recipe.

Cheesy Tomato Sauce Right before serving, stir in 1 cup cubed fresh mozzarella cheese, or use ½ cup ricotta or goat cheese for a creamier, milder sauce.

Puttanesca Sauce Skip the onion and in Step 1 put about 1 tablespoon chopped garlic in the oil along with a few oil-packed anchovies. Mash up the anchovies a bit as you stir; wait to add salt until the sauce is done. Just before adding the tomatoes, stir in 2 tablespoons drained capers, a pinch red pepper flakes if you like, and ½ cup pitted oil-cured black olives.

Meaty Tomato Sauce Start by cooking up to 1 pound ground beef, pork, lamb, chicken, or turkey with the oil and onion until it browns, 5 to 10 minutes, before adding the tomatoes. You can also use sausage; just break it up into chunks as it cooks. Adjust the heat so the meat browns without burning.

Spaghetti and Meatballs Make a recipe of Meatballs (page 282) and add them to the sauce in Step 2. Stir gently so they don't break.

Tomato Sauce with Seafood When the sauce is ready, stir in up to 1 pound peeled shrimp, lump crab- meat, or chopped cleaned squid or scallops. Reduce the heat so it bubbles gently, cover, and cook until the seafood is warmed or cooked through as necessary, 1 to 5 minutes. Or add a 6-ounce can of oil-packed tuna to the pan when you add the tomatoes.

Fresh Tomato Sauce This takes a few minutes longer to prepare than canned. For a "meatier" sauce, use roma (plum) tomatoes; slicing tomatoes have a brighter taste and thinner texture. Cherry tomatoes are fine if you cut them in half and don't mind the chewiness of the skins, but they'll never quite come together into a sauce the same way. In any case, figure about 2 pounds per recipe. I don't bother to peel or seed them (not worth the effort), but I do remove the cores. If you want to get rid of the seeds: Cut them in half— lengthwise if they're roma; around the equator if they're slicers—and gently squeeze out the watery interior. Then cut them into 1-inch chunks and proceed with the recipe.

Mushrooms, sliced thinly for sauce

Fresh thyme for herb sauce

Ingredients for Puttanesca Sauce

*Fresh mozzarella for
Cheesy Tomato Sauce*

Pasta with Broccoli and Sausage

This sauce, and its loads of variations, is probably the one I make most often.

TIME **40 minutes**

MAKES **4 servings**

Salt

1 pound broccoli

¼ cup olive oil, or more as needed

1 tablespoon minced garlic, or more to taste

½ pound Italian sausages (2 to 3 sausages), chopped

1 pound cut pasta like orecchiette, penne, ziti, or farfalle

Freshly ground black pepper

½ cup freshly grated Parmesan cheese, plus more for serving

1 Bring a stockpot of water to a boil and salt it. Trim the broccoli and cut it into pieces. Add the broccoli to the pot and return the water to a boil.

2 Meanwhile, put the oil in a large skillet over medium-low heat. When the oil is hot, add the garlic and the sausage. Cook, stirring occasionally, until the garlic is fragrant and the sausage is well browned, about 5 minutes. Remove it from the skillet and turn the heat off.

3 Start checking the broccoli after 5 minutes. You want it fully tender but not mushy; this could take up to 10 minutes. Use a slotted spoon or small strainer to scoop up the broccoli, draining off excess water, and transfer it to the skillet. (Keep the water boiling.)

4 Cook the broccoli over medium-high heat, stirring and mashing it slightly with a potato masher, until it is quite soft and breaks apart. If you need to, add a tablespoon or two of the boiling water to help soften the broccoli. Meanwhile, cook the pasta in the boiling water until it is tender but not mushy; start tasting after 5 minutes.

5 When the pasta is done, scoop out and reserve at least 1 cup of the cooking water, then drain it. Add the pasta, sausage, and a splash of cooking water to the broccoli; toss until combined, adding a little more water or olive oil if necessary to make a slightly creamy sauce. Taste and adjust the seasoning, adding lots of black pepper and the Parmesan cheese. Toss again and serve, passing more cheese at the table.

No need to go crazy—if a little skin remains, that's fine.

TRIMMING BROCCOLI After cutting off the dried-out end and pulling off any leaves, peel the stalk's tough skin with a sharp knife or vegetable peeler.

CUTTING BROCCOLI STALKS Now cut the stalk into roughly equal-size pieces so they'll cook evenly.

Tips

▶ The olive oil in this dish adds body and flavor to the sauce, so don't skimp. In fact, I add another tablespoon or two when tossing the pasta for richness, moisture, and flavor.

Variations

▶ **Pasta with Broccoli:** Skip the sausage and go directly from Step 1 to Step 3.

▶ **5 Pastas with Vegetables, with or without Sausage.** Use this same recipe with these vegetables instead of the broccoli; you'll need to vary the boiling time:

1 Kale, collards, or cabbage will take 5 to 10 minutes.

2 Cauliflower (which is fantastic) will take 10 to 12 minutes.

3 Broccoli raab and asparagus will take 3 to 5 minutes.

4 Chopped escarole, spinach, or arugula will take about 1 minute.

5 Mushrooms require no boiling—just trim and slice them, then cook them with the garlic and browned sausage until they shrink and their liquid evaporates, 5 to 10 minutes.

Learn More

▶ Mincing garlic (page 20), types of sausages (page 289), Pork Basics (page 284), Pasta Basics (page 172), Grating Cheese (page 176)

CUTTING BROCCOLI FLORETS
Break or cut the head into bite-sized (or slightly bigger) florets.

FINISHING THE SAUCE As you mash the broccoli until it breaks down into a sauce, stir in some of the boiling water from the stockpot to keep the pan from drying out.

Whole Wheat Pasta with Pesto

Pesto, of course, is a sauce you can use on anything, from vegetables to meats and fish.

TIME   **20 to 30 minutes**
MAKES   **4 servings**

Salt

2 loosely packed cups fresh basil leaves

1 garlic clove, or more to taste

2 tablespoons pine nuts

½ cup olive oil, or more to taste

½ cup freshly grated Parmesan cheese, plus more for garnish

1 pound any whole wheat pasta

1   Bring a stockpot of water to a boil and salt it. Put the basil, a pinch of salt, the garlic, the nuts, and about half of the oil in a food processor or blender. Turn the machine on, stopping a couple times to scrape down the sides of the container and gradually adding the rest of the oil. Continue processing or blending until you have a relatively smooth, thick consistency. If you're using a food processor, remove the blade. Stir in the cheese.

2   When the water boils, cook the pasta until it is tender but not mushy; start tasting after 5 minutes. When the pasta is almost done, thin the pesto by stirring in some of the pasta-cooking water—start with just a tablespoon so you don't overdo it. You're looking for the pesto to coat the back of a spoon.

3   When the pasta is done, scoop out and reserve at least 1 cup of the cooking water, then drain it. Return the pasta to the stockpot and quickly toss it with the pesto, adding more cooking water if necessary to coat the noodles. Taste and adjust the seasoning, top with more grated cheese if you like, and serve.

The smell is pretty fabulous right about now.

TRIMMING BASIL After rinsing basil well—it's often sandy—pull the leaves off the tough stems and measure them. (A few thin stems are fine.)

PURÉEING PESTO Slowly add the oil with the food processor running to achieve a smooth, even texture. Then remove the blade.

Tips

▶ I like the hearty texture and flavor of whole wheat pasta with pesto, but you can of course use regular pasta if you'd rather; any shape is fine.

▶ Basil pesto will keep in an airtight container in the refrigerator for up to several days or in the freezer for several months (but why wait?). To help the sauce stay fresh tasting, don't stir in the cheese until you're ready to serve it, and after putting it in the container, drizzle a layer of olive oil over the top.

Variations

▶ Make pesto from other light-tasting, grassy herbs like cilantro, parsley, mint, chives, or a combination. Just as with basil, use only the best leaves and tender stems.

▶ Pecorino Romano (which is saltier than Parmesan) is another good cheese for pesto. Or instead of a hard cheese, try goat cheese, feta, or ricotta. Or use no cheese at all.

▶ Change up the nuts—walnuts or pecans are nice—or for a nuttier pesto increase the quantity of nuts to 1 cup and decrease the basil to ½ cup.

Learn More

▶ Pasta Basics (page 172), Crushing and Peeling Garlic (page 247), Grating Cheese (page 176)

CHECKING TEXTURE After you stir in the cheese, the mixture should be fairly thick—kind of like yogurt.

CREATING A SAUCE Add cooking water to give the pesto the texture of heavy cream—just right for tossing with pasta.

Shortcut Macaroni and Cheese

Creamy, and beautifully browned and crunchy on top; not at all like the stuff from a box.

TIME **About 1 hour, mostly unattended**
MAKES **4 to 6 servings**

---

6 tablespoons (¾ stick) butter, softened

Salt

2½ cups milk

2 bay leaves

1 pound rigatoni, elbow, or other cut pasta

3 tablespoons all-purpose flour

6 ounces sharp cheddar cheese, grated (about 1½ cups)

Freshly ground black pepper

½ cup freshly grated Parmesan cheese

½ cup bread crumbs, preferably fresh

1 Heat the oven to 400°F and grease a 9 x 13-inch baking pan with 2 tablespoons of the butter. Bring a stockpot of water to a boil and salt it.

2 Put the milk and the bay leaves in a small saucepan over medium-low heat. When small bubbles appear along the sides of the pan, after about 5 minutes, turn off the heat and let the milk sit.

3 When the water boils, cook the pasta to the point where it is just becoming tender but is still quite underdone and firm in the center. Start tasting after 3 minutes. Drain the pasta and rinse it quickly in cold water to stop the cooking.

4 Fish the bay leaves out of the milk. Spread a third of the pasta evenly in the prepared baking dish. Sprinkle it with half of the flour (using your hands is easiest), dot with half of the remaining butter, cover with ½ cup of the cheddar, and sprinkle with salt and pepper.

5 Repeat this process once more. Finally, spread out the last of the pasta and top with the remaining cheddar and the Parmesan; sprinkle with the bread crumbs. Pour the heated milk over all. Bake until bubbling and browned on top, 30 to 40 minutes. Serve immediately.

When you bite or break into the noodle, the center will be white and chalky.

Look for steam and small bubbles just forming around the edge.

SCALDING MILK You want to heat it almost but not quite to boiling. Adding herbs or spices infuses the milk—and whatever you use it for—with wonderful flavor.

UNDERCOOKED NOODLES FOR BAKING You wouldn't want to eat pasta this underdone, but it's going to finish cooking in the oven.

Tips

▶ Most macaroni and cheese recipes start by making a cheese sauce; you can't just toss melting cheese with the pasta and expect it to become creamy and not stringy. This shortcut technique saves a step and creates a luxurious sauce as the noodles bake.

Variations

▶ Cut pasta is best because it grabs the sauce nicely, and elbows are most common. But you might also try shells, ziti, corkscrews, rigatoni, orecchiette, or farfalle.

▶ You want a flavorful, creamy melting cheese here. Besides cheddar, consider Emmental, Gruyère, manchego, or fontina.

Learn More

▶ Pasta Basics (page 172), Greasing a Pan with Butter (page 398), cheese for cooking (page 389), Grating Cheese (page 176), Fresh Bread Crumbs (page 386)

"DOTTING" WITH BUTTER This means exactly what it says: putting little bits of butter on the surface like polka dots.

LAYERING IN THE PAN By the time you get to the third layer, the baking dish is pretty full.

You can smell the bay leaves as you pour the milk.

Meaty Lasagne

This Italian-American version is always a hit at potlucks and parties.

TIME **About 45 minutes with prepared sauce**

MAKES **6 to 8 servings**

Salt

1 pound dried lasagne noodles

4 cups Meaty Tomato Sauce (page 180)

2 tablespoons olive oil

2 cups ricotta cheese

1 pound mozzarella cheese, grated (about 4 cups)

1½ cups freshly grated Parmesan cheese

Freshly ground black pepper

1 Put at least 5 quarts of water in a stockpot, bring it to a boil, and salt it. (If your pot isn't that big, cook the noodles in 2 batches.) When the water comes to a boil, add the noodles one at a time and cook, stirring frequently and gently, to the point where they just become pliable but are still quite underdone, 3 to 5 minutes. Drain the noodles carefully in a colander, then lay them flat on paper towels or clean dish towels. (Repeat with the second batch of noodles if necessary.) Heat the oven to 400°F.

2 Taste the sauce and make sure it has enough salt and pepper. Smear the bottom of a 9 x 13-inch baking pan with the oil and one-quarter of the meat sauce, then put in a layer of noodles, touching but not overlapping, trimming them as necessary. Dot about half of the ricotta over the noodles, then smear with another quarter of the meat sauce. Top with one-third of the mozzarella, one-third of the Parmesan, and a grinding of black pepper.

3 Repeat for one more layer; for the third layer, smear meat sauce directly on the noodles and end with the Parmesan. (At this point, you may refrigerate the dish for a day, well wrapped in aluminum foil or plastic wrap or freeze it for a month; defrost in the refrigerator for a day before cooking.)

4 Bake for 20 to 30 minutes, until the lasagne is bubbly and hot in the center. Remove the dish from the oven and let rest for 5 minutes before cutting and serving. (Or let cool completely, cover well, and refrigerate for up to 2 days or freeze for up to a month.)

If you taste a piece of noodle, it should be firm to the bite and still have a chalky center.

KEEPING THE NOODLES MOVING Gentle stirring guarantees that the noodles won't stick to each other (or the pot) as they cook. They're ready when they're still sturdy but can bend.

FITTING THE NOODLES IN THE PAN Trim off any excess with scissors or a knife; if you overlap or fold the edges, they will get unpleasantly hard during baking.

Tips

▶ Be careful when you drain the lasagne noodles: Because they're big and unwieldy, they have a tendency to trap water, which can splash and burn you.

▶ You can make the meat sauce up to a couple days ahead and keep it in the refrigerator before you make the lasagne. But you can also make it right before you start layering, in which case give yourself about an extra half hour and set the pot of water for the noodles to boil when the sauce is half done.

▶ Good ricotta is rich and creamy, not watery. Look for ricotta without food starch, xanthan gum, or guar gum. It's also soft and almost spreadable, but if you have trouble spreading it on the noodles, put it in a bowl and stir in ½ cup or so of the sauce to thin it out.

Variations

▶ **Vegetarian Lasagne:** Use the basic Tomato Sauce (page 178) or any of the meatless variations in Tomato Sauce Variations (page 180).

Learn More

▶ Pasta Basics (page 172), cheese for cooking (page 389), Grating Cheese (page 176)

LAYERING THE INGREDIENTS It's easier to spread tomato sauce on top of dots of ricotta than vice versa.

MAKING THE FINAL LAYER The very top should have noodles, sauce, mozzarella, and Parmesan, but no ricotta, or else it'll be too messy.

Asian Noodle Basics

The Noodles

Supermarkets usually carry one or two kinds; Asian markets offer an overwhelming array. Here are the most common:

Rice Noodles, Sticks, and Vermicelli White, almost translucent noodles, made from rice flour. You can soak rather than cook all but the thickest rice noodles. Check them frequently: The thinnest will be ready in 3 to 5 minutes; the widest will take 15 to 20 or even 30 minutes to soften. The thick, wide types can be boiled to speed things up a bit, but again, check them often; most are tender in 5 to 10 minutes.

Soba Noodles Japanese in origin, these are made from a combination of buckwheat and wheat flour. With a nutty flavor and grayish color, they're often served cold with a soy dipping sauce or in brothy soups. I like to add them to stir-fries too. Boil until tender, usually 5 minutes at most.

Udon Noodles Made from wheat flour, these chewy noodles are usually served in soups or stews, though you also see them served cold or in stir-fries. They range in thickness and length and should be boiled for 8 to 12 minutes. (*Somen* noodles are thinner and take much less time to get tender.)

Chinese Egg Noodles They're long, thin, and golden in color, made from wheat flour and sold fresh or dried. And they cook quickly: Dried take 3 to 5 minutes in boiling water, depending on thickness, and fresh take as little as 1 minute.

Bean Threads They go by various names, including *cellophane noodles* and *glass noodles*. These are long and translucent and made from the starch found in mung beans. Soften them by soaking for 5 to 15 minutes, unless you're using them in soup, in which case you can just toss them right in a few minutes before serving. In any case, you may want to use scissors to cut them up.

Cooking—or Soaking

Though you use the same equipment and similar technique, Asian noodles usually cook faster than Italian pastas, and rice and some other noodles require only soaking in boiling water to become tender. Like Italian pasta, you want them tender enough to eat but not at all mushy; check frequently, since the cooking times can vary wildly, even within the same type. When they're underdone, they are still too stiff to eat; overdone, they clump together and start to disintegrate. Here's how to get started:

1 Figure 2 to 4 ounces dried noodles per serving. Bring a stockpot of water to a boil and salt it. When the water comes to a boil, you have two choices:

For soaking (rice noodles, bean threads): Remove the pot from the heat and add the noodles (or put the noodles in a large bowl and add enough boiling water to cover). Stir to break them up with tongs or a big fork, then let them sit for a minute or two before you start checking. The thinnest noodles will be soft in as little as 3 minutes; thicker noodles can take up to 10 to 15 minutes.

For boiling (all other noodles): Add the noodles to the boiling water as you would for pasta and stir them with tongs or a big fork to break them up. Start checking after 3 minutes.

2 Drain the noodles in a colander when they are just tender. (You want to rinse rice noodles in cold water to cool them quickly and rinse off the starch, or they'll clump up in a terrible tangle.) If they seem too long and unwieldy, cut them up right in the colander with kitchen scissors. Use the noodles right away by dressing like salad or adding to soups or stir-fries. Or if the rest of the meal isn't ready, submerge them in a bowl of cold water for up to an hour, then drain again.

The Eating

Regardless of which you begin with, Asian noodles become fairly inter-changeable once you soak or boil them, and you can combine them with all sorts of ingredients. Here are three super-easy ideas:

CUP OF NOODLE SOUP For a single-serving treat, put 1 cup softened noodles (about 3 ounces dried) in a bowl and add 2 cups steaming-hot stock (vegetable, fish, chicken, and beef are all fine) or brewed green or black tea (for the adventurous). Chop up and add ½ small cucumber, ½ fresh hot chile, 2 or 3 scallions, and about ½ cup any cooked meat—or use any other ready-to-eat ingredients you have on hand. For fresh-tasting, crisp vegetables, eat the soup right away.

These are udon noodles.

STIR-FRY WITH NOODLES Cook or soak 8 to 12 ounces of any noodles. Reserve at least 1 cup of the boiling or soaking water when you drain the noodles. Add them to any stir-fry during the last moments of cooking (instead of serving the stir-fry on top of rice) and add just enough of the reserved liquid to help the ingredients come together and form a sauce. Taste and add more soy sauce, oil, and boiling or soaking water, just as you would season sauced pasta.

These are rice noodles.

FRIED NOODLES Cook or soak 8 to 12 ounces of any noodles and drain them well. Put 2 tablespoons vegetable oil in a large skillet over high heat. When it's hot, spread the noodles in the pan in an even layer. Wait to stir until the noodles smell toasty, about 1 minute. After that, toss the noodles with a spatula until they're brown and crisp in places. Adjust the heat as needed so they sputter but don't burn. Transfer to a plate and top with chopped steamed vegetables; simply cooked meat; or just a splash of soy sauce and hot sauce.

These are bean threads.

Cold Noodles with Peanut Sauce

Peanut butter, water, and seasonings make the simplest sauce on the planet.

TIME **30 minutes**

MAKES **2 main-course or 4 side-dish servings**

Salt

1 medium or 2 small cucumbers

½ cup peanut butter

2 tablespoons sesame oil

2 tablespoons sugar

3 tablespoons soy sauce, or more to taste

1 teaspoon grated or minced fresh ginger, optional

1 tablespoon rice vinegar or fresh lemon juice, or more to taste

3 drops hot sauce (like Tabasco), or more to taste

Freshly ground black pepper

12 ounces fresh or dried Chinese egg noodles

½ cup chopped scallions for garnish

1 Bring a stockpot of water to a boil and salt it. Peel the cucumbers, cut them in half lengthwise, and scoop out and discard the seeds with a spoon. Grate the cucumber with a box grater or the grating disk of a food processor.

2 Whisk together the peanut butter, sesame oil, sugar, soy sauce, ginger, vinegar, hot sauce, and pepper in a small bowl. Add ¼ cup of the hot water from the stockpot and continue to whisk. The sauce should be about the consistency of heavy cream; if it isn't, whisk in more hot water 1 tablespoon at a time.

3 When the water is boiling, cook the noodles until they are tender but not mushy; start tasting after 1 minute for fresh or 3 minutes for dried noodles. When the noodles are done, drain them and rinse with cold running water, then drain them again.

4 Toss the noodles with the sauce and cucumbers in a large bowl. Taste and adjust the seasoning, adding small amounts of salt, soy sauce, vinegar, hot sauce, or pepper as you like. (The noodles can be made up to 2 hours ahead and refrigerated; let sit at room temperature for a few minutes before serving.) Garnish with the scallions and serve.

The heat of the water helps melt the peanut butter.

GRATING SOFT VEGETABLES
When you grate watery vegetables like cucumber, you get a silkier texture than with chopping but retain some of the crunch.

WHISKING SOMETHING THICK WITH SOMETHING THIN Hot water and peanut butter reluctantly make a sauce. Keep at it and the mixture will eventually get smooth.

Tips

▶ You can make the peanut sauce—without the hot water—up to a day in advance; cover or transfer to an airtight container and refrigerate. When you're ready to serve, prepare the cucumber, whisk the hot water into the sauce, cook the noodles, toss, and serve.

Variations

▶ To make this a meal, add up to 1 cup sliced cooked chicken, beef, or pork; cooked whole shrimp or crabmeat; or cubes of firm tofu.

▶ **Cold Noodles with Sesame Sauce:** Use tahini (sesame paste) instead of peanut butter and add sesame seeds to the garnish.

▶ **Cold Noodles with Cashew Sauce:** Whirl ½ cup raw or roasted cashews in the food processor until they're puréed into a paste—it might take up to a few minutes, so be patient—and use that instead of the peanut butter. Add a sprinkle of salt if you used unseasoned nuts.

Learn More

▶ Asian Noodle Basics (page 190), seeding and chopping cucumbers (page 117), shredding vegetables in the food processor (page 121), preparing ginger (page 222), Preparing Scallions (page 295)

This clean swipe is the best way to test the thickness of all sorts of creamy sauces.

TESTING THE TEXTURE OF A CREAMY SAUCE The mixture should coat the back of a spoon but remain thick enough so that a line drawn down the spoon with your finger holds its shape.

Thai-Style Noodles with Shrimp

If you like pad thai, you'll love this.

TIME **30 to 40 minutes**
MAKES **4 servings**

Salt

12 ounces dried flat rice noodles, about ¼ inch wide

¼ cup vegetable oil

½ cup coconut milk (reduced fat is okay)

2 tablespoons soy sauce, or more to taste

2 tablespoons fresh lime juice

2 teaspoons sugar

¼ teaspoon crushed red pepper, optional

1 tablespoon minced garlic

2 scallions, cut into 1-inch lengths

3 eggs, lightly beaten

4 cups shredded Napa cabbage

½ pound medium shrimp, peeled

¼ cup chopped peanuts for garnish

½ cup chopped fresh cilantro leaves for garnish

1 Bring a stockpot of water to a boil and salt it. When the water is boiling, remove the pot from the heat and stir in the noodles. Soak until they are softened but not mushy; start checking after 5 minutes. Then drain the noodles, rinse them in cold water, and toss them with 1 tablespoon of the oil.

2 Whisk together the coconut milk, soy sauce, lime juice, sugar, and red pepper if you're using it in a small bowl.

3 Put the remaining 3 tablespoons oil in a large skillet over medium-high heat. When it's hot, add the garlic and scallions and cook, stirring once or twice, until they're fragrant and turning golden, 1 to 2 minutes. Add the eggs and cook without stirring for 30 seconds or so; when they begin to set, stir them and scrape the sides of the pan until they're pale yellow and opaque.

4 Add the cabbage and cook, stirring, until it begins to wilt, 3 to 5 minutes. Then add the shrimp and stir until it turns a little pink, 2 to 3 minutes. Add the coconut milk mixture and the noodles and toss with tongs or spoons until the noodles are warmed through and coated with the sauce. Taste and adjust the seasoning, adding more salt or soy sauce as you like. Transfer the noodles to serving plates, top with the peanuts and cilantro, and serve.

If the eggs stay soft and creamy, the heat under the pan isn't quite hot enough.

ADDING THE EGGS The garlic and scallions should be fragrant, glistening, and beginning to turn golden when you add the eggs.

ADDING THE SHRIMP The eggs should be fairly firm and the cabbage wilted by the time you add the shrimp. Keep stirring until it turns pink.

Tips

▶ Have all your ingredients prepared, measured, and within reach when you begin stir-frying—the cooking process will take only about 10 minutes, so you won't have time to mess with anything once the skillet gets hot.

▶ Coconut milk is widely available in both full- and reduced-fat types. Either is fine, but the dish will obviously be richer if you go for the former.

Variations

▶ **Vary the Vegetables:** Instead of the cabbage, try mung bean sprouts, grated carrots, broccoli florets, or green beans—alone or in combination, up to 4 cups total.

▶ **Almost Pad Thai:** Use mung bean or soybean sprouts instead of the cabbage and cubes of tofu for some of the shrimp. Instead of making the sauce with coconut milk and soy sauce, try combining fish sauce (nam pla, which is available at most supermarkets or Asian groceries) and tamarind paste (a sour concentrate, available in Asian markets and some supermarkets). Start with 2 tablespoons tamarind and ¼ cup fish sauce; add the sugar, lime juice, and crushed red pepper, then taste and go from there.

Learn More

▶ Asian Noodle Basics (page 190), Preparing Scallions (page 295), preparing cabbage (page 120), Peeling Shrimp (page 362), chopping nuts (page 19), Chopping Herbs (page 78)

Any size shrimp is fine here, or skip it entirely to make the dish vegetarian.

SAUCING AND TOSSING Add the noodles and the coconut milk mixture when the shrimp just begins to color. The dish will come together in the time it takes for the shrimp to finish cooking.

Rice Basics

Boiled Rice, Any Length, Any Color

Forget what you've heard about how tricky rice is to get right. The truth is you can cook almost all types of rice exactly the same way. The simmering time and the amount of liquid vary slightly depending on the kind of rice you're cooking, where it was grown, and how old it is. So it's best to learn what to look for as the rice cooks. This foolproof method will give you perfectly cooked rice most of the time and nearly perfect rice every other time. The yield is around 4 cups, so figure 4 to 6 servings.

RINSE THE RICE Put 1½ cups short-, medium-, or long-grain white or brown rice in a medium saucepan. Cover with water, swirl it around, and carefully pour off as much water as possible, leaving the rice in the pot. Repeat until the water looks almost clear. If you're making white rice, start with 2¼ cups water; for brown rice, add 2½ cups. Add a large pinch of salt. (To eyeball it, add enough water to the pot to cover the rice by about ½ inch.)

ADJUST THE HEAT Set the pot over high heat. Once the water boils, turn the heat to medium or medium-low so that it bubbles steadily but not violently. Leave the pot uncovered. You can now walk away for up to 15 minutes if you're cooking white rice, 30 minutes for brown.

CHECK FOR DONENESS Now check the rice every few minutes. When holes appear on the surface, taste the rice to make sure it's just tender and not crunchy. Tip the pot to see if liquid remains; the rice should be dry, but not sticking or burning. White rice takes 15 to 25 minutes; brown rice takes 40 to 50. If there's water and the rice is done, drain it and return it to the pot. If the pot is dry and the rice is firm, add ¼ cup water and return the pot to the heat; repeat until it's tender.

FLUFF THE RICE Once the rice is ready, cover the pot and remove it from the heat. Let the rice sit for at least 5 and up to 15 minutes. Just before serving, add a pat of butter or a drizzle of olive oil if you'd like—about 2 tablespoons for this quantity will do the trick. Then fluff and stir the rice with a fork. Taste, add more salt if needed, and fluff again.

SHORT-GRAIN

LONG-GRAIN

The Short and Long of It

Since there are literally thousands of different kinds of rice—more than enough to overwhelm even experienced cooks—let's group them all into two simple categories: long-grain rices and short- and medium-grain rices.

Long-Grain Rice These include the southern varieties (the most common rice in America), as well as aromatic rices like the nutty basmati and the floral jasmine. American aromatic rices (like Texmati) are also delicious and getting easier to find. All cook up into the fluffy familiar rice of side dishes and pilafs.

Short- and Medium-Grain Rice Plumper, starchier, and slightly sticky, these are the grains we know from dishes like risotto, paella, and sushi. Packages in supermarkets are often labeled simply *short-grain* or *medium-grain*. Risotto—the creamy Italian dish—is made with short-grain rices (the most common variety is Arborio), as is the classic Spanish dish known as *paella* (Valencia is the most common). The short-grain sticky rices used throughout Asia are increasingly available here in specialty markets. And a whole group of American short- and medium-grain rices are gaining popularity.

Brown Rice The name reflects the way the rice is processed, not its length or variety. All brown rice is minimally milled, so that its nutritious bran and germ remain attached; it's considered a whole grain. (White rice is not, since all of the outer layers are removed during milling.)

Brown rice takes about twice as long to cook as white rice. But if you parboil brown rice, you can use it interchangeably with white rice in any recipe, even risotto. Here's how: Boil the quantity in the recipe like pasta for 12 to 15 minutes. Then drain it and pretend that you're starting with raw white rice. (You can even store it in the fridge for up to a few days.) Amazing, but it works.

Rice Pilaf, Plain and Fancy

When you add fat, you add flavor: Toast the kernels first and everything changes.

TIME **45 to 60 minutes**
MAKES **4 servings**

1½ cups long-grain white rice, preferably basmati

2 to 4 tablespoons olive oil

1 medium onion, chopped

Salt and freshly ground black pepper

2¼ to 2½ cups water or chicken, beef, or vegetable stock

½ cup chopped fresh parsley leaves for garnish

1 Rinse the rice in a strainer and let it drain. Put 2 tablespoons of the oil in a large skillet over medium-high heat. When it's hot, add the onion. Cook, stirring occasionally, until the onion softens, 3 to 5 minutes.

2 Add the rice and turn the heat down to medium. Stir frequently until the rice is glossy, completely coated with oil, and starting to turn golden, another 3 to 5 minutes. Sprinkle with salt and pepper and add 2¼ cups water all at once. Stir once or twice just to incorporate the liquid and bring the mixture to a boil. Then adjust the heat so it bubbles gently; cover the pan.

3 Cook the rice until it is almost dry and craters appear on the surface, 15 to 20 minutes. Taste to make sure it's almost fully tender; if the liquid is absorbed but the rice is still too firm, add another ¼ cup water, cover, and cook for 5 more minutes, then taste again. Turn the heat as low as possible and let rest for 15 to 30 minutes.

4 Just before serving, stir in the remaining 2 tablespoons oil if you want to add even more richness and fluff the pilaf with a fork. Taste and adjust the seasoning, fluff again, sprinkle with the parsley, and serve.

Be patient: The rice should smell toasty but not burned.

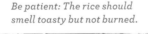

ADDING THE RICE Once the onion is soft, stir in the rinsed and drained rice.

TOASTING THE RICE The grains should turn noticeably translucent and begin to darken in color.

COOKING THE RICE Once the liquid is bubbling steadily but gently, put a lid on the pot and leave it for 15 minutes before checking to see if holes have formed on the surface.

Tips

▶ I go with basmati rice for pilaf because it's incredibly delicious and the grains stay separate long after cooking, but any rice will work. Pilaf made with short-grain rice is pleasantly sticky and perfect with stir-fries and other Asian-style dishes.

▶ Letting pilaf rest after cooking allows it to dry out and develop a light and airy texture. On a gas stove, set it over the absolute lowest possible heat. If you have an electric stove, turn the heat off and let the pan sit on the burner as it cools.

▶ Pilaf can be made ahead and reheated successfully; sprinkle the top with about 2 tablespoons water first, cover, and reheat gently on the stove or in the oven.

Variations

▶ **Brown Rice Pilaf:** Use brown basmati rice instead of white and increase the liquid to 2½ cups in Step 2. Cook for 30 to 40 minutes in Step 3 instead of 15 to 20. You might need to add even more water, so check it after about 20 minutes.

▶ **Garlicky Rice Pilaf:** Use 1 or 2 tablespoons minced garlic instead of the onion; it will soften in 1 or 2 minutes, so watch it. (Or try 2 large chopped shallots, 1 chopped leek, or 4 chopped scallions—all with slightly different results.)

▶ **Rice Pilaf with Vegetables:** Along with the onion, add 1 chopped celery stalk; 1 cored, seeded, and chopped bell pepper; or 1 chopped carrot.

▶ **Herbed Rice Pilaf:** Substitute other mild fresh herbs—like mint, basil, chervil, or dill—for the parsley.

▶ **Jazzed-Up Rice Pilaf:** When you fluff the rice, add other ingredients along with the parsley: up to 1 cup cooked and crumbled bacon or sausage, ½ cup flaked smoked salmon, ½ cup chopped nuts, ½ cup chopped dried fruit, or 1 tablespoon lemon, orange, or lime zest.

Learn More

▶ Rice Basics (page 196), chopping onions (page 19), Stock Options (page 156), Chopping Herbs (page 78)

Fried Rice

Leftover boiled rice makes a delicious comeback.

TIME   **30 minutes**
MAKES   **4 servings**

¼ cup peanut oil

1 medium onion, roughly chopped

1 medium bell pepper (preferably red), cored, seeded, and chopped

2 medium celery stalks, roughly chopped

Salt and freshly ground black pepper

1 tablespoon minced garlic

3 to 4 cups cooked long-grain white or brown rice, chilled for a few hours

2 eggs

2 tablespoons soy sauce, or more to taste

1 tablespoon sesame oil

Cold rice is best, since the starch in the rice needs to be dried out and firm to toast properly.

1 Put 1 tablespoon of the oil in a large skillet over medium-high heat. When it's hot, add the onion, bell pepper, and celery. Sprinkle with some salt and pepper and raise the heat to high. Cook, stirring occasionally with a spatula, until the vegetables begin to soften and brown, 8 to 10 minutes. Turn the heat down slightly if the mixture begins to burn. Transfer the vegetables to a bowl.

2 Add the remaining 3 tablespoons oil to the skillet and return it to high heat. When it's hot, add the garlic. Stir for about 15 seconds, then begin to add the chilled rice. Break up any lumps with the spatula, but resist the urge to stir it until the grains start to sputter and turn brown around the edges, 1 to 3 minutes. If at any point the rice begins to burn, lower the heat or remove the pan from the burner for a few seconds to slow down the cooking.

3 When the rice is sizzling, stir it around once and push it to the sides of the pan to make a well in the center of the pan. Crack the eggs on a flat surface and open them into the well, stir them quickly with the corner of the spatula to scramble them for about 30 seconds, then stir them together with the rice.

4 Add the vegetables back to the skillet and toss until they're combined with the rice and heated through, about 1 minute. Stir in the soy sauce and sesame oil. Taste, adjust the seasoning with more salt, pepper, or soy sauce, and serve.

CRUMBLING COLD RICE Give the garlic a little head start, then add the rice to the pan, separating the grains with your fingers above the pan and scattering them evenly.

SCRAMBLING THE EGGS They should solidify a bit before you combine them with the rice; otherwise they'll coat the grains instead of forming distinct curds.

Tips

▶ To start with raw rice: Cook a batch of Boiled Rice (brown or white) on page 196 and chill 3 to 4 cups for at least a couple of hours.

▶ To make a smaller batch: Cut the recipe in half if you have only 1½ to 2 cups of rice—perfect for 2 people.

Variations

▶ **5 Early Additions to Fried Rice.** In Step 1, use whatever vegetables you have handy or stir in any of these ingredients along with (or instead of) the raw vegetables:

1 1 medium zucchini or summer squash, chopped or grated

2 1 cup chopped eggplant

3 1 cup fresh or thawed frozen corn kernels

4 1 medium carrot, chopped or grated

5 1 cup bean sprouts

▶ **5 Last-Minute Additions to Fried Rice.** In Step 4, stir in any of these ingredients when you return the cooked vegetables to the skillet:

1 2 cups thinly sliced iceberg or romaine lettuce

2 1 cup fresh or thawed frozen peas

3 1 tomato, cut into thin wedges

4 1 cup chopped cooked poultry, meat, or fish

5 ½ pound firm tofu, cut into small cubes

Learn More

▶ Rice Basics (page 196), chopping onions (page 19), Preparing Bell Peppers (page 117), Boiled Rice (page 196)

Risotto with Butter and Parmesan

You've got to watch this and stir periodically, but it's not a big deal.

TIME **45 to 60 minutes**
MAKES **4 to 6 servings**

6 tablespoons (¾ stick) butter

1 medium onion, chopped

Large pinch saffron threads, optional

1½ cups Arborio or other short- or medium-grain white rice, rinsed

Salt and freshly ground black pepper

½ cup dry white wine (like Sauvignon Blanc or Pinot Grigio) or water

6 cups chicken, beef, or vegetable stock or water

½ cup freshly grated Parmesan cheese, plus more for serving

1 Put 2 tablespoons of the butter in a large pot over medium heat. (Leave the remaining 4 tablespoons butter at room temperature to soften.) When it's melted and the foam has subsided, add the onion and the saffron if you're using it and cook, stirring occasionally, until the onion softens and the saffron begins to dissolve, 3 to 5 minutes.

2 Add the rice and cook, stirring occasionally, until it is glossy and every grain is coated with the butter, 2 to 3 minutes. Sprinkle with salt and pepper, add the white wine, and stir until the liquid bubbles away, another minute or two.

3 Add ½ cup of the stock and stir; when the liquid is just about evaporated, add another ½ cup. As each addition of liquid is absorbed, add another, stirring often—but not constantly—after each addition. Adjust the heat so the liquid bubbles steadily but not too rapidly.

4 Begin tasting the rice after about 20 minutes of adding the stock; you might not have to use all of it. You want the texture to be creamy and the grains of rice tender but still with a tiny bit of crunch (it could take another 10 minutes or longer to reach this stage). When it's ready, stir in the remaining 4 tablespoons butter and the Parmesan. Taste, adjust the seasoning, and serve right away, passing additional Parmesan at the table.

A ½-cup metal measure (technically meant for dry ingredients) makes a convenient ladle.

COOKING THE RICE Keep stirring until the rice is shiny and uniformly coated in butter.

ADDING LIQUID The wine should be almost evaporated when you start adding more liquid.

Tips

▶ Saffron is undeniably expensive, but a good-size pinch (about ½ teaspoon) brings deep, haunting flavor and rich color to a dish. (Use too much, though, and you wind up with a medicinal taste.)

▶ Stock adds a lot of flavor here (and is especially valuable if you don't use saffron). But risotto made with water is still really good. Just be sure to taste for salt after adding the cheese.

▶ Risotto is traditionally made by ladling hot (not boiling) stock into rice, but I don't think preheating the stock or water is necessary, as long as you add it in small (about ½-cup) increments.

Variations

▶ **Seafood Risotto:** Skip the cheese and use fish stock for the liquid if possible. In Step 4, when the rice is almost done, stir in 1 pound seafood—like peeled medium shrimp, sliced cleaned squid, lump crabmeat, or roughly chopped scallops or thick firm fish fillets—alone or in combination. Cook until the seafood is opaque and tender, 2 to 5 minutes, then stir in the remaining butter and serve.

Learn More

▶ Rice Basics (page 196), chopping onions (page 19), Chicken Stock (page 154), Full-Flavored Vegetable Stock (page 152), Stock Options (page 156), Grating Cheese (page 176)

KNOWING WHEN TO ADD MORE LIQUID It's time to add more water or stock when you begin to see trails at the bottom of the pan when you stir. The rice should be barely sticking.

FINISHING RISOTTO Since the rice will continue to cook after you add the butter and cheese, make sure it's still got a bit of crunch and is a little soupier than you ultimately want it.

Paella with Chicken and Sausage

Spain's most famous dish, made easy enough for any day of the week.

TIME **About 1 hour**
MAKES **4 to 6 servings**

---

3 tablespoons olive oil

2 bone-in, skin-on chicken thighs, trimmed of excess fat

Salt and freshly ground black pepper

1 medium onion, chopped

2 tablespoons minced garlic

½ pound Spanish chorizo or other smoked sausage, chopped

2 cups any short- or medium-grain white rice, rinsed

2 teaspoons smoked paprika (pimentón)

½ cup dry white wine

3 to 3½ cups chicken, beef, or vegetable stock or water

1 cup chopped red bell pepper

½ cup chopped fresh parsley leaves for garnish

1 Heat the oven to 450°F. Put the oil in a large ovenproof skillet over medium-high heat. When the oil is hot, add the chicken, skin side down, and sprinkle with salt and pepper. Cook until the pieces are deeply browned and release easily from the pan, 5 to 10 minutes. Turn, sprinkle with salt and pepper, and cook on the other side, rotating the pieces as necessary until browned, another 5 minutes or so. Remove the chicken from the skillet.

2 Lower the heat to medium and add the onion, garlic, and chorizo to the pan. Sprinkle with salt and pepper and cook, stirring occasionally, until the vegetables soften and the sausage begins to crisp, 3 to 5 minutes. Add the rice and cook, stirring, until it is glossy and starts to smell toasty. Add the paprika and stir until it is fragrant, less than a minute. Stir in the wine and scrape up any browned bits from the bottom of the pan.

3 Pour 3 cups stock over the rice and tuck in the chicken pieces. Transfer the skillet to the oven and bake, undisturbed, for 15 minutes. Check to see if the rice is dry and just tender. If not, bake for another 5 to 10 minutes, until

it is. (If the rice is dry but not yet tender, add a little liquid—¼ cup or less—before baking for another 5 minutes; repeat if necessary.)

4 When the rice is ready, taste and stir in the bell pepper and more salt and pepper if you like; return the skillet to the oven. Turn off the heat and let the paella sit for at least 5 and up to 15 minutes.

5 When you're ready to serve, you can give the paella a crust: Put the pan over medium-high heat until the rice sizzles lightly and begins to smell toasted—but not burned—2 to 3 minutes. Garnish with the parsley and serve.

You could add another 2 to 4 chicken thighs without changing the recipe.

SEARING THE CHICKEN Keep the pieces moving so the chicken browns all over; this is the first step in flavoring the paella.

Tips

▶ Spanish chorizo is fully cooked—either smoked or cured—and has a fairly firm texture. If you can't find it, use another smoked sausage like kielbasa.

▶ Valencia rice is traditional for paella, but any short- or medium-grain white rice will do.

▶ Smoked paprika (*pimentón* in Spanish) is available in most supermarkets and has a distinctive robust flavor.

▶ To divide the chicken, pull the meat from the bones with a fork and serve everyone a bit.

Variations

▶ **Vegetarian Paella with Lots of Tomatoes:** Skip the chicken, sausage, and peppers and go directly to Step 2. Core 1½ pounds ripe tomatoes and cut them into wedges. In Step 3, put them on top of the rice and liquid before transferring the pan to the oven.

Learn More

▶ Rice Basics (page 196), Chicken Basics (page 306), types of sausages (page 289), Chicken Stock (page 154), Full-Flavored Vegetable Stock (page 152), Stock Options (page 156)

FLAVORING THE RICE Cooking the rice with the onions, sausage, and spices will help it develop smokiness throughout.

ADDING THE PEPPER When you stir it in, be careful not to dislodge any crust that may have formed around the edges. Tuck in the chicken again if you need to.

Grain Basics

How to Cook Any Grain

Many once unusual grains are now available in supermarkets, and fortunately, they're super-easy to cook. Start by ignoring the package directions: Trust your eyes and your teeth and treat all grains virtually the same way. (The exceptions are couscous—explained below—and grains ground into meal, like polenta—see page 212.) This recipe makes about 4 cups, or 4 to 6 servings.

Preparing Couscous

We treat couscous like a grain, but it's actually a kind of pasta that you steep in boiling water like tea. Here's what you do to get 4 servings:

For white couscous, put 2¼ cups water in a medium saucepan with a pinch of salt and bring to a boil. Stir in 1½ cups couscous, cover, and remove from the heat. Let it sit for at least 5 and up to 30 minutes. For whole wheat couscous, use 2½ cups water and let sit for at least 10 minutes. (Cook pearl or Israeli couscous as directed on this page; begin checking after 5 minutes.)

RINSE THE GRAINS Put 1½ cups of any whole, rolled, or cut grain with a pinch of salt in a medium saucepan, cover with water, and swirl them around. Let them settle to the bottom a bit, then pour off as much of the water as you can. Repeat the rinsing process until the water is no longer cloudy. (You can use a strainer and run water over them too.)

ADD WATER The water should cover the grains by about 1 inch if you want them a little soupy; about ½ inch if you want them to be drier. (Use a small saucepan if you're cooking a small quantity to make the eyeballing easier.) Bring to a boil over high heat, then adjust the heat so the water bubbles steadily but gently.

CHECK ONCE IN A WHILE Cook until the grains are tender, stirring with a fork once or twice to make sure the grains aren't sticking to the pot. This can take anywhere from 10 minutes to 2 hours or more, depending on the grain. Use the times listed on the facing page as guidelines and start tasting at the early end of the range.

TEST FOR DONENESS When craters appear on the surface and all the liquid is gone, taste a grain; it should have some bite without being chewy or crunchy. If not, add ¼ cup water and cook for 5 more minutes. (If they're done but still swimming, drain them in a strainer and put them back in the pot.) When they're tender, cover the pot, remove it from the heat, and let sit for 5 to 15 minutes. Just before serving, add 2 tablespoons butter or olive oil, fluff the grains with a fork, and serve within 10 minutes.

Common Grains and Their Cooking Times

The grains below only scratch the surface. For more on
how to cook specific grains, see the recipes that follow.

WHITE COUSCOUS
5 to 10 minutes
(steep in boiling water)

POLENTA AND
GRITS
20 to 30 minutes

WHOLE WHEAT
COUSCOUS
10 to 15 minutes
(steep in boiling water)

MILLET
20 to 30 minutes

ROLLED OATS
15 to 20 minutes

WILD RICE
45 to 60 minutes

STEEL-CUT OATS
30 to 45 minutes

WHEAT BERRIES
60 to 90 minutes *(faster
if you soak them over-
night first)*

QUINOA
About 20 minutes

HOMINY
2 to 4 hours *(faster if
soaked like beans)*

Quinoa Pilaf with Ginger and Chiles

The same technique you use for rice works perfectly for other grains too.

TIME **30 to 40 minutes**
MAKES **4 servings**

2 tablespoons vegetable oil

4 scallions, white and green parts separated and sliced

1 medium fresh hot chile (like jalapeño), seeded and minced

2 tablespoons minced ginger

Salt and freshly ground black pepper

1½ cups quinoa, well rinsed and drained

2¼ cups water or chicken, beef, or vegetable stock

1 teaspoon sesame oil

1 lime, quartered

1 Put the oil in a large skillet over medium heat. When it's hot, add the scallion whites, the chile, and the ginger. Sprinkle with salt and pepper and cook, stirring occasionally, until the vegetables begin to soften and turn golden, 3 to 5 minutes.

2 Add the quinoa and stir to coat with the oil. When the grains start popping and smelling toasted, 2 or 3 minutes later, add the water and bring to a boil. Lower the heat so the mixture bubbles steadily but gently, cover, and cook, undisturbed, for 15 minutes.

3 Taste the quinoa for doneness; the grains should be tender and have little rings around the edges. If the grains are still hard, make sure there's enough liquid to keep the bottom of the pan moist, adding a few tablespoons water if necessary, then cover, and check again in 2 or 3 minutes.

4 When the quinoa is ready, add the sesame oil and scallion greens, fluff with a fork, and taste and adjust the seasoning. Fluff again and serve immediately or at room temperature with the lime wedges.

This pilaf is so flavorful that water is fine, though stock will add another dimension of flavor.

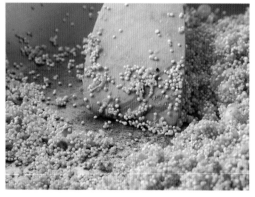

TOASTING QUINOA Stir the quinoa into the softened vegetables and cook and stir until it's translucent and starts to turn golden.

SIMMERING GRAINS Adjust the heat so the mixture bubbles steadily but not too vigorously. And don't stir the quinoa more than once or it will get sticky.

Tips

▶ Thankfully, this fantastic South American grain is now available in supermarkets. The small, delicate kernels have a subtle grassy flavor and cook up fluffy with a pleasant grittiness. And they are high in both protein and fiber.

▶ Quinoa can taste bitter unless you rinse it well, so this is one case where I use a strainer. Run the grains under cool water for a minute or two, using your fingers to stir the kernels so the water circulates.

Variations

▶ **Quinoa Pilaf with Caramelized Shallots:** Skip the scallions, ginger, and chile. Add 4 large sliced shallots to the hot oil in Step 1, lower the heat to medium, and cook until they soften and caramelize, 8 to 10 minutes. Continue with the recipe. In Step 4, stir in ½ cup chopped fresh parsley instead of the scallion greens.

Learn More

▶ Grain Basics (page 206), Preparing Scallions (page 295), Preparing Chiles (page 276), preparing ginger (page 222), Chicken Stock (page 154), Full-Flavored Vegetable Stock (page 152), Smarter Water (page 137)

Try not to stir too much so that the kernels stay fluffy and distinct.

RECOGNIZING DONENESS The quinoa is ready when it's just tender and the grains begin to burst—you'll see little rings around the outer rim.

Bulgur with Feta and Shrimp

An ideal one-bowl meal, super-simple to make but with a lot going on.

TIME   **30 to 40 minutes**
MAKES   **4 servings**

---

2 tablespoons olive oil

1 medium onion, chopped

1½ cups medium- or coarse-grind bulgur

Salt and freshly ground black pepper

1 cup chopped tomatoes (drained canned are fine)

½ cup dry white wine (like Sauvignon Blanc or Pinot Grigio) or water

2 cups water or chicken, beef, or vegetable stock

½ cup crumbled feta cheese

½ pound shrimp, peeled and cut into 1-inch pieces if large

½ cup chopped fresh parsley leaves for garnish

1 Put the oil in a large skillet over medium heat. When it's hot, add the onion and cook, stirring occasionally, until it softens, 3 to 5 minutes. Add the bulgur and stir until it is glossy and coated with oil; sprinkle with salt and pepper.

2 Stir in the tomatoes and wine and continue stirring for about 1 minute. Then add the water. Bring the liquid to a boil, then lower the heat so that it bubbles gently; cover and cook, undisturbed, for 5 minutes.

3 Taste the bulgur. If it seems dry, add 2 more tablespoons water and cook for another minute. When the bulgur is no longer gritty but still a little chewy, stir in the feta and shrimp with a fork, cover again, and cook for 5 minutes.

4 Turn off the heat and let the pan sit for at least 5 and up to 10 minutes. Taste, adjust the seasoning, and fluff the mixture with a fork. Serve garnished with the parsley.

When the package is labeled simply bulgur, *you're usually getting medium grind.*

IDENTIFYING FINE, MEDIUM, AND COARSE BULGUR Medium is the most common, but I like coarse for its chewiness, so grab it when you see it. Fine is best for hot breakfast cereal.

Tips

▶ Bulgur comes in different grinds, or sizes, sometimes identified by numbers: #1 is fine, #2 is medium, and #3 and #4 are coarse. The size of the grind affects how long it takes for bulgur to become tender: Including resting times, fine bulgur will become tender in 5 to 10 minutes, medium in 10 to 15 minutes, and coarse in 15 to 20 minutes.

▶ Don't skip the step where you let the bulgur sit after cooking; it will continue to soften and absorb liquid.

Variations

▶ **Bulgur with Parmesan and Spinach:** Skip the shrimp and use grated Parmesan instead of the feta. Roughly chop 1 pound fresh spinach and add it in Step 3 along with the cheese. (Just put it on top of the bulgur, where it will wilt.) Continue with the recipe.

Learn More

▶ Grain Basics (page 206), preparing tomatoes (page 80), Chicken Stock (page 154), Full-Flavored Vegetable Stock (page 152), Smarter Water (page 137), Peeling Shrimp (page 362)

CHOPPING SHRIMP To ensure the shrimp finish cooking with the bulgur, either use small shrimp or cut large shrimp into pieces no bigger than 1 inch.

FLUFFING GRAINS After stirring in the feta and shrimp with a fork, let the bulgur sit off the heat for no more than 10 minutes to avoid overcooking the shrimp.

Polenta with Mushrooms

In my humble opinion, better than mashed potatoes.

TIME **1½ hours**

MAKES **4 servings**

½ cup dried porcini
mushrooms (about
½ ounce)

2 cups boiling water

¼ cup olive oil

1 pound fresh button or
cremini mushrooms, sliced

Salt and freshly ground
black pepper

¼ cup red wine

1 tablespoon minced garlic

½ cup chopped fresh
parsley

1 cup medium or coarse
polenta

½ cup milk, preferably
whole

1 tablespoon butter

½ cup freshly grated
Parmesan cheese

1 Put the dried mushrooms in a medium bowl and pour in the boiling water. Press them down into the water now and then until they are soft, anywhere from 5 to 30 minutes depending on how dry they were. When it's time to cook with them, lift them out of the water with your hands or a slotted spoon and chop them roughly. Reserve the soaking water.

2 Put the oil in a large skillet over medium heat. When it's hot, add the soaked dried and fresh mushrooms and sprinkle with salt and pepper. Cook, stirring occasionally, until the mushrooms are tender and have released all their liquid, 10 to 15 minutes.

3 Add the wine and let it bubble away for 1 minute, then stir in the garlic, ¼ cup of the parsley, and 1 cup of the reserved soaking water. Cook until the liquid thickens a bit, another 2 or 3 minutes, then taste, adjust the seasoning, and turn off the heat under the skillet.

4 Put the polenta in a medium pot with 1 cup water and whisk to form a smooth slurry. Whisk in the milk and a large pinch of salt and set the pot over medium-high heat. Heat until the mixture boils, then lower the heat to medium and cook, whisking frequently and adding more water a little at a time to prevent lumps and keep the mixture somewhat soupy. Expect to add another 2½ to 3½ cups of water before the polenta is ready. The polenta will be done in 15 to 30 minutes, depending on the grind. It will be thick and creamy, with just a little grittiness, and the mixture will pull away from the sides of the pan when you stir. When the polenta is done, turn the heat under the mushrooms to medium to warm them quickly.

5 Stir the butter and cheese into the polenta, then taste and adjust the seasoning. Serve the polenta topped with the mushrooms and garnished with the remaining ¼ cup parsley.

You want to reserve the soaking liquid but leave the grit behind, so lift out the mushrooms rather than pouring to drain them.

SOAKING DRIED MUSHROOMS
The time needed to soften mushrooms depends on their size and age. They're ready when you can cut one easily with a paring knife.

Tips

▶ Polenta is a type of corn-meal; most kinds available now are medium or fine grind, which doesn't pull away from the pot as noticeably as coarse grind and has a smoother texture. Avoid using instant polenta or the cornmeal ground for baking, and taste frequently to check doneness.

▶ Like risotto, polenta requires some attention; you don't have to whisk constantly, but don't leave the stove unattended for more than a minute or two.

Variations

▶ Use grits instead of polenta. But not the quick-cooking or instant kind.

▶ **5 Other Toppings:**
1 Tomato Sauce or any of its variations (pages 178–181)
2 Fried Eggs (page 54)
3 Boiled Greens (page 218) with a drizzle of olive oil
4 Caramelized Onions (page 232)
5 Quick Skillet Beans with Tomatoes (page 252)

Learn More

▶ Grain Basics (page 206), types of mushrooms (page 231), preparing mushrooms (pages 100 and 230), mincing garlic (page 20), Chopping Herbs (page 78), Grating Cheese (page 176)

MAKING THE SAUCE When the mushrooms are tender and the wine has bubbled away, stir in the garlic, parsley, and soaking water.

MAKING POLENTA BY THE SLURRY METHOD When the slurry just starts to boil, turn it down a bit so it bubbles gently. Add more water and whisk or stir with a wooden spoon.

RECOGNIZING DONENESS When the polenta starts to pull away from the pan and is no longer gritty, it's time to stir in the butter and Parmesan.

Vegetables and Beans

Let's for a moment ignore the fact that vegetables come in a stunning variety of colors, flavors, textures, shapes, and sizes and focus instead on the techniques we use to prepare them: steaming, boiling, microwaving, sautéing, roasting, and grilling or broiling—in fact, every cooking method you can name. Make an effort to master just *one* of these skills and suddenly you can cook not only any vegetable but *every* vegetable. And when you get tired of that one method—or simply want to expand your horizons—you can begin to practice another, until soon you know how to cook all different kinds of vegetables in many ways.

In this chapter I also teach you how to think about vegetables in terms of how you intend to eat them: from barely cooked to soft enough to mash or purée. Then I take you through simple recipes for each cooking technique, building in degrees of difficulty as we go. If you're a true beginner, you can follow the steps for each recipe and end up with a broad repertoire of delicious, easy-to-make vegetable dishes. As you gain more experience (or if you have some already), you can put your own spin on the recipes by swapping out one vegetable for another.

The point is this: Cooking vegetables—and I'm counting beans in this category—is not as difficult as it seems at first glance, and there are so many ways to make them taste delicious that even the pickiest eaters will find a lot to like.

Vegetable Basics

Simplifying Vegetables

You can cook a different vegetable every day of the week and go a whole month without eating the same one twice. There are so many varieties that even an expert can't know everything about all of them. To make vegetables more manageable in the kitchen, I lump them into three groups—greens, tender vegetables, and hard vegetables—based on how fast they go from raw to mushy. This helps you substitute one for another in recipes and try things that may be unfamiliar. So when you encounter a new vegetable that resembles another, more familiar vegetable in the same group—think broccoli and cauliflower, for example, or beets and turnips—you have a point of reference. This method is far from scientific, but it works together with the techniques, tips, and variations in this chapter to demonstrate how easy it is to cook all sorts of vegetables.

10 Easy Toppings for Any Plain-Cooked Vegetables

You can cook vegetables without any seasonings (and little or no fat) and still make them super-appealing. Mix and match ingredients from the list below, then just before serving, sprinkle or splash them on top—and don't forget to add the salt and pepper!

1 A drizzle of olive oil or sesame oil
2 A pat of butter or drizzle of melted butter
3 A squeeze of lemon or lime juice
4 A splash of soy sauce
5 A handful of chopped fresh herbs
6 A dusting of grated Parmesan
7 A sprinkle of chopped nuts
8 A handful of toasted bread crumbs (page 387)
9 A pat of compound butter (page 236)
10 A splash of vinaigrette (page 114)

IS IT DONE YET?

One of the reasons to love vegetables is that you can cook them as much or as little as you like. All the recipes in this chapter offer ranges of time for proper cooking, but it's more valuable—and fun—to learn to recognize doneness by looking and tasting. Here's how:

RAW Raw vegetables are crunchy and hard; they're colorful but will become brighter as they cook.

BARELY COOKED These vegetables are less crunchy, easier to eat, and often brighter in color than raw. If you're pan-cooking, they'll start to get golden.

CRISP-TENDER Crisp-tender vegetables are bright and mostly tender, with just a little bit of pleasant crunch at the center. (If pan-cooked, they'll start browning.)

SOFT Soft vegetables have lost all crunch, and their color has faded slightly. (Pan-cooked vegetables will get more brown.)

SUPER-SOFT Super-soft vegetables will mash easily with a fork. This is how you want vegetables for puréeing.

MUSHY The color is dull and grayish and they're so soft that they break apart when you try to pick it up; there's no reason to cook them to this stage!

Think of Vegetables in Groups

Greens These vegetables cook in a flash—anywhere from 30 seconds to several minutes. In addition to the salad greens described on page 108 (you can even cook lettuces!) and the greens shown on page 218 (chard, watercress, collards, kale, mustard greens, and different bok choys), this group includes tatsoi and whatever you might encounter at farmers' markets and international grocery stores.

They all cook the same way. What varies is the time: The more delicate the leaves, the faster they soften. You can separate firm stalks from the leaves and give them a head start (see page 218). Boiling, steaming, stir-frying, and sautéing are the best cooking methods. Check them frequently and immediately remove them from the heat when they reach the softness you want.

Tender The vegetables in this group are firm but pliable when raw. The cooking time ranges from a couple minutes to 30 minutes or more, depending on how high the heat is. Celery, green beans, asparagus, snow and snap peas, broccoli, cauliflower, and mushrooms are examples. I also count vegetables that are pliable when you chop or slice them, like eggplant, zucchini, cabbage, onions, leeks, shallots, and fennel.

You have more options with tender vegetables than with greens; boiling (in some cases), steaming, stir-frying, and sautéing are all good choices, as are frying, roasting, grilling, and broiling. At high temperatures they soften quickly, so you still need to keep a close eye on them. When you lower the heat and let them progress more slowly, they can brown and become downright silky.

Hard This mix of root vegetables, tubers, and winter squashes (including potatoes, turnips, carrots, beets, celery root, and pumpkin) take much longer to become tender. Figure 5 to 10 minutes if they're grated or cut small and up to an hour if whole or in big chunks.

Like tender vegetables, you can boil, steam, stir-fry, sauté, fry, roast, grill, or broil them. Hard vegetables tend to work particularly well cut or sliced, then roasted or deep-fried, where their outsides will brown and crisp while the insides get soft. All can be roasted whole until soft (a knife or skewer can be inserted easily when they're ready). Then, after they cool a bit, it's easy to peel them and remove any seeds. (Winter squashes are great cooked that way.)

Boiled Greens

Bright, fresh tasting, full flavored: These are not your mother's boiled vegetables.

TIME   **10 to 30 minutes**
MAKES   **4 servings**

Salt

1½ pounds sturdy greens (like chard) or tender greens (like spinach)

Salt

2 tablespoons butter

Freshly ground black pepper

1 Bring a stockpot of water to a boil and salt it. Meanwhile, trim the greens and rinse them well. If you're using sturdy greens, separate the leaves from the stems and chop both separately. If you're using tender greens, roughly chop any big leaves.

2 To cook sturdy greens, first add only the stems to the boiling water; when the stems are almost tender, 3 to 4 minutes later, add the leaves. To cook tender greens, add everything to the boiling water all at once. Cook until the leaves are just becoming bright green and tender: 1 to 3 minutes for watercress and arugula, 3 to 5 minutes for spinach, 5 to 7 minutes for chard, and 7 to 10 minutes for kale, collards, and bok choy.

3 Drain the greens in a colander or strainer, pressing down lightly with a large spoon to remove as much excess water as possible. (Or "shock" them in a bowl of ice water to stop the cooking, then drain and squeeze them dry with your hands.) Transfer the vegetables to a large bowl and toss them with the butter and a sprinkle of salt and pepper. Taste, adjust the seasoning, and serve right away.

Rule of thumb: The sturdier the leaves and stems, the longer you cook 'em.

Cut on either side of the stalk to separate the leaf.

TRIMMING GREENS For sturdy greens, separate the stems and leaves and cut them both into bite-sized pieces. For tender greens, just remove any thick stem ends and chop the rest.

ADDING GREENS, WITH OR WITHOUT STEMS If you want the stalks (or "ribs") to get silky and tender, give them a bit of a head start. But don't bother if you want them to stay crunchy.

Tips

▶ By sturdy greens I mean those that have fibrous veins in the leaves and thick, celery-like stems. (Other examples besides chard are kale, collards, and bok choy.) You can eat some sturdy greens raw, but you'll have to chop them into small pieces. What I call tender greens are simply the kind you'd also use for salads (like arugula, watercress, spinach, dandelion, or escarole).

▶ Not only are boiled vegetables easy to prepare, but their flavor is also the most adaptable to any kind of seasoning. Other vegetables that are best for boiling: broccoli, Brussels sprouts, carrots, cabbage, cauliflower, corn, green beans, peas, potatoes, snap peas, sweet potatoes, and winter squash. Peel them if necessary and cut them up into pieces roughly the same size so everything cooks at the same time. Test them frequently; the tiny and delicate vegetables will cook in minutes.

▶ Vegetables that are terrible boiled: bell peppers, cucumber, eggplant, summer squash, and zucchini.

Learn More

▶ Vegetable Basics (page 216), Boiling (page 24), preparing greens (page 164), Shocking Vegetables (page 238), Trimming, Peeling, Chopping, and Slicing (pages 16–21)

TESTING FOR DONENESS Taste and test for doneness often and drain the greens when they're still a little crunchier than you'd like, since they'll keep cooking after you turn off the heat.

DRAINING GREENS Extract as much water as possible so the greens don't get soggy. Other options: Gently squeeze greens between your hands or shake the colander and let them sit.

Steamed Asparagus

Steaming is easier than boiling, more easily controlled, and perfect for asparagus.

TIME **10 to 15 minutes**

MAKES **4 servings**

1½ pounds asparagus

Salt

2 tablespoons butter or olive oil, or to taste

Juice of 1 lemon

Freshly ground black pepper

1 Trim the bottoms from the asparagus and peel them if they're thick. Stand the stalks upright in a stockpot, letting them lean against the sides at an angle. Add enough water to come 1 inch up the sides of the pan and a large pinch of salt. Cover and put the pot over high heat.

2 When the water boils, cook the asparagus for 2 minutes, then check them for the first time. They're ready when you can easily pierce the thick part of the stalks with a fork; this takes anywhere from 2 to 10 minutes, depending on how thick the asparagus are.

3 Transfer the asparagus to a serving platter with tongs, shaking them over the pot to remove excess water. Smear them with the butter (or drizzle with the olive oil) and sprinkle with lemon juice, more salt, and some pepper, then serve.

Cut in the spot where your knife doesn't meet much resistance.

TRIMMING ASPARAGUS I just cut the ends off the spears at the point where the tough, fibrous base becomes green and tender.

PEELING ASPARAGUS You don't have to peel the bottom of the stalks, but it does make them less fibrous, and it's a good idea if they're more than ½ inch thick.

Tips

▶ I like both thick and thin asparagus spears, but try to cook spears that are roughly the same size. You can buy a bunch that's all one size, or you can buy a mixed-size bunch and cook them in batches. Or you can cook everything together and pluck out thinner spears as they become tender. (Or you can be happy with some pieces being more tender than others, which isn't bad either.)

▶ Anything that you can boil you can steam. Vegetables with sturdy stems—like asparagus, broccoli, and cauliflower—can steam right in the pot. But for most vegetables, rig a steamer (see page 27) to keep them completely above the water so they don't get waterlogged.

Variations

▶ **Steamed Asparagus with Eggs:** Fry (page 54), poach (page 56), or hard-boil (page 51) 4 eggs. After you drizzle the spears with butter, put the eggs on top. Skip the lemon juice and try 1 tablespoon chopped fresh tarragon leaves for garnish if you've got some.

Learn More

▶ Vegetable Basics (page 216), Steaming (page 27)

If you decide to tie the asparagus, make sure the twine is loose enough so it doesn't cut into them.

STEAMING ASPARAGUS It's okay to lean the trimmed spears on the side of the pot, but if it bothers you or if they fall over, tie them in a loose bundle with kitchen twine.

Stir-Fried Cabbage with Ginger

This recipe is so versatile you might dub it "stir-fried anything with ginger."

TIME **20 to 30 minutes**
MAKES **4 servings**

---

1 medium head Napa or any cabbage (about 2 pounds)

2 tablespoons vegetable oil, or more as needed

2 tablespoons minced fresh ginger

1 tablespoon minced garlic

½ cup chopped scallions

½ cup water, vegetable stock, or white wine

2 tablespoons soy sauce

1 teaspoon sugar

Salt and freshly ground black pepper

1 Remove the outer leaves from the cabbage and remove the core by carefully cutting a cone-shaped section around the stem with a paring knife and pulling it out, using your knife for leverage if necessary. Switch to a chef's knife and cut the cabbage into halves or quarters, then thinly slice each piece; the slices will naturally fall into shreds. Cut the shreds into bite-sized pieces and rinse in a colander.

2 Put the oil in a large skillet over medium-high heat. When it's hot, add the ginger and garlic and cook, stirring, for 15 seconds. Add ¼ cup of the scallions and the cabbage to the pan and raise the heat to high. Cook, stirring occasionally, until the cabbage is soft and a little browned here and there, 5 to 8 minutes. If the pan looks too dry, add more oil (1 tablespoon at a time) as the cabbage cooks.

3 Lower the heat to medium and add the water, soy sauce, sugar, and a sprinkle of salt and pepper. Stir, then turn the heat back up to high and cook, stirring constantly to scrape up any browned bits from the bottom of the pan, until the liquid has thickened and partially evaporated. Taste and adjust the seasoning, garnish with the remaining ¼ cup scallions, and serve.

Don't go crazy— the pieces don't have to be tiny.

Peeling ginger with a paring knife is fast but a little wasteful. How you do it is your choice.

PEELING GINGER A vegetable peeler leaves a lot of ginger behind but can be tricky to handle.

MINCING GINGER Cut lengthwise into slices and lengthwise again into sticks, then use a rocking and pivoting motion over all to mince. The larger the pieces of ginger, the more intense their flavor.

Tips

▶ You can stir-fry lots of other vegetables the same way. Some ideas: broccoli or cauliflower (cut into florets), shredded Brussels sprouts, bell peppers (cut into strips), carrots cut into thin coins, celery slices, bean sprouts, or sturdy greens like chard or bok choy (keep the stems and leaves separate; add the stems to the pan 2 to 3 minutes before you add the leaves).

Variations

▶ **Stir-Fried Cabbage, Thai Style:** Substitute fish sauce (nam pla, available in supermarkets) for the soy sauce and finish the dish with a squeeze of fresh lime juice and a sprinkling of crushed red pepper.
▶ **Stir-Fried Cabbage, Mediterranean Style:** Skip the ginger, soy sauce, and sugar. Use olive oil instead of vegetable oil and add 1 more tablespoon garlic if you like.

Learn More

▶ Vegetable Basics (page 216), Stir-Frying (page 29), preparing cabbage (page 120), mincing garlic (page 20), Preparing Scallions (page 295), Full-Flavored Vegetable Stock (page 152)

STIR-FRYING AROMATICS
Everything happens fast when the heat is this high, so watch for the ginger and garlic (or what have you) to just begin to color, then quickly add the cabbage.

BROWNING, THEN SOFTENING
First char the cabbage with the aromatics to make it flavorful, then add liquid to make it soft.

Rosemary-Roasted Potatoes

One technique that works for any root—and many other—vegetables.

TIME   **1 to 1¼ hours,**
   somewhat unattended

MAKES   **4 servings**

2 pounds any potatoes

2 tablespoons olive oil, or more as needed

Salt and freshly ground black pepper

1 tablespoon chopped fresh rosemary or 1 teaspoon dried

1 Heat the oven to 400°F. Scrub and rinse the potatoes well and peel them if you like. Cut them into 1- to 2-inch chunks, put them on a baking sheet, and toss them with the oil and a sprinkling of salt and pepper. If they're too crowded, consider using 2 pans.

2 Put the potatoes in the oven and roast without stirring for 20 minutes, then check. If the potatoes release easily from the pan, stir or turn the pieces with tongs. If they look dry and are sticking to the pan, drizzle with 1 tablespoon more oil. Continue roasting, stirring or turning the potatoes once, until they're golden but still not tender

all the way through, another 20 minutes or so. Stir in the rosemary, then return the pan to the oven to finish cooking.

3 The potatoes are done when they're crisp on the outside and tender inside (a sharp, thin-bladed knife will easily pierce the center of one piece); this will take another 20 to 40 minutes depending on the type of potato and size of the chunks.

4 Remove the potatoes from the oven, taste, and adjust the seasoning with salt or pepper. Serve hot, warm, or at room temperature.

Do what's most comfortable: Work the tool away from—or toward—you.

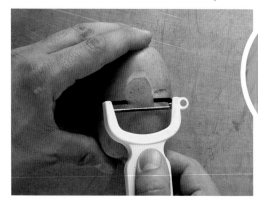

To cut potatoes in wedges, cut the halves lengthwise at an angle toward the center.

PEELING AND TRIMMING POTATOES It's optional: Use solid strokes and turn the potato as needed. Whether you peel or not, if there are any eyes or dark spots, dig them out with a paring knife.

CUTTING POTATOES Cut each potato into quarters lengthwise. Then cut across the spears to make equal-sized 1- to 2-inch chunks.

Tips

▶ You can roast any type of potato, but the results will be slightly different for each: Waxy potatoes (like red or white ones) get crisp on the outside and creamy on the inside; starchy potatoes (like the big dark brown russets you use for baking) turn quite dark and get pleasantly mealy inside; all-purpose potatoes (like the popular Yukon Gold variety) are somewhere in between.

▶ Peeled potatoes give you more crisp edges. Unpeeled will have a more rustic look and taste. Try both ways and see which you like.

▶ Root vegetables—carrots, celery root, sweet potatoes, and so on—are the most common for roasting. But you can even use this recipe for things you might not expect, like celery, eggplant, mushrooms, or even sturdy greens like kale. Chop them into large pieces and roast them as described here; start checking greens or tender vegetables after 10 minutes.

Variations

▶ **Garlic-Roasted Potatoes:** Substitute 1 tablespoon (or more) minced garlic for the rosemary—or add it along with the herb.

Learn More

▶ Vegetable Basics (page 216), Roasting (page 33), types of potatoes (page 235), Stripping Leaves from Hard Herb Stems (page 141), Chopping Herbs (page 78)

TURNING The potatoes will release easily when they're ready. If they stick a little but don't look dry, give them a few more minutes. If they stick a lot and do look dry, add a little more oil.

ADDING SEASONINGS The best time to add the rosemary is when the potatoes are turning golden but not quite done—if you add it too soon, it'll burn.

Grilled or Broiled Tomatoes

Extreme heat yields super-juicy results and a new way to enjoy tomatoes.

TIME **20 to 30 minutes**
MAKES **4 servings**

4 large ripe tomatoes

¼ cup olive oil, or more as needed

Salt and freshly ground black pepper

¼ cup freshly grated Parmesan cheese

1 Prepare a grill or turn on the broiler; the heat should be medium-high and the rack about 4 inches from the fire. Core the tomatoes and cut each horizontally into 3 or 4 thick slices. Spread them out on a rimmed baking sheet, drizzle or brush with the olive oil, turning to coat them all over, and sprinkle with salt and pepper.

2 The goal is to end up with tomatoes that are slightly charred and soft but not mushy.

To Grill: Transfer them to the grates over the fire and cook, undisturbed, until they start to brown underneath and ooze some juice, 3 to 4 minutes. Carefully turn and cook them on the other side until they're also darkened but you can still lift them from the grill without their falling apart, anywhere from 1 to 4 minutes more depending on the thickness of the slices and the heat of the grill.

To Broil: Put the baking sheet under the broiler and cook them without turning until the tops are browned and bubbling, 5 to 8 minutes. Either way, if at any point they start to look dry and stick, drizzle the tomatoes with a little more olive oil.

3 To serve, transfer the tomatoes to a serving platter or individual plates, sprinkle with the cheese, and serve hot, warm, or at room temperature.

Use your hands or a brush.

A serrated knife works best, unless you have a razor-sharp paring or chef's knife.

SLICING TOMATOES Use a gentle back-and-forth motion to cut horizontal slices, which are easier to maneuver and better looking than vertical slices.

COATING WITH OIL Coat the slices thoroughly with oil on both sides to keep them from sticking.

Tips

▶ Keep the heat relatively high; a hot flame will char the tomatoes, while a moderate fire will only make them mushy. If you can't control the heat on your broiler and it seems like they're not cooking fast enough, move the tomatoes closer to the heat source by putting the baking sheet on a broiler rack or an upside-down roasting pan.

▶ Grilling or broiling will improve the flavor of any tomato—even canned—but this dish is best in late summer and early fall, with ripe tomatoes at the peak of their season.

▶ Other sliced vegetables to try grilling or broiling: mushrooms, eggplant, zucchini or summer squash, bell peppers.

Variations

▶ **3 Ways to Vary Any Grilled or Broiled Vegetable:**

1 Instead of Parmesan, try topping them with crumbled blue cheese or a smear of ricotta cheese.

2 Before serving, sprinkle about ¼ cup chopped fresh basil, dill, parsley, or mint leaves over everything.

3 For an Asian twist, substitute 2 tablespoons vegetable oil mixed with 2 tablespoons sesame oil for the olive oil and use a drizzle of soy sauce instead of the Parmesan.

Learn More

▶ Vegetable Basics (page 216), Grilling (page 35), Broiling (page 34), Coring Tomatoes (page 80), Grating Cheese (page 176)

TRANSFERRING TO THE HEAT Put the tomatoes directly under or over the heat; they'll cook quickly, so keep an eye on them.

COOKING THE TOMATOES If you're broiling, there's no need to turn them. For grilling, turn the tomatoes while they're still firm; the longer you wait, the more difficult they are to flip.

Maple-Glazed Carrots

Braising vegetables takes virtually no effort, and the delicious sauce makes itself.

TIME **30 minutes**
MAKES **4 servings**

---

1 pound carrots

2 tablespoons butter

3 tablespoons maple syrup

Salt and freshly ground black pepper

¼ cup chopped fresh parsley leaves for garnish, optional

1 Trim the tops and bottoms from the carrots and peel them if the outsides are tough. Then cut them into coins or sticks about ¼ inch thick. Put them in a large pot with the butter, maple syrup, ½ cup water, and a sprinkling of salt and pepper; set over high heat and bring to a boil.

2 Stir once, then lower the heat so the mixture bubbles gently but steadily and cover the pan. Cook, undisturbed, until the carrots are just beginning to get ten-

der and have absorbed almost all of the liquid, 10 to 15 minutes. They're ready when you can spear them with a fork but still meet some resistance.

3 Remove the lid and keep cooking until the remaining liquid thickens into a glaze and coats the carrots, then remove from the heat. Taste, adjust the seasoning with salt or pepper, and serve hot or warm, garnished with the parsley if you like.

Smooth, clean-looking carrots need only a scrubbing.

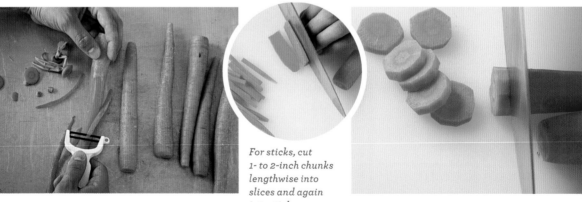

For sticks, cut 1- to 2-inch chunks lengthwise into slices and again into sticks any width you like.

PEELING CARROTS Be careful not to peel away too much of the carrots; just take one stroke with the peeler all the way around.

CUTTING COINS AND STICKS Whether you cut the carrots into coins or sticks, be sure that the pieces are all about the same width so they get tender at the same time.

Tips

▶ The thumb-sized nubbins labeled *baby carrots* are actually just peeled and cut regular carrots. They're convenient but aren't as flavorful as whole carrots you cut yourself.

▶ Carrots keep in the fridge for several weeks, but if you can bend them they're past their prime. Remove green tops (if they came with them) before storing, since they're not edible and will sap nutrients and moisture out of the carrots.

▶ If you're serving these at room temperature, use vegetable oil instead of butter—butter will harden as it cools, which isn't as appealing.

Variations

▶ **Maple-Glazed Vegetables:** You can cook lots of other things like this. Try parsnips, turnips, celery root, green beans, beets, Brussels sprouts, red or green cabbage, and winter squash. Cut into ¼-inch pieces (except for green beans, which you can leave whole).

Learn More

▶ Vegetable Basics (page 216), Braising (page 31), Maple Syrup (page 42), Chopping Herbs (page 78)

BRAISING THE CARROTS Make sure the liquid is bubbling steadily—but not too vigorously—before you put the lid on the pan.

GLAZING THE CARROTS Check the carrots once or twice as they cook, watching for the liquid to be syrupy; if the pan is dry, add more water 1 tablespoon at a time.

Pan-Cooked (Sautéed) Mushrooms

Not just mushrooms, but virtually any vegetable takes well to sautéing.

TIME **30 to 45 minutes**

MAKES **4 servings (about 2 cups)**

1 pound any fresh mushrooms

¼ cup olive oil

Salt and freshly ground black pepper

¼ to ½ cup dry white wine or water

1 teaspoon minced garlic

¼ cup chopped fresh parsley leaves

1 Rinse the mushrooms thoroughly and trim them. Set them round side up and cut downward into slices as thick or thin as you want (¼ inch thick is a good place to start).

2 Put the oil in a large skillet over medium heat. When it's hot, add the mushrooms and sprinkle them with salt and pepper. Cook, stirring occasionally, until the mushrooms have released their liquid, become tender, and the pan is beginning to dry out again, 10 to 15 minutes.

3 If you want the mushrooms to have a little sauce, pour in ½ cup wine. For moist mushrooms without any sauce, stir in ¼ cup. Let the liquid bubble and evaporate for 1 minute, stirring the bottom of the pan to scrape up any browned bits, then turn the heat down to low.

4 When the mushrooms are done as you like, stir in the garlic and parsley and cook for just 1 minute more. Taste and adjust the seasoning with salt or pepper and serve hot, warm, or at room temperature.

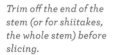

Trim off the end of the stem (or for shiitakes, the whole stem) before slicing.

SLICING MUSHROOMS Set each trimmed mushroom on the cutting board so it's stable, then slice downward; push the mushroom under the blade again and repeat.

EVAPORATING THE LIQUID Mushrooms will give off a lot of liquid after a few minutes; just keep the heat steady until it all evaporates before continuing.

DRIED PORCINI
The most intense. For directions for using them, see the polenta recipe on page 212.

CREMINI
Also known as baby portabellas—with a more robust flavor and deep color than button mushrooms.

SHIITAKE
Intensely flavorful and silky when cooked, but mostly water, so they shrink a lot. Remove the stems to use in stock.

PORTOBELLO
Popular and huge, with an earthy flavor and meaty texture.

BUTTON
The most common and blandest mushroom; best mixed with other, more flavorful varieties.

Tips

▶ For crisp, chewy mushrooms, don't add liquid in Step 3; instead, keep cooking until they darken and become crisp around the edges, another 10 to 15 minutes.

▶ Use the techniques described in this recipe to pan-cook—sauté—all sorts of other vegetables. Most won't release as much water as mushrooms. And since some will become tender in just a couple minutes, check them frequently for doneness. In order of how fast they cook: spinach or other tender greens, peas and snow peas, bean sprouts, zucchini, green beans, eggplant, cabbage, and sturdy greens like kale or chard (remove and chop the stems and give them a head start if you don't want them too crisp).

Variations

▶ **Asian-Style Sautéed Mushrooms:** In Step 2, use peanut oil instead of olive oil, add 1 small dried hot chile to the skillet along with the mushrooms, and use lots of black pepper. In Step 3, use water instead of wine. In Step 4, add 1 tablespoon soy sauce along with the garlic and use cilantro instead of parsley.

Learn More

▶ Vegetable Basics (page 216), mincing garlic (page 20), Chopping Herbs (page 78)

COOKING WITH WINE It helps food develop a more complex flavor, but let most of it bubble away or else the food will taste too alcoholic. (Or just use water if you prefer.)

ADDING GARLIC AND HERBS Garlic and parsley add a nice flavor boost so long as you keep cooking for only a minute or so after you add them.

Caramelized Onions

Golden and silky or jammy, these are great.

TIME **30 to 60 minutes or a little longer**
MAKES **4 servings (1½ to 2 cups)**

2 pounds any onions (6 to 8 medium)

2 tablespoons olive oil or butter, or more as needed

Salt and freshly ground black pepper

1 Trim the root ends from the onions and peel them. Cut the onions in half from top to bottom, then lay each half flat side down and cut it into thin slices (it doesn't really matter which direction you slice).

2 Put the onions in a large skillet over medium heat. Cover and cook, stirring every 5 minutes or so, until the onions are dry and beginning to stick to the pan, 15 to 20 minutes.

3 Add the oil and a large pinch of salt and turn the heat down to medium-low. Cook, uncovered, stirring occasionally, until the onions are soft, tender, and as browned and soft as you want them, another 5 to 40 minutes. As they cook, add a little more oil if necessary to keep them from sticking—no more than 2 additional tablespoons—and lower or raise the heat so that they sizzle gently without burning.

4 When they're as you want them, taste and adjust the seasoning, adding some black pepper. Serve hot or at room temperature. (They'll keep in the fridge for a week.)

Adjust the heat as needed to make sure they don't burn.

ADDING SLICED ONIONS TO THE PAN This looks like a lot of onions, but they'll cook down to less than half of this volume.

SOFTENED ONIONS After the first 20 minutes, they're tender and mild but not yet caramelized. Add the fat and give them at least 5 more minutes or, for darker, softer onions, keep going.

BROWNED, SHRUNKEN ONIONS After another 20 minutes, the onions will have browned considerably and reduced in size, but the slices will still be distinguishable from one another.

After a full hour, the onions will be silky, deep brown, and practically melted together; jammy, in other words.

Tips

▶ Caramelization is a process, not a final destination: What "caramelizes" is a food's natural sugars; this starts to happen as soon as you apply heat. The first time you try this recipe, taste frequently and stop cooking when you get a flavor and texture you like.

▶ Some ideas for using caramelized onions: When they're just soft and barely colored, try tossing them with noodles or rice. A little more golden and silkier, they're good on top of some simply cooked steaks, burgers, or chops. After they become brown and jammy, I like them smeared on bread or mixed into mashed potatoes.

Variations

▶ **Creamed Onions:** Slice the onions thickly (about ½ inch) and use butter instead of olive oil. In Step 3, add 1 cup cream to the pan along with the butter; cook, stirring occasionally, until the onions absorb most of the liquid and the sauce is thick, 20 to 25 minutes.

▶ **Caramelized or Creamed Leeks, Shallots, or Garlic:** Slice the vegetables as you would the onions and follow either the main recipe or the preceding variation. Check the vegetables frequently and lower the heat as necessary, since these vegetables are prone to scorch more quickly than onions.

Learn More

▶ Vegetable Basics (page 216), Trimming (page 16), Slicing (page 21), Sautéing (page 28)

Mashed Potatoes

All it takes is a fork. And you can mash many other veggies this way too.

TIME **30 to 45 minutes**

MAKES **4 servings**

---

2 pounds starchy or all-purpose potatoes

Salt

1 cup milk, or more as needed

4 tablespoons (½ stick) butter

Freshly ground black pepper

1 Scrub the potatoes and rinse them well. Put them in a large pot and add cold water to cover by about 2 inches; add a large pinch of salt. Put over high heat and bring to a boil. Cook until the potatoes are tender (you'll be able to insert a sharp, thin-bladed knife with virtually no resistance), 15 to 30 minutes depending on the size of the potatoes.

2 Drain the potatoes in a colander and let them sit to dry out for at least 5 minutes or up to an hour, then peel them if you like. Cut the potatoes into big chunks.

3 Rinse out the pot and put it back on the burner over medium-low heat. Add the milk and butter and sprinkle with salt and pepper. When the milk is hot and the butter is melted, 3 to 5 minutes, take the pot off the heat. Put the potatoes back in the pot and mash them with a potato masher (or put them through a ricer) until they are as lumpy or as smooth as you like. Put the pot back over medium-low heat and stir gently with a wooden spoon or rubber spatula until the potatoes reach the consistency you like; add more milk (2 tablespoons at a time) to make them thinner. Taste, adjust the seasoning, and serve hot or warm.

MASHING POTATOES Get a masher that has a disk with holes at the business end.

Or mash the potatoes with a fork and a little more elbow grease.

Overworking the potatoes makes them like glue.

ADJUSTING CONSISTENCY Stir the mashed potatoes gently, adding more milk slowly until you get the consistency as fluffy or creamy as you like.

WAXY POTATOES
May be red, white, or even purple. These are best for roasting, boiling, steaming, grilling, and whenever you want potatoes to hold their shape—as in salads. If you want to mash them, just smash lightly, or they'll get gummy.

STARCHY OR RUSSET POTATOES
What we typically use for baking whole. They cook up with a fluffy, mealy texture that's also good for mashed potatoes, gratins, and fries.

ALL-PURPOSE POTATOES
Like Yukon Gold. The interior is a little starchy and a little waxy and makes creamy, fluffy mashed potatoes. They're also good for salads, gratins, and boiling or steaming.

Tips

▶ Try not to poke the potatoes too much during boiling; they'll get waterlogged. If you're cooking potatoes of various sizes, the smaller potatoes will become tender before the larger ones are, so pluck them from the pot as they finish cooking.

▶ Fat makes mashed potatoes creamy, so if you don't have whole milk, add a little more butter or a splash of cream. You can also use buttermilk in place of some or all of the milk; it adds a pleasantly tangy flavor.

▶ Other vegetables to mash this way: carrots, beets, parsnips, rutabagas, turnips, or winter squash. Peel and trim them before boiling.

Variations

▶ **Garlic Mashed Potatoes:** Put the peeled cloves from 2 garlic bulbs in the pot along with the potatoes in Step 1.

▶ **Cheesy Mashed Potatoes:** In Step 3, add 1 cup grated Parmesan, cheddar, or Gruyère cheese to the pot with the milk. Blue cheese tastes good, too, but gives the potatoes a gray tint.

▶ **Mashed Sweet Potatoes:** Use sweet potatoes instead of potatoes and add 1 tablespoon ground ginger to the pot along with the milk and butter in Step 3.

Learn More

▶ Vegetable Basics (page 216), Dairy—and Not (page 42)

Corn on the Cob with Chile Butter

With flavored butter, you do virtually nothing and everyone is impressed.

TIME **15 to 20 minutes**
MAKES **4 servings**

4 tablespoons (½ stick) butter, softened

1 tablespoon minced fresh hot green chile (like jalapeño)

Salt and freshly ground black pepper

8 ears fresh corn

1 Put the butter in a small bowl, add the chile and a sprinkle of salt and pepper, and stir until well combined.

2 Peel the husk from the corn and remove as much of the silk as possible. Break or cut off the stem.

3 Put a large pinch of salt in a stockpot with enough water to come 1 inch up the sides, then add the corn; it's okay if some of the ears sit in the water and some sit above it.

4 Cover the pot, put it over high heat, and bring to a boil. The fresher the corn, the less you want to cook it, so start checking about 3 minutes after the water boils. You want the corn hot and just tender, but not tough, so don't let it go longer than 10 minutes. To serve, drain the corn, then smear the ears with the chile butter.

To make the butter sliceable, roll it into a log with wax or parchment paper and refrigerate until firm (or freeze it for up to 3 months).

MAKING COMPOUND BUTTER
Mixing seasonings (like chile) into softened butter is a handy way to intensify flavors. (See the Variations for more ideas.)

SHUCKING CORN Pull down the strips of the husk. When you get to the bottom of the cob, tug hard to remove them.

Tips

▶ As everyone knows, super-fresh corn is best, so get it from a farmstand or farmers' market if you can. (Some supermarkets get frequent deliveries too.) Look for ears with taut green husks and soft, supple silks; they should feel firm, even up at the top.

▶ You can shuck corn up to 3 hours in advance; put it in cold water to keep the kernels from drying out.

▶ The cobs will stay warm and tender in the pot for up to 20 minutes after cooking.

Variations

▶ **5 Compound Butter Flavors.** For plain-cooked vegetables, meat, fish, or poultry, add the following to 4 tablespoons (½ stick) butter:

1 2 tablespoons chopped fresh herb leaves (like parsley, chives, cilantro, dill, or sage)

2 1 teaspoon minced garlic

3 2 teaspoons smoked paprika (pimentón) or curry or chili powder

4 2 tablespoons chopped capers, olives, or anchovies (you probably won't need salt)

5 1 to 2 tablespoons honey or maple syrup

Learn More

▶ Vegetable Basics (page 216), Preparing Chiles (page 276)

REMOVING SILK FROM CORN
Once you've removed the husk, use your fingers to remove the silk. (Getting every last bit isn't essential.)

STEAMING CORN No need to bother with any additional setup. Don't worry: The kernels will all cook in the same time whether they're under water or not.

Green Beans with Crisp Shallots

Boiling and then sautéing vegetables gives you more control over doneness.

TIME **30 to 40 minutes**
MAKES **4 servings**

Salt

1½ pounds green beans

1 tablespoon olive oil

1 tablespoon butter

2 medium shallots, thinly sliced

Freshly ground black pepper

¼ cup sliced almonds, optional

1 Bring a stockpot of water to a boil and salt it. Fill a large bowl with cold water and lots of ice cubes and keep a colander handy. To trim the beans, snap or cut off the stem end and any brown spots. Cut them into 2-inch pieces or leave them whole.

2 Add the green beans to the boiling water and cook until they just start to get tender but remain quite crunchy, 3 to 5 minutes depending on the size of the beans. Drain the beans and immediately plunge them into the ice water. Let them sit for a minute to cool thoroughly, then drain them. (You can prepare the beans up to a day before finishing the dish; cover well and refrigerate.)

3 Put the oil and butter in a large skillet over medium-high heat. When the butter melts, add the shallots and cook, stirring once or twice, until they're golden brown and crisp, 5 to 10 minutes. Transfer the shallots to a plate lined with paper towels. Leave the fat in the pan.

4 Add the green beans to the skillet, sprinkle with salt and pepper, and cook, stirring occasionally, until the beans are crisp-tender, 3 to 5 minutes. Taste and adjust the seasoning and serve hot or warm with the shallots on top and almonds sprinkled over if you're using them.

To cheat, you can run them under cold water, but they won't cool as quickly.

TRIMMING GREEN BEANS The tip end is edible, but you need to remove the tough stem end. Snapping is simplest, but for more accuracy you could use a paring knife or shears.

SHOCKING VEGETABLES This step locks in a vegetable's bright color and instantly stops the cooking process.

Tips
▶ Fresh green beans should be crisp and smooth, with few brown spots. Try breaking one in half; if it doesn't snap, forget it. (They're not called snap beans for nothing.)

▶ Some lingo: Boiling vegetables until they're partially done is known as *parboiling*, and plunging them right into ice water to stop the cooking is called *shocking*. The parboil-and-shock method is perfect whenever you want to make sure vegetables stay crisp and vibrant. It's also great for entertaining, since you can do some of the work way ahead and finish right before serving.

▶ Other vegetables that work well with this treatment: asparagus, broccoli, carrots, cauliflower, snow and snap peas, any leafy greens, and turnips. Drain them well and keep them refrigerated until you're ready to use them, or use them right away sautéed in butter or olive oil (as with this recipe), in stir-fries, in salads, or as crudités with dip.

▶ Don't have any shallots? Use a medium red onion.

Learn More
▶ Vegetable Basics (page 216), Crudités with Warm Olive Dip (page 74)

REMOVING INGREDIENTS FROM THE PAN Try to keep most of the fat in the pan when you remove the shallots—you'll need it to cook and flavor the beans.

COOKING THE VEGETABLES AGAIN The partially cooked beans will become crisp-tender—or fully tender if you let them stay in the pan longer—as you cook them for a second time.

Garlicky Sweet Potatoes

These are a real treat, sweet and savory at once, and quick to make too.

TIME   **About 30 minutes**
MAKES   **4 servings**

2 pounds sweet potatoes

¼ cup olive oil

2 tablespoons minced garlic

Salt and freshly ground black pepper

1 Peel the sweet potatoes and grate them by hand or with the grating disk of a food processor; you should have about 5 packed cups; save any extra for another use.

2 Put 2 tablespoons of the oil in a large skillet over medium-high heat. When it's hot, add half the sweet potatoes, spread them out in an even layer, and sprinkle with half of the garlic and some salt and pepper. Cook, without stirring, until the potatoes begin to brown on the bottom and release easily from the skillet, 3 to 5 minutes.

3 Continue cooking, stirring every 2 to 3 minutes, until the potatoes are mostly golden brown and tender but not mushy; begin checking after about 5 minutes. When they're ready, transfer them to a serving plate.

4 Repeat with the remaining ingredients. Add the second batch of sweet potatoes to the first and toss to combine. Taste, adjust the seasoning, toss again, and serve.

Be careful with a box grater: It's better to throw away the end of the vegetable than to cut yourself.

It's surprising how much grating vegetables increases their volume.

GRATING SWEET POTATOES
Push the sweet potato up and down over the largest holes of a box grater. (You can also use a food processor fitted with a grating disk.)

ADDING POTATOES TO OIL They should sizzle but not spatter or smoke; if it does, turn down the heat. Then spread the potatoes out in an even layer to maximize browning and crisping.

Tips

▶ Moisture will put a crimp in the browning process; if the potatoes seem wet after you grate them (unlikely, but it can happen), put them on a towel and squeeze them dry before cooking.

▶ Other vegetables to try here: waxy potatoes, celery root, winter squash, parsnips, ruta-bagas, kohlrabi, or turnips.

Variations

▶ **Garlicky Sweet Potatoes with Bacon:** Skip the olive oil and start by cooking 4 ounces bacon until crisp (see page 43), then remove the bacon with a slotted spoon. In Step 2, cook the potatoes in the bacon fat. (Before cooking the second batch, add a little olive oil if the pan looks dry.) In Step 4, crumble the bacon back into the pan while cooking the second batch.

Learn More

▶ Vegetable Basics (page 216), peeling sweet potatoes (page 17), shredding vegetables in the food processor (page 121), mincing garlic (page 20)

When you cook vegetables in batches, you avoid crowding the pan, which would cause them to steam instead of brown and crisp.

BROWNING POTATOES Resist the urge to stir too much. You want to give the uncooked parts a chance to brown. Just adjust the heat to keep them sizzling but not scorching.

Curried Butternut Squash

A shortcut braise that turns sturdy vegetables into a saucy stew.

TIME **45 to 60 minutes**
MAKES **4 servings**

1½ pounds butternut squash

2 tablespoons butter

1 tablespoon minced garlic

1 tablespoon minced or grated ginger

1 tablespoon curry powder

1 cup coconut milk

Salt and freshly ground black pepper

¼ cup chopped fresh cilantro leaves for garnish

¼ cup chopped scallions for garnish

1 lime, quartered, for serving

1 Cut both ends off the squash and cut it into 2 sections: the cylindrical top and the bulbous bottom. Peel both sections, then cut the bottom in half lengthwise and scoop out the seeds with a spoon. Cut the flesh from both sections into 1-inch chunks (or cubes if you're feeling fastidious). You should have about 5 cups.

2 Put the butter in a large skillet over medium heat. When it melts, add the garlic and ginger and cook, stirring occasionally, until they soften and turn golden, 2 to 3 minutes. Add the curry powder and stir until it becomes fragrant, just 1 minute or so.

3 Stir in the squash, coconut milk, and some salt and pepper. Turn the heat to high, bring to a boil, then lower the heat to a gentle bubble. Cover and cook, stirring once or twice, until the squash is tender (you'll be able to pierce it easily with a sharp, thin-bladed knife), 15 to 20 minutes.

4 Remove the lid and raise the heat to medium-high. Cook, shaking the pan occasionally and stirring the squash just a few times, until the liquid thickens a bit, no more than 5 minutes. Taste and adjust the seasoning, garnish with the cilantro and scallions, and serve with the lime wedges.

If some stubborn strings remain, it's not a big deal.

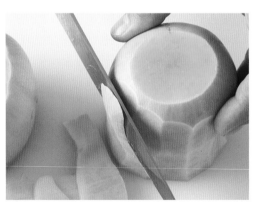

PEELING SQUASH Stand each piece of squash on the flat end for stability and cut downward, going slowly and trying not to take off too much of the flesh.

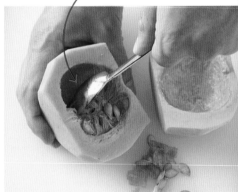

SEEDING SQUASH You need to scrape pretty hard to remove the seeds and stringy pulp from winter squash; a spoon is the best tool.

Tips

◗ Of all the winter squashes, the skin of butternut is the thinnest, and in some cases you might be able to get it off with a vegetable peeler, especially if yours is razor-sharp. But be prepared to use a knife, as you'll certainly need to with most winter squashes. Either way, take off the pale, green-striped layer just inside the peel, but try not to remove too much of the edible orange flesh.

◗ Other vegetables you can use here: sweet potatoes, potatoes, turnips, rutabaga, celery root, or any other winter squash, including acorn, kabocha, and pumpkin (but not spaghetti squash, which will fall apart). Or try a combination.

◗ If you don't want a creamy curry, substitute vegetable stock (or even water) for the coconut milk. To take the dish over the top in richness, use cream or half-and-half.

Learn More

◗ Vegetable Basics (page 216), Braising (page 31), mincing garlic (page 20), preparing ginger (page 78), Dairy—and Not (page 42), Chopping Herbs (page 78), Preparing Scallions (page 295)

CUBING SQUASH Cut crosswise or downward into slices, following the contours of the squash, then cut each slice into cubes of roughly the same size so they'll cook evenly.

BRAISING VEGETABLES After stirring in the liquid and squash, cover the pan so the moisture helps make the vegetables meltingly soft.

Panfried Breaded Eggplant

A classic: crisp and crumbly outside, super-tender and creamy within.

TIME **1 to 2 hours, partially unattended**

MAKES **4 servings**

---

4 small or 2 large eggplant (about 2 pounds)

Salt

3 eggs

Freshly ground black pepper

1 cup all-purpose flour

3 cups bread crumbs, preferably fresh

Vegetable or olive oil as needed for frying

¼ cup chopped fresh parsley leaves for garnish

2 lemons, quartered, for serving

1 Trim off the stem end from the eggplant and cut it crosswise into slices about ½ inch thick. If you have some extra time, put the eggplant in a colander in the sink, sprinkle with 1 tablespoon salt, and toss to coat the slices on both sides. Let the eggplant rest for at least 20 minutes and up to 1 hour.

2 Heat the oven to 200°F. Beat the eggs with some salt and pepper in a shallow bowl or pie plate. Put the flour and bread crumbs on separate plates, with the eggs in between them. Have a baking sheet and several rectangles of wax or parchment paper ready.

3 If you salted the eggplant, rinse and dry it well with paper towels. Coat a slice in the flour, dip in the egg, then coat in the bread crumbs. You want a thin, even layer of each coating; shake off any excess. Spread the eggplant on the baking sheet in a single layer, top with wax or parchment paper, and repeat with the remaining slices. Transfer the pan to chill in the refrigerator for at least 10 minutes and up to 3 hours.

4 Put a large skillet over medium heat and pour in enough oil to come about ½ inch up the sides. While the oil heats, line a plate with paper towels. The oil is ready when a pinch of flour sizzles immediately.

5 Put a few of the eggplant slices in the hot oil without crowding the pan. When the bottoms turn brown, after 2 to 3 minutes, turn them over and cook the other side for 2 to 3 minutes, adjusting the heat to keep the oil sputtering without smoking or burning the eggplant. As each piece is done, put it on the paper towels to drain, turning them if the tops need blotting too. Transfer them to an ovenproof platter and keep them warm in the oven while you finish cooking the remaining eggplant. In between batches, add more oil to maintain a depth of ½ inch and let it heat up a bit.

6 When all the pieces are cooked, garnish with the parsley and serve with the lemon wedges.

Don't worry: You rinse off most of the salt.

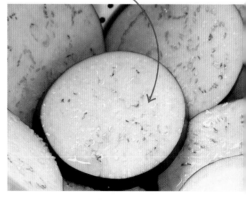

SALTING EGGPLANT This step improves the texture and flavor of eggplant (and other watery vegetables, like zucchini and cabbage). But it isn't necessary.

Tips

▶ Big eggplant are more common than small ones, but also more likely to be bitter. Either way, look for very firm eggplant with green, fresh-looking stems and use them ASAP.

▶ Salting eggplant—which pulls out excess moisture and mellows the flavor—is optional; if you don't have time, fine. If you opt not to salt, expect the texture to be a little spongier and perhaps more bitter, especially if the eggplant is big and has a lot of seeds. (This is a good reason to look for smaller, firmer eggplant.)

▶ Some people prefer to peel eggplant before cooking it. To me that's silly unless it's thick and bitter: I like the skin, sometimes more than I like the flesh.

▶ Vegetable oil can take a little more heat than olive oil before it begins to smoke, but olive oil tastes better. So if you decide to use olive oil, just keep an eye on how the eggplant cooks and be prepared to lower the heat if it's browning too fast or if the oil starts to smoke.

▶ Other vegetables to try panfrying like this: zucchini or other summer squash, celery root, rutabaga, green (unripe) tomatoes. With all, salting is optional.

Learn More
▶ Vegetable Basics (page 216), Panfrying (page 36), Beating Eggs (page 52), Fresh Bread Crumbs (page 386), Chopping Herbs (page 78)

DREDGING EGGPLANT *Dredge* means "to coat." Put the slices first in flour, then in egg, and finally in bread crumbs, tapping any excess back onto the plate.

STACKING EGGPLANT After you finish all the dredging, let the coating set in the fridge for at least a few minutes to set.

FRYING THE EGGPLANT The pieces are ready to turn when they're golden brown and crisp on the bottom. Adjust the heat so they take no more than a couple minutes per side but don't burn.

Cauliflower Gratin with Blue Cheese

Roasted cauliflower is sensational, and this recipe gives you plenty of options.

TIME **30 minutes**
MAKES **4 servings**

---

1 medium cauliflower
(about 1½ pounds)

2 garlic cloves, unpeeled

3 tablespoons olive oil

Salt and freshly ground
black pepper

1 cup crumbled blue cheese

½ cup bread crumbs,
preferably fresh

1 Heat the oven to 425°F. Trim the outer leaves from the cauliflower and cut the florets from the core. It's okay if they're not all perfectly separated, but you want them about 1 inch across, so cut through some if necessary.

2 Put the garlic on the cutting board and hold a chef's knife above them, parallel. Press down lightly to crush the garlic a bit; remove the peel and trim the flat end.

3 Put the cauliflower in a large gratin dish; drizzle with the olive oil and sprinkle with salt and pepper. Toss to coat the cauliflower with the oil and spread it out in an even layer. Nestle the garlic among the cauliflower florets and transfer the dish to the oven; cook until the florets are beginning to turn brown and the stems are crisp-tender (you'll be able to pierce them with a thin-bladed knife, but they'll offer some resistance), 10 to 15 minutes.

4 Remove the dish from the oven and remove and discard the garlic. Sprinkle the blue cheese evenly on top of the cauliflower, then sprinkle with the bread crumbs. Put the dish back in the oven and cook until the cheese is bubbling and the bread crumbs are golden brown, another 10 to 15 minutes. Serve hot or warm.

Break big florets into bite-sized pieces with your fingers or cut them.

TRIMMING CAULIFLOWER Once you remove the outer leaves, it's easy to see where the floret stems grow out of the core.

CUTTING FLORETS Begin at the base of the cauliflower and work your way to the top of the core, leaving some of the stem on each piece. When the core comes free, discard it.

Tips

▶ A gratin is anything—sliced, chopped, or whole vegetables, but also noodles, fish, whatever—usually with a topping, baked or broiled until nicely browned. To save a step you can precook the cauliflower right in the baking dish (as I do here), but you can also steam, boil, grill, broil, or pan-cook vegetables before turning them into gratins. (Or use leftovers, for sure.)

▶ Some other vegetable ideas: sturdy greens like cabbage, chard, or kale; broccoli; winter squash; potatoes or sweet potatoes; celery or fennel.

▶ Adding smashed garlic cloves to vegetables while they cook (and then removing them before serving) infuses vegetables with a hint of garlic without overwhelming them.

Variations

▶ **Broccoli Gratin with Parmesan:** Use broccoli florets instead of cauliflower and substitute grated Parmesan for the blue cheese.

Learn More

▶ Vegetable Basics (page 216), Fresh Bread Crumbs (page 386)

CRUSHING AND PEELING GARLIC
Press hard enough to flatten the clove a little and hear it pop, but not quite hard enough to turn it to mush. Afterward the skin comes off easily.

ADDING GRATIN TOPPING The cauliflower should be just lightly browned when you add the topping—more than that and it may burn before the cheese melts and the bread crumbs crisp.

Zucchini Pancakes

Vegetable pancakes turn everyday ingredients into a special treat.

TIME **30 to 40 minutes, plus time to chill**

MAKES **4 servings**

2 pounds zucchini

½ medium onion

2 eggs

¼ cup all-purpose flour or bread crumbs, preferably fresh, or more as needed

½ cup freshly grated Parmesan cheese

Salt and freshly ground black pepper

¼ cup olive oil, or more as needed

1 Trim off the ends of the zucchini. Grate the zucchini and onion on the large holes of a box grater or with the grating disk of a food processor. Squeeze as much water out of it as possible in a mesh sieve or with your hands.

2 Beat the eggs with a fork in a large bowl and add the vegetables, along with the flour, Parmesan, and a sprinkling of salt and pepper. If the batter looks too watery, add more flour, 1 tablespoon at a time. (The mixture can be refrigerated for up to an hour.)

3 When you're ready to cook, put 2 tablespoons of the oil in a large skillet over medium-high heat. When the oil is hot, carefully drop large spoonfuls of batter into the pan and spread them out with a fork to flatten them a little. You'll need to work in two or three batches to avoid overcrowding the pan.

4 Cook, undisturbed, until the pancakes are browned on the bottom, 5 to 8 minutes, adjusting the heat as necessary so they sizzle without burning. Turn them over and cook for another 5 to 8 minutes on the second side. As the pancakes finish cooking, transfer them to paper towels to drain, add 1 tablespoon more oil to the pan if it looks dry, and repeat the process until the batter is gone. Serve the pancakes hot or at room temperature.

Zucchini gives off lots of liquid, but the flour or bread crumbs will soak it up, so the pancakes get crisp.

Peek underneath with a spatula to check on the color.

CORRECT BATTER CONSISTENCY
The batter should plop from a spoon easily but not be too runny; add more flour or bread crumbs—a little at a time—to reach this consistency.

COOKING VEGETABLE PANCAKES
The heat should be high enough to brown both sides in the same amount of time it takes for the insides to cook through.

Serve plain or with a little sour cream or yogurt or salsa on the side for dipping.

Tips

▶ Hand grating results in slightly differently shaped shreds than food-processor grating, but both work.

▶ You can make the patties bite-sized (for hors d'oeuvres or snacks) or big (for a main course or sandwich filling)—but don't make them more than ½ inch thick or they won't cook through.

▶ Other vegetables to use for pancakes (start with about 2 pounds raw): grated carrots, celery root, beets, fennel, sweet potatoes, or winter squash; cooked spinach or other greens (squeezed between your hands to remove excess water); and chopped bean sprouts.

Variations

▶ **Vegetable Pancakes with Asian Flavors:** Skip the cheese and add 1 tablespoon grated or minced fresh ginger, 1 table-spoon minced garlic, and ¼ cup chopped scallions to the batter. Use vegetable oil instead of olive to fry the pancakes.

Learn More

▶ Vegetable Basics (page 216), Judging the Pan's Heat (page 66), Grating Soft Vegetables (page 192), Drying Grated Vegetables (page 104), Fresh Bread Crumbs (page 386), Grating Cheese (page 176)

Bean Basics

To Soak or Not to Soak?

Soaking beans before cooking is useful if you prefer super-soft beans, or if you want to cut cooking time slightly. (I rarely bother, however.)

Lentils and split peas never need soaking. With other beans you have two choices: For a shorter soak, put them in a large pot, cover with 3 to 4 inches of water, and boil for 2 minutes, then cover and turn off the heat. Let them sit for 30 minutes to 2 hours.

For a longer soak, cover the beans with 5 to 7 inches of water. Let sit for 6 to 12 hours—no longer or they'll turn mushy and bland—then drain. After either method, they're ready to use in any recipe, but they'll cook faster, so start checking after 15 minutes.

How to Cook Any Bean

Dried beans come in all shapes, sizes, and colors, but when it comes to cooking and serving they are essentially interchangeable—especially with this impossible-to-mess-up method. Figure 1 cup of dried beans will yield 2½ to 3 cups cooked, or 3 to 4 servings; a pound of dried beans will yield 5 to 6 cups cooked, or 6 to 8 servings. All beans keep for months in the pantry.

3 or 4 inches is about the length of an average index finger.

RINSE THE BEANS All beans should be cleaned before cooking. As you run them under water, rake through them with your hands and take out any withered, broken, or discolored beans or any pebbles. (If you're soaking the beans before cooking, rinse and pick over them beforehand.)

COOK SLOWLY IN PLENTY OF WATER Put the beans in a large pot with enough water to cover them by 3 to 4 inches. (Beans swell to twice their original size.) Start them out on high, then adjust the heat so they barely bubble, and cover. Vigorous boiling or inadequate water will make them bump into each other, which will rip their skins and cause them to fall apart. The bigger the bean, the longer the cooking time—lentils and split peas can cook in as little as 20 minutes, while chickpeas may need 2 hours or even more. The time can vary wildly depending on how old and dried out the beans are.

Canned Beans

Canned beans are more expensive, mushier, and less flavorful than dried beans you cook yourself. But when you need to make a quick weeknight dinner and don't have any home-cooked beans handy, they're undeniably convenient.

To use canned beans in any recipe: Figure on using 2½ cups (that's one standard can) of beans for every ½ pound of dried beans called for in the recipe. (In recipes that call for cooked beans, substitute canned in the same measure.) Dump them in a colander or strainer to drain off their liquid and rinse them well under cold running water. In recipes that start with dried beans, wait to add canned beans until the last 5 minutes or so of cooking.

Just tender *Soft* *Creamy*

CHECK THEM OCCASIONALLY Cook the beans until there's no trace of crunch and they're as tender as you want them, from just barely soft to creamy and falling apart. The only way to know for sure is to taste. If they're small (like lentils), start tasting the beans after 20 minutes or so and try again every 10 to 15 minutes. If they're larger (like kidney beans), start tasting after 30 minutes. As they cook, keep the beans covered by at least 2 inches of water, adding more if necessary and adjusting the heat to keep the water barely bubbling. When the beans begin to turn tender, add a big pinch of salt and as much pepper as you like.

DRAIN THE BEANS Drain them in a sieve or colander over a bowl or fish them out of the pot with a slotted spoon. The idea is to reserve the cooking liquid—it's flavorful and comes in handy when you're reheating beans (you can also use it in place of stock in many recipes). Use the beans right away or transfer them to a sealed container, cover them with bean-cooking liquid, and refrigerate for up to 5 days (or freeze for up to 6 months).

11 Additions to the Pot

To give beans extra flavor, add any of the following with the water. When the beans are done, fish out whatever is inedible.

1 1 to 2 small dried red chiles
2 1 whole lemon, lime, or orange
3 1 sprig fresh thyme or rosemary
4 Several sprigs fresh parsley, cilantro, basil, or mint
5 A leftover rind from a chunk of Parmesan cheese
6 4 bay leaves
7 3 to 4 garlic cloves
8 1 meaty pork bone
9 ½ pound chopped raw or smoked sausage
10 Several slices of smoked bacon
11 ½ pound raw pork shoulder (fattier is better; no need to trim)

Quick Skillet Beans with Tomatoes

A fast, saucy dish that's just as good warm or at room temperature as it is hot.

TIME **About 30 minutes**

MAKES **4 servings**

2 tablespoons olive oil

1 small onion, chopped

1 tablespoon minced garlic

1½ cups chopped tomatoes (canned are fine; don't bother to drain)

2 cups frozen shelled lima beans or edamame (no need to thaw)

Salt and freshly ground black pepper

2 tablespoons chopped fresh oregano leaves for garnish, optional

1 Put the oil in a large skillet over medium-high heat. When it's hot, add the onion and garlic and cook, stirring occasionally, until the onion begins to soften, 3 to 5 minutes.

2 Add the tomatoes and adjust the heat so the mixture bubbles gently. Cook, stirring occasionally, until the tomatoes begin to break apart and look saucy, 10 to 15 minutes. Add water, 2 tablespoons at a time, if the tomatoes ever look too dry.

3 Stir in the beans and sprinkle with salt and pepper. Cook until they're tender and hot all the way through, 5 to 7 minutes. Taste and adjust the seasoning with salt or pepper, sprinkle with the oregano if you're using it, and serve.

Cooked this way, tomatoes are the seasoning.

Canned diced tomatoes are fine here, especially when fresh ones aren't in season.

ADDING TOMATOES TO THE PAN It's okay if the onion and garlic aren't totally soft when you add the tomatoes; they'll continue to soften as the tomatoes bubble.

ADDING FROZEN BEANS TO THE PAN The tomatoes will break down, get watery, and start to thicken. That's when to add the beans.

To make this dish more substantial, serve it over thick-sliced toast, rice, or noodles.

Tips

▶ There are a handful of beans that we can sometimes find fresh or frozen. Lima beans and edamame (young soybeans) are most common. But whenever you see black-eyed peas, pigeon peas, fava beans, or cranberry beans—either frozen or fresh, in or out of their pods, at farmers' markets—grab them; they're a treat and totally different from their dried counterparts. They cook faster than dried beans, too; generally in less than half the time (but check them frequently, be-

cause the timing can vary quite a bit). If you find fresh beans in the pod, split the shell open and pop out the beans—a bit of work but worth it. (For favas, you need to peel off the skin of each bean, too; sometimes you can find them frozen, already peeled, which is nice.)

▶ To substitute canned beans for frozen in this recipe, try a somewhat firm bean like cannellini or chickpeas. Drain and rinse them and cook them for only 5 minutes in Step 3— just enough time to heat them through.

Variations

▶ **Quick Skillet Edamame with Japanese Flavors:** Use edamame, which are traditionally eaten in Japanese cuisine, not lima beans. Substitute vegetable oil for the olive oil, ½ cup chopped scallions for the onion, and soy sauce for the oregano.

Learn More

▶ Bean Basics (page 250), chopping onions (page 19), mincing garlic (page 20), preparing tomatoes (page 80), Chopping Herbs (page 78)

Chickpeas, Provençal Style

Chickpea-cooking liquid is so delicious you need bread to soak it up.

TIME **1 to 2 hours,
mostly unattended**

MAKES **4 servings**

**1½ cups dried chickpeas
(about 12 ounces), rinsed
and picked over**

**Salt and freshly ground
black pepper**

**4 thick slices French or
Italian bread (day-old
is fine)**

1 tablespoon minced garlic

**¼ cup olive oil, plus more
for drizzling**

**½ cup chopped fresh
parsley leaves for garnish**

1 Put the chickpeas in a large, deep pot and add enough water to cover them by about 3 inches; bring to a boil over high heat. Adjust the heat so the beans bubble gently and cover. Cook, stirring occasionally, for 30 minutes, then taste a chickpea to check for doneness. If the chickpeas have begun to soften, add a large pinch of salt and several grinds of black pepper; if they're still hard, return the lid to the pot, keep cooking, and check them every 10 or 15 minutes until it's time to add the salt.

2 Continue cooking, checking and stirring every 15 minutes or so, until the chickpeas are quite tender but still intact, anywhere from 15 to 45 minutes after you've added the salt. If at any point when you check the beans they look dry, add enough water to keep them covered by about 1 inch.

3 While the beans cook, heat the oven to 400°F. Roughly tear or cut the bread into bite-sized pieces and spread them out on a baking sheet. Bake the bread, turning once, until it's lightly toasted, 10 to 15 minutes. It doesn't have to be warm when you serve it, so just let it sit until serving time.

4 Meanwhile, keep checking the chickpeas every 15 minutes or so. When they're fully tender and just starting to break apart, stir in the garlic and the olive oil; taste and adjust the seasoning. To serve, put the bread in shallow bowls and spoon in the beans and some of the cooking liquid; drizzle with about 1 tablespoon more olive oil if you like and garnish with the parsley.

CHECKING BEANS You wouldn't want to eat this bean yet; it's still too firm. But as soon as you can mash one between your fingers, it's time to add the salt and pepper.

CUTTING THE BREAD Cutting the bread into uneven chunks with a serrated knife makes the dish pleasantly rustic.

Tips

▶ You can make the components for this dish up to 3 days before you're ready to assemble and serve it. Refrigerate the beans in their cooking liquid and store the bread in an airtight container. Reheat the chickpeas and broth just before serving. And like all beans, chickpeas freeze perfectly for months.

▶ The cooking time for chickpeas can vary even more than most beans. I've cooked some that were tender in 30 minutes, while older ones can take well over 2 hours. Taste frequently and be patient.

Variations

▶ **4 Ways to Vary These Chickpeas:**

1 Add 4 ounces chopped prosciutto, smoked ham, or cooked sausage or chorizo to the pot when you add the garlic in Step 4.

2 Garnish with chopped almonds or hazelnuts instead of or along with the parsley.

3 Sprinkle the top with freshly grated Parmesan cheese.

4 When you add the garlic, add ½ cup dried tomatoes to the pot.

Learn More

▶ Bean Basics (page 250), Bread and Sandwich Basics (page 382), mincing garlic (page 20), Chopping Herbs (page 78)

For the most flavorful broth, try to keep the chickpeas submerged by no more than 1 inch of water as they near the end of their cooking time.

RECOGNIZING TENDER CHICKPEAS
I like chickpeas a little creamy and falling apart. For firmer beans, stop cooking sooner.

Spanish-Style Lentils with Spinach

Here's how to take a simple pot of lentils in a few different global directions.

TIME **45 to 60 minutes**
MAKES **4 servings**

---

2 tablespoons olive oil

½ pound smoked chorizo, chopped

1 medium onion, chopped

1 tablespoon minced garlic

1 tablespoon smoked paprika (pimentón) or ½ teaspoon crumbled saffron threads

1 cup dried brown lentils, rinsed and picked over

2 bay leaves

½ cup fruity red wine

2 cups water or chicken, beef, or vegetable stock, or more as needed

1 pound spinach, roughly chopped

Salt and freshly ground black pepper

1 Put the oil in a large pot over medium heat. When it's hot, add the chorizo and onion. Cook, stirring occasionally, until the onion is soft and the sausage begins to brown, 5 to 7 minutes. Add the garlic and paprika and continue to stir and cook until fragrant, 1 minute.

2 Stir in the lentils, bay leaves, wine, and water; raise the heat to high and bring to a boil. Adjust the heat so the mixture bubbles gently. Cover and cook, stirring occasionally and adding more water if necessary to keep the beans submerged, until the lentils are no longer crunchy but are still a little too firm to eat, 20 to 30 minutes. (You can make the dish to this point up to 2 days ahead; gently reheat the lentils before continuing.) Fish out the bay leaves.

3 Stir in the spinach, sprinkle with salt and pepper, and keep cooking until the lentils are fully tender, the spinach is wilted, and the mixture is saucy and thick, another 5 to 10 minutes. Taste and adjust the seasoning. Serve hot or warm.

Nothing smells better than spices toasting in oil.

ADDING GARLIC AND SPICES If you put everything in the hot oil at the same time, the less sturdy garlic and spices will burn; they need only about a minute to toast and unleash their flavor.

ADDING LIQUID AND LENTILS The lentils take on the flavors of whatever goes in the pot. And once you get the lid on, you have to check on them only once or twice during cooking.

It's easier to find the bay leaves and fish them out before adding the spinach.

ADDING SPINACH The spinach won't take long to cook, so don't stir it in until the lentils are almost tender.

Tips

▶ Trust your teeth—not the clock—to tell you when the lentils are ready. (*Always* good advice!)

Variations

▶ **French-Style Lentils with Peas:** Use the green French "Le Puy" lentils here if you can find them. Substitute chopped thick-cut bacon for the chorizo and frozen peas for the spinach. Skip the paprika. When you stir in the peas in Step 3, add 2 tablespoons Dijon mustard and 1 teaspoon chopped fresh tarragon.

▶ **North African–Style Lentils with Carrots:** Skip the chorizo and use 4 medium chopped carrots instead of the spinach. For the paprika, substitute 1 teaspoon ground turmeric, 1 teaspoon ground cinnamon, and 1 teaspoon ground cumin. In Step 2, replace the wine and 1 cup of the water with 1 large can (28 ounces) diced tomatoes, including the juice. Continue with the recipe.

Learn More

▶ Bean Basics (page 250), types of sausages (page 289), chopping onions (page 19), mincing garlic (page 20), Buying, Preparing, and Storing Salad Greens (page 109)

Baked Black Beans with Rice

A surprisingly simple one-pot meal you finish in the oven for a crisp crust.

TIME **About 2 hours, mostly unattended**

MAKES **4 to 6 servings**

2 tablespoons olive oil

1 medium onion, chopped

1 medium red bell pepper, cored, seeded, and chopped

1 tablespoon minced garlic

¾ cup dried black beans, rinsed and picked over

1½ cups long-grain white rice

Salt and freshly ground black pepper

½ cup chopped fresh cilantro leaves for garnish

1 Put the oil in a large ovenproof pot over medium heat. When it's hot, add the onion, bell pepper, and garlic and cook, stirring occasionally, until the vegetables are soft, about 5 minutes.

2 Stir in the beans, add enough water to cover them by about 2 inches, and raise the heat to high. Bring to a boil, then adjust the heat so the mixture bubbles gently. Cover and cook, stirring occasionally and adding water if necessary to keep the beans submerged, until the beans are softening but still hard in the middle, 45 to 60 minutes.

3 Heat the oven to 350°F. Roughly mash some of the beans in the pot with a fork, the back of a spoon, or a potato masher; you want to leave at least half of them intact.

4 Add the rice and a good sprinkling of salt and pepper and stir well to combine. Let the beans and rice settle back to the bottom of the pot. They should be covered by 1 inch of liquid; if not, add enough water so they are. (If there's too much in the pot, spoon some of it out and reserve it to add later if you need it.)

5 Transfer the pot—uncovered—to the oven and cook until the rice and beans are tender, about 1 hour, adding water (or the reserved cooking liquid) ¼ cup at a time if the mixture becomes dry before the rice and beans are done. Taste and adjust the seasoning, fluff with a fork, and serve garnished with the cilantro.

Check the beans frequently as they cook. You've got to bite or break into one to judge the texture inside.

COOKING BEANS PARTIALLY
They're ready for the oven when the exterior of the beans is tender but they're a bit firm in the very center.

ADDING THE RICE After stirring and letting it settle, check that the amount of liquid on top is no more than 1 inch. Better to add some later than have the dish get too soupy.

Tips

▶ This is a great dish to make ahead. When it's done and cooled, cover and refrigerate for up to 2 days, then reheat in a 350°F oven—covered—until hot, 30 to 45 minutes.

▶ Canned beans are a good option here and let you get dinner on the table in half the time. Drain and rinse two 15-ounce cans black beans. Stir them in when you would the dried beans (along with enough water to cover by 1 inch) and cook to warm them for 5 minutes before moving on to Step 3.

Variations

▶ **Black-Eyed Peas with Rice:** A shortcut on the classic southern dish known as hoppin' John. Substitute black-eyed peas for the black beans and add 1 cup chopped smoked ham or sausage and 1 tablespoon chopped fresh thyme leaves along with the rice in Step 4. Garnish with parsley instead of cilantro.

Learn More

▶ Bean Basics (page 250), chopping onions (page 19), Preparing Bell Peppers (page 117), mincing garlic (page 20), Rice Basics (page 196), Chopping Herbs (page 78)

Bean Burgers

These are amazing—so good you'll want to double the recipe and freeze some.

TIME   30 to 40 minutes
       with cooked beans
MAKES   4 to 8 servings

2 cups cooked or drained
canned white, black, or
red beans or chickpeas or
lentils

1 medium onion, cut into
chunks

½ cup rolled oats, or more
as needed

1 tablespoon chili powder

Salt and freshly ground
black pepper

Bean-cooking liquid or
water as needed

2 tablespoons olive oil, plus
more as needed

1 Line a baking sheet with parchment or wax paper. Put the beans, onion, oats, and chili powder in a food processor with a sprinkle of salt and pepper. Let the machine run, stopping occasionally to scrape down the sides, until the mixture is thoroughly combined but not puréed, about a minute. (If you don't have a machine, use a potato masher and a large bowl.)

2 Let the mixture sit in the processor for 5 minutes. You want a moist consistency that will easily form cakes. If the mixture is too wet, add more oats, 1 tablespoon at a time. If it's too dry, add bean-cooking liquid or water 1 tablespoon at a time. Pulse (or mash) after each addition.

3 Shape the bean mixture into 4 large or 8 small patties and put them on the baking sheet. Let them sit for another 5 minutes.

4 Put the oil in a large skillet over medium heat. When the oil is hot, add the patties. Cook, undisturbed, until brown and crisp on one side, 3 to 8 minutes. Add more oil if the pan looks dry, then turn them over carefully with a spatula and cook on the other side until the burgers feel firm and are browned on the other side too, another 3 to 5 minutes. Serve hot or warm with side dishes or on buns with the usual burger fixings.

The less you handle them, the better. If you mess up, return the patty to the bowl and start over.

PROCESSING THE BEAN MIXTURE
Pinch a bit between two fingers:
If it's too wet, add more oats,
1 tablespoon at a time; if it
crumbles, add liquid 1 tablespoon
at a time.

FORMING PATTIES If the burgers are sticking, wet your hands with a little water before you shape them.

Tips

▶ Canned beans work well here, since their super-soft texture and their mild flavor makes them very amenable to other seasonings.

▶ Letting the bean mixture and the patties rest for a few minutes helps keep the burgers from falling apart. If you have time, you can put the patties in a container with a tight-fitting lid and refrigerate them for an hour (or up to a day), or freeze for up to a month; let them return to room temperature before cooking.

Variations

▶ **Bean Burgers with Cheese:** Remove the food processor blade and stir in ¾ cup freshly grated Parmesan, cheddar, Swiss, Jack, or mozzarella cheese to the other ingredients in the food processor right before forming the patties in Step 3.

▶ **Bean Burgers with Greens:** Add 1 cup cooked greens to the other ingredients in the food processor in Step 1. Be sure you press them dry first (see page 219).

Learn More

▶ Bean Basics (page 250)

TESTING OIL It's important that the oil be hot when you add the patties so that they form a crust quickly. If you're not sure, add a morsel to the skillet; it should sizzle immediately.

FLIPPING THE BURGERS Raise them high enough off the pan to leave plenty of room to turn them. They'll hold together, but they're not as sturdy as burgers made from meat.

Meat

I eat far less meat today than I used to, for the same reasons many others do: Less meat is better for your health, the environment, and of course your budget. So I look at meat as a treat, and when I do cook it I want it to taste good. That means buying meat from a reliably good source, selecting the right cut for the cooking method, seasoning it well, and cooking it as well as I can: all stuff you'll learn in this chapter.

Judging doneness can be intimidating to all but the most experienced cooks. Everyone seems to think there's some trick to getting a steak medium-rare or a rib fall-off-the-bone tender, but the truth is that cooking meat is like cooking anything else: You need to know which technique to choose for your ingredient (or, in this case, which cooking method to use for the animal and cut you have) and then practice until you get a feel for the process. Meanwhile, if things don't come out quite the way you'd hoped, you'll likely still be pleased: You cooked the food yourself, after all.

Here are the easiest, most efficient ways to grill, broil, roast, pan-sear, braise, and stir-fry. You'll learn how to flavor meat before, during, and after cooking. Most important, you'll discover that handling meat isn't a big deal. And since the techniques are the same whether you're cooking beef, lamb, or pork, you'll expand your recipe repertoire quickly and enormously.

Beef Basics

Buying Meat

Most of the meat in this country—beef, pork, lamb, chicken, turkey, whatever—is produced industrially. The sad and often inhumane process includes routine antibiotic treatment, growth hormones, an unnatural diet, and often bad living conditions. Since labels don't help much, if you want to know where an animal came from and how it was raised, you've got to ask or do some digging. Your best bet is usually to buy your meat from a farmers' market, butcher, co-op, or directly from a farm. If you seek out good, ethically raised meat, your eating experience will improve dramatically.

Ground Beef

If you have a food processor, consider grinding your own meat, as shown with The Burger on page 268. For the times you buy preground, some tips: Most supermarket "ground beef" is a mix of many parts of many cows, so you have no idea—zero—what cut you're getting. Look for label details like *ground round*, *ground sirloin*, or *ground chuck*, which correspond to specific cuts. (Or ask for help.) There should also be a ratio on the package, something like 75/25, 80/20, 85/15, or 90/10. This is the proportion of meat to fat. (Sometimes the label will say just *90% lean*.) For juicy, flavorful ground beef, shoot for 80 to 85 percent. Yes, it's going to have more calories than the leaner mixtures (it'll also cost less). But if you eat meat as "a treat," then when you do cook it, you want it to taste good.

IS IT DONE YET?

You can either insert a thermometer into the thickest part or make a small cut and peek inside. For maximum juiciness, take steaks, roasts, and burgers off the heat one stage (about 5°F) before the desired doneness and let them rest for 5 to 10 minutes to come up in temperature.

RARE 120–125°F. Bright red center.

MEDIUM-RARE 130–135°F. Bright pink center.

MEDIUM 140–145°F. Light pink center.

MEDIUM-WELL 150–155°F. No traces of pink.

WELL DONE 160°F and above. Dark brown/gray throughout.

TENDERLOIN

RIB-EYE STEAK

CHUCK ROAST

Cooking the Common Beef Cuts

FOR ROASTING
Large cuts, with most of the fat around the outside:
Prime rib (rib roast)
Tenderloin
Sirloin roast
Tri-tip
Top round
Rump roast
Round roast

FOR GRILLING, BROILING, AND PAN-COOKING
Small cuts, with most of the fat around the outside:
Rib-eye steak
Porterhouse steak
T-bone steak
Sirloin steak
Flank steak
Skirt steak
Strip steak
Filet mignon

FOR BRAISING OR SLOW ROASTING
Fatty "stew meat," whole or cut into chunks:
Chuck roast
Chuck steak
Arm roast
Shoulder roast
Brisket
Round steak
Short ribs

Grilled or Broiled Steak

In a nutshell: salt, pepper, meat, heat, eat.

TIME   **20 to 25 minutes**
MAKES   **2 to 4 servings**

---

2 strip, rib-eye, or other steaks (about 1 inch thick and ½ pound each), at room temperature

Salt and freshly ground black pepper

1   Prepare a grill or turn on the broiler; the heat should be medium-high and the rack about 4 inches from the heat source. If you're broiling, put a large ovenproof skillet on the rack 10 minutes before you're ready to cook.

2   Blot the steaks dry with a paper towel and sprinkle the top with salt and pepper.

3   Put the steaks—seasoned side down—on the hot grill or under the broiler and sprinkle the top with salt and pepper. Cook, undisturbed, until they release easily, about 3 minutes.

Turn and cook the other side, checking for doneness by peeking inside with a sharp knife and checking the same spot frequently. For medium-rare, figure about 3 more minutes (if they're over an inch thick, you'll need a little more time; if they're under an inch, you'll need a little less).

4   When the steaks are still a little bit redder than you want them, remove them from the heat and let them rest for at least 5 minutes. Sprinkle the steaks with more salt and pepper if you like and cut them in half crosswise or leave whole and serve.

If you're broiling, the pan is hot enough when a few drops of water evaporate almost immediately.

PREPARING STEAKS Wet steaks will steam instead of sear. So they cook evenly, start them out at room temperature—not straight from the fridge.

HEATING THE COOKING SURFACE The steaks should sizzle when you put them on the grill or in the pan. If they don't, the surface isn't hot enough yet.

You can have slightly different degrees of doneness in the same piece of meat.

NICKING TO CHECK DONENESS
Just a little cut, not a massacre. It's the only sure way; a thermometer doesn't give an accurate reading with thin cuts like steaks.

Tips

▶ When the steaks are done, don't cut into them right away. Let the meat rest for at least 5 minutes; they'll cook from the residual heat and reach the next level of doneness.

Variations

▶ **Pan-Cooked Steak:** A little more forgiving than using the higher-heat method: Put 2 tablespoons olive oil in a large skillet over medium-low heat. Prepare the steaks through Step 2. When the oil is warm, put the steaks in the pan (they won't sizzle), seasoned side down, and sprinkle the tops with salt and pepper. Cook until the edges begin to turn brown, 5 to 10 minutes, then turn and cook until the steak is at least 1 shade redder (or pinker) than you like, another 3 to 5 minutes. Turn the heat to medium-high and cook, turning once, until each side is seared a little, less than a minute total. Remove from the pan, let rest, and serve with the pan drippings poured over all.

▶ **Pepper Steak (*Steak au Poivre*):** Before Step 1, coarsely grind 1 tablespoon black pepper and melt 1 tablespoon butter. Salt and pepper the steaks as described in Step 2, pressing the extra pepper into the raw steaks, then brush both sides with the butter.

Learn More

▶ Beef Basics (page 264), Grilling (page 35), Broiling (page 34)

The Burger

Best with meat you grind yourself.

TIME   20 minutes
MAKES   4 or 6 servings

1½ pounds boneless chuck steak, cut into 1-inch chunks, or preground beef

½ small white onion, cut into chunks, optional

Salt and freshly ground black pepper

6 ounces cheddar cheese, grated or thinly sliced, optional

Hamburger buns, hard rolls, or English muffin, toasted if you like, optional

Lettuce, tomato, sliced onion, pickles, and condiments as you like

1   Prepare a grill or turn on the broiler; the heat should be medium-high and the rack about 4 inches from the heat source. If you're broiling, put a large ovenproof skillet on the rack 10 minutes before you're ready to cook.

2   To make your own ground beef, put the meat, onion if you're using it, and a generous sprinkle of salt and pepper into a food processor (in batches if your machine is small) and pulse until coarsely ground—finer than roughly chopped, but not much—this will take only a few pulses.

If you're starting with preground beef, mince the onion if you're using it and fold it into the meat with a generous sprinkle of salt and pepper.

3   Handling the ground beef mixture as little as possible, lightly shape the meat into 4 large or 6 small burgers. (You can make them up to several hours ahead of cooking. Cover tightly with plastic wrap or foil and refrigerate; bring them to room temperature before continuing.)

4   Put the burgers on the hot grill or under the broiler and cook, undisturbed, until they release easily, 3 to 5 minutes. Turn and cook the other side the same way, topping with the cheese if you're using it. Check for doneness frequently by taking a peek with a sharp knife or using a thermometer if the burger is more than 1 inch thick. For medium-rare, figure about 3 more minutes (if they're over an inch thick, you'll need a little more time; if they're under an inch, you'll need a little less). Serve on buns, topped however you like.

Don't grind it into mush.

GRINDING YOUR OWN MEAT Pulsing the machine helps you avoid overprocessing; the meat should just begin to come together in the bowl.

SHAPING BURGERS When forming the patties, handle them only enough to keep them together, using your thumbs to form rough rounds. Mash or knead them and they'll be tough for sure.

Tips

▶ Lean ground meat (any kind) cooks up dry and mealy. Whether you grind your own or not, choose meat well marbled with fat. You should be able to see it.

▶ Season with conviction. Start with a generous sprinkling of salt and pepper and taste it (to check the taste, fry up a spoonful in a skillet and taste it that way). Add more as needed.

Variations

▶ **Pan-Cooked Burgers:** After shaping the burgers, follow the directions for Pan-Cooked Steak on page 267.

▶ **Other Burgers:** Try using pork, lamb, turkey, chicken (yes, with the skin!), or even seafood instead of beef. (Cook turkey, chicken, and seafood until no pinkness remains inside but not until they're gray and dry.)

▶ **Seasoned Burgers:** Stir in chopped fresh herbs, like rosemary, sage, or basil. Add spices, like curry powder, chili powder, or ground cumin. Or try a splash of soy sauce, Worcestershire, or Tabasco.

Learn More

▶ Beef Basics (page 264), Grilling (page 35), Broiling (page 34)

Pressing down on the patties squeezes out their juice—don't even think about it!

FLIPPING BURGERS When they brown on the bottom and develop a crust, they'll release easily. Don't fuss with them.

MAKING CHEESEBURGERS Put the cheese on top right after you flip the burgers; the heat from the cooked side will melt it.

Stir-Fried Beef with Basil and Chiles

A Thai-inspired dish that will get you hooked on stir-frying.

TIME **15 minutes, plus time to freeze and marinate the meat**

MAKES **4 to 6 servings**

About 1½ pounds flank, sirloin, or strip steak

1 cup loosely packed fresh basil leaves

1 teaspoon plus 1 tablespoon vegetable oil

1½ tablespoons minced garlic or more to taste

Salt

¼ teaspoon crushed red pepper, or to taste

1 tablespoon soy sauce

Juice of ½ lime

½ cup chopped peanuts, optional

1 Put the meat in the freezer for 15 to 30 minutes. Meanwhile, if the basil leaves are large, roughly chop them.

2 Once the meat is firm, slice it across the grain as thinly as you can, then cut the slices into thin strips no more than 3 inches long. Combine the beef, basil, and the 1 teaspoon oil in a bowl, cover, and refrigerate for about 30 minutes so the flavor of the basil accents the beef. (If you don't have time to let the beef marinate, just mix the beef and basil together—skip the oil.)

3 When you're ready to cook, put a large skillet over high heat until it begins to smoke, 3 to 4 minutes. Lower the heat to medium and add the remaining 1 tablespoon oil. Swirl it around to coat the bottom of the pan and add the garlic; stir once or twice. As soon as the garlic begins to color—10 to 15 seconds—return the heat to high and add the beef-basil mixture; sprinkle with a little bit of salt and the crushed red pepper.

4 Stir frequently but not constantly, just until the meat loses its red color, 1 or 2 minutes. Add 2 tablespoons water, then the soy sauce and lime juice, and stir to make a little sauce. If the mixture looks dry, add 1 or 2 tablespoons water. Turn off the heat, garnish with the chopped peanuts if you're using them, and serve.

Slicing across the grain always results in a more tender texture than cutting in the same direction as the grain.

SLICING ACROSS THE GRAIN
Look for faint parallel lines running in one direction along the meat. Cut across them—not parallel to them.

SWIRLING THE OIL This gets the oil hot quickly and evenly. The pan will stay hot even after you turn down the heat.

Tips

▶ Freezing any meat for 15 to 30 minutes makes it easier to slice thinly.

▶ White or brown rice is most common, but you can serve stir-fries tossed with Asian noodles. Save a little soaking or cooking water as you drain the noodles; add the noodles to the pan with the stir-fry and toss, using the reserved water to keep everything moist.

Variations

▶ **Stir-Fried Beef with Vegetables:** Cut enough bell peppers, carrots, or celery into thin slices to get about 3 cups. Heat 2 tablespoons oil in the pan and cook them, stirring, until they're brightly colored but still crisp, 2 to 3 minutes. Remove them and continue with the recipe from Step 1. Just before serving, return the vegetables to the pan and stir a few times to warm them.

Learn More

▶ Beef Basics (page 264), Stir-Frying (page 29), mincing garlic (page 20), chopping nuts (page 19), Boiled Rice (page 196), Asian Noodle Basics (page 190)

To make sure the beef browns, stir only enough to keep it from burning.

ADDING THE MEAT As soon as the garlic begins to color, it's time. If you wait any longer, the garlic will burn.

Grilled or Broiled Beef Kebabs

There's something festive about skewers, and they're also a smart way to grill.

TIME   **45 minutes**

MAKES   **4 to 6 servings**

---

3 tablespoons olive oil

2 tablespoons fresh lemon juice

1 tablespoon balsamic vinegar

1 tablespoon minced garlic

1 tablespoon minced fresh thyme leaves or 1 teaspoon dried

Salt and freshly ground black pepper

1 pound button mushrooms

2 large onions, quartered

1½ pounds sirloin steak or roast, cut into 2-inch chunks

2 tablespoons chopped fresh parsley leaves for garnish

1 You'll need 16 to 24 skewers. If yours are wooden, soak them in warm water while you get everything together. Prepare a grill for indirect cooking so that there are hot coals on half and nothing on the other half. Or turn on the broiler. The heat should be medium-high and the rack about 4 inches from the heat source.

2 Whisk together the oil, lemon juice, vinegar, garlic, thyme, and a sprinkle of salt and pepper in a small bowl. Thread the vegetables and meat separately, using 2 skewers side by side and brush them all with most of the marinade.

3 Put the kebabs over the hot side of the grill or on a rimmed baking sheet under the broiler. The beef will cook faster: Cook, turning when the meat releases from the grill or broiler pan, until each of the 4 sides turns brown, 1 to 3 minutes per side. To avoid overcooking, cut a chunk in half after 5 minutes to see how it's doing; you want the inside to be pink and the outside nice and crisp. Transfer them to a platter.

4 While the meat cooks, keep an eye on the vegetable kebabs so they don't burn. Every few minutes, brush them with a little of the remaining marinade and move them to a cooler part of the grill or broiler to prevent them from burning. Keep cooking the vegetable kebabs, turning and moving as necessary, until they begin to brown and become tender, 10 to 15 minutes. As they finish, put them on the platter with the beef. When all the kebabs are cooked, garnish with the parsley and serve.

Food slides around less on wood than metal skewers.

THREADING MEAT ON SKEWERS
Using 2 skewers per kebab is a little more work up front, but it makes them easier to handle and cook evenly. Leave a bit of space between pieces of food.

Tips

▶ For a splurge, use tenderloin instead of sirloin—it has a milder flavor and softer texture.

▶ Kebabs can be assembled in advance and refrigerated. For best results, bring them to room temperature before cooking.

Variations

▶ **Other Vegetables to Try:** Chunks of tomato, eggplant, and bell pepper are classic. You can also try unexpected kebabs made with cabbage wedges, radishes, or whole small chiles.

▶ **Other Meats to Try:** Lamb or pork shoulder is ideal; both are tender, and their fat gives them great flavor. Lamb leg and pork tenderloin are leaner and will dry out if overcooked; cook them only until pink inside.

▶ **Fish Kebabs:** Cut big chunks—at least 2 inches across. You can use any steak, like salmon, swordfish, or halibut, as well as shrimp or scallops. All cook very quickly, in as little as 3 to 5 minutes total.

Learn More

▶ Beef Basics (page 264), Grilling (page 35), Broiling (page 34), Trimming (page 16), Mincing (page 20), Stripping Leaves from Hard Herb Stems (page 141), Peanutty Chicken Kebabs (page 316)

THREADING VEGETABLES ON SKEWERS I like to keep most foods on separate sets of skewers. But for things that cook at about the same rate, you can mix and match them on the same kebab.

TURNING SKEWERS Grab hold of the sturdiest, largest food on the skewer, lift a bit, then roll the kebab over.

Perfect Roast Beef

Prime rib, cooked so there's a slice just right for everyone.

TIME 1½ hours,
   mostly unattended
MAKES 6 to 8 servings

1 bone-in beef rib roast
(5 to 6 pounds)

2 garlic cloves, optional

Salt and freshly ground
black pepper

2 cups beef or chicken
stock, red wine, or water

1 Remove the meat from the fridge an hour before you want to cook it so it comes to room temperature.

2 Heat the oven to 450°F. Put the meat, bone side down, in a roasting pan. If you're using garlic, cut the cloves into slivers; use a paring knife to poke small holes in the meat and insert the garlic into them. Sprinkle the roast generously with salt and pepper.

3 Put the roast in the oven and cook, undisturbed, for 15 minutes. Turn the heat down to 350°F and continue to roast for 1 hour. Spot-check the meat by inserting a quick-read thermometer in several places. You want readings 5 to 10 degrees below your desired final temperature (so 125°F for medium rare).

Check every 5 minutes. But in no case let the temperature of the meat go above 155°F.

4 Take the pan out of the oven. Carefully transfer the meat to a platter with two forks to rest. Pour off all but a few table-spoons of the fat from the pan and put the pan on 2 burners over medium-high heat. Add the stock and cook, stirring and scraping up any browned bits from the bottom of the pan, until the liquid is reduced by half, 5 to 10 minutes.

5 Put the meat on a cutting board and pour any accumulated juices from the platter into the sauce. Cut the meat free from the bone, then slice it crosswise into thick or thin slices. To serve, splash a little of the sauce on the meat and pass the rest at the table.

RUBBING MEAT WITH SEASON-INGS Be generous and really rub it into the meat, especially if you're not using the garlic.

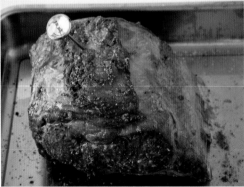

USING A THERMOMETER Most thermometers register a few millimeters from the tip. Keep that in mind and take aim, being careful to avoid fat and bone, which will skew your readings.

CARVING BONE-IN ROAST Use a sawing motion, with the blade flat against the bone, to cut the meat free. Then slice crosswise, against the grain, into any thickness you like.

Tips

▶ For a really crisp exterior, turn the heat back to 450°F for a few minutes right at the end of cooking; this won't affect the internal temperature too much but will give you a nice crust.

▶ Especially with an expensive cut like this, it's better to check early—and often—than to risk overcooking. If you don't have a thermometer, make a small incision on the side somewhere and peek inside. Bright red juices are another clue that the meat inside is rare.

▶ While the roast is in the oven, cook up a batch of roasted potatoes, steam a load of asparagus, and you have a fancy meal with hardly any fuss.

Variations

▶ **Perfect, Less Expensive Roast Beef:** Instead of prime rib, get a boneless rump roast that weighs 4 to 5 pounds. Follow the recipe through Step 2. In Step 3, start checking it after 40 minutes.

Learn More

▶ Beef Basics (page 264), Trimming Fat from a Roast (page 302), Roasting (page 33), Stock Options (page 156), Rosemary-Roasted Potatoes (page 224), Steamed Asparagus (page 220),

Chili from Scratch

A highly seasoned favorite. To speed things up, use canned beans (see the variations).

TIME **2 to 3 hours, mostly unattended**

MAKES **6 to 8 servings**

---

3 tablespoons vegetable oil

1 pound ground beef, pork, or a combination

Salt and freshly ground black pepper

1 large onion, chopped

1 tablespoon minced garlic

2 teaspoons chili powder

1 teaspoon ground cumin

1 tablespoon chopped fresh oregano leaves or 1 teaspoon dried

2 cups chopped tomatoes (diced canned are fine; don't bother to drain)

1 or 2 fresh or dried hot chiles, seeded and minced

1 pound dried pinto or kidney beans, rinsed and picked over, and soaked if you like

½ cup chopped fresh cilantro leaves for garnish

1 Put the oil in a large pot over medium-high heat. When it's hot, add the ground meat and sprinkle with salt and pepper. Adjust the heat so it sizzles steadily and cook, stirring occasionally to break it up, until the meat browns all over, 5 to 10 minutes.

2 Add the onion and cook, stirring every once in a while, until it softens and turns golden, 3 to 5 minutes. Add the garlic, chili powder, cumin, and oregano and cook, stirring constantly, until the mixture becomes fragrant, just another minute.

3 Add the tomatoes, chile, and beans to the pot, along with enough water to cover everything by 2 to 3 inches. Bring to a boil, then lower the heat so the mixture bubbles steadily but not furiously, and cover. Cook, undisturbed, for 30 minutes. After that, stir the chili every 20 minutes or so and adjust the heat so it continues to bubble gently; add more water, ½ cup at a time, if the chili ever starts to stick to the bottom of the pot.

4 When the beans begin to soften (this will take 30 minutes to 1 hour, depending on the type of bean and whether or not you soaked them), sprinkle with salt and pepper. Continue to cook, stirring occasionally and adding water if the pot looks too dry, until the beans are quite tender but still intact—this will take about the same amount of time as it took for them to soften. When the beans are very tender, taste, adjust the seasoning, and serve, garnished with the cilantro.

PREPARING CHILES Hold the stem and cut a slice from the core and seeds with a paring knife; turn and repeat. To mince, rock and pivot a chef's knife over the chile.

Taste a teeny bit to check the heat. The seeds are the hottest part, so keep or ditch them as you like.

BROWNING It's not a bad idea to cook the ground meat until it begins to crisp and the onions until they start to turn color; that will help develop more flavor.

Tips

▶ When you're working with chiles, do not touch your eyes or any other tender areas, and be sure to wash your hands well—with warm water and soap—after you've handled them. Wash them twice for that matter. (If you've got rubber gloves that are thin enough so you can safely wield a knife while wearing them, consider going that route.)

Variations

▶ **Chili with Canned Beans.** This cuts the cooking time down to about 35 minutes and is an easy adjustment: Drain and rinse about 4 cups (two 15-ounce cans) canned beans; add them instead of the dried beans in Step 3. Don't add any water. Bring the mixture to a boil, reduce the heat to a bubble, cover, and cook, stirring occasionally, until everything thickens, 20 minutes or so. Then continue with Step 4.

▶ **Chili with All Sorts of Beans:** Try black beans, white beans, chickpeas, or even lentils (which will be ready 30 minutes after you add them to the pot).

▶ **Chunky Chili:** Instead of ground beef, use pork butt or beef chuck, cut into 1-inch chunks. Brown the pieces on all sides in Step 1 and continue with the recipe.

Learn More

▶ Bean Basics (page 250), Grinding Your Own Meat (page 268), chopping onions (page 19), preparing tomatoes (page 80), chopping herbs (page 78)

At this point you need to stir a lot so it doesn't burn.

ADDING LIQUID Here it's okay to eyeball the amount of water—don't worry about precise measuring. As long as the beans are covered by a couple inches to start, they'll be fine.

DEVELOPING THICKNESS If the beans are done and the chili is still a little watery, remove the lid, raise the heat, and boil off some liquid. If it's too thick, add more water.

Braised Beef with Red Wine

French style. Be patient: The meat isn't done until it's almost falling apart.

TIME 2½ to 4 hours, mostly unattended

MAKES 4 servings

---

2 tablespoons olive oil

1½ pounds boneless beef chuck, cut into 2-inch chunks

Salt and freshly ground black pepper

2 onions, chopped

1 large or 2 medium carrots, chopped

1 celery stalk, chopped

½ cup red wine, or more as needed

½ cup chicken, beef, or vegetable stock or water, or more as needed

¼ cup chopped fresh parsley leaves for garnish

1 Heat the oven to 250°F. Put the oil in a large pot over medium-high heat. When it's hot, add some of the meat, working in batches to avoid crowding; sprinkle with salt and pepper. Cook until the meat is browned on all sides, adjusting the heat and turning the pieces as needed so they don't burn, about 10 minutes for each piece. As they brown, transfer them to a platter; repeat until all the meat is browned.

2 Pour off all but 3 tablespoons of the fat; lower the heat to medium. Add the onions, carrot, and celery, sprinkle with a little salt and pepper, and cook, stirring occasionally, until the vegetables begin to soften, 5 to 10 minutes.

3 Stir in the wine and stock, scraping up any browned bits from the bottom of the pot, and add the browned meat. The braising liquid should come about halfway up the sides of the meat. If it doesn't, add more liquid until it does. Raise the heat and bring to a boil; then lower it so that the mixture barely bubbles. Cover the pot and transfer it to the oven. Cook, stirring every 45 minutes and adding liquid to keep the meat half submerged, until the meat begins to get tender, at least 1½ hours and more likely more than 2 hours.

4 Now begin to check the meat every 15 minutes or so, adding a spoonful more liquid only if the pot looks too dry. The braise is done when the meat is very tender and almost falling apart, at least another 30 minutes. Taste and adjust the seasoning, garnish with the parsley, and serve.

MAKING STEW MEAT I prefer to cut my own, but you can buy it already done. The chunks shouldn't be smaller than 2 inches; this is a hearty dish.

TESTING THE OIL Dip a corner of the first piece of meat into the oil; if it doesn't sizzle loudly, wait a little bit longer.

Tips

▶ If the mixture is too wet when the meat is done, transfer the pieces to a serving bowl with a slotted spoon, turn the heat to high, and let the sauce thicken and reduce. Spoon it over the meat to serve.

▶ Braises and stews are even better the next day: When the dish cools a bit, cover and store it in the refrigerator for up to a few days (or in the freezer for months). The fat will harden on top for easy removal. Be sure to warm the dish gently on the stove in a covered pot so it doesn't burn.

Variations

▶ **Shortcut Braised Beef:** I do this without hesitation when I don't have time; it may not be *quite* as flavorful, but it's still really good: Skip Steps 1 and 2 and put the raw meat and all the other ingredients—except the parsley—into the pot. Pick up the recipe again in Step 3 and continue as directed.

▶ **Other Cuts to Try:** Whole or cut-up beef brisket, shoulder or arm roast, short ribs, lamb or beef shanks, or even oxtail. If you use a bone-in cut, plan on 3 to 4 pounds for 4 servings.

▶ **Other Vegetables to Try, Alone or in Combination:** Chopped fennel or chunks of parsnip, turnip, rutabaga, or celery root; figure about 4 cups total.

Learn More

▶ Beef Basics (page 264), Braising (page 31), Stock Options (page 156), Eyeballing Fat in a Pan (page 324)

COOKING IN BATCHES To avoid crowding, keep rotating pieces in and out of the pot: browned pieces out, raw pieces in.

If the pot looks too dry, add some more liquid to bring the level up.

CHECKING DONENESS AND LIQUID Whenever you uncover the pot, make sure the meat isn't left high and dry.

Pot Roast with Potatoes

Tender sliced meat and a load of delicious vegetables—cooked at the same time.

TIME   2½ to 4 hours,
      mostly unattended
MAKES   6 to 8 servings

1 garlic clove, peeled

1 boneless beef chuck or
rump roast (3 to 4 pounds)

2 bay leaves

Salt and freshly ground
black pepper

2 tablespoons olive oil

2 large onions, chopped

2 large or 3 medium
carrots, sliced

2 celery stalks, sliced

½ cup red wine or water

2 cups beef, chicken, or
vegetable stock or water,
or more as needed

1 pound small waxy red or
white potatoes, scrubbed
and halved

1 Cut the garlic clove into slivers; use a paring knife to poke small holes in the meat and insert the garlic into them. Crumble the bay leaves as finely as you can and mix them with salt and pepper. Rub this mixture all over the meat.

2 Put the oil in a large pot over medium-high heat. When it's hot, add the roast and cook, adjusting the heat and turning as needed so the meat doesn't burn, until it's nicely browned on all sides, about 20 minutes. Transfer the meat to a plate.

3 Add the onions, carrots, and celery to the pot, turn the heat up to medium-high, and cook, stirring frequently, until softened and somewhat browned, 5 to 10 minutes. Add the wine and cook, stirring and scraping up any browned bits from the bottom of the pan; continue cooking until the wine has just about evaporated, 5 to 10 minutes. Add 1½ cups of the stock, return the roast and its juices to the pot, and bring to a boil. Lower the heat so the liquid barely bubbles and cover the pot.

4 Cook, turning the roast every 30 minutes, until the meat is tender enough to pierce easily with a fork. This will take anywhere from 1½ to 3 hours, depending on the thickness of your roast and how low the heat is. Be careful not to overcook the meat or it will become tough and rubbery. If at any point the pot looks dry, add more stock or water, ¼ cup at a time.

5 Heat the oven to 200°F. Transfer the meat to an ovenproof platter, loosely cover with foil, and put in the oven to keep it warm. Spoon any excess fat from the surface of the remaining liquid and add the potatoes; they should be half submerged in liquid; if not, add more stock or water until they are. Turn the heat up to medium-high, cover, and cook, stirring occasionally and scraping the bottom of the pot, until the potatoes are tender when pierced with a knife and the liquid is the consistency of thin gravy, 10 to 20 minutes. Taste and adjust the seasoning. Slice the meat across the grain and serve it with the potatoes and sauce.

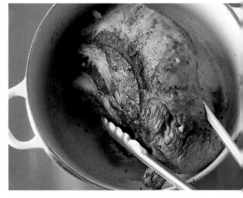

BROWNING POT ROAST Brown the seasoned roast in the hot oil, one side at a time. Turn when it releases easily from the pot and adjust the heat as needed so it doesn't burn.

Tips

▶ Low heat is important to keep pot roast tender. Most take between 2 and 3 hours to cook, but very thick cuts may need up to 4 hours; just check and add liquid as necessary. Once the fat cooks out of it, the meat will turn dry (even good gravy won't cover that up), so stop cooking when the meat is fully tender.

Variations

▶ **Other Cuts to Try:** Beef brisket, short ribs, shin, or cheeks; pork shoulder (bone in or boneless; use the chicken, not beef, stock). The thicker the cut—or if it has a bone—the longer it takes to cook.

▶ **Rosemary Pot Roast with Tomato Sauce:** In Step 1, add 1 tablespoon chopped fresh rosemary leaves to the seasoning rub. In Step 3, skip the carrots and celery and add one 28-ounce can diced tomatoes (don't bother to drain), 3 whole garlic cloves, and another 2 fresh rosemary sprigs with the onions. Use only 1 cup stock (add ½ cup at first) and omit the potatoes. Instead, serve the pot roast over thick slices of toasted Italian bread.

Learn More

▶ Beef Basics (page 264), Stock Options (page 156), Slicing Across the Grain (page 270)

CHECKING THE ROAST Don't walk away from the pot for too long. You need to turn the roast twice every hour so every side spends some time submerged in the liquid.

COOKING THE POTATOES Their starch helps thicken the sauce. Too little liquid and the sauce will pretty much disappear; too much and it will be too watery.

SLICING THE ROAST Put the roast on the cutting board so you can slice across the grain. To get thin, tender slices, work the knife back and forth.

Meat Loaf (or Meatballs)

The best ever, super-flavorful and always moist.

TIME **45 minutes to 1¼ hours, mostly unattended**
MAKES **6 to 8 servings**

1 tablespoon olive oil, optional

½ cup bread crumbs, preferably fresh

½ cup milk

1 pound ground beef

1 pound ground pork

1 egg, lightly beaten

½ cup freshly grated Parmesan cheese

¼ cup chopped fresh parsley leaves

1 teaspoon minced garlic

½ onion, chopped

1 teaspoon chopped fresh sage leaves or 1 pinch dried

Salt and freshly ground black pepper

4 slices bacon, optional

1 Heat the oven to 350°F. Grease a rimmed baking sheet or roasting pan with the olive oil. Soak the bread crumbs in the milk in a large bowl until the milk is absorbed, about 5 minutes.

2 Add the meats, egg, Parmesan, parsley, garlic, onion, sage, and some salt and pepper and gently fold everything into the meat with your hands or a rubber spatula. Mix just enough to distribute the flavorings without overworking the meat or it will become tough.

3 For meat loaf: Turn the meat mixture onto the prepared baking sheet, gently shaping it into an oval mound. Drape the bacon over the top if you're using it. Bake for 45 to 60 minutes, brushing occasionally with the rendered pan juices. When done, the meat loaf will be lightly browned and firm. To check, insert a quick-read thermometer into the center; it should read 160°F. Let the loaf rest for 5 minutes before slicing with a serrated knife.

For meatballs: Shape the mixture into balls of any size and put them on the prepared baking sheet or roasting pan. It's okay if they touch a little; they'll shrink as they cook. Figure that 2-inch meatballs will take 25 to 35 minutes to cook and add another 10 to 15 minutes for every additional inch in size.

Free-form loaves get much crisper than those baked in a loaf pan.

MIXING MEAT LOAF MIXTURE
Go easy: Too much handling and you'll end up with a tough brick.

SHAPING MEAT LOAF Try to give it a little height (at least 3 inches) so you wind up with nice big slices.

Tips

▶ Soaking bread crumbs in milk seems like a strange step, but it really helps. The bread soaks up the milk and redistributes it throughout the meat, keeping it moist.

Variations

▶ **Other Ground Meats to Try:** Veal, lamb, pork, turkey, and chicken all make an excellent base. Chicken and turkey could definitely use the bacon topping since they're so low in fat.

▶ **Pan-Cooked Meatballs:** This requires more attention, but the outsides become supercrisp. Heat 2 tablespoons olive oil in a large skillet over medium heat and add some of the meatballs, being careful not to crowd the pan. Turn them as they release to brown on all sides and transfer them to paper towels to drain as they finish cooking.

▶ **Spaghetti and Meatballs:** Add cooked meatballs to a batch of gently bubbling tomato sauce while you set pasta water to boil.

Learn More

▶ Fresh Bread Crumbs (page 386), Grinding Your Own Meat (page 268), Grating Cheese (page 176), Chopping Herbs (page 78), mincing garlic (page 20)

Use just enough pressure to shape—not squish—them.

DRAPING WITH BACON Put the slices on top however they fit best; tuck in the edges. For super-crisp bacon, set the finished loaf under the broiler for a few minutes.

MAKING MEATBALLS The bigger the meatballs, the longer they take to bake.

Pork Basics

Buying Pork

All of my suggestions in Buying Meat (page 264) apply to pork, but there's one more thing to discuss: fat. Pork was once super-fatty, but now the stuff you find in the supermarket is so lean it tastes more like chicken. Fortunately fat is making a comeback: The best meat has flecks of white fat integrated into the lean and a real strip on the outside. Those are signs of flavor and often an indication that the pig was raised more traditionally.

Ground Pork and Sausage

As with beef, I often grind my own pork (see page 268), but buying from a supermarket that grinds its own—or from a high-quality small producer—is a good alternative. The meat should be fatty enough to stay moist after cooking. You can use ground pork for burgers, meatballs, meat loaves, sausage patties, or stir-fries. Store-bought sausages should also be relatively fatty and can range from awesome to awful depending on where you get them, so when you find a source you like (and trust), stick with it. The meat should be packed in natural casings (you might have to ask) and look pink, not brown; and you should see small globs of white fat and some seasonings through the casings.

IS IT DONE YET?

Pork is generally not eaten quite as rare as beef or lamb, but I like steaks, chops, and roasts when they're still pink and juicy inside, not gray and dry. Check it as you do beef (see page 264), then yank it off the heat one stage (about 5°F) before your desired doneness and let it rest a few minutes before serving.

Most desirable.

Probably dry.

MEDIUM-RARE 145°F. Light pink center.

MEDIUM 150°F. Slightly pink but moist.

WELL DONE 160°F. No traces of pink.

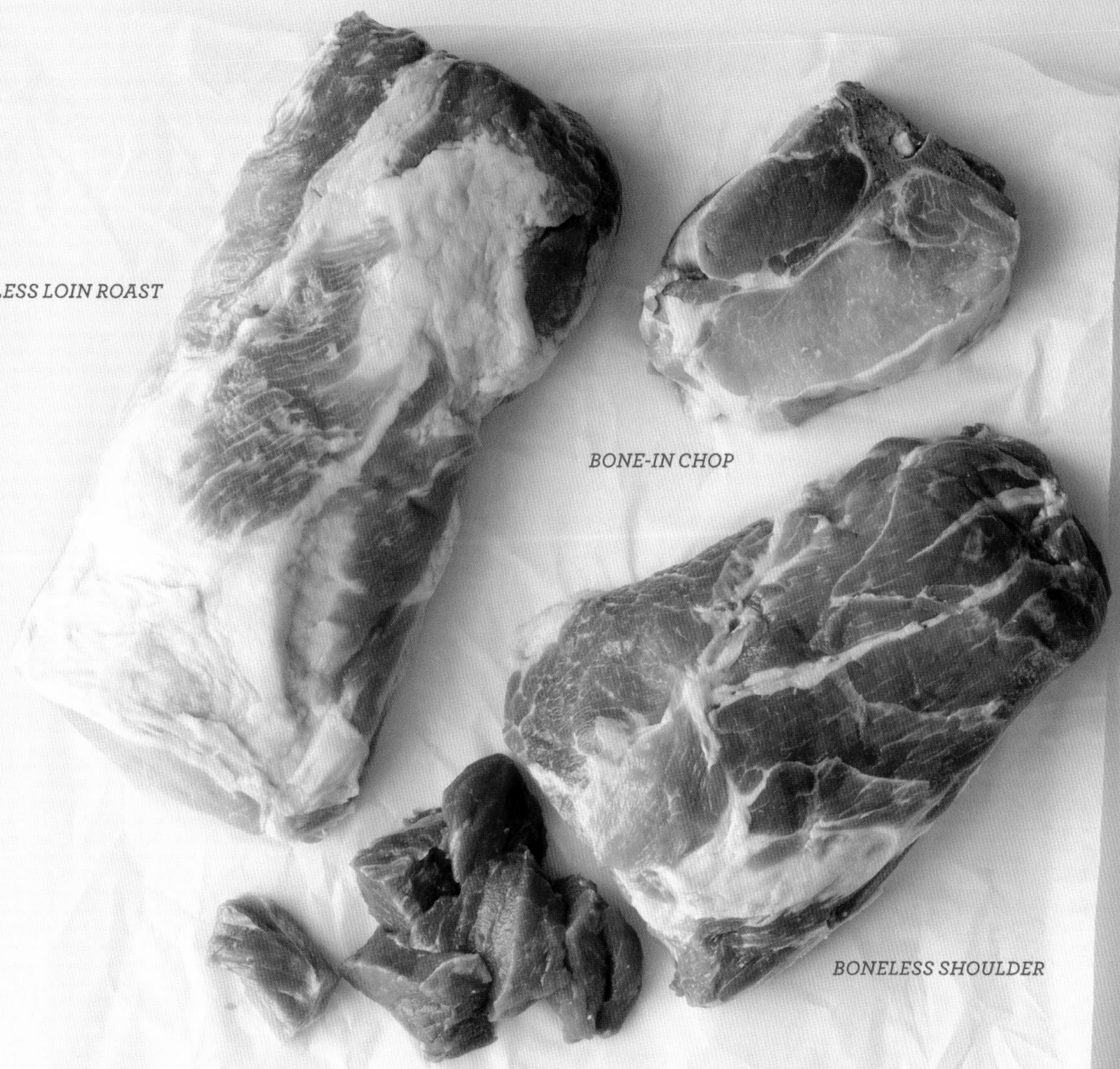

BONELESS LOIN ROAST

BONE-IN CHOP

BONELESS SHOULDER

Cooking the Common Pork Cuts

FOR ROASTING Large cuts, with most of the fat around the outside:
Loin roast
Tenderloin
Ham roast
Sirloin roast

FOR GRILLING, BROILING, AND PAN-COOKING Small cuts, with most of the fat around the outside:
Loin chops (all kinds)
Cutlets (from the loin, shoulder, or sirloin)
Ham steaks
Sliced bacon
Sausages
Ground pork

FOR BRAISING OR SLOW ROASTING Fatty "stew meat," whole or cut into chunks:
Shoulder
Butt
Spare or "baby back" ribs
Shanks
Hocks

Pork Stir-Fry with Greens

Far better—and even faster—than any takeout.

TIME **15 minutes, plus time to freeze the meat**

MAKES **4 servings**

---

1 pound boneless pork shoulder

1 pound greens (like bok choy or mustard)

2 tablespoons vegetable oil

1½ tablespoons minced garlic

2 tablespoons soy sauce

Juice of ½ lime

¼ cup stock or water, optional

½ cup chopped scallions for garnish

1 Put the pork in the freezer for 15 to 30 minutes; once it's firm, slice it across the grain as thinly as you can, then cut the slices into bite-sized pieces. Rinse the greens well and trim any thick stems if necessary; roughly chop them.

2 Heat a large skillet over high heat until it begins to smoke. Add 1 tablespoon of the oil, swirl the pan, then add all the pork. Cook, stirring occasionally, until the pork browns and loses its pink color, 2 to 3 minutes. Transfer the pork to a bowl with a slotted spoon and lower the heat to medium.

3 Add the remaining tablespoon of oil to the skillet. Swirl it around and add the garlic. Stir once or twice. As soon as the garlic begins to color—10 to 15 seconds—return the heat to high and add the greens and 2 tablespoons water. Stir frequently, just until the greens wilt, 2 or 3 minutes longer.

4 Add the pork back to the skillet and stir for 1 minute. Add the soy sauce and lime juice, stir, turn off the heat, and taste, adding more soy sauce if you like. If the mixture is drier than you like, add the stock and heat through. Garnish with the scallions and serve immediately.

Adding water helps steam and soften greens, especially the stems.

SEARING THE PORK Once it's browned all over, use a slotted spoon to take it out so any rendered fat stays in the skillet.

ADDING THE GREENS It looks like a lot, but the pile will soon collapse on its own, without too much stirring.

FINISHING THE DISH Right before serving you might need to add an extra tablespoon of liquid to help create a sauce.

WATERCRESS

KALE (RED)

BOK CHOY (BABY)

CHARD (RED)

MUSTARD GREENS

COLLARDS

Tips

▶ You can use any greens in this recipe—tender or sturdy—or any of the more unusual greens available at farmers' markets and Asian grocers. Sometimes, if greens have thick stems, I separate them from the leaves and give them a head start, but here I just chop them up to cook all together, which gives you both crunchy and tender pieces.

Variations

▶ **8 Other Vegetables to Try.** Increase or decrease the cooking time in Step 3 so that they're still a little crisp when you return the pork to the pan:
1 Bean sprouts
2 Carrots
3 Celery
4 Snow peas
5 Snap peas
6 Green beans
7 Turnips
8 Radishes

Learn More

▶ Pork Basics (page 284), Stir-Frying (page 29), Slicing Across the Grain (page 270), rinsing greens (page 109), mincing garlic (page 20), Preparing Scallions (page 295)

Sausage and Peppers

As good tossed with a batch of pasta as it is stuffed into a long crusty roll.

TIME **30 to 45 minutes**
MAKES **4 servings**

2 tablespoons olive oil

1 pound fresh Italian sausage links, sweet or hot

1 large onion, halved and sliced

2 large bell peppers of any color, cored, seeded, and sliced

Salt and freshly ground black pepper

4 oblong hard rolls, split in half lengthwise, optional

1 Put the oil in a large skillet over medium heat; when it's hot, put the sausages in the skillet, pricking each in a few places with a fork. Cook, turning frequently, until nicely browned all over, 10 to 20 minutes. Total cooking time will depend on the thickness of the sausages. The best way to check is to cut into one—when they are firm and the juices run clear, they are done. Transfer the sausages to a plate.

2 Add the onion and peppers to the skillet, sprinkle with salt and pepper, and cook, stirring occasionally, until they are soft and lightly browned, 10 to 15 minutes. Return the sausages to the skillet for a minute to heat them through. Serve the sausages with the peppers and onions on top, in long rolls if you like.

The sausage on top is perfect.

If you want a little pan juice, add ½ cup water—or, for more flavor, stock, beer, or wine—and stir until the liquid thickens a bit.

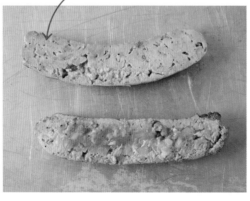

KEEPING THE SAUSAGES IN SHAPE Prick the sausages a few times with a fork; this allows some of the juices to escape during cooking so the sausages don't burst or squirt.

CHECKING DONENESS FOR FRESH SAUSAGES They should be firm, with no hint of pink in their juices. Remove them from the pan, and cook the vegetables.

FINISHING THE DISH Once the peppers and onions are done, turn the sausages around in the pan to warm them through.

FRESH POLISH SAUSAGE

SWEET OR MILD ITALIAN SAUSAGE

HOT ITALIAN SAUSAGE

FRESH BRATWURST (BRATS)

SPANISH CHORIZO

Tips

▶ Sausages come three ways: fresh (like the ones in this recipe), smoked or otherwise precooked (like andouille, kielbasa, and summer sausage), or cured (like salami and pepperoni)—which are essentially air-dried and safe to eat as is. Some are prepared multiple ways: Spanish chorizo can be cured and/or smoked, and brats and Polish sausage come fresh, smoked, or cured, so be sure you know what you're getting.

▶ You can also chop the sausages and toss everything with cooked pasta or beans.

Variations

▶ **Other Sausages to Try:** Italian sausages are the classic here, but you can really use any kind of uncooked sausage that you like. Or you can use smoked sausage, which you need only brown on the outside and warm through in Step 1.

▶ **Sausage and Grapes:** Instead of the onion and bell peppers, use about 1 pound red or green seedless grapes and 1 tablespoon minced garlic. In Step 2, add the garlic and grapes to the pan and cook them just long enough for the garlic to soften and the grapes to crack, 2 to 3 minutes. Return the sausages to the pan to warm.

Learn More

▶ Pork Basics (page 284), Preparing Bell Peppers (page 117), slicing onions (page 19)

Skillet Pork Chops with Apples

The sweet and savory combination of pork, apples, and onions is among the best in fall cooking.

TIME **30 minutes**

MAKES **4 servings**

Four 1-inch-thick pork chops, preferably bone in (6 to 8 ounces each)

2 tablespoons olive oil

Salt and freshly ground black pepper

½ cup dry white wine or light-bodied beer

2 tablespoons chopped shallot or red onion

3 medium apples, peeled, cored, halved, and sliced

1 large onion, halved and sliced

½ cup chicken stock or water, or more as needed

1 tablespoon fresh lemon juice

1 tablespoon butter

2 tablespoons chopped fresh parsley leaves for garnish

1 Blot the chops dry with a paper towel. Put a large skillet over medium-high heat and add the olive oil. When it's hot, add the chops, turn the heat to high, and sprinkle with salt and pepper. When they brown and release from the pan easily, turn the chops, season again, and cook this side the same way. The whole process should take about 2 minutes per side or 3 to 5 minutes total.

2 Reduce the heat to medium and add the wine—be careful here; the wine may splatter a bit when it hits the hot oil—and the shallot and cook, turning the chops once or twice, until the wine is almost evaporated, 1 or 2 minutes. Transfer the chops to a plate and return the pan to the heat.

3 Add the apples and onion to the hot pan and stir until they start to stick, 1 or 2 minutes. Add the stock, stirring and scraping up any browned bits from the bottom of the pan. Return the chops to the pan, along with any juices accumulated on the plate. Bring the mixture to a boil, reduce the heat so it bubbles steadily, then cover.

4 Cook, stirring occasionally and turning the chops once or twice, until the chops are tender, 5 to 10 minutes; add another ½ cup stock or water if the apples start to stick. When the chops are done, they will be firm to the touch, their juices will run just slightly pink, and when you cut into them the color will be rosy at first glance but turn pale within seconds. By this time the apples and onions will also be soft. Stir in the lemon juice and butter and taste and adjust the seasoning. Serve the chops with the sauce on top, garnished with the parsley.

Seasoning food before adding it to the pan only causes you to dirty more dishes and cutting boards.

SEASONING THE EASY WAY You can sprinkle with salt and pepper while the meat, poultry, fish, or vegetables are cooking without any noticeable difference in the flavor of the finished dish.

Tips

▶ There are three kinds of pork chops, cut from different parts of the animal: shoulder, center, and sirloin. Center cut is the leanest and least flavorful.

▶ Bone-in chops have more flavor and stay juicier than boneless chops.

▶ This sear-sauce-simmer technique (essentially a quick braise) is perfect for pork chops: The browning develops flavor, while the moisture keeps the meat tender and juicy. It also works with cuts that are a little fatty and can stand up to longer cooking without drying out—like sausages, bone-in chicken pieces, or boneless chicken thighs.

Variations

▶ **4 Other Ways to "Smother" Pork Chops:**

1 Use only onions.

2 Pair onions with peppers or mushrooms (1 pound total).

3 Use one 28-ounce can diced tomatoes (don't bother to drain).

4 Use 3 cups sauerkraut (and replace the wine with beer).

Learn More

▶ Pork Basics (page 284), preparing apples (page 454), slicing onions (page 232), Chicken Stock (page 154), Chopping Herbs (page 78)

SEARING PORK CHOPS When you remove the chops from the pan, they should be nicely browned but not cooked through.

DEVELOPING A SAUCE Giving the apples and shallots a minute or two head start before adding liquid helps the sauce develop better color and flavor.

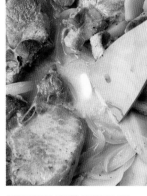

ENRICHING WITH BUTTER Stir the butter into the apple sauce as best as you can while working around the chops. (It's so good, feel free to add a little more.)

Roast Pork with Herb Rub

The most bang for your buck of any roast you can make.

TIME 1½ to 2 hours,
  mostly unattended
MAKES   6 to 10 servings

1 teaspoon salt

½ teaspoon freshly ground
black pepper

2 tablespoons chopped
fresh herb leaves or
2 teaspoons dried

1 tablespoon sugar

1 tablespoon minced garlic

1 boneless pork loin roast
(2 to 3 pounds)

1½ cups dry white wine,
chicken or vegetable
stock, or water, or more as
needed

2 tablespoons cold butter,
cut into pieces, optional

1 Heat the oven to 450°F. Combine the salt, pepper, herbs, sugar, and garlic in a small bowl; rub the roast all over with the mixture. Put the meat in a roasting pan and transfer to the oven. Roast, undisturbed, for 15 minutes.

2 Lower the heat to 325°F and pour ½ cup of the wine over the roast. Continue to cook the roast, checking every 15 minutes or so and adding ¼ cup of the remaining liquid to the bottom of the pan each time. Once the pork's exterior has crusted a bit, start brushing the meat with these pan juices whenever you check on the roast.

3 After 1 hour at the lower temperature, check the roast with a quick-read thermometer; insert it into the center in a couple different places to make sure you get an accurate reading. When the roast is ready is will read 140°F for medium rare. Remove and transfer the meat to a platter to rest (it will rise another 5 degrees as it sits).

4 Put the roasting pan on the stove over 1 or 2 burners over medium-high heat. If there is at least about 1 cup liquid in it, leave it; if the pan is almost dry, add 1 cup liquid. Bring the juices to a boil, scraping up any browned bits from the bottom of the pan. When the sauce is reduced to about ¾ cup, stir in the butter if you're using it.

5 Slice the roast crosswise into slices as thick as you like and serve the slices drizzled with the sauce.

Don't forget to season the ends.

RUBBING WITH HERBS They help form a crust that both seasons the meat and keeps the interior moist.

FORMING THE CRUST High heat at the beginning helps crisp and dry the outside of the roast.

Tips

▶ Pork roasts are usually cut from the loin. Boneless cuts are extremely convenient, but they dry out a little more quickly than the bone-in kind, so look for a piece that has a layer of fat on the outside to help keep the meat moist while it cooks.

▶ If the roast comes tied with string, great. If not, don't worry. It's fine to roast it untied.

▶ Choose a pork-friendly herb like rosemary, parsley, mint, thyme, oregano, or sage. Or use a combination; garlic is a must.

Variations

▶ **Roast Pork Tenderloin:** Prepare two tenderloins since they're much smaller than a loin roast; put them on a rack in the roasting pan. Roast for only 5 minutes at 450°F, followed by 15 to 25 minutes at 325°F. Check for doneness frequently because these are lean and will start to dry out as soon as they're cooked.

Learn More

▶ Pork Basics (page 284), Roasting (page 33), Trimming Fat from a Roast (page 302), Chopping Herbs (page 78), Chicken Stock (page 154), Stock Options (page 156)

BASTING THE ROAST Once you lower the heat and add the wine, brush with the pan juices to help thicken the crust and season the roast.

REDUCING THE SAUCE Make sure there is a good amount of liquid in the pan to start; everyone loves sauce, so you don't want to come up short.

Pork Stew with Chinese Flavors

Easier than beef stew, more exotic, and really delicious.

TIME **2 to 3 hours,
      mostly unattended**
MAKES **4 servings**

**2 pounds boneless pork
shoulder, cut into 2-inch
chunks**

**3 cups chicken, beef, or
vegetable stock or water**

**2 tablespoons soy sauce,
or more to taste**

**1 tablespoon dark
sesame oil**

**3 large or 4 medium
carrots, cut into large
chunks**

**1 inch fresh ginger, cut
crosswise into thin coins**

**1 or 2 small fresh hot green
chiles (like Thai), minced**

10 garlic cloves

**Salt and freshly ground
black pepper**

**¼ cup chopped fresh
cilantro leaves for garnish**

**¼ cup chopped scallions
for garnish**

1 Put the pork, stock, soy sauce, sesame oil, carrots, ginger, chiles, garlic, and some salt and pepper in a large pot. Bring to a boil, then adjust the heat so the mixture bubbles steadily but not furiously. Cover and cook, stirring every 30 minutes or so, until the meat is very tender and just about falling apart—1½ to 2 hours.

2 Transfer the meat and vegetables to a large bowl with a slotted spoon and turn the heat under the pot juices to high. Continue cooking until the liquid has thickened slightly and reduced to a cup or even less—you want the liquid to be the consistency of thin gravy.

3 Lower the heat so the mixture bubbles gently, then return the meat and vegetables to the sauce to reheat. Taste and adjust the seasonings, adding more soy sauce if you like, and serve garnished with the cilantro and scallions.

*Barely bubbling,
then lid on.*

*If you leave the meat in
the pot while reducing
the liquid, it will get
tough and watery.*

SKIPPING THE BROWNING For braised dishes with extremely flavorful ingredients like these, you can skip searing and put everything into the pot at once.

REMOVING THE MEAT AND VEGETABLES You're bound to leave some of the vegetables behind in the sauce. No big deal.

Tips

▶ This dish can be served over white rice or tossed with soba or rice noodles. It's also good served on an eggy roll, like Sloppy Joes.

▶ If you want to try this recipe with some other meat, use any other fatty cut, like beef chuck or brisket (the cooking time might be up to 30 minutes longer), bone-in or boneless chicken thighs (about 30 minutes shorter), or lamb shoulder (about the same).

Variations

▶ **Pork Stew with Oregano and White Wine:** In Step 1, skip the soy sauce and sesame oil. Replace 1 cup of the stock with 1 cup dry white or red wine, the ginger with 1 chopped onion, and the chile with 4 sprigs fresh oregano. In Step 3, replace the cilantro and scallions with ¼ cup chopped fresh parsley leaves. Serve the stew with boiled potatoes or buttered noodles.

Learn More

▶ Pork Basics (page 284), Braising (page 31), Chicken Stock (page 154), Stock Options (page 156), preparing ginger (page 222), Preparing Chiles (page 276)

RETURNING THE MEAT AND VEGETABLES Once the liquid has reduced to the consistency of a thin gravy, stir the pork and vegetables back in to warm and coat them in the sauce.

PREPARING SCALLIONS After trimming the tops and bottoms, remove any tough outer layers. Slice crosswise into lengths of any size. For small bits, chop with a rocking motion, as for herbs.

Barbecued Spareribs in the Oven

Crisp, sticky, and tender. And you learn to make barbecue sauce in the bargain.

TIME 2¼ to 4 hours,
      mostly unattended
MAKES 6 to 8 servings

2 medium racks pork
spareribs (about 6 pounds)

Salt and freshly ground
black pepper

2 teaspoons ground cumin

2 teaspoons paprika

2 cups ketchup

½ cup dry red wine or water

¼ cup wine vinegar or rice
vinegar

1 tablespoon
Worcestershire sauce

1 tablespoon chili powder

1 small onion, chopped

1 tablespoon minced garlic

Hot sauce, optional

*Never underestimate
the power of ketchup.*

1 Heat the oven to 250°F. Put the ribs in a large rimmed baking sheet or roasting pan. Sprinkle salt and pepper over all sides and rub them in a little bit. Put the pan in the oven.

2 Cook the ribs, turning them every 30 minutes or so, until they release most of their fat and start to look meaty and dry, 2 to 3 hours, depending on how fatty they are. You'll know they're ready when a fork slides in and out of the meat easily but the meat is not falling off the bones. Remove the pan from the oven and turn the heat up to 400°F.

3 While the ribs are roasting, make the barbecue sauce. Combine the cumin, paprika, ketchup, wine, vinegar, Worcestershire, chili powder, onion, and garlic in a small saucepan over medium-high

heat. Bring to a boil, then lower the heat so the mixture bubbles gently but steadily. Cook, stirring occasionally, until the onion softens and the flavors blend, 10 to 20 minutes. Taste and add a little salt, pepper, and hot sauce if you like. Remove the pot from the heat.

4 Spoon most of the fat out of the roasting pan, leaving behind a thin film on the bottom. When the meat is cool enough to handle, cut between the bones to separate the ribs, brush generously on all sides with barbecue sauce, and return the pan to the oven. Cook, turning the ribs every 5 minutes or so, until they become crisp and charred in places, 15 to 20 minutes. Serve hot or at room temperature with any remaining sauce on the side.

MAKING BARBECUE SAUCE You'll know when it's ready: It will look a lot like bottled sauce. (It'll taste a lot better.)

RECOGNIZING DONENESS When the ribs are ready to sauce, they'll be semicrisp and leave behind a load of fat.

Tips

▶ Buy trimmed spareribs—sometimes called *St. Louis cut*—so they lie flat and get super-crisp and are esier to cut.

▶ Figure about a pound per person, though less is fine if there's going to be a lot of other food on the table. Or serve as a party snack; this recipe yields 22 to 26 ribs.

▶ Real barbecued ribs are cooked over a low, slow indirect fire and require many hours of attention. This oven technique lets you cook them thoroughly without fussing (you can do this up to 2 days in advance). Then you sauce and brown them at the last minute so they're tender inside and crisp outside.

Variations

▶ **Barbecued Baby Back Ribs in the Oven:** Follow the recipe, but reduce the cooking time in Step 2 to 1 to 1½ hours.

▶ **Asian-Style Barbecue Sauce:** Keep the ketchup as a base and replace the wine with white wine or sake; use rice vinegar instead of wine vinegar and soy sauce instead of Worcestershire. Instead of chili powder, try Chinese 5-spice seasoning. Keep the onion, garlic, and hot sauce and stir in 1 tablespoon dark sesame oil after you remove the sauce from the heat.

Learn More
▶ Pork Basics (page 284)

CUTTING UP THE RACK When the racks are cool enough to handle, separate them for eating by cutting down firmly on the meaty part between each rib.

FINISHING THE RIBS Brush or smear the pieces with sauce on all sides. Then wait for the oven to come to 400°F and pop them in for a final crisping.

Oven-Seared Lamb Chops

Using the oven gives you perfect lamb chops with less work and far less mess.

TIME   **20 to 30 minutes**
MAKES   **4 servings**

---

1 garlic clove, optional

2 pounds bone-in lamb chops (any kind, at least 1 inch thick)

Salt and freshly ground black pepper

2 lemons, quartered, for serving

1 Turn the kitchen fan on and, if you can, open a window. Heat the oven to its maximum temperature, ideally 500°F, and set a rack in the lowest possible position (if you can, put it directly on the oven floor). Set a large ovenproof skillet on the rack and let it heat in the oven until it is almost smoking, 5 to 15 minutes, depending on your oven.

2 While the pan is heating, cut the garlic clove in half if you're using it and rub it all over the meat. Carefully remove the heated pan from the oven, sprinkle its surface with a generous pinch of salt, add as many of the chops as will fit without overcrowding, and immediately return the pan to the oven.

3 Roast the chops until seared and dark brown underneath; they're ready to turn when they release from the pan easily, 2 to 5 minutes, depending on the thickness of the chops. Cook on the other side to the desired doneness, another 2 to 5 minutes; start checking the inside with a sharp knife after 2 minutes. Remove the chops from the pan, sprinkle with pepper, and let them rest for at least 5 minutes; if you're cooking in batches, pour any juices over the meat and repeat with the remaining chops. Serve with the lemon.

If you had added the garlic to the pan instead of rubbing it over the meat, it would burn immediately.

My favorite are shoulder chops, which have the most complex flavor and texture by far. (They're also the least expensive!)

KNOWING YOUR LAMB CHOPS
Starting at the top, clockwise: loin chop, shoulder chop, rib chop.

HEATING THE PAN Both the pan and the oven will get incredibly hot, so wear a heavy oven mitt and take your time.

Tips

▶ Lamb chops can come from the ribs, loin, or shoulder. Rib and loin chops are both bone in with a small amount of fat and cook up quite tender. They're best eaten rare to medium-rare. Since they're small, figure 2 or more per person. Rib chops are the most familiar: They have little bones (like handles) sticking out of the ends, and when they're still attached in a single roast, they're known as *rack of lamb*. If you can, get them 2 ribs thick so they don't cook too fast. Loin chops are like mini T-bone steaks with the bone in the center. Chops cut from the shoulder, which are less expensive, fattier, and more flavorful, are best cooked to medium so more of the gristle softens. They're much bigger than other chops, so 1 per person is usually enough.

▶ The key to browning—as opposed to steaming—the chops is to first make sure the pan is indeed smoking hot; then choose a coarse salt, like kosher, which will dissolve more slowly than table salt.

Learn More
▶ Roasting (page 33), Trimming (page 16)

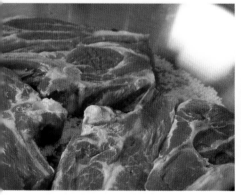

ADDING THE CHOPS TO THE PAN
The salt sprinkled onto the bottom of the pan will stick to the chops and form a flavorful crust on the outside.

TURNING THE CHOPS It won't take more than a couple minutes for the chops to form a deep brown crust and release from the pan; once they do, flip them over.

Lamb Curry

The basic, classic, and altogether Indian dish, far simpler to make than you might think.

TIME 1½ to 2½ hours, mostly unattended

MAKES 4 to 6 servings

2 tablespoons vegetable oil

2 pounds boneless or 3 pounds bone-in lamb shoulder, cut into 2-inch chunks

Salt and freshly ground black pepper

1 large onion, halved and sliced

1 tablespoon minced garlic

1 tablespoon minced fresh ginger or 1 teaspoon ground

2 tablespoons curry powder

½ teaspoon cayenne, optional

1 cup chicken or vegetable stock or water, or more as needed

½ cup yogurt

¼ cup chopped fresh cilantro leaves for garnish

1 Put the oil in a large pot over medium-high heat. When it's hot, add about half of the meat and sprinkle with salt and pepper. Cook, adjusting the heat and turning the pieces as needed so the meat doesn't burn, until it's nicely browned on all sides, 10 to 20 minutes. As the meat browns, transfer it to a platter and continue adding, seasoning, and cooking pieces until all the meat is browned.

2 Pour off all but 2 tablespoons of the fat and turn the heat down to medium. Add the onion, sprinkle with a little more salt and pepper, and cook, stirring occasionally, until the vegetables begin to soften, 3 to 5 minutes. Add the garlic, ginger, curry powder, and cayenne if you're using it and cook, stirring constantly, until fragrant, about 1 minute.

3 Stir in the stock, scraping up any bits from the bottom of the pot; add the browned meat. The braising liquid should come about halfway up the sides of the meat; if it doesn't, add more liquid. Raise the heat and bring to a boil; then lower it so that the mixture barely bubbles. Cover and cook, stirring every 30 minutes and adding small amounts of liquid if necessary, until the meat slides off a fork, at least 45 minutes and more likely up to 90.

4 If the curry looks too watery, remove the lid, raise the heat a bit, and cook, stirring frequently, until it thickens. If it looks too dry, add a little more stock or water and raise the heat until bubbly. Remove from the heat and stir in the yogurt. Taste and adjust the seasoning, garnish with the cilantro, and serve.

You can brown and cook the bone along with the meat for extra flavor.

CUTTING LAMB If you've got a bone-in piece, cut the meat into large pieces, as close to the bone as possible; cut those into chunks.

WORKING IN BATCHES Give the chunks of meat (and bone if you've got one) space so they brown, not steam. Rotate pieces in and out of the pan as they cook.

Tips

▸ Lamb shoulder is just like pork shoulder: fatty. Use already cut stew meat if that's easier for you to find. To get whole shoulder, you'll probably need to visit a butcher. If you're cutting the meat yourself, trim big pieces of fat away as you make the chunks, being careful not to remove too much of the lean at the same time.

Variations

▸ **Chicken Curry with Vegetables:** In Step 1, replace the lamb shoulder with about 3 pounds bone-in chicken parts. Follow the recipe, but in Step 3, after the mixture has cooked for about 15 minutes, add 1 pound waxy red or white potatoes, peeled and cut into 2-inch chunks, and 3 large or 4 medium carrots, peeled and cut into 2-inch chunks. When the chicken and vegetables are tender, in 20 to 30 minutes, stir in 1 cup fresh or frozen peas. Continue with the recipe.

▸ **Lamb or Chicken Curry with Coconut Milk:** In Step 2, pour off all the fat after the lamb is browned and cook the sliced onion in 3 tablespoons butter. In Step 4, use 1 can coconut milk instead of the stock and skip the yogurt in Step 4. If the curry starts to look dry as it cooks, add stock or water.

Learn More

▸ Braising (page 31), preparing ginger (page 222), Chicken Stock (page 154), Stock Options (page 156)

COOKING SPICES UNTIL FRAGRANT Heating the curry powder and other spices helps develop deeper flavor and removes that raw taste.

FINISHING THE CURRY Stir in the yogurt until it's fully combined (the curry will turn a few shades lighter), then serve right away. It's okay if the yogurt curdles.

Roast Leg of Lamb with Vegetables

Beautiful, wonderful, and always a welcome classic at holidays.

TIME **2 hours, mostly unattended**

MAKES **6 to 8 servings**

---

1 bone-in leg of lamb
(5 to 7 pounds)

2 pounds waxy red or white
potatoes, peeled and cut
into 2-inch chunks

3 large or 4 medium
carrots, cut into 2-inch
chunks

2 onions, quartered

¼ cup olive oil, or more
as needed

Salt and freshly ground
black pepper

1 Heat the oven to 425°F. Remove the thickest pieces of fat from the lamb's surface with a sharp knife. Scatter the vegetables in the pan and drizzle with the oil. Put the meat on top; rub the meat all over with a generous sprinkle of salt and pepper.

2 Roast the lamb for 30 minutes, then turn the heat down to 350°F. At the same time, check the vegetables; if they seem to be drying out, drizzle with a bit more oil.

3 After another 30 minutes, start checking the internal temperature of the lamb with a quick-read thermometer. Try several places—especially the thickest parts—to make sure you get an accurate reading, and make sure you don't hit the bone.

4 Continue to check every 10 minutes, spooning the pan juices over the vegetables to keep them moist. The total cooking time will be between 60 and 90 minutes, depending on the size of the roast. When the internal temperature at the thickest point is 125°F, the meat is still very rare, but it will heat up to 130°F (rare) as it rests. (And other sections will be more done.)

5 Remove the pan from the oven and let the meat rest for at least 5 minutes before carving. If the vegetables aren't quite done, return them to the oven for 5 to 10 more minutes. Serve slices with the vegetables and pan juices.

Work with the blade pointing away from you in case it slips.

TRIMMING FAT FROM A ROAST
It's much better to leave on a chunk of fat than to accidentally cut off a chunk of meat, so don't get too ambitious.

ROASTING WITH VEGETABLES
Since the potatoes help keep the lamb off the bottom of the pan and out of the pan juices, you don't need a rack for this roast.

Tips

▶ With lamb, all the temperatures for doneness are about 5 degrees lower than for beef. (And remember, all meat keeps cooking as it rests.) So if you want rare meat (130°F), remove it at 125°F; medium-rare (135°F) at 130°F; and so on. But don't let the meat roast too much longer than very rare at the thickest part or you'll have nothing pink left to offer. The great thing about leg of lamb is that its odd shape means that if the thickest parts are rare, the thinnest are well done, so everyone is happy.

▶ If possible, get a leg of lamb without the lower part—known as the shank—attached; it's cheaper this way and will fit easily in a roasting pan. If you can only buy the whole thing, ask someone at the store to remove it for you anyway and save it for later; it's good for braising.

Variations

▶ **Boneless Roast Leg of Lamb with Vegetables:** This cut usually comes rolled and tied with string or netting. A 3- to 5- pound roast will serve 6 to 8 people. Start checking for doneness in Step 2 after 30 minutes at high heat. The vegetables won't be ready when the roast is, so remove the meat and put the pan back in the oven until they are. To carve, remove the string and cut crosswise.

Learn More

▶ Roasting (page 33), types of potatoes (page 235)

REMOVING 3 BIG PIECES Hold the leg at an angle and cut downward below your hand until you hit the bone. Work your knife along the bone to remove a big slab. Turn the roast and repeat twice.

CUTTING SLICES Put one slab of meat flat on the board and cut downward, as thickly or thinly as you like. (You can save the bone for soup.)

Poultry

Chicken is mild tasting, inexpensive, relatively low in fat, and fast cooking, all of which contribute to Americans' eating more chicken over the course of the year than any other meat. (And don't forget, we devote an entire holiday to turkey.) So it makes sense that knowing the best ways to season and cook birds will expand your repertoire in ways everyone will appreciate.

It's easy enough, because you can use any cooking technique—grilling, broiling, stir-frying, roasting, sautéing, braising, and frying—with chicken. And I'll introduce them all here, while explaining which cooking methods work best with different parts of the bird.

These recipes also demonstrate smart, fast ways to season chicken (and turkey). And since poultry has such a mild taste, I'll introduce simple companion ingredients that enhance the flavor without overpowering it. You'll learn how to make some super-simple pan sauces too, and the extra section on Thanksgiving takes the fear out of cooking turkey—with all the trimmings.

If you're already comfortable working with chicken and turkey, use this chapter to test your boundaries: Change up your go-to seasonings, try new techniques or ingredients, and sharpen your butchering and carving skills.

Chicken Basics

Preparing Chicken

TRIM EXCESS FAT Flaps of fat—common on whole birds and thigh meat—can drip and burn, so I usually trim them. Stretch the skin with one hand to make it taut. Then, working away from you, cut through it with kitchen scissors (or saw through with a paring knife).

BLOT CHICKEN DRY Pat whole birds or individual parts with a paper towel to remove moisture and make sure the meat browns properly. (You can skip this step if you're steaming or boiling the chicken.)

Chicken Doneness and Safety

You want to cook your chicken enough to kill anything in the meat that might make you sick—like salmonella and other harmful bacteria—but not so much that it dries out. Try to catch the meat when it just turns from pink to opaque: Either insert a quick-read thermometer into the thickest parts of the breast and thigh (avoiding the bone) or cut a slit with a sharp knife and peek inside. The government (overcautious, in my opinion) recommends that chicken be cooked to 165°F—a temperature that virtually guarantees dryness, especially with breast meat. I suggest removing the chicken when the thermometer registers at least 155°F but less than 165°F. (If you like your chicken well done, steer toward the higher end of that range.)

BREAST

LEG

THIGH

WING

Chicken Lingo

"Natural" Virtually meaningless on labels, since the government's definition doesn't tell you anything specific about how a chicken was actually raised, fed, or processed. This description can—and is—used for a whole spectrum of chickens from regular supermarket birds to ones of higher quality.

Free Range A somewhat better choice: These birds technically must "have access to outdoor space" to be labeled this way. But unless you're provided (or ask for) more info, you're still lacking helpful details about their living conditions or diet.

Organic This certification is defined and regulated by the United States Department of Agriculture (USDA). It won't tell you everything, but it indicates the birds can move around at least some of the time, aren't given antibiotics or other drugs, and don't eat genetically modified feed.

Heritage or Local Neither is a government-recognized labeling distinction, but the terms are used in the same way as *heirloom vegetables*, and indicate chicken varieties that are valued for their taste and texture. You can find them at farmers' markets, some natural food stores, and directly from producers; be prepared to pay more for them.

Grilled or Broiled Boneless Chicken

The fastest, most flavorful way to cook boneless chicken.

TIME   **20 minutes**
MAKES   **4 servings**

4 large boneless, skinless chicken breasts (about 1½ pounds)

3 tablespoons olive oil

Salt and freshly ground black pepper

1 or 2 lemons, quartered, for serving, optional

1 Prepare a grill or turn on the broiler; the heat should be medium-high and the rack about 4 inches from the heat source. If the thickness of the breasts is noticeably uneven when you spread them out, put each between 2 sheets of plastic wrap and pound each breast to uniform thickness; blot them dry with paper towels.

2 If you're grilling, put the chicken in a pan or on a plate, toss with the oil, and sprinkle with salt and pepper. If you're broiling, do the same on a rimmed baking sheet. If you have time, cover and marinate the chicken for an hour to develop the flavor.

3 Put the chicken directly on the grill grates or in the pan under the broiler and cook until the side facing the heat browns, 3 to 5 minutes. Turn and repeat on the other side. To check for doneness, cut into a piece with a thin-bladed knife; the center should be white or ever so slightly pink. Serve right away or at room temperature, with lemon if you like.

You could also use a mallet or the bottom of a cast-iron skillet.

CHOOSING BONELESS CHICKEN
Thighs (left) are dark meat; so they're fatty, delicious, and take longer to cook. Breasts (right) are like mini white-meat roasts. Tenders (center) cook super quickly.

POUNDING BONELESS CHICKEN
For even cooking, spread the meat out on plastic wrap, cover with more plastic, then pound until the thickest part is the same height as the thinnest.

RECOGNIZING WHEN TO TURN
The first side should be nicely browned on the surface. (If grilling, the meat will release easily from the grates.)

Tips

▶ Thin, boneless cuts of meat are also known as *cutlets*. Boneless breasts are done so quickly that they're almost impossible to undercook; boneless thighs take a few minutes longer.

▶ If you like chicken salad (page 336), this is a good basic recipe for cooking the meat.

Variations

▶ **Grilled or Broiled Boneless Chicken Thighs:** Follow the recipe, but let them cook a little longer, 7 to 10 minutes per side, depending on their thickness.

▶ **Grilled or Broiled Chicken Tenders:** Follow the recipe; they'll take only 2 or 3 minutes per side to cook.

▶ **Grilled or Broiled Boneless Chicken with Herbs:** Rub herbs or spices into the chicken along with the salt and pepper. Choose whatever you like; the quantity depends on your taste, but a good rule of thumb is 1 tablespoon chopped fresh herb leaves or 1 teaspoon ground spices.

Learn More

▶ Chicken Basics (page 306), Grilling (page 35), Broiling (page 34), Building Flavor (page 12)

PEEKING AND CHECKING With thin cutlets like this, a thermometer isn't as reliable as making a small cut and looking inside occasionally.

RECOGNIZING DONENESS Chicken goes from raw to done quickly. The piece on top is opaque and still juicy. The piece shown on the bottom is still raw inside.

Perfectly cooked chicken has just turned from pink to white.

Stir-Fried Chicken with Broccoli

Infinite possibilities—all faster (and better) than takeout.

TIME **30 minutes**
MAKES **4 servings**

---

1 pound broccoli

2 tablespoons minced garlic

1 tablespoon grated or minced fresh ginger

1 medium onion, halved and sliced

½ cup water, chicken stock, or dry white wine

1 pound boneless, skinless chicken breasts or thighs

¼ cup vegetable oil

Salt and freshly ground black pepper

1 teaspoon sugar, optional

2 tablespoons soy sauce

1 Trim the broccoli and cut it into 1- to 2-inch pieces. Make sure the garlic, ginger, and onion are ready in advance, as well as the liquid.

2 Blot the chicken dry with paper towels and cut it into bite-sized chunks roughly the same size.

3 Put 2 tablespoons of the oil in a large skillet over medium-high heat. When it's hot, add the chicken, sprinkle with salt and pepper, and stir it once, then let it sit until it starts to sizzle and brown before stirring again, at least 1 minute. Scatter the garlic, ginger, and onion on top. Cook, stirring occasionally, until the chicken has lost its pink color and the vegetables are soft, 3 to 5 minutes. Remove everything from the pan with a slotted spoon.

4 Add the remaining 2 tablespoons oil to the pan, swirl it, then add the broccoli right away and raise the heat to high. Cook, stirring frequently, until the broccoli starts to char in some spots and turns bright green, 1 or 2 minutes. Add ¼ cup of the water and stir to scrape up any browned bits from the bottom of the pan. Taste a piece of broccoli; it should be just tender but not at all mushy. If not, keep cooking for another minute or two.

5 Return the chicken mixture to the pan and toss once or twice. Add the sugar if you like a little sweetness, the soy sauce, and the remaining ¼ cup water if the mixture looks dry; toss again. Taste and adjust the seasoning and serve.

CUTTING BITE-SIZED PIECES
By *bite-sized* I mean ½- to ¾-inch chunks.

STIRRING OR NOT You don't need to stir in the vegetables right away if you want the chicken to brown. If you like it lighter colored, with a springy, less chewy texture, keep it moving as it cooks.

Tips

▶ If you're making rice or noodles, get them going before you start the stir-fry. That's how fast this dish comes together.

Variations

▶ **Stir-Fried Chicken with Vegetables:** Try this recipe with other sliced, chopped, or whole vegetables, like mushrooms, snow peas, carrots, celery, greens, bell peppers, bean sprouts, or mixed vegetables. Their exact cooking times depend on how small the pieces are and how firm they are raw, so be sure to taste frequently in Step 4.

Learn More

▶ Chicken Basics (page 306), Stir-Frying (page 29), preparing broccoli (page 182), mincing garlic (page 20), preparing ginger (page 222), Chicken Stock (page 154)

Water is fine here, but chicken stock and white wine—or even beer or sake—are more flavorful alternatives.

STIR-FRYING VEGETABLES The idea is to sear the broccoli, then add a little liquid, which helps it steam a bit. The result is crisp-tender. Tasting is the only way to know when it's done.

ADDING MORE LIQUID I prefer stir-fries that are well coated with a little sauce. Add enough liquid to get the consistency you like.

Chicken Cutlets with Quick Pan Sauce

Quick, dependable, rich, and rather elegant.

TIME   20 to 30 minutes
MAKES   4 servings

1 cup all-purpose flour

1½ pounds boneless, skinless chicken breasts, thighs, or tenders

Salt and freshly ground black pepper

2 tablespoons olive oil

3 tablespoons butter

½ cup dry white wine

½ cup water, chicken stock, or vegetable stock

¼ cup chopped fresh parsley leaves, plus 2 tablespoons for garnish

1 lemon, quartered, for serving

1 Heat the oven to 200°F. Put the flour on a plate or in a shallow bowl next to the stove. If necessary, put each cutlet between 2 sheets of sheet of plastic wrap and pound to uniform thickness; blot the chicken dry with a paper towel and sprinkle with salt and pepper.

2 Put the oil and 2 tablespoons of the butter in a large skillet over medium-high heat. When the butter has melted, turn a piece of the chicken in the flour to coat it on all sides; shake off any excess. Add the floured chicken to the pan, then repeat with the next piece; work in batches if necessary to avoid crowding the pan.

3 Cook, adjusting the heat as needed so that the fat is always bubbling but the chicken doesn't burn. After 2 minutes, rotate the chicken so that the outside edges are moved toward the center and vice versa (don't flip them; you want the same side in contact with the fat). When the bottom of each piece is brown, after 3 to 4 minutes, turn them over.

4 Cook on the second side, adjusting the heat as described in Step 3, until the chicken is firm to the touch but still a bit pink inside, another 3 to 4 minutes. To check for doneness, cut into a piece with a thin-bladed knife and take a peek. Transfer the chicken to an ovenproof platter and put it in the oven.

5 Add the wine to the skillet, keeping the heat at medium-high. Let it bubble away as you stir and scrape the bottom of the pan, until about half the wine has evaporated, a minute or two. Pour in the water and continue to stir until the liquid has thickened slightly and reduced to ¼ cup, another 2 or 3 minutes. Add the remaining tablespoon of butter to the skillet and swirl the pan around until the butter melts; turn off the heat.

6 Remove the chicken from the oven, and if any juices have accumulated on the platter, add them to the skillet along with the ¼ cup parsley. Stir, taste the sauce, and adjust the seasoning. Spoon the sauce over the chicken, garnish with the remaining 2 tablespoons parsley, and serve with the lemon quarters.

DREDGING IN FLOUR Pace yourself: Dredging the pieces and adding them to the pan one at a time helps prevent the coating from getting soggy and keeps the oil hot.

Tips
▶ This is a recipe for which it helps to be organized. Especially until you get the hang of dredging, set up everything before you start.

Variations
▶ **Any Cutlets with Quick Pan Sauce:** Try turkey, pork, or veal cutlets; or fish fillets here. Cooking times will vary by up to a couple of minutes per side, but the clues for knowing when to turn them and how to recognize doneness remain the same.
▶ **Chicken Cutlets with Balsamic Sauce:** In Step 5, stir in 1 tablespoon balsamic vinegar just before adding the butter.

Learn More
▶ Chicken Basics (page 306), Pounding Boneless Chicken (page 308), Chicken Stock (page 154), Full-Flavored Vegetable Stock (page 152), Chopping Herbs (page 78)

TIMING AND SPACING If you overcrowd the pan, the chicken won't brown; it's okay to cook a batch and then repeat. If the oil stops sizzling and you start to see steam, the pan is overcrowded.

ROTATING AS YOU COOK As soon as the chicken starts to brown in places, rotate (don't flip) each piece so that the outside edges are now at the pan's center.

DEGLAZING THE PAN TO MAKE SAUCE Let the wine bubble away while you scrape the browned bits from the bottom of the pan.

Roasted Chicken Cutlets

Crisp bread crumbs on top, tender and juicy inside—without stovetop cooking.

TIME   **30 to 40 minutes**
MAKES   **4 servings**

2 tablespoons butter, melted, plus butter for greasing the pan

1½ pounds boneless, skinless chicken breasts, tenders, or thighs

1 cup bread crumbs, preferably fresh

¼ cup chopped fresh parsley leaves

Salt and freshly ground black pepper

1 egg

2 lemons, quartered, for serving

1 Heat the oven to 400°F and grease a rimmed baking sheet with a little butter. If necessary, spread the chicken between 2 pieces of plastic wrap and pound each to uniform thickness; blot them dry with a paper towel.

2 Combine the bread crumbs, melted butter, and parsley in a shallow bowl and sprinkle with salt and pepper; toss until mixed. Lightly beat the egg in another shallow bowl.

3 Dip the smooth side of each chicken breast first in egg and then in the bread crumb mixture, pressing down to make sure the bread crumbs stick. Put each breast, crumb side up, on the baking sheet. If there's any leftover topping, sprinkle it on top of the breasts and press down again so it sticks.

4 Put the chicken in the oven and roast until the cutlets are firm to the touch with little or no pink inside, 15 to 25 minutes, depending on thickness. To check for doneness, cut into a piece with a thin-bladed knife and take a peek. To serve, transfer the cutlets to plates and serve with lemon.

This is a topping, rather than a coating.

SEASONING BREAD CRUMBS Toss just enough to evenly distribute the bread, butter, parsley, salt, and pepper.

DIPPING IN EGG The egg acts like the glue for the bread crumbs, so make sure to coat the smooth side completely.

SPACING PROPERLY Spread them out a bit so they brown and your work is done until the cutlets finish cooking.

Tips

▶ For crunch and flavor it's hard to beat your own bread crumbs, made from good-quality rustic-style bread. But coarse panko (or Japanese-style bread crumbs) are a solid second choice, and they're available in supermarkets. Avoid finely ground store-bought bread crumbs; they taste like dust.

Variations

▶ **4 Different Dredging Mixtures:**
1 Add ¼ cup freshly grated Parmesan to the bread crumb mixture.
2 Replace the parsley with 1 tablespoon chopped fresh tarragon, oregano, rosemary, cilantro, or mint leaves.
3 Skip the parsley and add ½ cup ground or finely chopped nuts to the bread crumb mixture.
4 Replace the egg with ¼ cup miso. Spread a thin coating of the paste all over the chicken, then follow the recipe from Step 3.

Learn More

▶ Chicken Basics (page 306), Pounding Boneless Chicken (page 308), Fresh Bread Crumbs (page 386), Chopping Herbs (page 78), miso (page 145)

Peanutty Chicken Kebabs

Reminiscent of Thai satay, minus the hassle of pounding the chicken until thin.

TIME **40 minutes, plus time to marinate**

MAKES **4 servings**

1½ pounds boneless, skinless chicken thighs

1 onion, roughly chopped

2 tablespoons minced garlic

¼ cup fresh cilantro leaves

Grated zest and juice of 1 lime

1 tablespoon vegetable oil, plus more for greasing

1 tablespoon soy sauce

¼ teaspoon cayenne

2 tablespoons peanut butter

Salt

2 limes, quartered, for serving

If you're using wooden skewers, start soaking them in warm water now.

1 You'll need 4 long or 8 short skewers. If you're using wooden ones, soak them in warm water while you prepare the chicken. Cut the meat into 1½-inch chunks.

2 For the marinade, put the onion in a food processor or blender along with the garlic, 2 tablespoons of the cilantro, the lime zest and juice, oil, soy sauce, cayenne, peanut butter, and a pinch of salt. Purée the mixture until relatively smooth, adding a few drops of water if necessary to keep the machine moving. Put the chicken in a large bowl, pour the marinade over it, and cover it with plastic wrap. Let it sit for at least a few minutes or up to an hour at room temperature or refrigerate it for up to 12 hours.

3 When you're ready to cook, prepare a grill or turn on the broiler; the heat should be medium-high and the rack about 4 inches from the heat source. If you're broiling, grease a large rimmed baking sheet with some oil. Thread the chicken onto the skewers, leaving a little space between pieces.

4 To grill, put the kebabs on the grates directly over the fire. To broil, put them on the prepared pan under the heat. Cook, turning once or twice with tongs, until the chicken is cooked through, 12 to 15 minutes total. To check for doneness, cut into a piece with a sharp, thin-bladed knife; the center should be white or slightly pink. Garnish with the remaining 2 tablespoons cilantro and serve with the lime wedges.

CUTTING CHICKEN INTO CHUNKS Try to keep the pieces fairly uniform in size for even cooking.

MARINATING CHICKEN IN A THICK MIXTURE Toss the chicken well so all the pieces are coated with the marinade.

Tips

▸ Chicken thighs are much more forgiving when grilled or broiled than white meat.

▸ As you thread the skewers, be sure to leave about ¼ inch between pieces of meat so the heat can circulate. For easier turning, run 2 parallel skewers through the pieces. You can incorporate vegetables, but it's easier to control cooking times if you put different ingredients on separate skewers. If you want to mix meat and vegetables, choose vegetables that you expect will cook in about the same time as the meat.

Variations

▸ **Mediterranean Chicken Kebabs:** Skip all of the ingredients except the chicken and the salt. Instead, in Step 2, combine 3 tablespoons olive oil with 1 teaspoon balsamic or sherry vinegar, ½ cup chopped fresh basil leaves, and a pinch of salt and pepper (there is no need to purée the marinade). Marinate the chicken in this mixture as described in Step 2, then thread the chicken onto the skewers alternately with 1 pint whole cherry tomatoes. Grill or broil as described in Step 4.

Learn More

▸ Chicken Basics (page 306), mincing garlic (page 20), Chopping Herbs (page 78), Grilled or Broiled Beef Kebabs (page 272)

SKEWERING CHICKEN The pieces will brown properly only if there's a little space between them.

COOKING CHICKEN KEBABS
The meat on a single skewer will sometimes spin around a little bit. That's okay; just turn the individual pieces over so both sides cook evenly.

Roasted Buffalo Chicken Wings

All the flavor of bar food, easily done at home.

TIME 1½ hours,
 mostly unattended
MAKES 6 to 8 servings

1 cup yogurt, sour cream, or mayonnaise

½ cup crumbled blue cheese

2 teaspoons fresh lemon juice

Salt and freshly ground black pepper

1 to 4 tablespoons hot sauce

4 tablespoons (½ stick) butter, melted

2 tablespoons wine vinegar

1 tablespoon minced garlic

3 pounds chicken wings

2 tablespoons vegetable oil

8 to 12 celery stalks, cut into sticks

1 Heat the oven to 400°F. To make the dressing, whisk together the yogurt, blue cheese, and lemon juice and sprinkle with salt and pepper. Refrigerate it while you make the wings or for up to a few hours. Combine the hot sauce, butter, vinegar, and garlic in a small bowl.

2 If the wings are not already divided into 2 pieces, cut them apart through the center of the joint with a chef's knife or scissors. If the pointed tips are still attached to the lower sections, remove them to save for stock or discard.

3 Put the chicken wings in a large roasting pan, drizzle with the oil, and sprinkle with salt and pepper. Toss to coat, then spread the wings out in a single layer. Put the pan in the oven and roast, undisturbed, until the bottom is coated with fat and the wings are beginning to brown, 25 to 35 minutes. Brush the wings with some of the drippings, then carefully spoon out as much of the liquid as possible. If the wings are still sticking to the bottom of the pan, return them to the oven until they release easily, another 5 to 10 minutes.

4 Turn the wings over, brush again with drippings, then spoon off any more fat. Return the wings to the oven until browned and again release easily, 15 to 20 minutes.

5 Raise the oven temperature to 450°F. Spoon off fat for the last time. Drizzle the wings with the hot sauce mixture and toss to coat; spread them out in a single layer, and return them to the oven. Cook, tossing once or twice, until crisp all over, 5 to 10 more minutes. Serve hot or at room temperature, with the celery and blue cheese dressing.

Sharp shears make this even quicker work.

SEPARATING CHICKEN WINGS To separate the section of the wings easily, be assertive when you cut through the center of the joint.

Tips

▶ For the tangiest, lightest dipping sauce, choose yogurt. Sour cream and mayonnaise are both richer, with their own distinctive tastes. Want tang and richness? Use a combo.

▶ Hot sauce is a matter of preference. For this recipe, use as little or as much of whatever type you like.

▶ The wings will tell you when it's time to turn them: They'll release easily. If you have to yank, they're not ready.

Variations

▶ **Roasted Chicken Wings with Spicy Soy Glaze:** Skip the blue cheese dressing, hot sauce, and melted butter. Replace the vinegar with lemon juice. When you make the glazing sauce in Step 1, add 1 tablespoon minced fresh ginger, 1 minced fresh hot green chile (like Thai), ¼ cup soy sauce, and 2 tablespoons dark sesame oil. Continue with the recipe, using this sauce to coat the wings in Step 5.

Learn More

▶ Chicken Basics (page 306), cutting celery sticks for dipping (page 74)

After coating the wings, be sure to spread them out again.

SPACING WINGS FOR ROASTING As long as the wings aren't piled up on top of each other, it's okay if they overlap a little in the pan; they'll shrink.

SPOONING OFF FAT When you check the wings, tip the pan a bit and carefully spoon off the excess fat; otherwise they won't brown and crisp.

BASTING AND CRISPING Now that you've raised the temperature and added the sauce, the wings will crisp quickly, so check them frequently and turn as necessary.

Grilled or Broiled Chicken Parts

A go-to recipe for life. Change the herb and change the flavor.

TIME **30 to 50 minutes,**
depending on the
cooking method
MAKES **4 servings**

5 sprigs fresh oregano,
parsley, or thyme or a
combination

1 whole cut-up chicken or
about 3 pounds parts

Juice of 2 lemons

Salt and freshly ground
black pepper

1 lemon, quartered, for
serving

1 Either prepare a grill for indirect
cooking so that there are hot coals on
half and nothing on the other half and
put the rack about 4 inches from the
heat source or turn the broiler to high
and put the rack about 6 inches from
the heat source.

2 Pull the herb leaves from the stems
with your fingers and discard the stems.
Reserve a pinch of the leaves to use as a
garnish.

3 Put your fingers between the skin
and the meat of each piece of chicken
to loosen the skin; insert a few leaves of
the herb between the skin and the meat.
Rub the chicken all over with the lemon
juice and sprinkle it generously with salt
and pepper.

4 To grill: When the fire is ready, put
the chicken pieces skin side up on the
cool side of the grill and cover. When
the chicken fat begins to melt and drip
down, after about 10 minutes, turn the
chicken and cover again; if the fire flares
up, move the chicken to an even cooler
part of the grill or turn it with a pair of
tongs so the skin side is up again. When
the skin has lost its raw look and most
of the fat has melted, usually after 20 to
30 minutes, it's safe to move the chick-
en directly over the fire. Cook uncovered, turning now and then, until both
sides are nicely browned and the flesh
is firm and cooked through, 5 to 10 minutes longer.

To broil: Put the chicken skin side down
on a rimmed baking sheet and broil,
checking every few minutes to make
sure the pieces do not burn. If they are
cooking too fast, move the rack farther
away from the heat source. When the
chicken is nearly done, after 15 to 20
minutes, turn the pieces with tongs and
cook until the skin is brown, 5 to 10 minutes longer. Whether you broil or grill,
to check for doneness, cut into a piece
close to the bone with a sharp, thin-
bladed knife; the juices should run clear.

5 While the chicken is cooking, chop
the reserved herb leaves. Serve hot,
warm, or at room temperature, garnished with the chopped herbs and
lemon wedges.

With this technique, you
season the meat, the sea-
sonings don't burn, and
the skin stays crisp.

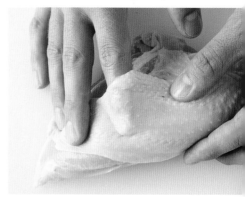

LOOSENING THE SKIN Carefully
run your fingers between the
meat and the skin to create a
space between them. Don't worry
if you tear the skin.

Tips

▶ Trust your nose when you grill or broil bone-in, skin-on chicken: If it smells like it's burning, it is—which usually means the outside will be charred while the inside is still raw. It's better to start with the skin away from the heat source and make sure the chicken is cooked through, then crisp the skin as the last step.

Variations

▶ **Grilled or Broiled Chicken Parts Teriyaki Style:** Skip the herbs and lemon juice. In Step 2, combine ⅓ cup soy sauce, ⅓ cup sake (or slightly sweet white wine), 3 tablespoons honey, 2 tablespoons sugar, 3 tablespoons water, and a sprinkle of salt and pepper in a small saucepan and put it over medium-high heat. Bring to a boil and cook for a couple minutes, until it begins to thicken. Brush the soy sauce mixture all over the chicken pieces; continue with Step 4. Every 5 minutes or so, brush the chicken pieces with a little sauce and turn them. When the meat is done, turn them once more to crisp on both sides and serve hot or at room temperature.

Learn More

▶ Chicken Basics (page 306), Grilling (page 35), Broiling (page 34), Stripping Leaves from Soft Herb Stems (page 78) or Hard Herb Stems (page 141)

INSERTING HERBS BETWEEN SKIN AND MEAT After you separate the skin from the meat, stick a few herb leaves in the gap, trying not to break through the skin.

SEASONING WITH LEMON Rub the chicken all over to help keep it moist during high-heat cooking.

TURNING THE CHICKEN It's ready to flip when it's browned, firm to the touch, and the juices are running clear.

Chicken Stew with Softened Garlic

The soft, mellow garlic is almost as good as the tender, juicy chicken.

TIME 1¼ hours,
    mostly unattended

MAKES 4 servings

---

2 tablespoons olive oil

1 whole cut-up chicken or about 3 pounds parts

Salt and freshly ground black pepper

2 large garlic bulbs, separated into cloves but not peeled

½ teaspoon ground cinnamon

¾ cup water, dry white wine, or chicken stock

1 loaf crusty bread, sliced, for serving

1 Put the oil in a large skillet over medium-high heat. When it's hot, add the chicken, skin side down. Sprinkle with salt and pepper and cook, undisturbed but adjusting the heat so the chicken sizzles but doesn't burn, until the pieces release easily from the pan, 5 to 10 minutes. Then turn and rotate them every few minutes to brown them evenly. As the chicken pieces brown, after another 5 to 10 minutes, remove them from the pan and spoon out all but about 2 tablespoons of the fat.

2 Add the garlic and cinnamon, sprinkle with more salt and pepper, and pour ½ cup of the liquid over all. Bring to a boil, then adjust the heat so the mixture bubbles gently but steadily.

Garlic fanatics: Feel free to add another bulb or even two.

3 Cover and cook for about 30 minutes, then check and add the remaining liquid if the pan looks dry. Cover and cook until the chicken and garlic are very tender, another 25 to 35 minutes. (At this point, you may refrigerate the stew for up to a day; reheat gently.) Transfer the chicken, garlic, and pan drippings to a deep platter and serve, spreading the softened garlic cloves on bread slices.

BROWNING CHICKEN PIECES
The fit is a little snug, but as long as you let the chicken brown on one side before you start moving it, you'll get a good sear.

ADDING TONS OF GARLIC It seems like a lot, but it mellows and makes a delicious sauce.

ADJUSTING THE HEAT FOR BRAISING You want a gentle but steady bubble.

Tips

▶ Searing the chicken first develops a little extra flavor and gives the skin a crisper texture, but it's not necessary. If you feel lazy, just dump all of the ingredients into the pot at once, bring the mixture to a boil, and go from there.

▶ The skins help keep the cloves intact and flavor the sauce.

▶ Bread is the simplest accompaniment for this stew, but it's also nice over boiled—and buttered—egg noodles or rice.

Variations

▶ **Braised Chicken with Shallots:** Instead of the garlic, trim and peel 10 shallots, but leave them whole. Follow the recipe.

Learn More

▶ Chicken Basics (page 306), Braising (page 31), Smarter Water (page 137), Rotating as You Cook (page 313), Eyeballing Fat in a Pan (page 324)

Braised Chicken, Mediterranean Style

A bright-tasting stew, light enough for summer.

TIME **1 hour**

MAKES **4 servings**

2 tablespoons olive oil

1 whole cut-up chicken or about 3 pounds parts

Salt and freshly ground black pepper

2 medium onions, chopped

2 anchovy fillets or 1 tablespoon drained capers, optional

1 teaspoon minced garlic

One 28-ounce can diced tomatoes (don't bother to drain)

½ cup dry white wine, chicken stock, or water

1 cup Niçoise or kalamata olives, pitted

1 tablespoon fresh thyme leaves or 1 teaspoon dried

2 tablespoons chopped fresh parsley leaves for garnish

1 Put the oil in a large skillet over medium-high heat. When it's hot, add the chicken, skin side down. Sprinkle with salt and pepper and cook, undisturbed but adjusting the heat so the chicken sizzles but doesn't burn, until the pieces release easily from the pan, 5 to 10 minutes. Then turn and rotate them every few minutes to brown them evenly. As the chicken pieces brown, after another 5 to 10 minutes, remove them from the pan.

2 Reduce the heat under the skillet to medium and pour or spoon off all but about 2 tablespoons of the fat. Add the onions and anchovies if you're using them and cook, stirring frequently, until the onions soften and the anchovies break up, 3 to 5 minutes. Add the garlic and tomatoes and turn up the heat just a little. Cook until the mixture starts to bubble and the tomato thickens a bit, 1 to 2 minutes. Pour in the wine, stir, and let the mixture bubble for another 2 minutes.

3 Add the olives and thyme, along with some pepper. (The olives are so salty that you may not need to add more salt, but if you do, you can always add it later.) Return the chicken pieces to the pan, tucking them into the sauce a bit. Adjust the heat so the liquid bubbles gently but steadily, then cover the skillet.

4 Cook, checking every 5 minutes to turn the pieces, until the chicken is tender and cooked through, 20 to 30 minutes, adding a tablespoon of liquid if the sauce looks too dry. The meat is done when a quick-read thermometer inserted into the thickest part of a thigh reads 155–165°F. Remove the chicken from the pan and taste the sauce; adjust the seasoning, spoon it over the chicken, garnish with the parsley, and serve.

As the chicken braises it will continue to release fat. So, to prevent the sauce from becoming too greasy, you need to remove some.

EYEBALLING FAT IN A PAN I don't expect you to measure what's left; the idea is to leave enough to create a thin film in the bottom of the pan.

Tips
▶ If fresh tomatoes are in season (and ripe), use them, chopped—skin, seeds, and all. Figure 3 cups. For a rich, thick sauce, use roma (plum) tomatoes; slicers will be brighter tasting and more watery.

Variations
▶ **Braised Chicken with Chile and Orange:** Skip the anchovies, olives, and thyme. Replace the olive oil with vegetable oil and the wine with orange juice. In Step 2, add a teaspoon of chili powder along with the onions. Continue with the recipe and garnish with cilantro.
▶ **Braised Barbecue Chicken:** Skip the anchovies, olives, and thyme. Replace the wine with beer and add a tablespoon of chili powder and ¼ cup brown sugar along with the onions. Continue with the recipe.

Learn More
▶ Chicken Basics (page 306), Rotating as You Cook (page 313), chopping onions (page 19), mincing garlic (page 20), Pitting (page 431), Stripping Leaves from Hard Herb Stems (page 141)

COOKING WITH ANCHOVIES Try them, at least once. They dissolve into the sauce, leaving behind a rich, briny flavor. If you're still squeamish, try adding capers instead.

BRAISING CHICKEN IN SAUCE The tomato mixture should be fairly liquid when you return the chicken to the pan.

Chicken and Rice

One of the world's great one-pot dishes.

TIME **About 1 hour**
MAKES **4 servings**

2 tablespoons olive oil

1 whole cut-up chicken or about 3 pounds parts

Salt and freshly ground black pepper

2 medium onions, chopped

1 tablespoon minced garlic

1½ cups short-grain white rice

Pinch saffron threads, optional

3½ cups water, chicken stock, or vegetable stock, or more as needed

1 cup peas (frozen are fine; no need to thaw them)

2 limes, quartered, for serving

1 Put the oil in a large skillet over medium-high heat. When it's hot, add the chicken, skin side down. Sprinkle with salt and pepper and cook, undisturbed but adjusting the heat so the chicken sizzles but doesn't burn, until the pieces release easily from the pan, 5 to 10 minutes. Then turn and rotate them every few minutes to brown them evenly. As the chicken pieces brown, after another 5 to 10 minutes, remove them from the pan.

2 Reduce the heat under the skillet to medium and pour or spoon off most of the oil so that only 2 tablespoons remain. Add the onions to the pan and cook, stirring frequently, until they soften, 3 to 5 minutes. Add the garlic and rice; cook, stirring, until the rice is glossy and coated with oil. Crumble in the saffron threads if you're using them.

3 Return the chicken to the pan, add the water, and stir gently to combine everything. Bring the mixture to a boil, then reduce the heat so it bubbles gently but steadily. Cover the skillet and cook, undisturbed, for 20 minutes, then check the rice and chicken. The goal is

to have the liquid absorbed, the rice tender, and the chicken cooked through. If the rice is dry but nothing is ready, add another ¼ cup water and cook for another 5 to 10 minutes. The meat is done when a quick-read thermometer inserted into the thickest part of the thigh reads 155–165°F.

4 Remove the skillet from the heat. Taste the rice and adjust the seasoning. Add the peas, then cover the pan again and let it sit for 5 to 15 minutes. Fish the chicken out of the pan and transfer it to a serving platter. Fluff the rice with a fork, spoon it around the chicken, add the lime wedges, and serve.

CRUMBLING SAFFRON You need only a pinch of saffron; too much is overpowering. If you don't have it, use a teaspoon of ground cumin or smoked paprika (or both).

Tips

▶ Saffron (as you probably know if you're using it) is not cheap. Fortunately a little goes a long way.

▶ Don't be intimidated by cooking chicken and rice in the same pan. It's no harder than cooking either ingredient on its own. You may need to monitor the moisture in the pan toward the end of cooking, but as long as you resist the urge to uncover the skillet and stir, it will come out great.

▶ Short-grain rice is classic here, but if you like rice less sticky and more fluffy, use long-grain rice. You'll probably need to add the extra liquid in Step 3.

Variations

▶ **Chicken and Lentils:** Skip the peas and use lemon instead of lime. Replace the rice with 1 cup dried brown or green lentils (rinsed and picked over) and continue with the recipe.

Learn More

▶ Chicken Basics (page 306), Braising (page 31), Rotating As You Cook (page 313), Rice Basics (page 196), Eyeballing Fat in a Pan (page 324)

Check the rice: it should have absorbed all of the liquid and be tender but not too wet.

ADDING THE LIQUID Get everything evenly distributed in the pan without roughing it up too much by overstirring.

RESTING TIME After turning off the heat, add the peas and cover. This important step also makes the dish perfect for entertaining, since you can wait up to 15 minutes before serving.

Fried Chicken

Undeniably messy but an irresistible treat.

TIME **40 minutes**

MAKES **4 to 6 servings**

Vegetable oil as needed

1 whole cut-up chicken or about 3 pounds parts

2 cups all-purpose flour

1 tablespoon salt

1 tablespoon freshly ground black pepper

2 tablespoons ground cinnamon

1 Put about ½ inch of the oil in a large skillet. Dry the chicken well with paper towels. Mix together the flour and seasonings in a large plastic bag or bowl. Toss the chicken in the mixture, 2 or 3 pieces at a time, until they are well coated. Tap off the excess flour and put them on a rack as you finish. Turn the heat under the oil to medium-high.

2 Add a pinch of flour to the oil; it will sizzle when the fat is ready. Add the chicken pieces, slowly and skin side down. The fit might be a little snug, but as long as the chicken is sizzling but not burning, that's okay. Throughout the process, adjust the heat and add oil, 2 tablespoons at a time, as necessary to maintain that balance. Cover and cook until you can smell the skin browning, 5 to 10 minutes.

3 Uncover the skillet and tug gently on a piece with tongs. If it releases easily, turn it; if not, cover the pan again and cook for another minute or two. Once all the chicken has been turned, cook, uncovered, until the other side is well browned, 5 to 10 minutes.

4 The smaller pieces will be done first. To check, remove one and cut into it close to the bone; the meat should be firm and the juices run clear. Keep cooking and turning (again, adjusting the heat as needed) until all the chicken is done inside, another 5 to 10 minutes. As the pieces finish cooking, transfer them to paper towels to drain. Serve hot, warm, or at room temperature.

Follow your instincts: Adjust the heat and add oil whenever you think you should.

COATING CHICKEN PARTS A zipper bag is handy. For the crispest skin, make sure the coated chicken isn't gunked up with too much flour.

TESTING THE OIL TEMPERATURE You don't need a thermometer. The flour should sizzle but not burn immediately.

KNOWING WHEN TO TURN The chicken is ready when it releases easily from the pan and has a nice toasty smell.

Tips

▶ Dredging the chicken in a plastic bag (instead of a bowl) is the best way to completely coat the pieces and is much easier to clean up.

Variations

▶ **Fried Boneless Chicken:** Use about 1½ pounds of boneless chicken breasts, tenders, or thighs. Pound them to an even thickness, dredge them, and heat the oil as described in Step 1. But cook them uncovered, for just 3 to 5 minutes per side. They're done when the outside is crisp and the interior is white or very slightly pink.

▶ **Fried Chicken with a Thick Coating:** Soak the chicken in 4 cups buttermilk—either for several hours in the fridge or for up to 1 hour on the counter. Before adding a piece to the flour mixture, hold it over the bowl for a few seconds to let some of the liquid drain off. Then continue with the recipe.

Learn More

▶ Chicken Basics (page 306), Panfrying (page 36), vegetable oil (pages 2 and 112), Pounding Boneless Chicken (page 308)

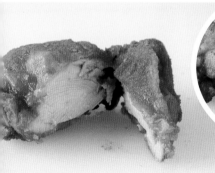

CHECKING FOR DONENESS If the chicken is cooked through, the juices will run clear; if it isn't done, they will run pink.

If you check inside and it's still pink, like this, just put the piece back in the hot fat and check another piece in a few minutes.

Roast Chicken

Crisp, delicious skin, tender, moist meat, and no-sweat carving.

TIME **1 hour,
    mostly unattended**
MAKES **4 servings**

1 whole chicken (3 to 4
pounds)

3 tablespoons olive oil

Salt and freshly ground
black pepper

1 Heat the oven to 400°F with a rack
in the lower third. Put a large ovenproof
skillet on the rack. While it heats, trim
the excess fat from the chicken, pat it
dry with a paper towel, rub the outside
with the oil, and sprinkle it with salt and
pepper.

2 When the pan is scorching hot, 10
or 15 minutes later, carefully put the
chicken in the pan with the breast side
up. Roast, undisturbed, until the chick-
en is cooked through, 40 to 60 minutes,
depending on its size. It's done when a
quick-read thermometer inserted in
the thickest part of one of the thighs
registers 155–165°F or you cut into a
thigh down to the bone and the juices
run clear.

*Remember: Mistakes
are still edible!*

3 Carefully remove the pan from the
oven. Tip the pan slightly to let any
juices from the bird's cavity flow into
the pan, then transfer the chicken to a
cutting board and let it sit for at least
5 minutes. Pour the pan juices into a
clear measuring cup and let it sit for a
few minutes, until the fat rises to the
top; use a spoon to skim off some of the
excess fat. Cut up the bird and serve it
with the warm pan juices.

*If you hit bone, gently
pull on the thigh so you
can see the joint, where
it's easiest to cut and
separate the pieces.*

**POURING JUICES FROM THE
CHICKEN CAVITY** Hold the bird
with a fork so it doesn't slide
around in the pan when you tip it.

CARVING CHICKEN IN HALF Cut
straight down one side between
the breast and the bone. Hack
through the small rib bones to
free the breast, wing, leg, and
thigh. Repeat on the other side.

QUARTERING CHICKEN Cut
between the breast and thigh,
aiming for the joint, to divide each
half in two pieces. The breast and
wing are still connected, as are
the leg and thigh.

Tips

▶ Heating the pan first helps accelerate cooking the dark meat and ensures a moist chicken with a gorgeous skin without turning the bird during roasting.

▶ The visual way to gauge doneness: Tip the bird so juices flow from the cavity. If they're reddish or pink, it's not ready. Check again every 5 minutes until they look golden. Use the leftovers for salad, or just eat whole pieces cold.

▶ Don't let carving intimidate you. Once you get a sense of where the joints connect, it becomes second nature.

Variations

▶ **5 Ways to Add Flavor:**
1 Put a few sprigs of fresh herbs—like rosemary, thyme, parsley, or sage—in the cavity.
2 Sprinkle the skin with up to 1 teaspoon dried herbs—like thyme or oregano—when you add the salt and pepper.
3 Put fresh herb leaves under the skin (see page 321).
4 After you skim the fat from the pan juices, stir in 1 tablespoon Dijon-style mustard.
5 Or stir in 1 tablespoon balsamic or sherry vinegar.

Learn More

▶ Chicken Basics (page 306), Roasting (page 33), Skimming Fat from Pan Juices (page 343)

SEPARATING THE WING FROM THE BREAST Find the joint where the wing meets the breast and cut through it. You can also cut the breast in half crosswise to make smaller pieces.

SEPARATING THE LEG AND THIGH Move the parts to locate the joint that connects them and cut through it.

Chicken in a Pot with Soy Broth

Chinese-style chicken soup, deconstructed.

TIME **1½ hours,
mostly unattended**
MAKES **4 servings**

---

1 whole chicken (3 to 4 pounds)

6 to 8 cups water or chicken stock

¼ cup soy sauce, plus more to taste

1 bay leaf

10 black peppercorns

2 cloves

3 carrots, cut into thick coins

3 celery stalks, cut into 2-inch chunks

1 bunch scallions, cut into 2-inch pieces

1 Put the chicken in a stockpot with enough water or stock to cover by at least 1 inch. Add the soy sauce, bay leaf, peppercorns, and cloves and bring to a boil. Immediately turn the heat down so the liquid bubbles gently. Cover and cook, undisturbed, for 15 minutes.

2 Add the carrots, celery, and scallions to the pot. Return the lid and cook until the vegetables are tender and the chicken is cooked through, 10 to 20 minutes longer. The meat is done when a quick-read thermometer inserted into the thickest part of one of the thighs reads 155–165°F.

3 When the chicken is ready, use tongs to carefully transfer it to a large bowl. Fish the vegetables out of the stock with a slotted spoon and put them on a large serving platter. Raise the heat under the pot to high and let the broth bubble vigorously until it has thickened slightly and partially evaporated—the volume of broth should decrease by about 25 percent—10 to 15 minutes.

4 After the chicken has cooled enough to handle, separate the meat from the skin and bones and put it on the platter with the vegetables. Pour the broth through a strainer into a large bowl or ceramic pitcher; taste and adjust the seasoning with salt, pepper, or more soy sauce. To serve, put some chicken and vegetables in soup bowls and pour a splash of the broth over all.

The chicken is going to be heavy and hot, so be ready for a splash in case it plops back into the pot.

BRINGING LIQUID TO A SIMMER
When you put the lid on, the liquid should be bubbling steadily but gently, or the chicken may get tough and stringy.

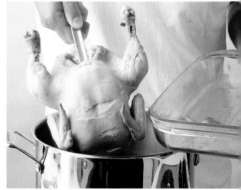

TRANSFERRING THE CHICKEN
Before you try moving the bird, carefully tilt it to empty the cavity of hot stock and the odd steaming carrot.

Tips

▶ Water works quite well here since the chicken and vegetables create a broth all by themselves. But using stock ratchets up the flavor dramatically.

▶ If your stockpot is so large that 6 to 8 cups liquid doesn't cover your chicken, you have two choices: Don't submerge the chicken, but turn it a couple times during cooking. Or add more liquid and then allow extra time to reduce the broth.

▶ Be patient: Reducing the broth takes some time, and you want to intensify the flavors as much as possible. Keep tasting; you'll know when it's ready.

▶ This dish is good with simply boiled Chinese egg noodles or plain white or brown rice.

Variations

▶ **More Traditional Chicken in a Pot:** Skip the soy sauce and cloves. In Step 1, add 2 pounds small waxy red or white potatoes to the pot along with the chicken. After reducing the broth in Step 3, stir in ½ cup cream if you like and add 1 cup peas.

Learn More

▶ Chicken Basics (page 306), Simmering (page 25), Smarter Water (page 137), Chicken Stock (page 154), Asian Noodle Basics (page 190), Boiled Rice (page 196)

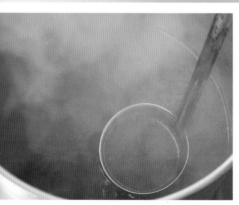

REDUCING THE BROTH Boil it vigorously until at least one-quarter of the water evaporates and the flavors intensify.

PULLING CHICKEN Hands are the best tool to remove the meat and shred it, but if you're not crazy about the idea, use 2 forks. (The result is called *pulled chicken*.)

Grilled or Broiled Split Chicken

Flatten the bird for fast cooking without burning.

TIME **About 1 hour**
MAKES **4 servings**

---

1 whole chicken (3 to 4 pounds)

1 tablespoon minced fresh rosemary leaves or 1 teaspoon dried

2 teaspoons salt

1 tablespoon minced garlic

2 tablespoons olive oil

2 lemons, quartered, for serving

1 Either prepare a grill for indirect cooking so that there are hot coals on half and nothing on the other half and put the rack about 4 inches from the heat source, or turn the broiler to high and put the rack about 6 inches from the heat source. Remove the backbone and split the chicken: With the breast facing up, cut down each side of the backbone, front to rear, with a chef's knife or kitchen shears. Once the backbone is removed, lay the chicken out and press down firmly to flatten it. Turn it over, then press down again.

2 Mix together the rosemary, salt, garlic, and 1 tablespoon of the olive oil. Put your fingers between the skin and the meat of the breast to loosen the skin of the chicken and tuck about half of the herb mixture under the skin; rub the remainder all over the chicken.

3 To grill: Put the chicken on the cool side of the grill, skin side up, cover, and cook until the meat is almost done, 20 to 30 minutes. Turn the chicken so that the skin side is over direct heat. (If the fire flares up, reduce the flame if it's a gas grill; with a charcoal fire, move the chicken back to indirect heat.) Cook, turning and moving the chicken once or twice more, until most of the fat has been rendered and the bird is done, 10 to 15 minutes more (if using a charcoal fire, add more coals if necessary).

To broil: Put the chicken on a rimmed baking sheet, skin side down, and broil; you might need to move it to a lower rack to prevent burning. When the chicken looks opaque, in about 25 minutes, turn and cook until the skin is brown, 10 to 15 minutes more. Move the chicken close to—or away from—the heat as needed so it cooks through without burning. Turn the skin side down if it's browning too quickly, but finish with a final crisping of the skin.

4 The meat is done when a quick-read thermometer inserted into the thickest part of a thigh reads 155–165°F or the juices run clear when you make a small cut near the bone. Let it rest for a few minutes, then cut it into serving pieces. Drizzle with the remaining 1 tablespoon olive oil and serve with the lemon.

SPLITTING WHOLE RAW CHICKEN
The bones are easy to cut through if you use the heel of the knife for leverage; just make sure your fingers aren't nearby.

Tips

▶ Splitting the chicken is another good place to use kitchen shears.

Variations

▶ **Tandoori-Style Grilled or Broiled Split Chicken:** Skip the rosemary, salt, garlic, and olive oil. In Step 2, put in a blender or food processor 1 quartered medium onion, 2 cloves garlic, a ½-inch piece of fresh ginger (or 1 teaspoon ground), 1 tablespoon ground cumin, 1 teaspoon ground coriander, ¼ teaspoon cayenne, 1 teaspoon salt, and 1 cup yogurt. Blend until smooth. Put the chicken in a large baking dish with the marinade and turn to make sure it's well coated; refrigerate for 12 to 24 hours, turning occasionally. Scrape off most of the marinade before cooking and continue with the recipe; serve hot.

▶ **Chipotle-Lime Grilled or Broiled Split Chicken:** Skip the rosemary, salt, and garlic. Replace the lemons with limes. In Step 2, combine ¼ cup chopped or puréed canned chipotles in adobo and the juice of 2 limes along with the olive oil. Rub the mixture all over the chicken as described in Step 2. Serve with the quartered lime.

Learn More

▶ Chicken Basics (page 306), Grilling (page 35), Broiling (page 34), carving a chicken (page 330), seasoning under the skin (page 321)

FLATTENING SPLIT CHICKEN You should hear the breastbone crack if you press down hard enough. Remember to turn and flatten both sides.

TURNING SPLIT CHICKEN Wait to turn the chicken skin side down until it releases easily from the grates and is firm.

If you're broiling, you'll be turning the skin side up in this step.

Chicken (or Turkey) Salad

You may never want to eat the store-bought version again.

TIME **20 minutes with cooked chicken or turkey**

MAKES **4 servings**

¼ cup mayonnaise

2 tablespoons Dijon-style mustard

2 tablespoons olive oil

Juice of 1 lemon

Salt and freshly ground black pepper

1 pound shredded or cubed cooked chicken or turkey meat (about 1½ cups)

1 cup chopped celery

¼ cup chopped scallions

¼ cup chopped almonds, optional

1 Whisk together the mayonnaise, mustard, olive oil, lemon juice, and a sprinkle of salt and pepper in a large bowl until well combined.

2 Add the chicken, celery, scallions, and almonds if you're using them and stir until everything is coated with the dressing. (At this point, you may refrigerate the salad for a day or two; take it out of the fridge 15 minutes or so to take the chill off before continuing.) Taste, adjust the seasoning, and serve.

As the salad rests (or chills), it will absorb dressing. Every now and then, stir it to give everything a fresh coating.

Shredding makes a softer salad.

CUTTING CHICKEN FOR SALAD
You can cut the chicken into small cubes with a knife or pull it into shreds with your fingers, depending on the texture you like.

STIRRING THE SALAD Make sure everything is evenly coated. If you have time, let the salad chill for an hour or more to blend the flavors.

Tips

▶ Using leftovers is handy, but don't hesitate to cook chicken or turkey solely for the purpose of making salad. In fact, the meat soaks up the dressing better when it's still a little warm.

▶ If mayo isn't your thing, use Vinaigrette (page 114) to dress this salad.

▶ Leftovers that have been seasoned or cooked with vegetables make an excellent cold salad. Consider chopping up the vegetables and including them, and wait to add salt and pepper until you finish and can get a good taste.

▶ It's always nice to serve chicken or turkey salad over crisp lettuce leaves, with tomato wedges on the side.

Variations

▶ **6 Possible Additions:**
1 1 cup grapes (red or green)
2 1 chopped apple or pear
3 ½ cup pecans or walnuts
4 ⅓ cup dried cranberries
5 2 chopped hard-boiled eggs
6 1 tablespoon chopped strong fresh herbs, like mint or tarragon

Learn More

▶ Chicken Basics (page 306), Grilled or Broiled Boneless Chicken (page 308), Roast Chicken (page 330), Roast Turkey (page 338)

Roast Turkey

Have fun: You always remember your first.

TIME **3 to 4 hours**
MAKES **8 to 12 servings**

---

1 turkey (12 to 14 pounds)

8 tablespoons (1 stick) butter, softened

Salt and freshly ground black pepper

1 cup roughly chopped onion

1 cup roughly chopped carrot

½ cup roughly chopped celery

Stems from 1 bunch fresh parsley, tied together with kitchen string, optional

1 Heat the oven to 500°F. Rinse the turkey under cool running water and remove the giblets from the cavity. Trim off the excess fat and wing tips if you like. Pat the bird dry with a paper towel, smear the butter all over the skin, and sprinkle it well with salt and pepper.

2 Put the turkey on a rack in a large roasting pan with the breast facing up. Pour ½ cup water into the bottom of the pan and add the onion, carrot, celery, and parsley, along with the turkey neck, whatever giblets you want (or not), and the wing tips if you removed them. Put the turkey in the oven, legs first if possible.

3 Roast until the top of the turkey begins to brown, 20 to 30 minutes, then lower the oven heat to 325°F. Continue to roast, checking and brushing the bird with the pan juices every 30 minutes or so. If the bottom of the pan gets dry, add about ½ cup water; there should be a little liquid in the bottom of the pan at all times.

4 The turkey is done when a quick-read thermometer inserted into the thickest part of one of the thighs measures 155–165°F; figure 2½ to 3½ hours. If the top looks like it's getting too brown too quickly, press a piece of aluminum foil directly onto it. If the top looks like it's not browned enough, turn the heat back up to 425°F for the last 20 to 30 minutes of roasting.

5 When the turkey is ready, tip the juices out of the cavity into the pan, transfer the bird to a cutting board, cover loosely with a tent of aluminum foil, and let it rest for at least 20 minutes before carving. If you're serving the turkey with pan juices, strain them from the pan into a glass measuring cup. When the fat rises to the top, skim it off and warm the juices before serving (you can add them to several cups of chicken or turkey stock if you want more). If not, hang on to the roasting pan and all its contents; you're going to need it to make gravy.

Using the giblets (which are the edible internal organs) is optional, but if you do, cook them with the turkey.

PREPARING TURKEY FOR THE OVEN All this extra stuff is going to flavor the pan juices and become the backbone of the gravy.

Tips

▶ Most whole turkeys on the market are standard birds, which are raised much like conventional chickens and are of similar nondistinct quality. (Self-basting turkeys, pumped full of flavored vegetable oil and/or water, are absolutely to be avoided.) True wild turkeys are scrawny birds that are rarely available commercially. Other than that, the same labeling standards (and lack of standards) that apply for chicken work for turkeys. See page 307 for some details.

▶ If you're starting out with a frozen bird, let it defrost thoroughly before getting started. Figure a 12- to 14-pound turkey will take at least 48 hours to defrost in the refrigerator. If you're in a hurry, put it in a sink (or large bowl) full of cold water and soak the bird for 8 to 12 hours, changing the water every couple of hours or so. But don't put it in warm or hot water and don't just let it sit out on the counter.

Learn More
▶ Chicken Basics (page 306), Thanksgiving Basics (page 340), Roasting (page 33)

CARVING WHITE MEAT The easiest way is to simply cut thick slices from the breast.

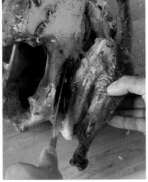

REMOVING THE LEG AND THIGH This part is like carving a whole roast chicken: Cut through the joint that connects them to the backbone.

CARVING DARK MEAT Put the leg and thigh—still connected—on a cutting board so they're stable; cut slices off with downward strokes.

Thanksgiving Basics

Stuffing in a Pan

Both turkey and stuffing will be infinitely better if you cook them separately. That way they'll roast—not steam—and become crisp in all the right places; also, your pan juices won't have a bunch of unwanted stuff(ing) floating in them. Finally, a stuffed turkey takes a long time to heat through, making it a legitimate food safety risk. Here's a delicious stuffing (enough for 8 to 12 servings) that comes together quickly the night before and is then reheated while the bird rests.

MAKE BREAD CRUMBS

1 Heat the oven to 375°F; grease a 9 x 13-inch pan with 2 tablespoons butter. (You'll need 16 tablespoons or 2 sticks total for this recipe.)

2 Cut a large loaf of bread into 1-inch slices. (Wheat or white doesn't matter as long as it's of the quality you'd choose to eat on its own. It's okay if it's dried out. And I leave the crust on; it adds texture.)

3 Pulse a few slices in a food processor until they form crumbs the size of peas; dump them into a bowl and repeat until all the bread is pulverized. You should have 8 cups.

ASSEMBLE THE STUFFING

1 Put what's left of the 2 sticks butter in a large pot over medium heat. When it melts and foams, add 1 chopped large onion and 4 chopped celery stalks and cook, stirring occasionally, until the vegetables soften, 3 to 5 minutes. Add 1 cup chopped walnuts and cook, stirring almost constantly, until they begin to brown, 2 or 3 minutes.

2 Add the bread crumbs and 2 tablespoons chopped fresh sage leaves (or 2 teaspoon dried) and toss to combine. The bread should be slightly wet but not soggy. Stir in chicken stock or water, ½ cup at a time, if the stuffing looks too dry (you won't need more than 1½ cups).

3 Sprinkle with salt and pepper, toss again, then taste and adjust the seasoning. Turn off the heat.

BAKE (AND REHEAT) THE STUFFING

1 Transfer the stuffing to the prepared pan. Bake until the top is golden (but not too brown) and the inside is steaming hot, 40 to 50 minutes. Cool, cover with foil, and refrigerate.

2 On Thanksgiving Day, take the stuffing out of the fridge about 1 hour before the turkey is ready so it comes to room temperature. When you take the bird out of the oven, lower the heat to 375°F. Put the stuffing in the oven (if the pan is glass, make sure it's no longer cold) and bake until hot throughout (a quick-read thermometer will register 160°F), 15 to 20 minutes.

3 Remove the foil and continue baking until the top is browned and crisp, another 5 to 10 minutes.

Making Gravy

Whatever drips down from the turkey into the bottom of the roasting pan provides the backbone for incredible gravy. To add volume, you'll need stock. (This is one of those times when water just doesn't cut it.) Thicken it a bit and away you go.

PREPARE THE PAN AND GIBLETS After you remove the turkey from the roasting pan, take out the giblets and chop them up; put them back in the pan along with the neck. Spoon some of the fat off the top of the pan liquids, leaving as many of the solids and as much of the dark liquid behind as possible. Put the roasting pan over 2 burners and turn the heat to high.

DEGLAZE THE PAN When the solids in the pan start to sizzle, add 6 cups turkey or chicken stock. (To make your own turkey stock, see page 156.) Scrape the bottom of the pan to get up any browned bits. Reduce the heat so the stock bubbles and cook, stirring frequently, until fragrant, about 5 minutes. Meanwhile, whisk ⅓ cup cornstarch with ¼ cup water in a small bowl until smooth.

FINISH THE GRAVY Strain the stock through a mesh sieve into a large pot and discard the solids. Bring to a boil and add the cornstarch slurry to the bubbling gravy, stirring constantly. It should thicken almost immediately. Taste and adjust the seasoning and serve hot.

You can keep gravy warm over low heat for up to 10 minutes.

Timing the Big Dinner

I have two suggestions for destressing this meal: Grab a couple helpers to get the meal—and guests—to the table. And remember that only the gravy needs to be served piping hot; everything else can be served from the fridge or at room temperature. Here's how:

▶ The turkey shouldn't go right from the oven to the table. It is big enough that it can rest for up to an hour without cooling down too much. So once it's out, cover it loosely with a tent of aluminum foil and let it rest on a rimmed baking sheet or platter (to catch the juices).

▶ Casseroles and gratins can either be cooked ahead and warmed or assembled the day before and popped into the oven to cook when the turkey comes out. Refrigerate them in the baking dishes (covered tightly) that you plan to use for cooking and serving; that way you don't have to scramble.

▶ Once casseroles and gratins are in the oven, check on things once in a while and rotate pans and dishes as needed to keep them cooking or warming evenly. Pull them out when they're done and tent with foil. They'll stay warm enough.

▶ Figure it takes about as long to make gravy (15 to 20 minutes) as it does to get both the whole meal and the whole family to the table.

Turkey Parts Braised in Red Wine

Showing turkey in a different, delicious light.

TIME **About 1½ hours**
MAKES **4 to 6 servings**

3 tablespoons olive oil

3 to 4 pounds turkey thighs
or legs

Salt and freshly ground
black pepper

1 large onion, chopped

1 medium carrot, chopped

1 celery stalk, chopped

1 tablespoon minced garlic

2 cups fruity red wine

¼ cup red wine vinegar

3 whole cloves or a pinch
ground

1 bay leaf

1 tablespoon chopped
fresh rosemary leaves or
1 teaspoon dried

1 piece orange peel (about
1 x 3 inches)

1 Put 2 tablespoons of the oil in a large pot over medium-high heat. Pat the turkey thighs dry with a paper towel. When the oil is hot, add the thighs to the pan; to avoid crowding the pan, work in batches if necessary. Sprinkle with salt and pepper and cook, undisturbed, until they release from the pan, 5 to 10 minutes. Adjust the heat as necessary so the fat sizzles but the turkey doesn't burn. Turn them, season the other side, and cook, turning and rotating the pieces every few minutes to brown them evenly all over, another 10 to 15 minutes. As the pieces finish, remove them from the pan. Carefully pour off all but 1 tablespoon of the fat and wipe out the pan with paper towels.

2 Put the pot back on the burner, turn the heat to medium, and add the remaining 1 tablespoon oil. When it's hot, add the onion, carrot, celery, and garlic. Cook, stirring frequently, until the vegetables soften, 5 to 10 minutes. Pour in the wine and turn the heat back up to medium-high. Bring the wine to a steady bubble and cook, stirring, for about 1 minute. Stir in the vinegar, cloves, bay leaf, rosemary, orange peel, and some salt and pepper. Add the thighs back to the pot, skin side up, turn the heat down to low, and cover. Adjust the heat so that the liquid bubbles very slowly.

3 Uncover the pot every 15 minutes to turn the turkey thighs and make sure the liquid is still bubbling and the pan doesn't seem dry (if it does, add ¼ cup water); replace the lid. After the turkey has cooked for 30 minutes, heat the oven to 200°F.

4 The turkey is done when a quick-read thermometer inserted into the thickest part of one of the thighs measures 155–165°F. When it's ready, transfer the thighs to an ovenproof platter and put it in the oven. Spoon the fat off the surface of the remaining liquid with a large spoon and raise the heat to high; let the liquid bubble vigorously until it has thickened slightly and reduced by about half—15 to 20 minutes. Taste, adjust the seasoning, spoon the wine sauce over the turkey, and serve.

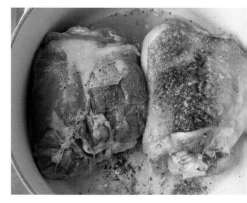

BROWNING TURKEY THIGHS The deeper the color, the deeper the flavor. Keep them moving to crisp all sides.

Fish out the cloves, bay leaf, and orange peel before serving.

Tips

▶ This is another one of those braised dishes that you can cook without browning the meat first without ruining it. So if you're in a hurry, skip Step 1 and cook the thighs for slightly longer in Step 3.

▶ If you don't want to use alcohol, try homemade chicken, turkey, or vegetable stock.

Variations

▶ **Turkey Thighs Braised with Fresh and Dried Mushrooms:** Before Step 1, put 1 ounce dried porcini mushrooms in a small bowl and cover them with hot water. Let them soak while you continue with Step 1. In Step 2, add ½ pound stemmed and sliced fresh shiitake mushrooms along with the other vegetables. When they have softened, remove the soaked dried mushrooms (be careful not to include the sediment that has gathered at the bottom), chop them roughly, and add them to the pot. Pour most of the soaking liquid into the pot, leaving the sediment in the bottom of the bowl. Continue with the recipe from Step 3.

Learn More

▶ Chicken Basics (page 306), Braising (page 31), Rotating as You Cook (page 313), Eyeballing Fat in a Pan (page 324), Reducing the Sauce (page 293)

MONITORING THE LIQUID If the pan ever looks too dry while the turkey is still cooking, stir in a little water; the sauce will be reduced anyway.

SKIMMING FAT FROM PAN JUICES Start at the edges and slide the spoon just beneath the surface of the liquid; you'll capture the fat but not the juices.

Seafood

Learning how to cook seafood is one of the most useful things you can do. First of all, fish is the healthiest animal product that you can eat. It's also incredibly rewarding to cook: The variety of flavors and textures is astounding, yet you need to know only a few basic techniques to cook them all. And seafood rarely takes more than 10 minutes of heat, so those rewards come fast. Simple, quick, healthy, and never boring: What could be better than that?

The frustrating truth is that buying fish and shellfish is much harder than cooking it. We know that many types are endangered, and we know that many are farm-raised; it's often impossible for us to tell which fish are wild, which are sustainable, which are farmed, or which came from local waters and which were shipped from the other side of the world. This chapter will go over some basic guidelines for buying species that are fresh, flavorful, and environmentally responsible.

Once you have quality seafood in your kitchen, the possibilities are unlimited. Here you'll learn a variety of ways to cook seafood simply and quickly—from grilling and broiling to frying and roasting to steaming and boiling. You'll also learn how to group similar kinds of fish into categories—like steaks, thick fillets, thin fillets, and shellfish—and how to tell when each of them is cooked just the way you like.

After you learn which methods and cooking times work for which kinds of fish, you'll be able to perfectly cook almost anything you can find in the sea.

Fish Basics

5 Rules for Buying and Storing Seafood

1. Follow Your Nose Buy fish from a clean store that doesn't smell bad, where the fish is displayed on ice, not in packages. This might be the counter at a supermarket or a fishmonger. Once you find that place, make friends.

2. Be Flexible For every fish you can think of, there are others much like it; they're interchangeable. So instead of focusing on individual species, think of fish in the three groups shown on the next page, then choose what looks best in each category.

3. Be Picky Buy what smells briny and sweet—like the sea—not stinky or acrid like chemicals. Avoid anything mushy, dried out, or "gaping"—where the flesh is separating. If you're not sure, ask your new friend behind the counter to let you have a whiff and a close look.

4. Choose Safe and Sustainable Seafood Many species of seafood have been overfished or polluted to near extinction, and farmed fish isn't always the best alternative. Several reputable organizations can help you decide what fish and shellfish to avoid, using lists that fluctuate along with the fish populations themselves. Check out Monterey Bay Aquarium, for one: montereybayaquarium.org/cr/seafoodwatch.aspx.

5. Keep Seafood Cold To help maintain good quality, hurry home (or have the store pack the fish in ice); cook thawed seafood within a day. Frozen seafood degrades with time, so eat it within a couple months.

Think of Fish in Groups

When you cook fish, the species matters less than the type and thickness of the cut. Here's how to cook the different cuts shown on the opposite page.

Thick Fish Fillets A good place for beginners to start: All should be at least 1 inch thick—sturdy enough to turn during cooking if you need to. Sometimes the skin is still on and helps hold the fillet together. A piece cut from the tail end may not be totally uniform, so just remember that one part will cook faster than the other. But in general, figure a total of 8 to 10 minutes of cooking time per inch of thickness.

Thin Fish Fillets Some of the fish on this list, most notably the so-called flatfish (like flounder and sole) are about ¼ inch thick and cook in as little as 2 minutes; others are a little thicker. You can always substitute the sturdier fillets in recipes that call for a thin cut (just cook them a little longer). But if you try to treat these delicate fish like the sturdy thick ones, they will break apart during cooking.

Fish Steaks When the fish is cut all the way through into a piece that's essentially a cross section, this is what you get. With really large fish—like tuna and swordfish—a steak is boneless. With smaller species—like salmon or halibut—there will be bones and skin. Steaks are fairly sturdy (some more than others), which means that they'll hold up on the grill, and since they're of uniform thickness, they usually cook evenly, at a rate of 8 to 10 minutes per inch of thickness.

Fish and Doneness

Fish dries out quickly, so it's better to undercook it—and take peeks inside—than to overcook it: Most species are best cooked to medium, so the interior is still a little translucent and just beginning to break into flakes. Some—like high-quality tuna—are even better cooked rare, so that the inside still looks raw. Each recipe will help you determine doneness case by case until you get the hang of it.

The more you cook fish, the better you'll become at visually recognizing doneness before you decide to nick-and-peek. Eventually you'll get to the point where you can determine doneness by poking the thickest part with your finger.

STEAK *(Salmon)*

THICK FILLET *(Halibut)*

THIN FILLET *(Trout)*

Three Groups of Fish

Different species may be cooked the same way within groups, but their flavor and texture vary. Here's a quick summary of the most common kinds:

Thick Fish Fillets

SALMON Same flavor as steaks.

HALIBUT Mild flavored with a firm, large flake.

STRIPED BASS Medium flavored, meaty, and flaky.

COD Mild flavored with big flakes and fairly firm flesh.

CATFISH Dense texture, strong (some say muddy) flavor.

SEA BASS (Thick and thin fillets.) Medium flavored, quite firm. (Red snapper is similar.)

MACKEREL Dark, fatty, flavorful.

Thin Fish Fillets

SOLE Mild, almost sweet, and delicate.

FLOUNDER Tender (sometimes soft) and mild flavored.

TROUT Sturdy, like a light, freshwater version of salmon.

SEA BASS (Thick and thin fillets.) Medium flavored, very firm flesh. (Red snapper is similar.)

TILAPIA Farm-raised, increasingly available, but uninteresting flavor and texture.

Fish Steaks

SALMON Distinctive strong flavor, usually pleasantly fatty; wild is preferable to farmed.

HALIBUT Sturdy and mild flavored.

COD More delicate; a good substitute for halibut.

SWORDFISH Meaty and flavorful.

TUNA Often eaten raw or rare. Meaty but tender, almost sweet flavor.

Grilled or Broiled Fish

As fast as chicken cutlets and as fancy as beef steaks.

TIME **20 minutes**

MAKES **4 servings**

---

4 small or 2 large fish steaks or thick fillets (at least 1 inch thick; 1½ pounds total)

2 tablespoons olive oil, or more as needed

Salt and freshly ground black pepper

2 lemons, quartered, for serving

1 Prepare a grill or turn on the broiler; the heat should be medium-high and the rack about 4 inches from the heat source. Brush both sides of the fish generously with olive oil and sprinkle with salt and pepper.

2 To grill: Put the fish directly on the grill over the hot coals. Cook until it is lightly charred on the first side, 3 to 4 minutes. Wait for the edges to become opaque and a crust to form on the bottom. Then turn carefully with a spatula and cook on the other side until the steak is just cooked through, another 2 to 4 minutes.

To broil: Put the fish on a rimmed baking sheet under the broiler. It won't get as brown as with grilling, but you also won't have to turn it. Watch for the top to become opaque and the flesh to feel firm. Figure anywhere from 2 to 10 minutes, depending on the thickness of the steak and the intensity of your broiler.

3 To see whether the fish is done, stick a paring knife between the layers of flesh; when the knife meets little resistance and just a touch of translucence remains in the center of the fish, it's ready. Serve right away with the lemon wedges and any accumulated pan juices if you broiled it.

PEEKING TO CHECK DONENESS
The only sure way to check doneness is to make a small incision and look inside. If the fish isn't ready, check the same area in another minute.

JUDGING DONENESS For most species, take the fillet off the heat when the center is still slightly translucent. The residual heat will bring it to fully opaque.

This is really good "sushi-grade" tuna, which I like to cook so it's crusty outside and almost raw inside. The fire has to be really hot—or your broiler pan close to the heat—to get it this way.

▶ Scrape the grates clean with a wire brush right before putting the fish on. They're easier to clean when hot, and clean grates help prevent the fish from sticking.

▶ The cooking times depend on how hot your grill or broiler is, the thickness of the fish, and how done you like it. For rarer fish, cook for 2 to 3 minutes per side; for more well done, 4 to 5 minutes. For me, fish is better too rare than overcooked, but ultimately you'll decide.

Variations

▶ **Grilled or Broiled Fish with Soy-Lime Marinade:** Use vegetable oil instead of the olive oil and skip the salt and pepper. Before Step 1, combine the oil with 2 tablespoons soy sauce and the juice of 1 lime; soak the fish in this mixture, turning once or twice, for 15 to 30 minutes. Remove the steaks from the marinade, pat them dry, and continue with the recipe. Serve with lime wedges.

▶ **Fish Kebabs:** Before Step 1, cut the steaks into chunks about 1½ inches thick. Thread them on skewers, brush with oil, sprinkle with salt and pepper, and continue with the recipe.

Learn More

▶ Fish Basics (page 346), Grilling (page 35), Broiling (page 34), grilling or broiling kebabs (page 272)

Oven-"Fried" Fish Fillets

All the crunch without all the work.

TIME **25 minutes**

MAKES **4 servings**

---

4 tablespoons (½ stick) butter, melted, or olive oil

1½ pounds thick fish fillets

1½ cups milk, buttermilk, or yogurt

2 cups bread crumbs, preferably fresh, for dredging

Salt and freshly ground black pepper

2 lemons, quartered, for serving

1 Heat the oven to 450°F with a rack in the top third. Smear half of the butter on a rimmed baking sheet. While the oven heats, cut the fillets crosswise into 4 or 8 manageable pieces and put them in a large bowl with the milk; let them soak for a few minutes. Put the bread crumbs on a plate and sprinkle with salt and pepper.

2 When the oven is hot, remove the fish from the milk and let some of the liquid drip off. While the fillets are still wet from the milk, dredge them on both sides in the bread crumbs, pressing them gently into the fish, then shaking off any excess. Transfer the fillets to the prepared pan and drizzle the remaining 2 tablespoons butter over the fish.

3 Put the baking sheet in the oven and bake until the fish is crisp on the outside and tender and opaque on the inside, but not dry, 8 to 15 minutes, depending on the thickness of the fish. Serve immediately with the lemon wedges.

Using buttermilk or yogurt will make the fish a bit tangier. Remove the excess by shaking gently—or wiping with your hands.

CUTTING FILLETS You want the pieces to be easy to handle and serve, so cut them into large or small pieces, depending on how big they were to start with.

DIPPING FILLETS IN MILK This helps the bread crumbs adhere to the fish, but the pieces don't need to be sopping wet.

Variations

▶ **Panfried Fish Fillets:** Even crispier. Put half of the butter in a large skillet over medium heat. When it's hot, add some of the fish pieces without overcrowding (you'll probably need to work in batches) and cook, turning once, until both sides are golden and crisp and the inside is opaque, 8 to 15 minutes total. Repeat, adding more fat to the pan as necessary; keep cooked fillets warm in a 200°F oven.

▶ **Cornmeal-Crusted Oven-"Fried" Fish Fillets:** Use cornmeal or a combination of half cornmeal and half all-purpose flour instead of the bread crumbs.

▶ **Chile-Lime Oven-"Fried" Fish Fillets:** Skip the milk and the bread crumbs. In Step 1, rub the fillets all over with the juice of 1 lime and combine 1 cup all-purpose flour with 1 tablespoon chili powder and the salt and pepper in a shallow plate. In Step 2, dredge the fillets in the chili-spiked flour and continue with the recipe. Serve with lime wedges.

Learn More
▶ Fish Basics (page 346), Fresh Bread Crumbs (page 386)

DREDGING FILLETS IN CRUMBS
To guarantee crispness all over, make sure the coating is distributed evenly but not too thick. Tap gently to shake off excess bread crumbs.

DRIZZLING WITH FAT Pour the butter or oil over the fillets as evenly as you can; it helps the bread crumbs brown.

Crisp Sesame Fish Fillets

Sesame seeds make an irresistibly crunchy crust for delicate fish.

TIME **20 minutes**
MAKES **4 servings**

4 thin fish fillets (about 1½ pounds)

Salt and freshly ground black pepper

1 cup sesame seeds

1 tablespoon dark sesame oil

2 tablespoons vegetable oil, or more as needed

2 tablespoons chopped fresh mint or cilantro leaves for garnish

2 limes, quartered, for serving

1 Heat the oven to 200°F. Sprinkle the fillets with salt and pepper on both sides. Put the sesame seeds on a plate and dredge the fillets in the sesame seeds on both sides, pressing them gently into the fish, then shaking off any excess.

2 Put the sesame and vegetable oils in a large skillet over medium-high heat. When they're hot, add 2 of the fillets to the skillet.

3 Adjust the heat as necessary so the fish sizzles but doesn't burn and cook until the seeds on the bottom are toasted and the top begins to turn opaque, 2 or 3 minutes. Then carefully turn the fillets to cook on the other side, another minute or two.

4 Transfer the finished fillets to an ovenproof plate and put it in the oven to stay warm. If necessary, add more vegetable oil to maintain a thin coating in the bottom and let it heat; then cook the remaining 2 fillets the same way. To serve, garnish the fish with the mint and serve right away with the lime wedges.

COATING THE FILLETS Pat the sesame seeds onto both sides of each fillet, then pick it up from one end and gently shake off the loose seeds.

You can test the oil by putting a couple seeds in first; they should sizzle and sputter.

HEATING THE PAN If the oil isn't fully heated, the sesame seeds won't crisp quickly enough. Put the fish in after the oil shimmers but before it smokes.

Adjust the heat as necessary to prevent the seeds from getting too dark.

PEEKING UNDER THE FILLETS They cook fast, and this is the only way to know for sure that the crust isn't burning.

Tips

▶ Thin fish fillets tend to take up a lot of space, so plan to work in two batches.

Variations

▶ **Crisp Sesame Fish Fillets with Soy Glaze:** After removing the fillets from the skillet in Step 4, lower the heat to medium and add 1 tablespoon dark sesame oil, ¼ cup soy sauce, ¼ cup water, and 2 tablespoons sugar to the skillet. Cook, stirring and scraping all the brown bits off the bottom of the pan, until the sugar dissolves, a minute or two. Pour the sauce over the fillets and garnish with cilantro and lime wedges, and ¼ cup chopped scallions if you like.

▶ **Sesame-Crusted Tuna, Done Rare:** Use tuna steaks, which are a good deal thicker than the fillets. But since you want tuna to be very rare, you can follow the recipe and cook the pieces for about the same amount of time, just until the sesame seeds are toasted.

▶ **Crisp Pistachio-Crusted Fish Fillets:** Use olive oil instead of the sesame and vegetable oils; instead of the sesame seeds, grind 1 cup pistachios until fine in a food processor or blender. Dredge the fillets in the pistachios and continue with the recipe. Serve with lemon wedges.

Learn More

▶ Fish Basics (page 346), Panfrying (page 36), Chopping Herbs (page 78)

Steamed Fish with Ratatouille

The vegetables make a perfect "steamer" and create a built-in side dish.

TIME **1 hour**

MAKES **4 servings**

---

1 large or 2 medium zucchini

1 medium or 2 small eggplants

1 medium red bell pepper, cored

2 medium or 3 small tomatoes, cored

3 tablespoons olive oil, or more as needed

1 tablespoon minced garlic

1 large onion, chopped

Salt and freshly ground black pepper

1 tablespoon fresh thyme leaves

½ cup Niçoise or kalamata olives, pitted, optional

4 thick fish fillets or steaks (about 1½ pounds)

½ cup roughly chopped fresh basil leaves

1 Trim and cut the zucchini and eggplant into 1-inch chunks. Cut the pepper into strips. Roughly chop the tomatoes, reserving their juice.

2 Put 2 tablespoons of the oil in a large skillet over medium-high heat and immediately add the garlic. When it begins to sizzle, add the onion and sprinkle with salt and pepper. Cook, stirring occasionally, until the onion begins to soften, 3 to 5 minutes.

3 Add the zucchini, eggplant, bell pepper, and another sprinkle of salt and pepper. Lower the heat a bit to keep the vegetables from burning and cook, stirring occasionally, until the eggplant is fairly soft, another 10 to 15 minutes. Add the tomatoes and their juice, the thyme, and the olives if you're using them and cook, stirring occasionally, until the tomatoes begin to break down, another 5 to 10 minutes. Taste and adjust the seasoning.

4 Sprinkle the fish with salt and pepper and lay it on top of the vegetables. Adjust the heat so the mixture simmers. Cover and cook until the fish is opaque throughout and a paring knife inserted into the fish at its thickest point meets little resistance. This will take anywhere from 5 to 12 minutes, depending on the thickness of the fish.

5 Transfer the fish to a platter, then stir the basil into the vegetables. Spoon the vegetables around the fish, drizzle everything with the remaining 1 tablespoon olive oil (plus a little more if you like), and serve.

SOFTENING THE VEGETABLES
They'll take longer to cook than the fish. Wait until they're tender and lightly browned before adding the tomatoes.

ADDING THE FISH Give the tomatoes a few minutes to break down; it's their juice that will create the steam that cooks the fish. Then keep the mixture bubbling gently when you add the fillets.

Once the fish is ready, remove it from the pan or it will keep cooking.

RECOGNIZING DONENESS The knife should slide in and out of the fillet fairly easily, and the interior should be opaque but not dry looking.

Tips

▶ Be careful not to cook swordfish and tuna too long when steaming; other fish won't dry out as quickly.

▶ Giving slower-cooking foods a head start is a valuable technique you can try with chicken breasts and other quick-cooking cuts of meat.

Variations

▶ **Steamed Fish with Leeks:** Skip the zucchini, eggplant, pepper, tomatoes, thyme, and olives. Trim and slice 1½ pounds leeks (the white and light green parts) and rinse them in a colander to remove all grit. Begin the recipe with Step 2 and cook the leeks in the hot oil, stirring occasionally, until they're tender and begin to turn golden, 5 to 10 minutes. Add ½ cup white wine or water and bring to a gentle bubble. Continue with the recipe from Step 4.

▶ **Steamed Fish with Bok Choy:** Skip the zucchini, eggplant, pepper, tomatoes, thyme, and olives. In Step 2, add about 1 pound roughly chopped bok choy, ¼ cup soy sauce, and ½ cup water to the skillet. Cook, stirring, until the greens begin to wilt, 3 to 5 minutes. Continue with the recipe from Step 4.

Learn More

▶ Fish Basics (page 346), Chopping (page 19), Preparing Bell Peppers (page 117), preparing tomatoes (page 80)

Roasted Salmon with Butter

This dish is perfect for entertaining—you can serve it hot or at room temperature.

TIME   **20 minutes**
MAKES   **6 to 8 servings**

---

4 tablespoons (½ stick) butter

Salt and freshly ground black pepper

1 salmon fillet (2 to 3 pounds), skin on if you like

2 tablespoons chopped fresh parsley leaves for garnish

1 Heat the oven to 475°F. When the oven is hot, put the butter on a rimmed baking sheet and sprinkle with salt and pepper. Put the pan in the oven for the butter to melt, about 1 minute. Watch it the whole time: As soon as the foaming stops, remove the pan.

2 Put the salmon in the seasoned butter, skin side down, and sprinkle the top with more salt and pepper. Return the pan to the oven.

3 Roast until the salmon is just cooked through, 8 to 12 minutes. To see whether the fish is done, stick a paring knife between the layers of flesh; the center should be bright pink and still a little translucent. Garnish with the parsley and serve.

The fish will brown a little more, but don't expect it to develop a crust.

If you let the interior get any paler than this, it will become overcooked and dry.

MELTING THE BUTTER Watch the butter in the oven: It will bubble for a few seconds; when the foam subsides, carefully take the pan out and tip it to coat the bottom, then add the salmon.

CHECKING THE FISH Salmon is dark pink or orange inside when raw, even though the outside might be opaque. But keep checking frequently for the color to brighten; it cooks quickly.

RECOGNIZING DONENESS Perfectly cooked salmon will separate into big, soft flakes and still be vibrant pink in the center. It will continue to cook a little more off the heat.

Tips

▶ Salmon is one of the most popular types of fish in the United States, and deservedly so. It's got beautiful, tender flesh (as long as you don't overcook it) and amazing flavor. Wild salmon, which at this point comes pretty much exclusively from the Pacific Northwest (mostly Alaska), is the best choice for the environment and is leaner, darker, and better tasting than farm-raised salmon.

Variations

▶ **Herb-Roasted Salmon:** Skip the parsley for garnish. In Step 1, use 2 tablespoons olive oil and 2 tablespoons butter. In Step 2, add 2 tablespoons minced shallot and ¼ cup chopped fresh parsley or basil leaves or 2 tablespoons chopped fresh tarragon, thyme, or dill leaves to the pan along with the salmon. Continue with the recipe.

▶ **Salmon Roasted with Olives and Thyme:** Skip the parsley for garnish. Before Step 1, pit and chop 1 cup kalamata olives. In Step 1, sprinkle the salmon with pepper, but skip the salt (olives have plenty). In Step 2, add the olives and 2 tablespoons chopped fresh thyme leaves to the pan along with the salmon. Continue with the recipe.

Learn More

▶ Fish Basics (page 346), Roasting (page 33), Chopping Herbs (page 78)

Panfried Trout with Tartar Sauce

Campfire food in your own kitchen.

TIME **25 minutes**

MAKES **2 servings**

½ cup mayonnaise

2 teaspoons Dijon-style mustard

2 tablespoons chopped pickles, capers, or a combination

Salt and freshly ground black pepper

Vegetable oil for panfrying

2 whole trout (about 12 ounces each), cleaned, head and tail removed

½ cup cornmeal

½ cup all-purpose flour

2 lemons, quartered, for serving

1 In a small bowl, whisk together the mayonnaise, mustard, pickles, and a sprinkle of salt and pepper. Cover and refrigerate for up to a day or keep at room temperature while you cook the trout. Line a baking sheet with paper towels.

2 Put about ¼ inch of oil in a large skillet over medium heat. Sprinkle the fish inside and out with salt and pepper. Combine the cornmeal and flour on a large plate, sprinkle with salt and pepper, and toss with a fork. Dredge both sides of the fish in the cornmeal mixture.

3 When the oil is hot, carefully lay the fish in the pan. Cook, turning once, until it is nicely browned on both sides and the interior turns white, 8 to 12 minutes total. Adjust the heat so the fish sizzles without burning and add more oil, 1 tablespoon at a time, if the pan looks dry.

4 Drain on the paper towels and serve immediately with the tartar sauce and lemon wedges.

Save the head and tail in the freezer for stock!

You can also cook 4 fillets in two batches; they'll be ready to turn in 3 to 5 minutes.

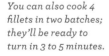

GETTING TO KNOW WHOLE FISH Removing the head and tail makes the fish easier to handle. Ask the fishmonger to do it, or cut them off yourself. (Or just leave them on if you'd like.)

CUTTING WHOLE FISH To remove the head, cut right below the gills. To remove the tail, cut right above where the tail connects to the body.

HEATING THE OIL Don't mess with a thermometer when you use shallow oil for frying; a pinch of the flour mixture will sizzle when the oil is ready.

CHECKING DONENESS Use a spatula to peek inside the cavity; make sure the flesh is opaque throughout.

Tips

▶ The whole trout that you are likely to find will already be scaled, gutted, and perhaps even butterflied. They may, however, still have the head and tail on. I think it's kind of cool to cook the whole thing, but if you want them gone, just cut them off with a sharp knife.

▶ The cooked fish pulls away from the bones easily, leaving you with a fillet.

Variations

▶ **Panfried Trout with Bacon:** Roughly chop 4 ounces thick-cut bacon. In Step 2, add the bacon to the pan with the oil and cook, stirring, until crisp; remove with a slotted spoon and continue with the recipe. Serve the fish with the bacon crumbled on top.

▶ **Lemon-Roasted Whole Trout.** Try this instead of the main recipe: Heat the oven to 425°F. After seasoning the fish, thinly slice 1 lemon crosswise and fill the opening in the belly of the trout. Add several fresh parsley and thyme sprigs if you like. Smear the fish with 2 tablespoons olive oil and put on a rimmed baking sheet. Roast until the fish is opaque and flaky, 15 to 20 minutes. Serve the fish drizzled with the pan juices.

Learn More

▶ Fish Basics (page 346), Panfrying (page 36)

Shellfish Basics

Shrimp

If you're lucky enough to live in a place with fresh local shrimp, there's nothing better. If not, the shrimp you'll see is either wild imported (from abroad or the southern United States) or farmed, mostly likely from Asia (this is the most common).

Almost all shrimp (which is a crustacean) is frozen before shipping. And 99 percent of the time I buy unpeeled frozen shrimp—it's less convenient than peeled and cleaned, but way more flavorful. You can use any size shrimp in the recipes here. So get the best-quality medium to large shrimp you can find.

Frozen shrimp last in the freezer for about a month before their quality goes perceptibly downhill; thawed you should eat the same day. Defrost shrimp in the fridge for 24 hours. Or submerge them in cold water and change it every 30 minutes until thawed, usually within an hour or two.

Scallops

Scallops are creamy, briny, and sweet, with an incredible meaty (rather than flaky) texture. These are mollusks but are rarely seen in their shell; sea scallops are the most common.

Often scallops are frozen and sold thawed, usually soaked in a salt solution, which plumps them up and waters down their flavor. Rinse and dry them well. If you see scallops not packed in brine—*dry*, in other words—grab 'em; they're far better.

Mollusks

Mollusks—which includes the examples below—should be alive when you buy them raw. Their shells will be shut so tight you can't wiggle them. When they're dead, the shells will be open, cracked, or easily moved, and you should *not* buy them. If they're gaping a little, tap the shell with your fingers; those that close are fine; avoid those that stay open. Store them in the fridge in a bowl so they can breathe and eat them within a day or two.

Mussels, clams, and oysters can be wild or farmed, from anywhere in the world. Wild might taste better, but farmed can be quite good. Clams and mussels can both be cooked in the same way. For both, just rinse them under running water and scrub with a brush to remove any grit.

The best oysters are raised in cold waters. Shucking can be a bit of a pain but you must at least witness it being done and eat them within hours if you intend to eat them raw. (The one oyster recipe in this book calls for them shucked for cooking.)

SEA SCALLOPS

FROZEN

WHOLE

MUSSELS

CLAMS

OYSTERS

PEELED AND CLEANED

LOBSTER

CRAWFISH

SQUID

BLUE CRAB

Crustaceans

Crustaceans are a type of shellfish that includes two of the best-tasting sea creatures: lobsters and crabs. All are easy to cook: You plunge them into boiling seasoned water. What takes a little work is what happens before and after—the shopping and the eating.

When buying lobster, make sure its claws are banded shut and that it's still lively. Crabs are available with both hard and soft shells and can be bought live, cooked, or frozen (raw or cooked), depending on the variety and where you live. If you're buying crabs to boil or steam, they should

be moving up until the time you put them in the pot. To heat cooked, frozen crab—right from the freezer—put them in boiling water for a few minutes; to serve cold, defrost in the fridge for a day or so. For crab cakes or crab salad, you'll want cooked lump or jumbo lump crab meat—usually sold in cans or plastic containers. Stick with the fresh stuff unless you're in a pinch.

Crawfish look—and cook—like mini lobsters. Like crab, you can get them live, precooked, or precooked and frozen.

Squid

Squid (a type of mollusk) is shockingly easy to cook. You can buy it frozen and keep it for a month in your freezer or buy it thawed and cook it within a day or two.

Either way, the squid should have white or purplish bodies and tentacles and a clean, sweet smell. Buying it cleaned is more convenient than messing with a squid's inedible parts.

People always say that you should cook squid for either 1 minute or 1 hour. That's about right. Anywhere in between and the squid will have the texture of a rubber band. Once it just turns opaque—no more than a minute or two after hitting the heat—it's done.

Shrimp Scampi

This dish is famous for two reasons: It's incredibly delicious and ridiculously easy.

TIME **20 minutes**

MAKES **4 servings**

⅓ cup olive oil, or more as needed

1 tablespoon minced garlic

1½ pounds medium or large shrimp, peeled

Salt and freshly ground black pepper

2 tablespoons fresh lemon juice or white wine

2 tablespoons chopped fresh parsley leaves

1 Put the olive oil in a large skillet over low heat. Add the garlic and cook, stirring frequently, until it just turns golden, 2 or 3 minutes.

2 Raise the heat to medium-high and add the shrimp, along with a sprinkle of salt and pepper. Spread them out in an even layer.

3 When the shrimp turn pink on one side, after 2 or 3 minutes, stir to turn them over. Continue cooking and stirring as necessary until the shrimp are pink all over and just barely translucent inside, another 2 or 3 minutes. Add a few drops of oil if the pan ever seems too dry.

4 Stir in the lemon juice and 2 tablespoons water and cook for another 30 seconds to thicken the sauce. Stir in the parsley and serve.

I don't bother to remove the thin black cord that runs along the top of the shrimp. This is deveining. *You can cut it out if you want to take the time.*

I just pinch the tail off, since it's not edible, but some people like to leave it on.

PEELING SHRIMP After pinching off the tail, split the shell down the center to remove it like a jacket. Run your finger along the shrimp to check for stray pieces.

FLAVORING THE OIL Cooking the garlic slowly keeps it from getting bitter and also intensifies the flavor it imparts to the oil.

Tips

▶ The advantage of peeling your own shrimp is that you have the makings of great stock. Freeze the shells if you're not going to make a batch in a day or so.

▶ The best way to tell whether shrimp is perfectly cooked is to slice into it. The flesh should be an opaque white all the way through, but not rubbery. If anything, err on the side of slight undercooking; the residual heat will finish cooking the shrimp before it gets to the table.

Variations

▶ **Pan-Cooked Shrimp with Garlic, Cumin, and Paprika:** Skip the parsley and use all water or wine instead of the lemon juice. In Step 2, stir in 1 teaspoon ground cumin and 1½ teaspoons paprika along with the shrimp.

▶ **Garlic Shrimp with Tomatoes and Cilantro:** Double the amount of garlic. In Step 2, add 4 chopped roma (plum) tomatoes to the skillet along with the shrimp. Use chopped fresh cilantro leaves instead of the parsley and lime juice instead of the lemon juice. The shrimp will take an extra minute or two to get pink.

Learn More

▶ Shellfish Basics (page 360), mincing garlic (page 20), Chopping Herbs (page 78), Making Quick Shrimp Stock (page 364)

TURNING PINK It might take only a minute for the shrimp to start changing color, but if they're big they could take a little bit longer to cook through.

CHECKING DONENESS If it is just barely translucent in the center, turn off the heat. The shrimp will finish cooking in the hot oil by the time it gets to the table.

Stir-Fried Shrimp with Celery

Fast, easy, healthy, and infinitely better than takeout.

TIME **20 to 30 minutes**
MAKES **4 servings**

1½ pounds medium or large shrimp, peeled (save the shells)

3 tablespoons vegetable oil

Salt and freshly ground black pepper

1 tablespoon minced garlic

1 tablespoon minced fresh ginger

1 small red onion, halved and thinly sliced

8 celery stalks, cut into sticks

2 tablespoons soy sauce

1 teaspoon dark sesame oil

¼ cup chopped cashews for garnish, optional

1 If you peeled the shrimp yourself, put the shells in a saucepan with 1 cup water, turn the heat to high, and bring to a boil. Turn the heat to low, cover, and let the stock simmer while you prepare the stir-fry. (If you bought peeled shrimp, skip this step.)

2 Put 2 tablespoons of the oil in a large skillet over high heat. When it's hot, add the shrimp and a sprinkle of salt and pepper. Cook, stirring frequently, until the shrimp are pink all over and almost opaque in the center, 3 to 4 minutes. Transfer them to a plate with a slotted spoon.

3 Add the remaining 1 tablespoon oil, then immediately add the garlic and ginger. Cook, stirring, for 15 seconds, then add the onion and celery. Cook, stirring frequently, until the celery has softened a bit but is still crunchy, 3 to 5 minutes. (If you made shrimp stock, strain it.)

4 Stir the shrimp back into the skillet, add ½ cup of the shrimp stock (or use water if you didn't have shells), the soy sauce, and the sesame oil, and cook until some of the liquid evaporates, another minute. (If the mixture looks too dry, add more liquid, 1 tablespoon at a time.) Turn off the heat, stir in the cashews if you're using them, and serve.

Keep the water at a gentle bubble.

MAKING QUICK SHRIMP STOCK
The shells release flavor quickly (in as little as 10 minutes). By the time you're ready to add liquid to the skillet, it will be good to go.

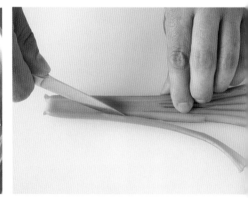

CUTTING CELERY INTO STICKS
Cut each celery stalk lengthwise into several strips with a paring knife or the tip of a chef's knife. Then cut crosswise into matchsticks about 1½ inches long.

Tips

▶ If you can, buy shell-on shrimp and peel them yourself. It's a little more work, but the quick shrimp stock adds a ton of flavor, so it's well worth the effort.

▶ I like to cut celery into long thin sticks for stir-fry, but you can chop it however you like.

▶ You can serve stir-fries with any rice or noodles. Your choice.

Variations

▶ **7 Other Vegetables You Can Stir-Fry with Shrimp.** In this recipe you have lots of options to substitute for the celery. The cooking times may vary a bit, so check for doneness frequently:

1 Carrots, cut into sticks or coins
2 Red bell pepper, sliced
3 Fennel (bulb only), halved and sliced
4 Asparagus, cut into 2-inch pieces
5 Green beans, whole or cut in half
6 Snow peas, trimmed
7 Bean sprouts

Learn More

▶ Shellfish Basics (page 360), Stir-Frying (page 29), Peeling Shrimp (page 362), mincing garlic (page 20), preparing ginger (page 222), slicing onions (page 232)

UNDERCOOKING THE SHRIMP Remove them from the pan just after they start to turn pink so they don't get rubbery when they cook again with the celery.

CHECKING FOR DONENESS Taste the celery to be sure it's ready for you to add the shrimp. It should be just a little less crunchy than raw.

MAKING A SAUCE Decide how saucy you'd like the stir-fry and remove the pan from the heat just a moment before it reaches the consistency you want.

Seared Scallops with Pan Sauce

You'll amaze yourself and your friends with this easy restaurant-style dish.

TIME **15 minutes**
MAKES **4 servings**

---

3 tablespoons butter

1 tablespoons olive oil

1½ pounds sea scallops

Salt and freshly ground black pepper

1 tablespoon minced garlic

Juice of 1 lemon

½ cup dry white wine or water, or more as needed

2 tablespoons chopped fresh chives

1 Cut 2 tablespoons of the butter into pea-sized pieces, put it on a small plate, and stick it in the freezer. Heat a large skillet over medium-high heat for 3 or 4 minutes. Add the remaining 1 table-spoon butter and the olive oil and wait for the butter to melt.

2 Pat the scallops dry with paper towels, add them to the pan, and sprinkle with salt and pepper; work in batches if necessary to avoid crowding the skillet. Cook, turning once, until they are well browned on both sides but not quite cooked through, 2 minutes per side (less if the scallops are under 1 inch across; more if they're over). Transfer the scallops to a plate.

3 Stir in the garlic, lemon juice, and wine and scrape all the brown bits off the bottom of the skillet with a spatula. Lower the heat to medium and cook until the liquid in the skillet thickens, a minute or two, then whisk in the butter you chilled in the freezer, one bit at a time, to make a creamy sauce, adding another tablespoon or two of liquid if necessary.

4 Return the scallops to the skillet and add the chives. Adjust the heat so the sauce bubbles gently and toss to coat the scallops with the sauce. To serve, transfer the scallops to a platter and spoon the sauce over all.

Press down gently while the scallops cook to encourage full contact with the pan, then listen for a hiss: That's moisture heating and evaporating.

RELEASING FROM THE PAN The scallops will offer no resistance when they're ready to turn.

GETTING A GOOD SEAR The idea is to brown the scallops well on both sides without overcooking them, so keep the heat as high as you can without creating too much smoke.

Tips

▶ Make sure you pat the scallops dry with a paper towel. Only a dry scallop will sear properly.

▶ A perfectly seared scallop should be nicely browned on the outside and buttery in the middle. A paring knife should slide in and out with almost no resistance, but as always, the best way to check it is to make a small slice into one and look (or taste). The inside should remain translucent. High-quality scallops are delicious raw and tend to dry out quickly: It's better to undercook than overcook.

Variations

▶ **Seared Scallops with Cherry Tomatoes And Basil:** Skip the lemon juice. Cut 1 pint cherry tomatoes in half. In Step 3, add the tomatoes with the garlic and wine and cook until they wrinkle a bit and release their juice, 2 or 3 minutes. Use chopped fresh basil leaves instead of the chives.

Learn More

▶ Shellfish Basics (page 360), mincing garlic (page 20), deglazing the pan (page 157), Chopping Herbs (page 78)

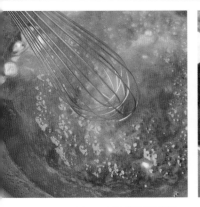

Nick-and-peek into one if you need to check for doneness.

BUILDING SAUCE WITH BUTTER
After you add the liquid and deglaze the pan, the addition of butter develops fantastic creaminess and richness.

FINISHING THE DISH As soon as the scallops are cooked through completely and coated with the sauce, remove the pan from the heat; they will continue to cook.

Bacon-Wrapped Scallops

Smoked pork is perhaps a scallop's most flavorful companion.

TIME **45 minutes**
MAKES **4 servings**

⅓ cup olive oil, plus more for greasing the pan

1 teaspoon minced garlic

Salt and freshly ground black pepper

1½ pounds sea scallops

About 1 pound thinly sliced bacon (16 to 24 slices)

2 lemons, cut into quarters, for serving

1 Soak wooden toothpicks (1 per scallop) in warm water while you prepare the remaining ingredients. Combine the oil, garlic, and a sprinkle of salt and pepper in a large bowl. Add the scallops to the marinade and toss gently to coat. Let the scallops sit in the bowl while you cook the bacon. Line a baking sheet with paper towels.

2 Prepare a grill or turn on the broiler; the heat should be medium-high and the rack about 4 inches from the heat source. If you're grilling, brush the grates clean and grease them well. If you're broiling, grease a rimmed baking sheet with a thin film of oil.

3 Put the bacon in a large skillet over medium-high heat; you will need to work in batches. Cook, turning and adjusting the heat as necessary so they

don't burn, until the slices are cooked lightly but flexible enough to wrap around a scallop, 5 to 10 minutes. Transfer the bacon to paper towels to drain. Repeat with the remaining bacon.

4 Cut the bacon into pieces that will wrap around the scallops without overlapping too much. Wrap each piece around a scallop and secure it with one of the soaked toothpicks, stuck horizontally through the center.

5 To grill: Put the scallops directly over the fire. To broil: Put the scallops on the prepared baking sheet and under the heat source. Cook, turning once, until they are lightly charred on both sides and a paring knife can be inserted with little resistance, 2 to 3 minutes per side. Serve right away, with the lemon wedges.

Better to cook too little than too brittle.

COOKING THE BACON FOR WRAPPING The bacon crisps as it cools, so remove it from the pan when it's still quite pliable.

WRAPPING WITH BACON How much bacon you use will depend on how big the scallops are. Encircle them snugly without changing their shape.

Tips
▶ If you end up cooking the bacon so that it's too crisp to use as a wrapping, just crumble it up and sprinkle it on top of the scallops after cooking.

Variations
▶ **Simply Grilled or Broiled Scallops:** Skip the garlic and bacon. Toss the scallops with the oil and a sprinkle of salt and pepper. Grill or broil as directed in Step 5.

▶ **Bacon-Wrapped Stuffed Scallops:** In Step 1, combine ½ cup very finely chopped fresh basil leaves with the garlic, 1 tablespoon of the olive oil, and a sprinkle of salt and pepper. Instead of marinating the scallops, make a deep horizontal slit in the side of each scallop with a paring knife, but don't cut all the way through. Fill each scallop with about ½ teaspoon of the basil mixture, then close. Put the remaining oil onto a plate and gently coat the scallops in it. Continue with the recipe.

Learn More
▶ Shellfish Basics (page 360), Grilling (page 35), Broiling (page 34)

SECURING WITH A TOOTHPICK
The tips of the toothpick should stick out from both sides.

CHECKING DONENESS The scallops are ready to turn when they're golden and the edges of the bacon are crisping.

Steamed Mussels or Clams

A classic seafood dinner that's totally fun and super-easy.

TIME **30 minutes**
MAKES **4 servings**

2 tablespoons olive oil

1 large shallot or small red onion, chopped

½ cup white wine, beer, or water

4 to 6 pounds mussels or hard-shell clams, well scrubbed, those with broken shells discarded

½ cup chopped fresh parsley leaves for garnish

2 lemons, quartered, for serving

1 Put the oil in a large pot over medium heat. When it's hot, add the shallot and cook, stirring occasionally, until it begins to soften, 3 to 5 minutes.

2 Add the wine along with the mussels, turn the heat up to high, and cover the pot. Cook, gently shaking the pot occasionally, until they all (or nearly all) open, 8 to 10 minutes for mussels and 10 to 15 minutes for clams. Remove the pot from the heat.

3 Scoop the mussels or clams into a serving bowl. Remove as many shallots as you can with a slotted spoon and scatter them on top. Pour or ladle the accumulated liquid over the mussels or clams, being careful to leave any sediment in the bottom of the pan. Garnish with the parsley and serve with the lemon wedges.

Most mussels will be clean shaven.

Like clams and oysters, only live mussels are fresh mussels.

REMOVING MUSSEL BEARDS
Hold the beard firmly between your thumb and forefinger and pull it along the opening between the shells toward the wide end and out.

TESTING MUSSELS AND CLAMS If the shells don't close when you press them together or flick them with your fingers, throw them out.

Tips

▶ Small to medium clams are best for steaming.

▶ To eat the mussels or clams, just hold the shell in one hand and scoop out the meat with a fork or your fingers or teeth.

▶ Good crusty bread is the very best thing to soak up the cooking juices, but you can also serve this dish on top of rice, noodles, or boiled potatoes.

Variations

▶ **Tomato-Basil Steamed Mussels or Clams:** Use garlic instead of the shallots, stir in 1 cup chopped tomatoes with the wine, and garnish with chopped fresh basil leaves.

▶ **French-Style Steamed Mussels or Clams:** Use butter instead of olive oil and stir in ½ cup heavy cream along with the mussels or clams.

▶ **Curry-Coconut Steamed Mussels or Clams:** Use butter instead of olive oil, 2 tablespoons minced fresh ginger and 2 tablespoons curry powder instead of the shallots, and 1 cup coconut milk instead of the wine. Garnish with chopped fresh cilantro leaves.

Learn More

▶ Shellfish Basics (page 360), Chopping Herbs (page 78)

CHECKING DONENESS When the majority of mussels are open, the batch is ready. (These aren't quite there yet.) Shaking the covered pot once in a while—like popcorn—encourages even cooking.

SERVING THE POT LIQUID There will probably be a little bit of sand at the bottom of the pot, so remove the juice from the top rather than pouring out the liquid.

Grilled or Broiled Shrimp Burgers

Of the three burgers in this book, this is the fanciest—but it's no more difficult.

TIME **30 minutes**
MAKES **4 servings**

Vegetable oil as needed

1 garlic clove, peeled

1½ pounds shrimp, peeled

1 small red onion, chopped

1 red or yellow bell pepper, cored, seeded, and chopped, optional

Salt and freshly ground black pepper

½ cup fresh parsley leaves

Hamburger buns or hard rolls, toasted if you like, optional

Lettuce, tomato, sliced onion, pickles, and condiments as you like

1 Prepare a grill or turn on the broiler; the heat should be medium-high and the rack about 4 inches from the heat source. If you're grilling, clean the grates with a wire brush. If you're broiling, grease a rimmed baking sheet with a thin film of the oil.

2 Combine the garlic and one-third of the shrimp in a food processor and process to a purée, stopping the machine to scrape down the sides of the container as necessary.

3 Add the remaining shrimp along with the onion, bell pepper if you're using it, a sprinkle of salt and pepper, and the parsley. Pulse until the shrimp is chopped, but not too finely. Shape the mixture into 4 patties and put on wax or parchment paper.

4 Brush the grill or the patties lightly with the oil. To grill: Put the burgers directly over the fire. To broil: Put them on the prepared baking sheet and under the heat source. Cook, undisturbed, until the side exposed to the heat develops a browned crust, 3 to 5 minutes. Carefully turn the burgers and repeat on the other side, cooking until the shrimp has turned opaque throughout, another 3 to 5 minutes. Serve on buns if you like, with mayonnaise, ketchup, or any other condiments you like.

This two-step process is the key to making any fish burger work.

PURÉEING SOME OF THE SHRIMP Purée the first batch until completely smooth.

PULSING THE REMAINING INGREDIENTS Pulse everything else until the remaining shrimp breaks into chunks about the size of peas.

Tips

▶ Shrimp contain collagen, which when puréed acts as the "glue" that holds these burgers together. Make sure you chop (not purée) the rest of the shrimp, or else you will get a burger that's all glue (sticky and mushy). And don't add too many more vegetables or the burgers might start to break apart when you cook them.

▶ For a switch from lettuce, try garnishing with whole basil leaves.

Variations

▶ **Grilled or Broiled Salmon Burgers:** Try substituting skinned salmon fillets in this recipe. They'll be a little more fragile but still hold together.

▶ **Thai-Style Grilled or Broiled Shrimp Burgers:** In Step 2, add 1 seeded fresh hot green chile (like jalapeño) and 2 tablespoons minced fresh ginger along with garlic and the first third of the shrimp. Add 2 teaspoons soy sauce and the juice of 1 lime along with the remaining shrimp. Replace half of the parsley with fresh basil leaves (preferably Thai basil). Continue with the recipe. Serve with mayonnaise spiked with hot sauce and lime wedges.

Learn More

▶ Shellfish Basics (page 360), chopping onions (page 19), Preparing Bell Peppers (page 117)

FORMING THE PATTIES Just like beef burgers, the more you handle the mixture, the tougher the burgers will be, so use a light touch.

FLIPPING THE BURGERS If you try to turn these before a dark crust forms and they release easily, they'll probably fall apart.

If you're grilling, wait for them to release easily from the grates.

Creamy Oyster and Potato Stew

Luxury in a bowl and the best way to serve cooked oysters.

TIME **45 minutes**

MAKES **4 servings**

1 pound small waxy red or white potatoes, halved

Salt

3 tablespoons butter

2 large or 3 medium shallots, sliced

Freshly ground black pepper

½ cup white wine or dry sherry

2 cups cream

16 to 24 oysters, shucked, liquid reserved, those with broken shells discarded (1 quart)

1 tablespoon chopped fresh tarragon leaves or 2 tablespoons chopped fresh chives

Don't bother with canned oysters; they taste tinny.

1 Put the potatoes in a large pot, add a pinch of salt and enough water to cover by 2 inches, and bring to a boil. Reduce the heat so the water bubbles vigorously. Cook, stirring once or twice, until the potatoes are just barely tender at the center; a paring knife will still meet some resistance when inserted. Drain, reserving 2 cups of the cooking liquid.

2 Return the pot to medium heat (no need to wipe it out) and add the butter. When it foams, add the shallots, sprinkle with salt and pepper, and cook, stirring, until soft and golden, 5 to 10 minutes.

3 Raise the heat to medium-high, add the wine, and stir until it almost all bubbles away, a minute or two. Add the cream, the reserved oyster liquid and potato cooking liquid, and the potatoes. Bring the mixture just to a boil, stirring occasionally to prevent sticking. Cook, stirring occasionally, until the mixture thickens a little, about 5 minutes, then lower the heat so it barely bubbles.

4 Slip the oysters into the pot, cover, and turn off the heat. After 5 minutes, take a peek; the oysters should be turning opaque; if not, put the lid on for another minute or two. Stir in the tarragon, taste and adjust the seasoning, and serve.

BUYING SHUCKED OYSTERS
Make sure they come from a source you trust. They should smell like the sea and come packed in their own juices—an almost clear, relatively thin liquid.

RESERVING THE POTATO WATER
You want to save the starchiest part. If you have more than 2 cups liquid after draining, let it settle, remove some from the top, then measure.

Tips

▶ Oysters have an incredibly delicate flavor and texture, which is why they're so good raw. Lightly poaching them in the warm cream—instead of blasting them over high heat—helps to preserve their natural character.

Variations

▶ **Lighter Oyster and Potato Stew:** Use 3 cups fish, chicken, or vegetable stock instead of the cream.

▶ **Shrimp Bisque:** Use 1½ pounds peeled shrimp instead of the oysters. If you have time (and peel your own shrimp), boil the shells and tails in the reserved potato water for 15 minutes; strain, then let the starch settle and continue with the recipe. Let the soup cool a bit, then carefully purée it in a blender and return it to the pot over medium-low heat to rewarm before garnishing and serving.

Learn More

▶ Shellfish Basics (page 360), types of potatoes (page 235), Dairy—and Not (page 42)

POACHING THE OYSTERS The whole idea is to heat them through without making them tough or stringy. This requires low heat, frequent checking—and not much time.

RECOGNIZING DONENESS Perfectly cooked oysters look puffed and opaque and are easily pierced with a knife but not quite falling apart.

Battered and Fried Squid

Perfectly cooked squid (or almost anything else for that matter) in a crisp coating.

TIME **40 minutes**
MAKES **6 to 8 servings**

Vegetable oil for deep frying

1 cup all-purpose flour for the batter, plus 1½ cups for dredging

1 egg

¾ cup sparkling water, beer, or cold tap water

Salt and freshly ground black pepper

1½ pounds cleaned squid, tubes cut into ⅓-inch rings, tentacles cut into bite-sized pieces

1 lemon, quartered, for serving

1 Put at least 2 inches of oil in a large pot over medium heat. (Use an oil thermometer clipped to the side if you have one.) While the oil heats, combine 1 cup of the flour, the egg, the sparkling water, and a sprinkle of salt and pepper in a bowl. Whisk together; the batter should be fairly thin (a little lumpy is fine). Put the remaining 1½ cups flour in a shallow bowl and stir in a sprinkle of salt and pepper. Line a baking sheet with paper towels.

2 The oil is ready at 350°F. If you don't have a thermometer, put a drop of batter into the oil: It should bubble vigorously but not turn brown right away. Adjust the heat as necessary. If the oil starts to smoke, remove it from the heat immediately to cool a bit.

3 A few pieces at a time, dredge the squid in the flour, shake off any excess, then dip it in the batter, shaking off any excess batter as well. Working in batches to avoid crowding the pan, carefully drop the squid into the oil. Cook, turning the pieces as necessary with a slotted spoon, until they are crisp and pale golden, just a minute or two.

4 As the squid finishes cooking, transfer the pieces to the paper towels to drain and sprinkle with a little salt. Repeat the dredging, battering, and frying process until all the squid is cooked. Serve right away with lemon wedges.

Add another splash of liquid if the batter is too thick; a tablespoon of flour if too thin.

MAKING BATTER FOR FRYING It should be the consistency of thin pancake batter.

COATING WITH BATTER Make sure all the pieces are coated thinly and evenly. (Dredging in flour first helps the batter stick.)

Tips

▶ I like to buy whole cleaned squid and cut it myself: Separate the tentacles with a sharp knife and remove any tough cartilage on them; slice the tubular bodies crosswise into rings about ⅓ inch thick.

▶ The carbonation of sparkling water or beer makes the batter fluffy, while the egg adds the richness of a classic American seafood coating. For a more delicate tempura-style batter, use just flour and ice water and skip the egg.

Variations

▶ **Deep-Fried Squid Marinara.** The classic combo: Serve with warmed Tomato Sauce (page 178) for dipping.

▶ **Deep-Fried Seafood, Chicken, or Vegetables:** This recipe works with all sorts of other foods. Try peeled shrimp or shucked oysters (patted dry with towels). For fish, cut 1- to 2-inch chunks of thick white fish fillets. Boneless chicken (cut into strips or chunks) or whole tenders will taste better than any fast food you've ever tried. And assorted raw vegetables—like carrot sticks, broccoli florets, onion rings, or sweet potato slices—are also great in this recipe. The cooking time for all will vary a little, but the visual cues remain the same.

Learn More

▶ Shellfish Basics (page 360), Deep Frying (page 37)

FRYING IN BATCHES To work fluidly, keep the process moving: By the time you get a few more squid dredged and battered, the first round will be done.

REMOVING FOOD FROM HOT FAT When the squid is golden brown, use a spoon, slotted spoon, or tongs to transfer it to paper towels.

Lobster (or Other Seafood) Boil

The perfect shore dinner, a summer one-pot meal like no other.

TIME **45 minutes**
MAKES **4 servings**

---

4 bay leaves

2 teaspoons dried thyme or 4 sprigs fresh

1 tablespoon black peppercorns

4 garlic cloves, sliced

1 tablespoon coriander seeds or 1 teaspoon ground

3 cloves

Salt

1 pound small waxy red or white potatoes, halved or left whole

2 large onions, quartered

4 ears fresh corn, shucked and cut in half

Four 1½-pound lobsters, 16 to 24 blue or rock crabs, 3 pounds whole crawfish, or 2 pounds unpeeled shrimp

2 lemons, quartered, for serving

8 tablespoons (1 stick) butter, melted, optional

1 Fill a stockpot halfway with water, add the bay leaves, thyme, peppercorns, garlic, coriander, cloves, a small handful (seriously) of salt, the potatoes, and the onions.

2 Bring the mixture to a boil. Cook the potatoes and onions until they are tender and can be speared easily with a sharp knife, 8 to 10 minutes from when the water comes to a boil. Fish the potatoes out of the pot with a strainer (trying to leave the onions and seasonings behind) and put them on a large platter.

3 Add the corn to the pot, bring the water back to a boil, and cook until it's bright yellow, about 2 minutes. Transfer the corn to the platter with tongs.

4 Add whatever seafood you're using to the pot (use tongs for the lobsters or crabs). Bring the water back to a gentle but steady boil, cover, and cook: The lobsters will take 10 to 12 minutes; crabs and crawfish 5 to 10 minutes; shrimp 3 to 5 minutes. When cooked, the lobster, crab, and crawfish will be bright red and the shrimp pale pink and opaque throughout. To make sure the lobster is fully cooked, insert a quick-read thermometer into the joint at the base of the tail and into the tail meat; it should read between 140°F and 150°F.

5 Transfer the seafood and onions with tongs or a small strainer to the platter with the potatoes and corn. Ladle some of the juices into a bowl to serve on the side along with the lemon wedges and some melted butter if you like.

GOING FISHING When you boil the ingredients in batches like this, a strainer and tongs are the best tools to shuffle things in and out of the pot.

ADDING THE SEAFOOD Put the lobsters in head first and count the cooking time starting from when the water comes back to a boil.

Tips

▶ The best way to eat lobster, crab, crawfish, or shell-on shrimp is with your hands: Break the pieces apart at the joints and pick at the meat until it separates from the shell. (Many people believe sucking the shells dry is the best part of this meal.) It's also helpful to have nutcrackers and picks (or small mallets) handy to get every last bit.

▶ Some serving suggestions: A seafood boil is meant to be a lot of fun to eat (it's often served directly on newspaper so you can bundle up the mess when you're done). Whatever way you go, don't use the fancy tablecloth or china, put out plenty of napkins (and lots of cold beer for the adults), and scatter loaves of crusty bread and bottles of hot sauce around the table.

Learn More

▶ Shellfish Basics (page 360), Boiling (page 24), types of potatoes (page 235), Melting Butter (page 70)

Sometimes you have to get a little rough to crack the shells.

CHECKING FOR DONENESS
Once the lobsters turn bright red, take one out and check the temperature just to be sure. The vegetables should all be tender and ready by this time.

GETTING AT THE GOOD STUFF
If your hands or a butter knife doesn't work, use a nutcracker or small hammer or mallet to gently crack open the shells.

Breads

There's no denying it: Sandwiches, bread, and pizza are the dishes home cooks—even experienced ones—are most likely to outsource. Sandwiches, tacos, and the like are America's most popular take-out food; bread is commonly thought to be difficult, time-consuming, and finicky to bake; and pizza is more closely affiliated with telephones than with home ovens.

My job is to change your mind about all of this, or at least some of it some of the time, and I'm going to try to do that with a collection of straightforward and rewarding recipes for breads of all kinds.

We start with a lesson on different types of bread and how to use them for croutons, sandwiches, tacos, and burritos. After that you'll start turning out biscuits, muffins, scones, and other quick breads—so called because they come together in an instant. (Really.) Then we move on to the simplest yeasted breads, rolls, and pizza, all easy enough to prove that baking can be a natural part of everyday cooking. Along the way you'll learn to master the measuring and mixing techniques that guarantee success.

Very few people get to the point where they make all of their own bread, but it's easy enough to add loads of baked goods to your regular repertoire: corn bread to go with weeknight chili, Sunday morning cinnamon rolls, and edible thank-you gifts like homemade banana bread. Or maybe you'll tap your inner baker and open up a whole new part of kitchen life. Hey, you never know until you try.

Bread and Sandwich Basics

How to Cut Bread for Sandwiches

Bakeries have mechanical slicers, which give perfectly uniform slices, though not much choice in thickness. To do it yourself, grab a long serrated knife and let's go.

SANDWICH LOAVES With slow, steady back-and-forth motion, cut into slices about ½ inch thick.

FLAT LOAVES Like baguettes, focaccia, bagels, and ciabatta: Cut it into manageable squares or lengths. Then—keeping your fingers out of the path of the blade—slice it horizontally.

PITA BREAD Cut pocket pitas in half and stuff; or if there is no pocket, just fold bread to enclose the fillings and eat like a taco.

10 Sandwich Fillings

Almost anything can go between two slices of bread, provided it's not too wet (it will make the bread soggy if it is), too thickly sliced (impossible to bite), or too finely chopped and loosely bound (small pieces will fall out the sides). Above all, don't overdo the fillings; a sandwich that falls apart during eating defeats the purpose. Cheese, deli meats, lettuce, tomatoes, and onions are the obvious choices, but I also like salads or lightly mashed beans as vegetarian options. Sandwiches are also an ideal vehicle for cold or reheated leftovers. Here are a few meat and non-meat ideas from elsewhere in the book:

1 Hard-Boiled Eggs (page 51), thinly sliced
2 Hummus (page 86)
3 Pesto (page 184)
4 Grilled or Broiled Steak (page 266)
5 Perfect Roast Beef (page 274)
6 Meat Loaf (page 282)
7 Roast Pork with Herb Rub (page 292)
8 Grilled or Broiled Tomatoes (page 226)
9 Panfried Breaded Eggplant (page 244)
10 Grilled or Broiled Boneless Chicken (page 308)

CRUMB Open means that it has a lot of big holes. Tight means the interior is fine-grained and dense.

CRUST Ranges from dark and crackling crisp to golden and chewy.

Crust and Crumb

Bread has a language of its own. The best way to learn is to eat, so start by trying several kinds at the best bakery you can find (it might be in a supermarket, but probably not).

The differences are pronounced: thick, chewy crusts; crumbly insides; lots of holes; breads with crackly crusts and chewy interiors; those that are soft and doughy, sweet and dense; and so on. Each has its own character and its own best uses, but ultimately you'll decide what you like.

Croutons

A big payoff: You turn leftover bread into a pantry staple.

TIME   15 to 25 minutes
MAKES   4 servings

½ large loaf any high-quality bread

2 to 4 tablespoons butter, softened, or olive oil

1 Heat the oven to 400°F. If the bread isn't sliced, cut it into slices about ½ inch thick (or thicker if you'd like). You should have 8 or more slices.

2 Smear 1 side of each slice with butter or brush with olive oil. Cut each slice into halves, quarters, or large or small cubes as you like. Spread the bread out in a single layer on a rimmed baking sheet; if they touch a bit, that's fine, but don't overlap them.

3 Put the pan in the oven and toast the bread, turning the slices or tossing the cubes with a spatula as needed, for 10 to 20 minutes, until all the sides are lightly browned, depending on how thick the pieces are. Let cool to room temperature and serve right away or store in an airtight container for up to several days.

If you're using olive oil instead of butter, dab them just a bit with the brush so they don't get soggy.

You don't have to stay glued to the oven, but don't wander too far away.

SMEARING BREAD WITH BUTTER Just a thin layer or the croutons won't crisp. This works only when the butter is softened; otherwise you'll tear up the slices.

MAKING CROUTONS Any size is fine, as long as they're all relatively the same.

CHECKING FOR DONENESS The smaller the pieces, the faster they'll brown. Figure you need to check for the first time after 10 minutes.

Tips

▶ You don't have to use any fat on the bread; it'll crisp up anyway. But the flavor is much improved if you do.

▶ To soften hard butter, put it in the microwave for 20 seconds at a time on low. Or just let it sit out at room temperature for a while.

Variations

▶ **Toast:** Ideal for a crowd. Cut the bread into slices about ½ inch thick. If you like, smear with butter or drizzle with olive oil before baking (or after). Spread the slices on the baking sheet as described in Step 2 and continue with the recipe.

▶ **Seasoned Croutons:** Before toasting, sprinkle the bread with salt and pepper, followed by 1 tablespoon chili or curry powder.

▶ **Garlicky Croutons:** In Step 2, stir 1 or 2 tablespoons minced garlic into the butter or oil before spreading or brushing on the bread.

Learn More

▶ Bread and Sandwich Basics (page 382), Roasting (page 33)

Fresh Bread Crumbs

You control everything, from the type of bread you start with to the texture you end up with.

TIME **10 minutes**
MAKES **1½ to 2 cups**

½ large loaf any bread, preferably 1 or 2 days old

1 Tear the bread into pieces about 2 inches across. Put half the bread in a food processor. Pulse 3 to 4 times to break up the bread, then let the machine run for a few seconds to chop the bread to the desired texture—coarse, fine, or somewhere in between.

2 Remove the crumbs and repeat with the remaining bread. Use right away or store at room temperature in an airtight container for up to 1 month or in the freezer for up to 3 months.

The bread should ideally be a bit dry but not rock-hard.

A little bit of unevenness like this makes for nice texture, so don't strive for perfection and overprocess, or you'll end up with dust.

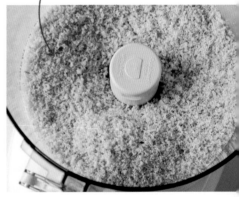

TEARING BREAD You'll get fluffy, evenly ground crumbs if you start with small pieces.

MAKING COARSE CRUMBS Pulse the machine several times, until the bread breaks down into pea-sized pieces.

MAKING FINE CRUMBS Let the machine run for several more seconds, until the bread looks like coarse grain.

Tips

▶ You can make bread crumbs out of almost any kind of bread—crust and all—but avoid using bread with solids such as seeds, fruit, or nuts.

▶ The only kind of store-bought bread crumbs I keep in the pantry (for emergencies, really) is panko, the coarse, airy Japanese-style variety, now available almost everywhere. If you see the kind made from whole wheat bread, grab it: It's hearty and super-crunchy.

Variations

▶ **Toasted Bread Crumbs:** For a crunchier crumb, heat the oven to 350°F. After pulverizing the bread, spread the crumbs in a single layer on a rimmed baking sheet and bake, shaking the pan occasionally, until they're lightly browned, about 15 minutes, depending on how fine they are.

▶ **Fried Bread Crumbs:** A super garnish, though not suitable for breading. Put ¼ cup olive oil in a large skillet over medium heat. When it's hot, add the bread crumbs and cook, stirring frequently, until they're toasted and crisp, 3 to 5 minutes. Use right away.

Learn More

▶ Bread and Sandwich Basics (page 382)

Grilled Cheese Sandwich

Use good ingredients for terrific results—no more effort than cooking with mediocre stuff.

TIME **10 minutes**

MAKES **1 sandwich**

---

2 ounces melting cheese, like cheddar or Gruyère

2 slices sandwich bread

1 tablespoon butter

1 Slice or grate the cheese. Put the cheese in an even layer between the bread slices, up to about ¼ inch from the edges.

2 Put the butter in a medium skillet over medium heat. When the butter melts, swirl the pan to spread it around a bit and put the sandwich in the skillet. Cook until the bottom of the sandwich is lightly browned and the cheese begins to melt, 2 to 5 minutes.

3 Turn the sandwich over and cook until the second side is also lightly browned and the cheese is fully melted, 2 to 3 minutes more. Cut in half (or into quarters if you like) and eat.

Packaged sliced or grated cheese is never top quality, dries out fast, and lacks flavor.

After turning, slide the sandwich around in the pan to sop up all the butter.

SLICING CHEESE For even slices, insert the knife at the desired thickness, then press down slowly, keeping the blade perpendicular to the board.

MAKING THE SANDWICH Be sure the bread isn't overfilled and the butter coats the center of the pan.

FLIPPING THE SANDWICH Before turning, press the uncooked piece of bread down to help "glue" it to the cheese. Then lift and flip.

EMMENTAL
Real "Swiss" cheese, medium-hard, nutty, and flavorful.

CHEDDAR
Yellow or white. When aged, it's sharp and complex, but even supermarket varieties make good sandwiches.

MOZZARELLA
Fresh or aged. Super-mild—almost bland—but wonderfully gooey when melted.

GRUYÈRE
Full flavored and really perfect when melted.

FONTINA
Italian mountain cheese. Nutty and mild at the same time.

Tips

▶ The cheeses shown here all melt easily and are good choices for cooking.

▶ You can use olive oil instead of the butter if you like, but the results won't be quite as rich.

Variations

▶ **Big-Batch Grilled Cheese Sandwiches:** Heat the oven to 400°F and multiply the recipe for as many sandwiches as you like. Grease a large baking sheet with half the butter and melt the rest. Put the sandwiches on the baking sheet so they have a little space between them. Brush the tops with the melted butter. Bake until the bread is golden and crisp on both sides and the cheese has melted, turning once or twice to promote even cooking, 15 to 20 minutes total.

▶ **5 Ways to Vary Grilled Cheese Sandwiches.** Be careful not to overload the sandwich or it won't hold together:

1 Smear the inside of the sandwich with mustard or mayonnaise.

2 Add a slice of tomato.

3 Smear 1 slice of the bread with pesto and use mozzarella.

4 Spread a spoonful of caramelized onions on 1 side of the bread.

5 Crumble a slice of bacon on top of the cheese.

Learn More

▶ Bread and Sandwich Basics (page 382), Simple Sandwich Loaf (page 410), Sautéing (page 28), Pesto (page 184), Caramelized Onions (page 232)

Bean Burritos

Refried beans and burritos in one fast recipe.

TIME **About 30 minutes**
MAKES **4 to 8 servings**

8 small or 4 large flour tortillas (8- or 12-inch diameter)

¼ cup olive oil

1 medium onion, chopped

1 tablespoon ground cumin, or more to taste

¼ teaspoon cayenne, or more to taste

Salt and freshly ground black pepper

3 cups drained cooked or canned pinto beans

1 cup grated cheddar, Jack, or other cheese

¼ cup sour cream

1 cup roughly chopped iceberg or romaine lettuce

1 cup salsa

1 Heat the oven to 300°F. Stack the tortillas on a sheet of foil and roll them up with the foil into a log. Warm them in the oven while you make the filling.

2 Put the oil in a large skillet over medium heat. When it's hot, add the onion and cook, stirring frequently, until it softens and begins to turn translucent, 3 to 5 minutes. Add the cumin, cayenne, and a sprinkle of salt and pepper and stir until the spices become fragrant, no more than 1 minute. Add the beans and mash them with a large fork or potato masher until they're mostly broken up but not completely smooth.

3 Cook, mashing and stirring, until the onion is quite soft and the beans are hot and creamy, 5 to 10 minutes; add water, a tablespoon at a time, if the mixture looks dry. Taste and adjust the seasoning, adding more spices if you like.

4 Remove the tortillas from the oven. Lay a tortilla on a flat surface and put about ¼ cup of the beans (or ½ cup for large tortillas) on the third closest to you. Sprinkle with about an eighth of the cheese, sour cream, lettuce, and salsa (or a quarter for large tortillas).

5 For small tortillas, fold the 2 sides of the tortilla in to cover the fillings partway, then roll up the tortilla to fully enclose them; put the burrito seam side down on a plate. Repeat with the remaining tortillas and fillings. For large tortillas, first fold the tortilla over the fillings to enclose them, then fold in the sides and roll. (You will have some leftover beans.) Serve right away.

MASHING REFRIED BEANS The beans should be mostly broken up, though some chunks vary the texture nicely. Add only enough water so they're creamy, not runny or soupy.

FILLING BURRITOS Put the fillings on one side of the tortilla so that they're in a compact pile not too close to the edges. Resist the urge to overfill.

Tips

▶ Another heating method: Wrap the tortillas in a damp towel and microwave for 30 seconds; check and heat for another 10 seconds or so, until they're hot but not soggy. To keep tortillas warm, wrap them in a dry kitchen towel.

▶ Try substituting bacon fat, lard, vegetable oil, or butter for the olive oil in the beans—all will result in slightly different flavors.

Variations

▶ **10 Mix-and-Match Fillings.** Instead of or in addition to the other ingredients; stick to about ½ cup total for each burrito:

1 Grated or crumbled Mexican-style cheese, like queso fresco
2 Scrambled eggs
3 Cooked chicken
4 Chunks of roasted potato
5 Cooked corn
6 Chopped scallions
7 Minced fresh chiles
8 Chopped olives, any kind
9 Chopped fresh tomatoes
10 Chopped avocados

Learn More

▶ Bean Basics (page 250), chopping onions (page 19), Grating Cheese (page 176), Salsa (pages 80–83)

ENCLOSING THE FILLING With small tortillas, start by folding the sides of the burrito about an inch over the fillings. For large burritos you start by enclosing the filling first.

ROLLING BURRITOS Then, keeping the sides tucked in, roll the tortilla up tightly. Keep pressure on the tortilla and fillings to keep the roll from falling apart.

Beef Tacos

Weeknight dinner made better—fresh tacos without mixes, all in one pan for easy cleanup.

TIME **45 minutes**
MAKES **4 servings**

½ cup vegetable oil, or more as needed

12 small (about 5-inch) corn tortillas

1 pound ground beef sirloin or chuck

Salt and freshly ground black pepper

1 medium onion, chopped

1 tablespoon minced garlic

1 fresh hot chile (like jalapeño), seeded and minced, optional

1 tablespoon ground cumin

2 tablespoons tomato paste

1 cup roughly chopped radishes for garnish

½ cup chopped fresh cilantro leaves for garnish

2 limes, quartered, for serving

1 Pour about ½ inch of oil into a large skillet and set over medium-high heat. When it's hot, put a tortilla in the pan and let it cook until it starts blistering but is still soft, less than 15 seconds. Flip it with tongs, then fold it over and hold it for a few seconds. Once the tortilla is crisp enough to hold its shape, cook it, turning it every few seconds, until it's crisp all over, 15 to 30 seconds more. Transfer to paper towels to drain. Repeat with the remaining tortillas, adjusting the heat and adding more oil as necessary.

2 Carefully pour all but 2 tablespoons of the oil out of the pan and lower the heat to medium. Add the ground beef, sprinkle with salt and pepper, and cook, stirring occasionally and breaking it up until it starts to brown, 5 to 10 minutes. Add the onion and cook, stirring occasionally, until it softens and begins to color and the meat is getting crisp in places, 5 to 10 minutes more.

3 Add the garlic and the chile if you're using it and cook until the vegetables soften, 1 to 3 minutes. Add the cumin and tomato paste and cook and stir until the mixture is fragrant, about 1 minute. Taste and adjust the seasoning.

4 Divide the meat among the taco shells and top with the radishes and cilantro. Serve with a squeeze of lime.

Tongs are the best tool, but be gentle so you don't rip the tortillas before they start to crisp.

SOFTENING TORTILLAS IN OIL Flip the shell while it's still soft, before it starts to get even a little crisp.

SHAPING TACO SHELLS Fold the tortilla in half, and hold it with tongs to set the shape. Then turn it as necessary to crisp both sides and the center fold. This all takes less than a minute.

Tips
▶ You can fry flour tortillas the exact same way.

Variations
▶ **More Taco Fillings:** You can use any ground meat you like in this recipe, from chicken to pork. Or make seafood tacos, using Grilled or Broiled Fish (page 348) or Shrimp Scampi (page 362).
▶ **5 Different Garnishes:**
1 Guacamole and chopped tomatoes
2 Shredded cabbage and chopped scallions
3 Drained black beans and red or green salsa
4 Shredded iceberg or romaine lettuce and crumbled queso fresco or feta cheese
5 Chopped avocado and red bell pepper

Learn More
▶ Beef Basics (page 264), chopping onions (page 19), mincing garlic (page 20), Preparing Chiles (page 276), Chopping Herbs (page 78)

As the meat cooks, break it up as much or as little as you like.

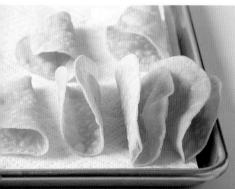

DRAINING THE TACO SHELLS
Remove them from the pan when both sides are golden and crisp. They'll crisp more as they rest.

FINISHING THE FILLING When the meat is fully browned and you've cooked the garlic and chile a bit, it's time to add the tomato paste and seasonings.

Bread-Baking Basics

Flour Fundamentals

All different kinds of flour are increasingly available in both natural food and regular grocery stores, ground from grains like rye, buckwheat, rice, and spelt. But when you're starting out, it's best to stick with the basics, and the recipes in this chapter work best with the flours detailed here:

All-Purpose Flour Made with wheat kernels milled so that the dark germ and bran is removed, creating a creamy-colored flour. (Bleached flour is bright white, but there's no reason to buy it.) It gets the name for good reason: You can use it in everything.

Cake (or Pastry) Flour With lower protein than all-purpose flour and a finer texture, this helps make many biscuit, cake, and cookie recipes become light and delicate. (Beware: Their doughs and batters are fragile.)

Bread Flour With more protein than all-purpose flour, this makes yeast breads more elastic, chewy, and crusty than those made with all-purpose flour. Not essential, but useful.

Whole Wheat Flour Milled (preferably stone ground) from whole wheat including the bran and germ, so it has more fiber, a denser texture, and a nuttier flavor than white flour.

You can substitute up to 50 percent whole wheat for white flour in most recipes and the results will be good. Buy all-purpose whole wheat for bread and whole wheat pastry flour for cakes and cookies.

Cornmeal Made from dried corn kernels and available in fine, medium, and coarse ground (in white or yellow, sometimes even blue; all are interchangeable). Look for medium stone-ground cornmeal (if it's just labeled stone-ground cornmeal, that's it), which tastes better and is more nutritious than steel-ground cornmeal.

Leavening

The magic ingredients that make dough rise and give it its appealing light texture. They work by generating carbon dioxide, which is in turn trapped by the structure formed by mixing flour and liquid into a batter or dough. Simple enough, right? There are some easy-to-understand differences among types of leavening:

Chemical leavening, like baking soda and baking powder, is used in quick breads, pancakes, waffles, cakes, and cookies. The reaction that makes the batter rise begins upon mixing, so the batter or dough must be baked right away. The results are tender and crumbly insides, not sturdy and chewy like yeast breads.

Yeast is a living organism (a fungus, actually), and breads made with it can vary from ultra-tender to super-tough. Yeast takes time to activate after you mix it into a dough (it's actually multiplying, by feeding on the flour), so recipes that call for it take a while. (Thus they're not "quick" breads!)

Here are more details:

Baking Soda An alkaline compound—sodium bicarbonate—that reacts when combined with an acidic liquid, like buttermilk, yogurt, vinegar, or lemon juice.

Baking Powder Baking soda mixed with a dry acidic ingredient, so it's activated by any liquid at all.

Instant Yeast Also called *rapid-rise* or *quick-rising* yeast, this convenient powdered yeast comes in individual pouches, large bags, or jars. It keeps almost indefinitely in the refrigerator and can be mixed right in with the dry ingredients. It's the only yeast I use.

Active Dry Yeast Also available in small envelopes or in bulk and looks much like instant yeast. The difference—and this is big—is that active dry yeast must be mixed with warm (110°F) liquid to become active; that's a step you can avoid as long as you use instant yeast, and in this book that's what I'm doing.

*ALL-PURPOSE
FLOUR*

*BAKING
SODA*

*BAKING
POWDER*

*KOSHER
SALT*

*WHOLE WHEAT
FLOUR*

Yes, You Can

The ingredients for almost all bread making are nothing special and are pretty much the same from recipe to recipe: flour, leavening (baking powder, baking soda, or yeast), water (or other liquid), salt, and sometimes fat or other ingredients for added flavor. As in other chapters, the recipes here build from simplest to most difficult, but really: These breads are easy enough for a complete beginner. (One suggestion: If you're totally new to this game, check out the directions for how to measure dry and liquid ingredients on pages 22 and 23.)

Corn Bread

My super-easy version, not too sweet or cakey, but moist, crunchy, and great with many foods.

TIME   45 to 50 minutes
MAKES   6 to 8 servings

1¼ cups milk, or more as needed

1 tablespoon white vinegar

4 tablespoons (½ stick) butter, melted, plus more for greasing the pan

1½ cups cornmeal

½ cup all-purpose flour

1 teaspoon baking soda

1 teaspoon salt

1 tablespoon sugar

2 eggs

1 Heat the oven to 375°F. Heat the milk in the microwave or in a pot on the stove until it reaches about 100°F; it will be a little hotter than lukewarm. Stir in the vinegar and let rest while you prepare the other ingredients. Grease a square baking pan with some butter.

2 Combine the cornmeal, flour, baking soda, salt, and sugar in a large bowl. Whisk the eggs into the soured milk. Stir the milk mixture into the dry ingredients just enough to combine everything. If the batter is very dry and doesn't come together easily, add another 1 or 2 tablespoons milk.

3 Add the 4 tablespoons butter and stir until just incorporated; avoid overmixing. Pour the batter into the prepared pan, spread into an even layer, and put in the oven.

4 Bake for 25 to 30 minutes, until the top is lightly browned, the sides have pulled away from the pan, and a toothpick inserted into the center comes out clean. Cut into squares and serve hot or warm.

When a liquid looks separated like this, it's called either curdled or broken.

The liquid mixture will still look curdled— from the soured milk.

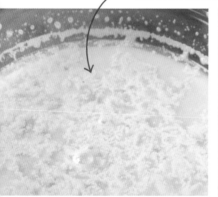

SOURING MILK Vinegar thickens milk and makes it acidic so it'll react with the baking soda and give the bread a tender crumb.

COMBINING DRY INGREDIENTS This key baking technique helps evenly distribute the leavening and minimizes the need to over-stir the batter.

COMBINING WET INGREDIENTS The wet ingredients should be mixed until evenly colored and textured.

Tips

▶ You can use either yogurt or buttermilk instead of the milk and vinegar mixture. The flavor will have a subtle tang, and the crumb will be a little more tender.

Variations

▶ **Sweeter Corn Bread:** Use up to ¼ cup sugar.
▶ **Corny Corn Bread:** Add 1 cup corn kernels, fresh or frozen (don't bother to defrost them first), to the wet ingredients in Step 2.
▶ **Jalapeño-Cheddar Corn Bread:** In Step 2, add ½ cup grated cheddar cheese and 1 tablespoon seeded and minced jalapeño chile to the dry ingredients after mixing.
▶ **Bacon Corn Bread:** You won't need all of the butter. Before starting, cook 4 to 6 slices of bacon until crisp. Drain the bacon on paper towels and use some of the fat from the skillet to grease the baking pan in Step 1. When you add the wet ingredients to the dry in Step 2, crumble the bacon into the batter. In Step 3, measure the remaining bacon fat and add enough melted butter to make ¼ cup total.

Learn More

▶ Bread-Baking Basics (page 394), Greasing a Pan with Butter (page 398)

FINISHING THE BATTER It should still be lumpy; when you no longer see streaks of flour, stop stirring. (If the batter isn't coming together, add milk, 1 tablespoon at a time.)

SPREADING BATTER IN A PAN The batter is fairly wet, but be sure to push some toward the edges so the bread's top becomes fairly even.

Banana Bread

Use those overripe bananas to make a quick bread that eats like cake.

TIME **About 1 hour**
MAKES **1 loaf (8 to 12 servings)**

---

8 tablespoons (1 stick) butter, softened, plus more for greasing the pan

2 cups all-purpose flour

½ teaspoon salt

1½ teaspoons baking powder

¾ cup sugar

2 eggs

3 very ripe bananas, mashed with a fork until smooth

1 teaspoon vanilla extract

½ cup chopped walnuts, optional

1 Heat the oven to 350°F. Grease a loaf pan with enough butter to coat the bottom and sides.

2 Mix together the flour, salt, baking powder, and sugar in a large bowl.

3 Put the stick of butter in a medium bowl and beat it with a whisk (or an electric mixer) until creamy and fluffy. Beat in the eggs and bananas until well combined. Stir this mixture into the dry ingredients just enough to combine everything. Gently fold in the vanilla and the nuts if you're using them.

4 Pour the batter into the prepared pan. Bake for 50 to 60 minutes, until it's browned on top and a toothpick inserted in the center of the bread comes out almost entirely clean. Cool the pan on a rack for 15 minutes, then carefully turn it upside down to release the loaf. Serve warm or at room temperature (or wrap in plastic and keep at room temperature for up to a couple days).

If you don't want to use your hands, try a brush or paper towel.

You can do this with an electric mixer too, but it's really not that much work.

GREASING A PAN WITH BUTTER Smear just enough butter to coat the inside bottom and sides.

CREAMING BUTTER WITH A WHISK The idea is to incorporate air by beating until it looks light and fluffy.

Tips

▶ Banana bread is perfect for overripe fruit you wouldn't dream of eating out of hand. The darker and softer—and the more brown spots—the better.

Variations

▶ **Whole Wheat Banana Bread:** Substitute ½ cup whole wheat flour for ½ cup of the all-purpose flour.

▶ **5 Substitutions for Walnuts:**

1 Chopped pecans
2 Chopped almonds
3 Raisins
4 Dried cranberries
5 Unsweetened shredded coconut

Learn More

▶ Bread-Baking Basics (page 394), chopping nuts (page 19), Combining Dry Ingredients (page 396), Combining Wet Ingredients (page 396)

Another doneness test: The top of the bread should be springy when you tap it lightly.

FOLDING INGREDIENTS INTO BAT-TER Scoop the finished batter up and over additional ingredients a few times to incorporate them.

TESTING DONENESS WITH A TOOTHPICK A toothpick inserted in the center of the loaf should be dry (or almost so). If it's coated in wet batter or crumbs, the bread isn't done yet.

Blueberry Muffins

The intersection of cupcakes and bread: slightly sweet and *very* tender.

TIME **About 40 minutes**
MAKES **12 muffins**

3 tablespoons vegetable oil, plus more for the pan

2 cups all-purpose flour

½ cup sugar

½ teaspoon salt

1½ teaspoons baking powder

1 teaspoon ground cinnamon

1 egg

1 cup milk, or more if needed

½ teaspoon grated lemon zest

1 cup fresh blueberries

1 Heat the oven to 375°F. Grease a 12-cup muffin tin with a little oil or line it with paper or foil muffin cups.

2 Mix together the flour, sugar, salt, baking powder, and cinnamon in a large bowl. Beat together the egg, milk, lemon zest, and oil in a medium bowl. Add the wet ingredients to the dry ingredients and stir just enough to combine everything. If the batter is very dry and doesn't come together easily, add another 1 to 2 tablespoons milk. Gently fold the blueberries into the batter.

3 Distribute the batter among the muffin cups, filling them about two-thirds full. Bake for 20 to 25 minutes, until the muffins are browned on top and a toothpick inserted in the center of a muffin comes out clean. Remove the pan from the oven and let rest for 5 minutes before removing the muffins. Serve warm or at room temperature (or cover tightly and keep at room temperature for up to a couple days).

You can line the tin with paper or foil cups instead.

GREASING A PAN WITH OIL The same as you do with butter: Smear enough to evenly coat the bottom and sides.

Tips

▶ Muffin batter should be lumpy, even before you add the blueberries. Overmixing the batter to make it smooth will make the muffins tough and rubbery.

Variations

▶ **Cornmeal-Blueberry Muffins:** Substitute cornmeal for ½ cup of the flour.
▶ **Cranberry-Nut Muffins:** Substitute fresh or frozen cranberries (no need to thaw) for the blueberries and orange zest for the lemon, and fold in ½ cup chopped walnuts along with the berries.

Learn More

▶ Bread-Baking Basics (page 394), Combining Dry Ingredients (page 396), Combining Wet Ingredients (page 396)

The batter will rise as it cooks.

FOLDING IN FRUIT Be gentle with the blueberries, or they'll break, and their juices will stain the batter with color.

FILLING MUFFIN CUPS Use 2 large spoons—or 1 large spoon and your finger—to fill the muffin cups two-thirds full.

Buttermilk Biscuits

The acidity of buttermilk or yogurt makes a tender crumb, as does cake flour if you have it.

TIME   20 to 30 minutes

MAKES   6 to 12 biscuits, depending on size

2 cups all-purpose or cake flour, plus more for shaping the biscuits

1 teaspoon salt

1 tablespoon baking powder

1 teaspoon baking soda

5 tablespoons cold butter, cut into ½-inch slices

¾ cup plus 2 tablespoons buttermilk or yogurt

1   Heat the oven to 450°F. Mix together the flour, salt, baking powder, and baking soda in a large bowl. Add the butter and press it into the flour mixture, breaking it into tiny pieces with your fingers until the mixture looks like coarse meal.

2   Add the buttermilk and stir just until the mixture comes together and forms a ball. Spread some flour (about ¼ cup) on a clean work surface and turn the dough out onto the flour. Knead the dough a few times, adding a little more flour to your hands only if the dough is very sticky.

3   Press the dough out ¾ inch thick and cut out 1½- to 2½-inch rounds with a biscuit cutter or drinking glass. Put the rounds on an ungreased baking sheet. Press together the scraps, pat them out ¾ inch thick, and cut out more biscuits. Repeat once more if possible.

4   Bake for 5 to 10 minutes, depending on size, until the biscuits are golden brown. Transfer the biscuits to a rack and serve within 15 minutes or wrap in foil and keep in a 200°F oven for up to an hour.

RUBBING BUTTER INTO FLOUR For flaky biscuits and pastry, mix in cold butter with your fingers—like you're making the hand sign for "cash."

You're done stirring when the dough looks like this.

MIXING BISCUIT DOUGH After adding the buttermilk, stir just enough for the ingredients to come together in a shaggy mass, then stop.

To avoid using too much flour, dust your hands, not the dough.

KNEADING LIGHTLY Quickly fold the dough over, press it away from you, and give it a quarter turn; repeat only until the dough becomes a little smoother than when you started.

Tips

◗ Since cake flour has less of the protein gluten than all-purpose flour, it ensures the biscuits will be flaky. But it can make the dough harder to work with, so if you're worried, try using a combination of both flours.

◗ If you prefer, you can use a rolling pin to spread the dough out ¾ inch thick instead of pressing it with your hands. The texture will be a little more even and breadlike.

Variations

◗ **Buttermilk Biscuits in the Food Processor:** In Step 1, put the flour, salt, baking powder, and baking soda in a food processor and pulse a few times to combine. Add the butter and pulse several times to incorporate it into the flour mixture. Transfer the mixture to a bowl and continue the recipe with Step 2.

◗ **Drop Biscuits:** Perfect if you're in a hurry, with either the hand-mixed or food processor method, but not quite as flaky: Increase the buttermilk to 1 cup and skip the kneading in Step 2; instead, drop heaping tablespoons of the dough onto a greased baking sheet and bake as directed.

Learn More

◗ Bread-Baking Basics (page 394), Dairy—and Not (page 42)

CUTTING BISCUITS Pat the dough out to about ¾ inch thick. If you have a round cookie or biscuit cutter, great; if not, improvise. Place it over the dough and press down.

ADJUSTING BISCUIT TEXTURE For golden and slightly crisp biscuits, leave more space between them. For soft and fluffy biscuits, arrange them so they almost touch.

Cherry-Almond Scones

This combo is amazing, but you can stir almost anything into this rich and delicate dough.

TIME 20 to 30 minutes
MAKES 8 or 10 scones

2 cups all-purpose or cake flour, or more as needed, plus more for shaping

½ teaspoon salt

2 teaspoons baking powder

3 tablespoons sugar

5 tablespoons cold butter, cut into ½-inch slices

1 egg

½ cup cream, or more as needed, plus more for brushing

⅓ cup dried cherries

⅓ cup sliced almonds

1 Heat the oven to 450°F. Mix the flour, salt, baking powder, and 2 tablespoons of the sugar in a large bowl. Add the butter and press it into the flour mixture, breaking it into tiny pieces with your fingers until it looks like coarse meal.

2 Stir in the egg and ½ cup cream. The mixture should form a slightly sticky dough. If it's too sticky, add a little flour, but very little; it should still stick a little to your hands. If it's too dry, add more cream, 1 tablespoon at a time.

3 Sprinkle 2 tablespoons flour on a work surface and turn out the dough. Sprinkle the cherries and almonds over it and knead only a few times to incor-

porate the fruit and nuts. If the dough is very sticky, add 1 to 2 tablespoons flour, but no more.

4 Press the dough into a ¾-inch-thick circle and cut across the diameter into 8 or 10 wedges.

5 Brush the top of each scone with a bit of cream, sprinkle with a little of the remaining 1 tablespoon sugar, and transfer them one by one to an ungreased baking sheet with a spatula, leaving at least 1 inch between them. Bake for 8 to 12 minutes, until the scones are golden brown. Transfer to a rack to cool a bit. Serve right away if possible, or at least the same day.

An egg beaten with a teaspoon of water is another common wash.

KNEADING IN INGREDIENTS Fold the dough over the fruit and nuts and press it away from you. Give it a quarter turn and repeat, trying to handle the dough as little as possible.

"WASHING" TOPS FOR BAKING Brushing the scones with a little cream gives them a subtle sheen.

SPRINKLING WITH SUGAR Wash and top the scones before putting them on the baking sheet. That way you won't spill sugar or cream on the pan, which can burn.

◗ As with Buttermilk Biscuits (page 402), using cake flour in this recipe will give you a super-tender and flaky crumb, but the dough will be a little more delicate and tricky to handle.

◗ In Britain (where scones originated) they're served with clotted cream, which can be hard to find here. Try using the creamy Italian cheese called *mascarpone* or sour cream—or just go with butter. And jam, of course.

Variations

◗ **5 Other Knead-Ins for Scones.** Instead of the cherries and almonds, try up to ½ cup of any of these:
1 Currants (this is classic)
2 Poppy seeds
3 Chopped dried apricots
4 Chocolate chips or chunks
5 Grated cheddar or Parmesan cheese (omit the sugar from the recipe)

Learn More

◗ Bread-Baking Basics (page 394), Chocolate, Butter, Sugar (page 422), Rubbing Butter into Flour (page 402)

Spicy Cheddar Shortbread

No junk food snack comes close to these easy savory cookies, a perfect finger food.

TIME   45 to 60 minutes

MAKES   30 to 40 cookies

8 tablespoons (1 stick) cold butter, plus more for greasing the pan

2 cups grated cheddar cheese

1½ cups all-purpose flour

1 egg, lightly beaten

½ teaspoon salt

½ teaspoon cayenne

1 Heat the oven to 400°F. Cut the stick of butter into chunks. Grease a baking sheet with more butter. Put all the ingredients in a food processor and pulse several times; as soon as the mixture resembles coarse meal, stop. Turn the dough onto a sheet of plastic, wrap it, and press it gently into a ball. Refrigerate the dough for at least 20 minutes or up to several hours.

2 Pinch off heaping tablespoon-sized pieces of the dough and roll them into 1-inch balls with your hands. Put the balls on the prepared pan, leaving 2 inches between them. Press down on each ball with your fingers to flatten it to ¾ inch thick. If there is dough left over when the sheet is filled, wait and cook a second batch.

3 Bake for 10 to 12 minutes, until the shortbreads are puffed and golden brown. When they're cool enough to handle, transfer them to a wire rack and bake the remaining dough. Serve right away or store covered at room temperature for up to 1 day.

The less you handle the dough, the more tender the shortbread will be.

If you pulse to the point where the dough starts to come together, you've gone too far.

MIXING SHORTBREAD Pulse all the ingredients until the dough is evenly colored and textured; there should be no big lumps.

GATHERING SHORTBREAD INTO A BALL The dough may crumble, but use the plastic wrap to press it into shape.

Tips

▶ Refrigerating makes the dough easier to handle and shape, but if you're in a real hurry, stick it in the freezer for 10 minutes or so.

Variations

▶ **Spicy Cheddar Shortbread by Hand:** Put all the ingredients in a large bowl and stir and mash them together with your fingers or a fork until they become moist and crumbly, then press the dough together into a ball, wrap it in plastic, and continue with the recipe from Step 2.

▶ **Other Cheeses for Shortbread:** Try Gruyère, Emmental, manchego, or another semi-hard melting cheese instead of the cheddar. Parmesan works well too.

▶ **Cumin-Scented Cheese Shortbread:** Skip the cayenne and add 1 tablespoon ground cumin.

Learn More

▶ Bread-Baking Basics (page 394), Greasing a Pan with Butter (page 398), cheese for cooking (page 389), Grating Cheese (page 176)

For a more uniform look, grease the bottom of a drinking or shot glass and use that.

ROLLING DOUGH BALLS Rotate your hands in opposite directions, using gentle pressure to roll pinches of dough into a ball shape.

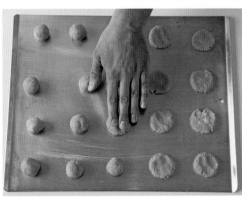

FLATTENING THE SHORTBREAD Use your hands to press down on the shortbread balls and you get a wonderful, rustic look.

No-Knead Bread

This is the real thing—crusty, delicious yeast bread. It's ideal for beginners.

TIME **24 hours,**
mostly unattended
MAKES **1 large loaf**
(4 to 8 servings)

4 cups all-purpose or bread flour, or more as needed

½ teaspoon instant yeast

2 teaspoons salt

Cornmeal as needed for dusting

1 Combine the 4 cups flour, yeast, and salt in a large bowl. Add 2 cups tap water (it should be about 70°F). Stir to combine; you'll have a shaggy, sticky dough (add 1 or 2 tablespoons tap water if it seems dry). Cover the bowl with plastic wrap and let the dough rest at room temperature until its surface is dotted with bubbles, about 18 hours (a couple hours less if your kitchen is warmer; more if your kitchen is cooler).

2 Spread about ¼ cup flour on a clean work surface, turn the dough out onto the flour, and fold it once or twice. Cover the dough loosely with plastic wrap and let it rest for 15 minutes.

3 Gently and quickly shape the dough with your hands into a round mass, adding just enough flour to keep the dough from sticking. Sprinkle a clean cotton (not terry cloth) towel with 2 table-spoons cornmeal, put the dough seam side down on the towel, and dust the top with 1 tablespoon more cornmeal. Cover with another cotton towel and let rest until the dough is more than doubled in size and doesn't spring back readily when poked with your finger, about 2 hours (longer if the room is cool).

4 When the dough is ready, heat the oven to 450°F and put a large covered ovenproof pot in the oven.

5 When the pot is scorching hot, carefully take it from the oven and remove the cover. Uncover the dough, slide your hand under the bottom towel, and use it to turn the dough over into the pot, seam side up. Cover the pot with the lid and bake for 30 minutes, then uncover and bake until the loaf is fully browned and crackled on top, 20 to 30 minutes. Carefully remove the bread from the pot with a spatula or tongs and cool on a rack for at least 30 minutes before cutting into thick slices.

The dough will never look dry enough to knead. It will always be sort of a blob.

MIXING BREAD DOUGH Stir until the flour, yeast, salt, and water are well combined and even in texture—the dough will still be sticky and rough and shaggy looking.

Tips

▶ This recipe was developed by New York baker Jim Lahey. I've streamlined the process a bit and highlighted the universal lessons the recipe teaches.

▶ The first few times you bake with yeast, use a thermometer to make sure you get the water temperature close to 70°F so the yeast will perform properly.

▶ If the dough starts to smell burned before the cooking time is over, lower the oven temperature to 425°F.

▶ To tell whether bread is done for sure, use a quick-read thermometer. It's done at 210°F.

Variations

▶ **Whole Wheat No-Knead Bread:** Use whole wheat flour for up to 2 cups of the all-purpose flour. You won't get quite as much rise, and the bread will be slightly denser and full flavored.

Learn More

▶ Bread-Baking Basics (page 394)

Let the towel do the work so your hands don't touch the hot pot.

FERMENTING BREAD This step develops flavor; the dough is ready to move on when the surface is dotted with bubbles and already has the yeasty smell of bread.

RISING THE DOUGH Let it sit between towels to increase in volume. It's ready to bake when it loses most of its springiness.

TRANSFERRING THE DOUGH The trick is not to hesitate: Use the towel to swiftly pick up the dough and turn it upside down in the pot. It will look uneven; that will fix itself.

Simple Sandwich Loaf

Perfect for slicing and toasting or all sorts of fillings.

TIME **3 to 4 hours,
mostly unattended**
MAKES **1 large loaf**

**1¼ cups whole or 2-percent
milk, or more as needed**

**3½ cups all-purpose or
bread flour, plus more for
shaping the dough**

1 teaspoon salt

**1 packet (2½ teaspoons)
instant yeast**

1 tablespoon sugar

**3 tablespoons vegetable
oil, plus more for greasing
the pan**

1 Heat the milk in the microwave or
in a pot on the stove until it reaches
about 100°F; it will be a little hotter than
lukewarm. Put the 3½ cups flour, salt,
yeast, and sugar in a food processor
and pulse a few times to combine.
With the machine running, add 2
tablespoons of the oil and the milk
through the feed tube and process until the dough is a well-defined, barely
sticky, easy-to-handle ball, about 30
seconds. If it is too dry, add milk 1 tablespoon at a time and process for 5 or 10
seconds after each addition. If it is too
wet, add flour 1 tablespoon at a time
and process for another 5 to 10 seconds.

2 Grease a large bowl with 1 tablespoon oil. Shape the dough into a rough
ball, put it in the bowl, turn it over once
(so that the top is coated lightly with oil),
and cover with plastic wrap. Let rest at
room temperature until the dough has
nearly doubled in size, 2 hours or more.
Punch down the dough to deflate it and
shape it into a ball again. Dust your work
surface with ¼ cup flour, put the dough
on the work surface, cover with plastic
wrap, and let rest for 15 minutes.

3 Grease a loaf pan with enough oil to
coat the bottom and sides. Flatten the
dough into a ¾-inch-thick rectangle,
then fold the long sides of the rectangle
into the middle. Pinch the seam closed

and transfer the loaf to the pan, seam
side down. (If the loaf is too long, fold
under the ends of the loaf.) Flatten the
top of the loaf with the back of your
hand to press the loaf firmly into the
pan. Cover with plastic wrap and let rise
until the top of the dough is nearly level
with the top of the pan, about 1 hour.

4 Heat the oven to 350°F. Brush the
top of the loaf lightly with water, then
put it in the oven. Bake for 40 to 50
minutes, until the loaf falls easily from
the pan and the bottom of the loaf
sounds hollow when you tap it. (A
quick-read thermometer will register
210°F.) Remove the loaf from the pan
and cool on a wire rack before slicing.

*Oil keeps the dough from
drying out as it rises.*

**RISING DOUGH THE FIRST
TIME** Turn the dough over in the
greased pan so that the top is
coated with oil, then cover with
plastic and let rise.

Tips

▶ The food processor does the kneading here. Or you can use a standing mixer with a dough hook, which also does a good job. Either makes better dough than almost anyone can achieve by hand, but to make this dough without a machine: Combine all the ingredients in a bowl with a wooden spoon until you can't stir anymore; then start using your hands to work the dough into a ball. Turn it onto a floured work surface and fold, press with the heel of your hand, and turn as with biscuits only much harder (see page 402), repeating for several minutes, until the dough is smooth. Continue from Step 2.

Variations

▶ **Honey-Wheat Sandwich Bread:** Substitute whole wheat flour for 1¾ cups of the all-purpose flour. Instead of the sugar, use 2 tablespoons honey and add it along with the oil and milk in Step 1.

▶ **New England–Style Anadama Bread.** With a slightly sweet and corny flavor: Substitute ½ cup cornmeal and 1 cup whole wheat flour for 1½ cups of all-purpose flour. Reduce the milk to 1 cup. Instead of the sugar, use ½ cup molasses and add it along with the oil and milk in Step 1.

Learn More

▶ Bread-Baking Basics (page 394), Greasing a Pan with Oil (page 400)

PUNCHING DOUGH DOWN You don't literally punch the dough (unless you really want to)—just press down with your fist hard enough to deflate it for the second rising in the pan.

SHAPING LOAF BREAD After you fold the rectangle, seal the seam by squeezing the sides together; tuck the edges under to make it fit. As it rises, the dough will fill the pan.

PRESSING DOUGH INTO THE LOAF PAN Flatten the dough gently so as it rises and bakes the top will become rounded.

Cinnamon Rolls

A fun baking project sure to make you the hero of your household.

TIME **3 to 5 hours, mostly unattended**

MAKES **15 rolls**

3½ cups all-purpose or bread flour, or more as needed, plus more for shaping the dough

1 tablespoon instant yeast

2 teaspoons salt

¾ cup plus 1 tablespoon granulated sugar

2 tablespoons cold butter

2 eggs

1 cup whole milk, or more as needed

7 tablespoons butter, softened, plus more for greasing the pan

2 tablespoons ground cinnamon

1½ cups powdered sugar

½ teaspoon vanilla extract

1 Put 3½ cups flour, the yeast, salt, 1 tablespoon of the sugar, and the cold butter in a food processor. Pulse the machine a few times until the butter is evenly distributed in the flour but not completely blended into a dough. Add the eggs and pulse a few more times. With the machine running, slowly add ¾ cup of the milk through the feed tube.

2 Process for about 30 seconds, adding more milk if necessary, 1 tablespoon at a time, until the mixture forms a ball and is sticky to the touch. If the mixture becomes too sticky, add flour, 1 tablespoon at a time, and process for 5 to 10 seconds after each addition.

3 Grease a large bowl with 1 tablespoon of the softened butter. Spread about ¼ cup flour on a clean work surface, turn the dough out onto the flour, and knead it 5 or 6 times. Shape the dough into a smooth, round ball. Put the dough in the prepared bowl, turn it over once (so that the top is lightly coated with butter), and cover with plastic wrap. Let rest at room temperature until the dough doubles in size, 1 to 2 hours.

4 Punch the dough down to deflate it and then form it into a ball. Put the ball on a lightly floured surface, sprinkle with a little flour, cover with plastic wrap, let rest about 20 minutes.

5 Grease a rectangular baking pan with enough softened butter to coat the bottom and sides. Combine the cinnamon and remaining ¾ cup sugar in a small

bowl. Press the dough into a rectangle the size of the baking pan. Spread the remaining 6 tablespoons softened butter all over the surface of the dough, then sprinkle the cinnamon sugar over the butter. Roll the dough lengthwise and pinch the seam closed. Cut the log into 15 slices. Put each slice, cut side up, into the pan. Cover with plastic wrap and let rest until the dough has doubled in size, 1 to 2 hours.

6 Heat the oven to 350°F. Uncover the pan and bake until the rolls are golden brown, 25 to 30 minutes. Whisk the powdered sugar with the remaining ¼ cup milk and the vanilla extract in a small bowl. Let the cinnamon rolls cool for a few minutes, then invert them onto another pan or platter. Smear the glaze over all and serve.

FILLING CINNAMON ROLLS Sprinkle the cinnamon sugar as evenly as possible over the butter, including all the way to the edges.

Tips

▶ If the dough seems too springy to press into a rectangle, let it rest for a few minutes; that'll make it less elastic and easier to shape.

▶ Use any cinnamon sugar that falls out of the dough as you're rolling or cutting the dough to sprinkle over the rolls once you get them in the pan.

▶ If you don't have anything large enough to invert the pan onto (or the finished rolls stick), just glaze them in the pan.

▶ If you glaze the rolls while they're still hot, the sugar will melt into them (they'll still taste good); if you want the glaze to stay white, wait for the rolls to cool a bit.

Learn More

▶ Bread-Baking Basics (page 394), working with yeast dough (page 410), kneading dough (page 411), Greasing a Pan with Butter (page 398)

ROLLING AND SEALING THE DOUGH Work slowly and roll the dough as tightly and evenly as possible. Then pinch the edge all the way down the roll with your fingers to seal the seam.

CUTTING THE ROLLS Slice with a gentle back-and-forth motion with a serrated knife so you don't squish the rolls.

Cheese Pizza

Infinitely better than delivery, and super easy if you make the dough ahead and refrigerate it.

TIME **2 to 3 hours, mostly unattended**

MAKES **2 medium pizzas (4 to 6 servings)**

---

3 cups all-purpose or bread flour, or more as needed, plus more for kneading

2 teaspoons instant yeast

2 teaspoons salt, plus more for sprinkling

3 tablespoons olive oil, plus more for greasing the pans

2 cups tomato sauce

2 cups grated mozzarella cheese

Freshly ground black pepper

1 Put the 3 cups flour, yeast, and salt in a food processor. Turn the machine on and add 1 cup tap water and 2 tablespoons of the oil through the feed tube. Process until the mixture forms a ball and is slightly sticky to the touch, about 30 seconds. If the mixture is too dry, add more water 1 tablespoon at a time and process for 5 to 10 seconds after each addition. If the mixture is too sticky, add more flour 1 tablespoon at a time and process for 5 to 10 seconds after each addition.

2 Sprinkle ¼ cup flour on a clean work surface. Turn the dough onto the flour and knead just enough times to form a smooth, round dough ball. Grease a large bowl with the remaining 1 tablespoon oil. Put the dough in the bowl, turn it over once (so that the top is lightly coated with oil), and cover it with plastic wrap. Let rest at room temperature until the dough doubles in size, 1 to 2 hours.

3 Punch down the dough to deflate it, divide it in half, and form it into 2 balls. Put the balls on a lightly floured surface, sprinkle with flour, and cover with plastic wrap. Let rest until the balls puff slightly, about 20 minutes. (Now's a good time to make the tomato sauce if you haven't already.)

4 Heat the oven to 500°F. Press one of the dough balls into a ½-inch-thick flat round, adding more flour to the work surface and the dough as necessary (use only as much flour as you need to keep it from sticking). Repeat with the remaining dough; let the disks sit for a few minutes. Grease 2 baking sheets with enough oil to coat them evenly, put 1 piece of dough on each baking sheet, and gently press each into a thin round or rectangle.

5 Spread the sauce over the pizzas. Sprinkle them with the cheese and some salt and pepper. Put the baking sheets in the oven and bake for 8 to 12 minutes, until the crust is crisp, the cheese melts, and the pies release. Let sit for several minutes before slicing. Serve warm or at room temperature.

Repeat pressing or rolling and resting until the dough is a little bit thinner than you want the finished crust.

SHAPING THE CRUST Press—or roll—the dough into an even round until it resists being stretched further before pressing or rolling again.

Tips

▶ Homemade dough deserves homemade sauce. Period. And making that sauce is so fast you can whip up a batch while the dough rises and still have time for other tasks. If you need a shortcut, drain a 14-ounce can of diced tomatoes for several minutes, toss them with 2 tablespoons olive oil and ½ cup chopped fresh basil leaves if you like, and use this mixture instead of the sauce.

▶ To cut pizza, rock a chef's knife back and forth in the same place until you hear the crust snap. A pizza cutter—essentially a sharp wheel tool—is a good investment if you make a lot of pizza. Then all you have to do is firmly press down and roll.

▶ If you make pizza often, considering investing in a pizza peel and stone. If you have one, assemble the pizza on the (cornmeal-dusted) peel and slide it directly onto the preheated stone (which can stay in the oven at all times).

Variations

▶ **Individual Pizzas:** Divide the dough into 4 or 6 pieces after punching it down in Step 3, press each into a thin round, and divide the ingredients among them.

Learn More

▶ Bread-Baking Basics (page 394), working with yeast dough (page 410), Tomato Sauce (page 178), Grating Cheese (page 176), Pizza Variations (page 416)

SPREADING THE SAUCE Not too thick a layer or the sauce will make the dough soggy; it's okay if you have a little left over.

TOPPING PIZZA Don't overload the pizzas with cheese—it should be in a relatively thin layer so that it gets browned and crispy on top and around the edges.

Pizza Variations

Homemade Pizza *Is* Convenient

Pizza dough is forgiving, so you can prepare the recipe in advance to work around your schedule. To keep the dough from puffing up too much—or *overproofing*—you can refrigerate it for up to a day or freeze it for up to 3 months. Be sure you wrap the pieces tightly in plastic wrap or a zipper bag, with as little air as possible. For reliable results, thaw the dough out in the fridge; depending on the size, it will take between 8 and 12 hours but will remain stable in the fridge for up to a day.

2 Other Things to Do with Pizza Dough

Focaccia Press the dough into a greased rectangular baking pan, cover, and let rise for 30 minutes. Dimple the surface of the dough with your fingers, drizzle with 2 tablespoons olive oil, and sprinkle with 1 tablespoon chopped fresh rosemary and 1 tablespoon coarse salt. Bake at 375°F for 30 to 40 minutes, until golden and spongy to the touch.

Calzone Divide the dough in half or into quarters and press or roll each into a large thin circle. Mix together 2 cups ricotta cheese, 1 cup grated mozzarella cheese, 1 cup freshly grated Parmesan cheese, and 1 cup crumbled cooked Italian sausage in a large bowl. Divide the mixture between the rounds, fold them over, press the edges together with your fingers, then fold them over to seal. Bake at 350°F for 30 to 40 minutes, until golden brown.

10 Pizza Toppings

Use the following ingredients, alone or in combination, on top of the Cheese Pizza on page 414. But beware the overloaded crust. Any more than 2 cups of total toppings and you run the risk of making the pizza soggy. I also like to keep the extra ingredients to two or three—too many competing flavors muddies the overall taste. And don't forget the salt and pepper!

1   Lightly cooked sausage, bacon, or other meat
2   Sliced salami, prosciutto, Spanish chorizo, or other cured meat
3   Small amounts of Gorgonzola or other blue cheese or fontina or other semisoft cheese; gratings of Parmesan cheese
4   Small dollops of soft goat cheese or ricotta
5   Minced raw or mashed roasted garlic
6   Minced fresh chile (like jalapeño) or hot red pepper flakes to taste
7   Pitted black olives, especially the oil-cured kind
8   Canned anchovy fillets, with some of their oil
9   Pesto (page 184)
10 Well-washed and dried tender greens, especially arugula, added after the pizzas come out of the oven

---

5 Ways to Vary Pizza Dough

Add any of the following ingredients to the dry ingredients at the beginning of Step 1 of Cheese Pizza on the preceding pages.

1   1 teaspoon chopped fresh strong herbs (like rosemary, thyme, or tarragon)
2   1 tablespoon chopped fresh mild herbs (like parsley, basil, or dill)
3   1 teaspoon (or more) minced garlic
4   1½ cups whole wheat flour (in place of 1½ cups of the flour)
5   ½ cup medium-grind cornmeal (in place of ½ cup of the flour)

Desserts

It's rare to find someone who doesn't have at least a little bit of a sweet tooth. Most of us have more than that; and making desserts from scratch is an impressive way to satisfy it.

There is a mystique that surrounds dessert making, which suggests that it's much harder than normal cooking. On a grand scale, there's some truth to that, but for home cooks? No way. Although precise measuring plays a greater role, much of dessert making is simply following the recipe. And, just as in savory cooking, after you learn a few basic techniques and principles you'll have plenty of leeway to customize and vary recipes to your liking.

In this chapter you'll learn all the important basic dessert techniques by using them to produce some all-time favorites: You'll cream butter for cookies, separate eggs for mousse, make and spread icing for cake, roll out dough for pie, and more. You'll quickly see that, while it's important to be precise, it's also easy to be precise.

One word about equipment: All of the recipes here can be made successfully by hand. But I won't kid you: Having a handheld electric mixer and a food processor will make the work go faster. If you're going to bake even occasionally, these are worthwhile investments.

My guess is that it will take only one or two recipes for your fear of dessert to evaporate. After that, all you'll have to worry about is learning to control your sweet tooth.

Brownies

Ridiculously easy, ridiculously good.

TIME   **30 to 40 minutes**
MAKES   **9 to 12**

---

8 tablespoons (1 stick) butter, plus a little more for greasing the pan

3 ounces unsweetened chocolate, roughly chopped

1 cup sugar

2 eggs

½ cup all-purpose flour

Pinch salt

½ teaspoon vanilla extract, optional

1 Heat the oven to 350°F. Grease a square baking pan with butter or line it by overlapping 2 pieces of parchment paper or aluminum foil crosswise and grease the lining.

2 Combine the stick of butter and the chocolate in a small saucepan over very low heat, stirring occasionally. (Or microwave them in a large microwave-safe bowl on medium for 10-second intervals, stirring after each.) When the chocolate is just about melted, remove the saucepan from the heat (or bowl from the microwave) and continue to stir until the mixture is smooth.

3 Transfer the mixture to a large bowl (or use the bowl you put in the microwave) and stir in the sugar. Then beat in the eggs, one at a time. Gently stir in the flour, salt, and the vanilla if you're using it.

4 Pour and scrape the mixture into the prepared pan and bake for 20 to 25 minutes, until just barely set in the middle. Cool on a rack until set. If you used parchment, lift it out to remove the brownies. If not, cut them in squares right in the pan. Store, covered, at room temperature, for no more than a day.

Stir the melted chocolate and butter until it's completely smooth and thin, like this.

GREASING THE PAN Whether you line the pan or not, make sure to cover the bottom as well as the sides. And don't be stingy or the brownies might stick.

MELTING BUTTER WITH CHOCOLATE When there's this much butter, the chocolate won't burn easily; just stir them both together in a small pot over the lowest possible heat.

Tips

▶ If you use parchment paper (or foil) to line the pan, leave an extra inch or two overhanging each end. When the brownies are cool, grab each flap and lift them out of the pan.

▶ Err on the side of underbaking: An overcooked brownie is dry and cakey, while an undercooked brownie is gooey and delicious.

Variations

▶ **Nutty Brownies:** In Step 3, substitute ¼ cup finely ground hazelnuts, almonds, walnuts, or pecans (use the food processor or blender to grind them) for ¼ cup of the flour and add 1 cup lightly toasted, roughly chopped nuts to the batter.

▶ **Cocoa Brownies:** After the brownies cool a bit but are still warm, put 2 tablespoons cocoa in a small strainer and shake it over the pan to dust the tops of the brownies.

Learn More

▶ Bread-Baking Basics (page 394), Chocolate, Butter, Sugar (page 422), melting chocolate (page 441)

AVOIDING OVERMIXING The batter should be relatively smooth and thick; some lumps are okay. If you work it too much, the brownies will be tough.

FAILING THE TOOTHPICK TEST A clean toothpick might signal some cakes are ready, but it means brownies are overcooked. Their signal: a crust on top with a slightly jiggly center underneath.

Chocolate, Butter, Sugar

Chocolate

Most chocolate is labeled by the percentage of cacao—sometimes called *cocoa solids*—it contains. Since the main ingredients in chocolate are cacao and sugar, this tells you just how sweet it is: The higher the percentage, the darker and less sweet.

Most of the recipes here just call for "chocolate" that you chop or melt yourself. Choose what you like to eat straight—milk, dark, or white—they're interchangeable in these recipes.

You don't need a scale; just buy a bar that's a little larger than the size you need and use the little squares to help you calculate the right quantity. (Nice: You're almost certain to have extra for a snack.)

▶ **Unsweetened Chocolate** 100 percent cacao—it contains no sugar—and too bitter to eat. If a recipe calls for unsweetened chocolate, use it.

▶ **Dark Chocolate** Anywhere from 35 to 99 percent cacao; the higher the number, the less sweet (and more crisp) it will be.

▶ **Milk Chocolate** Less than 35 percent cacao, so it's much creamier.

▶ **White Chocolate** Contains no cacao but is sweetened cocoa butter, which is also a component of the cocoa bean.

▶ **Cocoa** This is what's left when you separate the fat out of partially refined chocolate—and then dry it to a powder. It's intense, unsweetened, and good for baking.

MILK

DARK (this one is 70 percent cacao)

WHITE

COCOA

1 TABLESPOON

Butter

As far as I'm concerned there's only one kind of butter: unsalted. It has a fresh, creamy taste you'll never get with the salted kinds. Local butter is a special treat if you have access to it, but supermarket brands are fine too: Just make sure it's unsalted! (You can always add salt, of course.)

▶ **Some Measurements** 1 pound (the common supermarket package) contains 4 sticks. Each stick is ½ cup and measures 8 tablespoons—whether it's cold, softened, or melted. Use the marks on the wrapper as your guide or use a tablespoon to measure.

▶ **Some Translations** When a recipe calls simply for "butter," it can be either room temperature or out of the fridge. Softened butter is at room temperature. Cold or very cold butter is used in crusts and crumbles and should be quite hard; you'll usually be asked to cut it into bits and need a knife to get through it. (Butter that's put in a food processor is almost always cold.) Melted butter should be liquid but not browned or burned. To get it to that point, put it in a small pot over low heat or microwave it on medium for 10-second intervals and watch it like a hawk. You can measure butter before or after you melt it (the results are the same).

GRANULATED

BROWN

COLD

POWDERED

SOFTENED

Sugar

The recipes in this book call for three kinds of sugar:

▶ **Granulated** (Just *sugar* in recipes, unless it appears with another type.) This is common table sugar, which is best for baking since it dissolves reliably and has a simple sweet flavor.

▶ **Brown** Light (or *golden*) or dark, your choice. Both include molasses (dark has more) for more moisture and a deeper flavor. When you measure it out, press it into your measuring cup for accuracy—this is what is meant by a *packed cup*.

▶ **Powdered** Also sometimes called *confectioners'* sugar and labeled 10×, this is the kind used for frostings, glazes, and dusting. It's made by combining pulverized sugar with cornstarch so it dissolves easily without any grittiness.

Oatmeal Chocolate Chip Cookies

Crispy, chewy, and a little chocolaty—or not, depending on your mood.

TIME **About 30 minutes**
MAKES **3 to 4 dozen**

About ½ pound chocolate

8 tablespoons (1 stick) butter, softened

½ cup granulated sugar

½ cup packed brown sugar

2 eggs

1½ cups all-purpose flour

2 cups rolled oats (not instant oats)

½ teaspoon ground cinnamon

Pinch salt

2 teaspoons baking powder

½ cup milk

½ teaspoon vanilla extract

1 Heat the oven to 375°F. Chop the chocolate: Use a chef's knife with a rocking motion to cut the bars into pea-sized pieces. You should have about 1½ cups.

2 Use an electric mixer to cream together the butter and sugars in a large bowl until light and fluffy. Crack the eggs on a flat, hard surface, add them one at a time, and beat until well blended.

3 Mix the flour, oats, cinnamon, salt, and baking powder together in a small bowl. Alternating with the milk, add the dry ingredients to the butter mixture a little at a time, mixing on low. Stir in the chocolate and vanilla.

4 Drop tablespoon-sized mounds of dough about 3 inches apart in rows and columns on ungreased baking sheets. Bake for 12 to 15 minutes, until lightly browned. Cool for about 2 minutes on the sheets before using a metal spatula to transfer the cookies to racks to finish cooling. Store in a tightly covered container at room temperature for no more than a day or two.

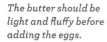
The butter should be light and fluffy before adding the eggs.

USING AN ELECTRIC MIXER
Always start slow, then increase the speed as the ingredients blend.

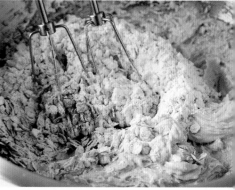

ALTERNATING INGREDIENTS
Start with the mixer on low to incorporate some of the dry ingredients, then add a little of the milk. Repeat until everything is combined.

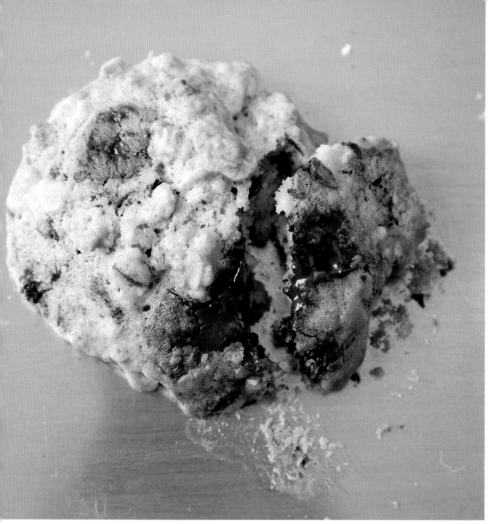

Tips

▶ Dark chocolate is my first choice for these cookies, but go ahead and use whatever kind you like to eat.

▶ You can always stir batters and doughs together by hand: Start with a whisk to handle butter, sugar, and eggs, then switch to a rubber spatula to add dry ingredients. But the electric mixer is much faster and usually gives better results. Try a handheld mixer that has several speeds and see how you like it. If you get hooked on baking, you'll probably want a standing (upright) mixer.

Variations

▶ **Oatmeal Raisin Cookies:** Skip the chocolate and use up to 1 cup raisins instead.

▶ **Peanut Butter Oatmeal Cookies:** Substitute ¼ cup peanut butter for 4 tablespoons (½ stick) of the butter. These cookies have a tendency to burn a bit more quickly, so keep an eye on them.

▶ **Coconut-Cherry Cookies:** Skip the cinnamon. Use coconut milk instead of the milk, 2 cups shredded unsweetened coconut instead of the oats, and ½ cup dried cherries instead of the chocolate.

Learn More

▶ Bread-Baking Basics (page 394), Chocolate, Butter, Sugar (page 422), Creaming Butter with a Whisk (page 398)

DROPPING COOKIES I use my finger to scrape the batter onto the pan, but a spoon works too. These will spread out a little during baking, so leave about 3 inches between them.

RECOGNIZING DONENESS Cookies are usually soft when they're ready to come out of the oven. The best way to check is to peek underneath and see if they're golden brown.

Butter Cookies

The blank canvas of baking—perfect for flavoring, decorating, and sandwiching.

TIME **About 30 minutes, plus time to chill**
MAKES **2 to 3 dozen**

16 tablespoons (2 sticks) butter, softened, plus more for greasing the pans

1 cup sugar

1 egg

1 teaspoon vanilla extract

3 cups all-purpose flour, plus more for dusting

1 teaspoon baking powder

Pinch salt

1 tablespoon milk, or as needed

1 Use an electric mixer to cream together the 2 sticks butter and the sugar until light and fluffy; add the egg and vanilla and beat until thoroughly blended.

2 Combine the flour, baking powder, and salt in a medium bowl. Add the dry ingredients to the butter mixture, beat for a few seconds, then pinch the dough to see if it holds together easily. If not, add some milk, 1 tablespoon at a time, beating and stopping to pinch the dough after each addition.

3 Divide the dough in half. Shape each piece into a log about 2 inches in diameter by rolling it on a flat surface. Wrap them in wax paper, parchment, or plastic and refrigerate for at least 2 hours or

up to 2 days (or wrap tightly in plastic wrap and freeze indefinitely).

4 Heat the oven to 400°F. Lightly grease 1 or 2 baking sheets with some butter. Cut each roll of cookie dough crosswise with a chef's knife into slices ⅛ to ¼ inch thick. Put the cookies on the prepared sheets, leaving about 1 inch of space between them.

5 Bake for 6 to 10 minutes, until the edges are lightly browned and the center is set. Cool for about 2 minutes on the sheets; then transfer the cookies to a rack with a spatula to finish cooling. Store in a tightly covered container at room temperature for no more than a day or two.

If the dough sticks, spread a light dusting of flour on top of the work surface.

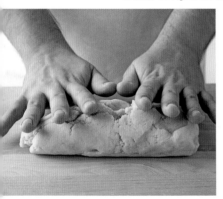

SHAPING THE ROLLS After you get the log shape started with your hands, use the work surface to even the dough out into a smooth roll.

SLICING THE DOUGH INTO COOKIES Try to make them all the same thickness so they bake evenly.

SPACING THE COOKIES These won't spread much, so you can put them close together. If you don't have 2 baking sheets, refrigerate the dough between batches.

Tips

▶ To decorate with frosting or glaze (see page 446), wait until the cookies are cool and leave them on the rack so the excess drips down, away from the cookies.

Variations

▶ **Cookie Cutter Cookies:** In Step 3, pat each dough half into a flat disk. In Step 4, dust the work space with flour and use a rolling pin to roll each disk until it's ⅛ to ¼ inch thick. Cut out the shapes you like by pressing a cookie cutter into the dough; then gather up and roll out any scraps and make some more. Continue with the recipe.

▶ **5 More Butter Cookies:**

1 Cocoa Cookies: Add ¼ cup cocoa to the dry ingredients in Step 2.

2 Butterscotch Cookies: Use ⅔ cup packed brown sugar instead of the granulated sugar.

3 Butter Cookies with Sea Salt: Sprinkle the tops of just-baked cookies with a few grains of coarse sea salt.

4 Ginger Cookies: Add 2 tablespoons or more chopped crystallized ginger to the finished dough.

5 Jam Sandwich Cookies: Smear ½ teaspoon of raspberry or strawberry jam between 2 baked cookies.

Learn More

▶ Chocolate, Butter, Sugar (page 422), creaming butter (pages 398 and 446), Combining Dry Ingredients (page 396), Greasing a Pan with Butter (page 398), Vanilla Glaze (page 447)

Use a whisk (or toothpicks or skewers) to drizzle glaze quickly over the cookies.

DECORATING COOKIES I don't go for anything too fancy, but it's easy to make a batch of glaze or frosting and have some fun.

Hazelnut Biscotti

Baked twice for incredible crunch, long-lasting flavor, and ideal dunking.

TIME 1¼ hours
MAKES About 2 dozen

4 tablespoons (½ stick) butter, softened, plus more for greasing the pans

2 cups all-purpose flour, plus more for dusting the pans

¾ cup sugar

2 eggs

1 teaspoon vanilla extract

1 teaspoon baking powder

1 cup blanched hazelnuts, toasted and chopped

Pinch salt

1 Heat the oven to 375°F. Grease a baking sheet with some butter and dust it with flour; turn the sheet upside down over the sink and tap to remove the excess flour.

2 Use an electric mixer to cream together the ½ stick butter and the sugar until light and fluffy; add the eggs, one at a time, and beat until well blended, then add the vanilla. Combine the flour, baking powder, nuts, and salt in a medium bowl. Add the dry ingredients to the egg-butter mixture a little at a time, beating until just combined.

3 Divide the dough in half, roll each half into a loaf about 2 inches wide, and put on the prepared baking sheet. Bake for 25 to 30 minutes, rotating the position of the pan in the oven if necessary so they cook evenly, until they're golden and beginning to crack on top. Cool the logs on the sheets for a few minutes, then transfer to a rack. Lower the oven temperature to 250°F.

4 When the loaves are cool enough to handle, carefully transfer them to a cutting board and use a serrated knife to slice each on the diagonal into ½-inch-thick slices. Put the cookies on the sheet, sliced side up; it's okay if they are close to each other. Return the pan to the oven, and bake 15 to 20 minutes, turning the biscotti once, until they dry out. Cool them on racks. They will keep in an airtight container for several days.

TESTING THE DOUGH Stop mixing when the dough holds little dimples after you poke and pinch it. There's no reason to keep beating after that.

SHAPING THE DOUGH Roll the loaves as uniformly as you can so the biscotti bake evenly.

Store dipped cookies in an airtight container between layers of wax or parchment paper.

Tips

▶ Hazelnuts (also known as *filberts*) have a dark skin that is a little bitter. Peeling them completely is a royal pain, so try to find them already blanched (or peeled). If you can't, toast them first, then roll them around in a towel to rub off what you can without too much hassle.

Variations

▶ **Other Nuts to Try in Biscotti:** Peanuts, almonds, pistachios, walnuts, or pecans

▶ **Chocolate-Dipped Biscotti:** While the biscotti are cooling, melt ½ pound chopped chocolate with 3 tablespoons butter in a small saucepan over low heat and put something under the wire rack to catch drips. Transfer the chocolate mixture to a cup or glass just big enough to hold it. When the biscotti are cool enough to handle, dip half of each cookie into the chocolate, tap against the rim to remove excess, then put them on the rack. As they continue to cool, the chocolate will harden a bit.

Learn More

▶ Chocolate, Butter, Sugar (page 422), Greasing a Pan with Butter (page 398), Dusting Pans with Flour (page 448), Toasted Nuts (page 73), chopping nuts (page 19), Combining Dry Ingredients (page 396)

BAKING THE LOAVES Don't let the loaves brown too much the first time around—just enough to dry the dough out and set them up.

CUTTING BISCOTTI Use a serrated knife to cut the loaves on the diagonal; this will give you long, gorgeous—and dippable—biscotti.

These slices are about ½ inch thick.

Preparing Fruit

Even though there are so many different kinds of fruit, their preparation remains the same. First remove the inedible (or undesirable) parts. Then cut or slice what's left into pieces that are relatively (but not obsessively) the same size.

Trimming

Be sure to stabilize round fruit on the cutting board and insert the knife securely before cutting.

Some fruit requires no more than pulling off a stem.

For other, sturdier fruits (like pineapple) you must cut off the top and bottom.

Coring

For medium cores, as in apples and pears, see page 454.

Small cores are easiest to remove by cutting a cone around them.

With larger fruit it's easier to peel and cut the fruit first, then remove the core from a smaller piece.

Peeling

For thin-skinned fruit like apples, pears, and mangoes, you can use a vegetable peeler and stroke either away from you or toward you, whichever feels more comfortable in your hands.

Another way is to trim, core, and quarter the fruit first, then hold the pieces in one hand and remove the peel with the other by pulling toward you with a paring knife.

Trim pineapple to stabilize it on the cutting board; then cut downward between the peel and the flesh, following the contours of the fruit. This technique works well for citrus and wedges of melon too.

Pitting

For small stone fruit—like cherries and olives—it's easiest to smash them first. (If you want to keep them intact, you've got to fish the pit out with a paring knife.)

With large stone fruit, slice around the equator, then wiggle the pit free. If it doesn't release easily, just cut slices downward into the flesh and pull them from the pit.

Melons are seeded like cucumbers and squash—with a spoon. (The exception is watermelon, where you have to poke and scrape with a fork.)

The only way to remove citrus seeds is to fish for them (and even then you won't get them all, so don't go crazy!).

Peach (or Other Fruit) Crisp

This will become one of your go-to desserts, since it's so versatile.

TIME **About 1 hour**
MAKES **6 to 8 servings**

---

5 tablespoons cold butter, plus more for greasing the pan

6 cups pitted, sliced peaches (2 to 3 pounds)

Juice of ½ lemon

⅔ cup packed brown sugar

½ cup rolled oats (not instant oats)

½ cup all-purpose flour

Pinch salt

¼ cup chopped nuts, optional

1 cup vanilla ice cream or whipped cream, optional

1 Heat the oven to 400°F. Cut the 5 tablespoons butter into ¼-inch bits and put in the fridge or freezer. Lightly butter a square baking pan. Toss the peaches with the lemon juice and 1 tablespoon of the brown sugar in a large bowl, and spread them out in the prepared pan.

2 Combine the chilled pieces of butter with the remaining brown sugar, the oats, the flour, the salt, and the nuts if you're using them in a food processor and pulse a few times, then process for a few seconds more, until everything is combined but not too finely ground. (To mix by hand, mash the mixture together between your fingers.)

3 Crumble the topping over the peaches and bake for 30 to 40 minutes, until the topping is browned and the peaches are tender and bubbling. Serve hot, warm, or at room temperature, with ice cream if you like.

Don't overprocess, or your topping will be gritty and tough.

MAKING A CRUMBLE TOPPING If you don't want to chop the oats up, mix them in by hand after pulsing the butter with the sugar and flour.

MAKING TOPPING BY HAND Squeeze the ingredients between your fingers until they are pretty well combined but still crumbly.

Tips

▶ Whether you are mixing the topping in the food processor or by hand, the idea is to combine all the ingredients, but not so much that the butter gets too mushy and warm.

▶ You can certainly eat crisp on its own, but in my opinion it was absolutely made for a scoop of vanilla ice cream or a dollop of whipped cream.

Variations

▶ **Other Fruit Crisps:** Apples, pears, plums, cherries, and berries all make classic crisps. Whichever you choose, start with about 6 cups fruit, sliced as needed. If you're using berries (which are a bit more watery), toss them with 2 tablespoons flour or cornstarch along with the lemon juice. This will help thicken the juices as the crisp bakes.

▶ **Individual Fruit Crisps:** Divide the fruit among individual ovenproof custard cups or ramekins (6- or 8-ounce is fine) and sprinkle some topping on each.

Learn More

▶ Preparing Fruit (page 430), chopping nuts (page 19), Dairy—and Not (page 42), Whipped Cream (page 447)

COVERING THE FRUIT Distribute the topping over the fruit, pinching bits into clumps and leaving holes here and there. It isn't supposed to cover the whole top.

JUDGING DONENESS The fruit should be bubbly and the topping brown. Let it cool for a few minutes before serving.

Blueberry Cobbler

Far easier than a pie and just as good (maybe even better).

TIME **About 1 hour**
MAKES **6 to 8 servings**

8 tablespoons (1 stick) cold butter, plus more for greasing the pan

About 6 cups blueberries, rinsed and well drained

1 cup sugar

½ cup all-purpose flour

½ teaspoon baking powder

Pinch salt

1 egg

½ teaspoon vanilla extract

1 Heat the oven to 375°F. Lightly grease a square baking pan with some butter. Toss the blueberries with ½ cup of the sugar in a medium bowl, and put them in the prepared pan.

2 Cut up the stick of butter into ¼-inch bits. Put the flour, baking powder, salt, and remaining ½ cup sugar in a food processor and pulse once or twice. Add the butter and process until the mixture is just combined (you should still see bits of butter), just a few seconds. By hand, beat in the egg and vanilla with a fork (you can do this right in the food processor—remove the blade first—or transfer the mixture to a bowl first if you like).

3 Drop this mixture onto the blueberries, 1 heaping tablespoon at a time, until you use it all up (space the mounds of dough as evenly as you can, but don't spread them out). Bake for 35 to 45 minutes, until the topping is just starting to brown and the blueberries are tender and bubbling. Serve hot, warm, or at room temperature.

A two-step process keeps the dough from getting overworked and tough.

PUTTING BLUEBERRIES IN THE PAN Press them down gently into an even layer, leaving enough room for the topping.

MIXING BY MACHINE, THEN HAND Stir in the egg and vanilla just until everything's combined; the batter will look like wet cookie dough.

LEAVING SPACE The dough will spread out a bit as it cooks, so make sure some of the berries show through.

Tips

▶ Don't overprocess the topping or you'll wind up with a tough, breadlike crust instead of a sweet, cookielike pastry.

▶ It's hard to beat cobbler served warm, with ice cream or whipped cream.

Variations

▶ **Apple Cobbler:** Instead of the blueberries, core and slice 2 pounds apples. (I don't bother to peel them.)

▶ **Peach Cobbler:** Instead of the blueberries, slice and pit 2 pounds peaches (peeled if you like).

▶ **Cherry Cobbler:** Instead of the blueberries, remove the pits from 6 cups sweet cherries.

▶ **Apricot Cobbler:** Instead of the blueberries, slice and pit 2 pounds apricots.

Learn More

▶ Chocolate, Butter, Sugar (page 422), Greasing a Pan with Butter (page 398), Whipped Cream (page 447)

Stovetop Pudding

Not much harder than so-called instant, but with infinitely more flavor.

TIME **About 20 minutes, plus time to chill**

MAKES **4 to 6 servings**

2½ cups half-and-half

⅔ cup sugar

Pinch salt

3 tablespoons cornstarch

2 tablespoons butter, softened

1 teaspoon vanilla extract

1 Combine 2 cups of the half-and-half, the sugar, and the salt in a small saucepan and stir. Put over medium-low heat. Cook until the mixture just begins to steam, 2 or 3 minutes.

2 Combine the cornstarch and the remaining ½ cup half-and-half in a bowl and whisk to make a slurry; there should be no lumps. Add the cornstarch mixture to the pan. Raise the heat a little if not much is happening and cook, stirring occasionally, until the mixture thickens and just starts to boil, 3 to 5 minutes. Reduce the heat to very low

and continue to cook, stirring constantly, until it thickens noticeably and starts to stick to the pan, another 3 to 5 minutes. Stir in the butter and the vanilla extract.

3 Pour the mixture into a bowl big enough to hold it or into 4 to 6 small ramekins or glasses. Put plastic wrap directly on top of the pudding to prevent the formation of a "skin," or, if you like pudding skin, leave it uncovered. Refrigerate until chilled, at least an hour, and serve within a day.

If any lumps remain, they'll make the pudding lumpy too.

For Chocolate Pudding, stir in chopped chocolate when you add the butter and vanilla.

MAKING THE SLURRY Whisk the cornstarch and half-and-half vigorously until completely smooth, then add it to the dairy mixture.

COOKING THE PUDDING Once the mixture comes to a boil, turn the heat down as low as you can so the pudding "plops" but the bottom of the pan doesn't scorch.

GETTING THE RIGHT CONSISTENCY The pudding is ready to remove from the heat when the mixture thickly coats a spoon and starts to actually look like pudding.

Tips

▶ The mixture of cornstarch and half-and-half is called a *slurry* (a term used to describe similar wet mixtures both in and out of cooking). Once it's stirred into the warm liquid it immediately starts to thicken the pudding. Just make sure the slurry is completely smooth before you add it (it's easy; that's the beauty of cornstarch), or the pudding will be lumpy.

Variations

▶ **Lighter Pudding:** Use milk instead of half-and-half and skip the butter.
▶ **Chocolate Pudding:** In Step 2, add 4 ounces chopped bittersweet chocolate to the thickened pudding. Make sure it has all melted before transferring it to the fridge.
▶ **Butterscotch Pudding:** Substitute packed brown sugar for the granulated sugar.

Learn More

▶ Dairy—and Not (page 42), Chocolate, Butter, Sugar (page 422), Testing the Texture of a Creamy Sauce (page 193)

Remember that for some people the skin is the best part.

AVOIDING SKIN (OR NOT) Pressing plastic wrap directly onto the pudding would prevent skin from forming as the mixture cools.

Rice Pudding in the Oven

The term *comfort food* is overused. But not here: There is nothing more soothing.

TIME **About 2 hours,**
mostly unattended

MAKES **At least 4 servings**

1/3 cup any white rice

1/2 cup sugar

Pinch salt

4 cups milk

1 Heat the oven to 300°F. Combine the rice, sugar, salt, and milk in a large gratin dish that holds at least 6 cups. Stir a couple of times and put it in the oven, uncovered. Bake for 30 minutes, then stir. Bake for 30 minutes longer, then stir again; at this point the rice might be swelling up and the milk should begin to develop a bubbly skin (if so, stir it back into the mixture).

2 Cook until the rice plumps and starts to become a more noticeable part of the mixture and the skin becomes more visible and darker, about 30 minutes more. Now the pudding is getting close to done, so check on it every 10 minutes, stirring each time (it should reach the right texture in 10 to 30 minutes, depending on the kind of rice you used).

3 The pudding will be done before you think it's done. The rice should be really swollen and the milk thickened considerably but still pretty fluid (it will thicken more as it cools). Serve warm, at room temperature, or cold.

Stirring helps the starch release from the rice and thicken the milk.

COMBINING THE INGREDIENTS
When it goes in the oven, you'll think there's no way it's ever going to become pudding.

STIRRING EVERY 30 MINUTES
Here's what the pudding will look like after 1 hour in the oven. Still quite thin but beginning to thicken and darken on top.

FORMING A SKIN The light brown covering that forms on top of the milk is loaded with flavor and helps thicken the pudding. Just stir it back in.

Tips

▶ You've got to use white rice in this recipe, but you have some choices: Long-grain aromatic rice (like basmati or jasmine) will deliver the most delicate texture and fragrance. Short- or medium-grain white rice (like Arborio) will be more thick and chewy. Supermarket long-grain rices will be somewhere in between.

Variations

▶ **5 Ways to Change the Flavor:**

1 Substitute coconut, soy, rice, or nut milk for the milk.

2 Stir in a piece or two of whole spice (cinnamon sticks, cloves, or nutmeg) at the beginning of cooking.

3 Stir in a teaspoon of grated citrus zest at the beginning of cooking.

4 Add 1 teaspoon vanilla extract after cooking.

5 Add up to ½ cup chopped toasted nuts right before serving.

Learn More

▶ Rice Basics (page 196), Dairy—and Not (page 42), chopping nuts (page 19), Toasted Nuts (page 73)

GETTING CLOSER TO DONE Almost there. Much thicker but still somewhat runny.

RECOGNIZING DONENESS When the pudding is ready, it falls from the spoon in soft clumps. It will thicken as it cools.

Chocolate Mousse

A few basic techniques are all you need to make this sublimely decadent classic.

TIME **30 minutes, plus time to chill**

MAKES **6 servings**

2 tablespoons butter

4 ounces chocolate, chopped

3 eggs, separated

½ teaspoon vanilla extract

¼ cup sugar

½ cup cream

1 Fill a small or medium saucepan about halfway with water and put over high heat. Find a bowl that sits comfortably in the pot so the bottom just touches the water (or is close). When the water comes to a boil, lower the heat so it bubbles gently. Put the butter and chocolate in the bowl and set it in the saucepan to rig a double boiler.

2 Cook, stirring occasionally, until the chocolate is almost completely melted. Remove it from the heat and stir the mixture until it's completely smooth. Let it cool until you can hold the bowl, then whisk in the egg yolks and the vanilla.

3 Put the egg whites and 2 tablespoons of the sugar in a medium mixing bowl and beat with an electric mixer until the mixture holds stiff peaks, 30 to 45 seconds. Wash the beaters; put the cream and the remaining 2 tablespoons sugar in a separate, smaller mixing bowl and beat with the electric mixer until the cream holds soft peaks, 20 to 30 seconds.

4 Stir a couple of spoonfuls of the egg whites into the chocolate mixture, then fold in the remaining whites thoroughly but gently with a rubber spatula. Fold in the cream just enough so that there are no streaks of white, then refrigerate until chilled. Eat within a day; to serve, transfer the mousse to a serving bowl or individual cups.

You can also use your hand; separate your fingers to let the whites slip through.

This is the best way to melt straight chocolate too.

SEPARATING EGGS After cracking the shell, transfer the yolk back and forth from one half to the other, letting the white fall into a bowl. Put the yolk in a separate bowl.

USING A DOUBLE BOILER This rig keeps chocolate—and butter and other delicate foods—from burning. Be careful: The bowl will get hot.

BEATING EGG WHITES These are *stiff peaks*: firm and slightly glossy but not dried out. It's okay if the tips curl over, but any more beating and they'll break apart and curdle.

Tips

▶ Melting chocolate is easy, but keep an eye on it. (Chocolate burns easily, especially if you're melting it by itself.) So watch the heat, be patient, and stir frequently.

▶ Folding ingredients together always works best when they're a similar density. Adding some of the whites to the chocolate helps lighten it for easier incorporation, but you'll still need to be patient when folding. Work from the bottom of the bowl with the spatula, lifting and folding like turning the pages of a book. Try to avoid using cutting or stirring motions as shortcuts and you'll be rewarded with a super-fluffy mousse.

Variations

▶ **Mocha Mousse:** Add 2 tablespoons very strong brewed coffee (espresso is best) to the chocolate mixture in Step 1 and reduce the cream in Step 3 to 6 tablespoons. Or add 2 teaspoons instant espresso powder to the chocolate mixture in Step 1 and use the same amount of cream.

▶ **White Chocolate Mousse:** Use white chocolate.

Learn More

▶ Chocolate, Butter, Sugar (page 422), Egg Basics (page 50), Dairy—and Not (page 42), beating cream to soft peaks (page 447)

STIRRING SOME WHITES INTO CHOCOLATE This step makes it easier to fold in the remaining whites and cream. The idea is to lighten the chocolate a little.

FOLDING IN WHIPPED CREAM
Keep gently lifting the spatula up and over—just until everything's the same color and there are no white streaks still visible.

Raspberry Sorbet

No ice cream maker? No problem!

TIME **10 minutes, plus optional freezing time**
MAKES **4 to 6 servings**

1 pound frozen raspberries

½ cup yogurt

¼ cup sugar

1 Put the raspberries, yogurt, sugar, and 2 tablespoons water in the food processor. Process, stopping to scrape down the sides of the bowl if necessary, until the raspberries break down and the mixture is just puréed. If the raspberries aren't breaking apart, add another tablespoon or two of water, but don't add too much and don't overprocess, or the mixture will liquefy.

2 Serve immediately or transfer it to a container and freeze for later. (If you're freezing it, let the sorbet soften in the fridge for an hour or so before serving, or if you're in a hurry, let it sit at room temperature for 10 to 15 minutes.)

You can freeze your own fruit or buy it already frozen.

If the sorbet freezes solid, thaw it out slowly in the fridge for the best texture.

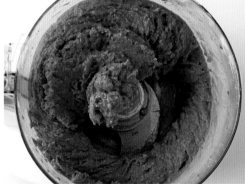

PURÉEING THE FRUIT It's okay if the sorbet has a little texture to it, but you don't want big hunks of frozen raspberries.

PERFECTING THE TEXTURE You want the mixture fairly smooth, thick, and cold. Add only enough water to keep the machine working.

FREEZING FOR LATER If this consistency is too loose for you to eat right away, transfer the mixture to a container or zipper bag and freeze it for 30 minutes (or up to several weeks).

Tips

▶ The food processor works incredibly well here. The key is to process the mixture just enough so the frozen fruit breaks apart but not so much that it begins to liquefy. You want the results to be frozen enough to eat with a spoon, not a drinking straw.

▶ Yogurt gives the sorbet a little creamy tang, which is nice, but not necessary. You can use water or juice instead. Or for an even creamier texture: cream.

Variations

▶ **Mango-Coconut Sorbet:** Use frozen mangoes instead of the raspberries and coconut milk instead of the yogurt.

▶ **Cherry-Chocolate Sorbet:** Use frozen pitted cherries instead of the raspberries. In Step 1, add 4 ounces chopped chocolate to the food processor along with the rest of the ingredients.

▶ **Raspberry Granita:** Essentially shaved, flavored ice. In Step 2, transfer the mixture from the food processor to a square baking pan and put it in the freezer. Every 30 minutes, stir and scrape the sorbet with a fork to break it into small crystals as it freezes. It's done when all of the crystals are fully frozen (kind of like a snow cone), about 2 hours. Scrape the granita into bowls or cups and serve.

Learn More

▶ Preparing Fruit (page 430), Dairy—and Not (page 42)

Pound Cake

Beloved with good reason: It's simple, delicious, goes with anything, and keeps well.

TIME **About 1½ hours**

MAKES **At least 8 servings**

16 tablespoons (2 sticks) butter, softened, plus more for greasing the pan

2 cups all-purpose flour

1½ teaspoons baking powder

Pinch salt

1 cup sugar

5 eggs

2 teaspoons vanilla extract

1 Heat the oven to 325°F. Grease a loaf pan with butter. Combine the flour, baking powder, and salt in a medium bowl.

2 Use an electric mixer to cream the butter in a large bowl until it's smooth. Add ¾ cup of the sugar and beat until it's well blended, then add the remaining sugar and beat until the mixture is light and fluffy. Beat in the eggs, one at a time. Add the vanilla and beat until blended.

3 Stir in the dry ingredients by hand just until the mixture is smooth; don't mix it too much and don't use the electric mixer.

4 Transfer the batter to the loaf pan and smooth out the top. Bake for 1 to 1¼ hours, until a toothpick inserted into the center comes out clean. Let the cake rest in the pan for 5 to 10 minutes before inverting onto a rack with a towel. Remove the pan, then turn the cake right side up. Cool before slicing. Serve warm or store at room temperature, wrapped in wax paper, for several days.

You want a natural dome to develop during baking, but too much batter in the center of the pan will bake unevenly.

PUTTING THE BATTER IN THE PAN After scraping whatever you can out of the bowl with a rubber spatula, smooth the top with a butter knife.

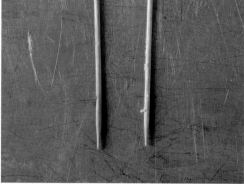

TESTING WITH A TOOTHPICK This method works well with cakes: Insert it in the center; if it comes out clean, it's ready.

TURNING OUT THE CAKE Keep the top of the cake in contact with the towel so it doesn't fall when it slides out. Use the towel to turn it upright on the rack to cool.

Tips

▶ Rarely—and only if your pans don't have a nonstick coating—a cake might not release from the pan right away. If so, give a few firm taps to the bottom or loosen the cake by carefully running a butter knife along the sides of the pan. You can also line the pan with parchment paper after you grease it in Step 1. To remove the cake, just use the overhanging parchment paper as handles and lift.

Variations

▶ **Lemon Poppy Seed Pound Cake:** Skip the vanilla. After beating in the eggs at the end of Step 2, beat in 1 tablespoon fresh lemon juice, 1 teaspoon grated lemon zest, and ¼ cup poppy seeds.

Learn More

▶ Bread-Baking Basics (page 394), Greasing a Pan with Butter (page 398), Egg Basics (page 50), Creaming Butter with a Whisk (page 398)

Icing on the Cake

Vanilla Buttercream

Adding ingredients gradually helps keep the butter fluffy.

CREAM THE BUTTER Put 8 tablespoons (1 stick) softened butter in a large bowl. (It's got to be soft enough to spread.) Beat with an electric mixer until the butter becomes light colored and, well, creamy.

ADD SOME SUGAR Measure out 4 cups powdered sugar and ½ cup cream or milk. Start by beating in 2 cups of the sugar.

For Chocolate Buttercream, reduce the vanilla to 1 teaspoon. Before adjusting the consistency, add 2 ounces melted (and cooled) unsweetened chocolate (see pages 422 and 429).

ALTERNATE SUGAR WITH CREAM After beating the sugar, add 2 tablespoons of the cream and another ½ cup of sugar. Repeat until all the sugar and cream are gone. After the last addition, beat in 2 teaspoons vanilla extract and a pinch salt.

ADJUST THE CONSISTENCY If the icing is too thick to spread, add a little more cream, 1 teaspoon at a time. If it's too thin (unlikely but possible), refrigerate; it will thicken as the butter hardens.

Vanilla Glaze

ASSEMBLE AND MEASURE This recipe makes about 3 cups—enough for any cake or batch of cookies. Put 3 cups powdered sugar in a large bowl with ¾ cup cream (or milk), ½ teaspoon vanilla extract, and a pinch of salt. Whisk or beat with an electric mixer.

KEEP MIXING The glaze should be smooth and barely pourable, about the consistency of thick maple syrup. If it's not quite there, add more liquid to thin it (or sugar to thicken it) 1 teaspoon at a time.

Whipped Cream

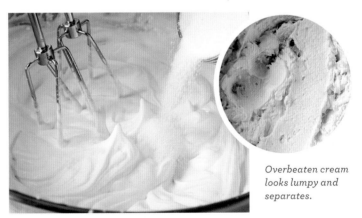

Overbeaten cream looks lumpy and separates.

BEAT BY HAND OR MACHINE Put 1 cup cream in a clean metal or glass bowl and use a whisk or an electric mixer to beat the cream until it reaches the consistency you like. Here it's almost like a sauce.

ADD SUGAR (OR NOT) After the cream begins to take shape, you can add up to ¼ cup sugar—slowly, as you continue to beat. Here the cream is whipped to *soft peaks* (which fall over when the beaters are raised). Don't go any further than stiff peaks.

Coconut Layer Cake

The classic yellow cake taken to a higher level.

TIME   **About 1 hour, plus time to cool**

MAKES   **At least 10 servings**

---

10 tablespoons (1¼ sticks) butter, softened, plus more for greasing the pans and paper

2 cups all-purpose flour, plus more for dusting the pans

1¼ cups sugar

4 eggs

1 teaspoon vanilla extract

2½ teaspoons baking powder

3 cups shredded unsweetened coconut

¼ teaspoon salt

¾ cup milk

1 recipe Vanilla Buttercream (page 446)

1 Heat the oven to 350°F. Grease the bottom and sides of two 9-inch round cake pans; cover the bottom with a circle of wax or parchment paper, grease the paper, and sift flour over the pans. Shake to distribute the flour evenly, turn the pans upside down, and tap over the sink to remove the excess flour.

2 Cream the 1¼ sticks butter with an electric mixer until smooth, then gradually add the sugar. Beat until light and fluffy, 3 or 4 minutes. Beat in the eggs, one at a time, then the vanilla. Combine the flour, baking powder, ½ cup of the coconut, and the salt; add to the egg mixture by hand, a little at a time, alternating with the milk. Stir after each addition just until smooth.

3 Pour the batter into the pans and smooth out the tops. Bake for 20 to 25 minutes, until a toothpick inserted in the center of the cakes comes out clean. Let the cakes cool in the pans for 5 minutes, then invert the pans and slide the cakes onto a rack to finish cooling.

4 Fill, stack, and frost the layers directly on a large plate: Figure one-third of the icing and ½ cup coconut for the middle, one-third of the icing for the top, and one-third of the icing for the sides. Press the remaining coconut into the icing all over the cake. Serve or store at room temperature, covered with a tent of foil, for a day or two.

DUSTING PANS WITH FLOUR A thin layer after greasing helps ensure that the cakes won't stick to the pans.

FILLING THE PANS They don't need to be totally smooth, but it helps the cakes cook evenly.

FROSTING BETWEEN THE LAYERS Put the bottom layer upside down on the plate so the flat side is facing up. Spread the frosting all the way to the edges, then sprinkle with coconut.

Tips

▶ The ideal tool for frosting cakes is an offset spatula or straight blade (a long, narrow, flat spatula). If you don't have either, just use a butter knife or rubber spatula. If you're not topping with coconut, wiggle your hand a little as you're frosting to create little peaks and swirls.

▶ A 9 x 13-inch pan also works for this recipe—resulting in a small sheet cake. You'll have a thick layer of icing and coconut on top.

▶ If you want a cleaner look, you can transfer the frosted cake to a clean plate with 2 spatulas held at 90-degree angles—a risk sometimes worth taking. Or you can just wipe the rim of the cake plate with a damp clean towel.

Variations

▶ **Birthday Cake:** Skip the coconut; bake the cakes and make the frosting. Tint ¾ cup of the frosting with a few drops food coloring and put it in a small zipper bag; use the rest of the frosting to ice the cake. Cut a small tip off one corner of the bag and squeeze out the tinted icing to write a message on top.

Learn More

▶ Bread-Baking Basics (page 394), baking equipment (page 10)

FROSTING THE TOP AND SIDES
Put the other layer face up. Smear the frosting in an even layer on top, being careful not to dig the knife. Then do the same around the sides.

ADDING THE COCONUT Put some coconut in your hand and press it against the frosting until it sticks. Pick up whatever falls on the plate and repeat until the cake is covered.

Pumpkin Pie

Silky filling in a crisp graham cracker crust. And super-easy.

TIME **About 1 hour**

MAKES **One 9-inch pie**
(about 8 servings)

½ cup plus 3 tablespoons sugar

6 ounces graham crackers, broken, or more as needed

5 tablespoons butter, melted, or more as needed

2 eggs

½ teaspoon ground cinnamon

¼ teaspoon ground ginger

⅛ teaspoon freshly grated nutmeg

⅛ teaspoon ground cloves

Pinch salt

1½ cups canned pumpkin purée

1¼ cups half-and-half, cream, or milk

1 To make the crust, heat the oven to 350°F. Combine 3 tablespoons of the sugar with the graham cracker pieces in the bowl of a food processor and process until they're finely ground. You should have about 1½ cups; add or remove some if not. Slowly add the butter and pulse a few times until they're all moistened by the butter (if the crumbs aren't all moistened, add a little bit more melted butter). Press the crumbs evenly into the bottom and sides of a 9-inch pie plate.

2 Bake the crust for 8 to 10 minutes, just until it begins to brown. Set the pie plate on a rack; the crust will crisp as it cools. Turn the oven up to 375°F.

3 While the crust is baking, use an electric mixer or a whisk to beat the eggs with the remaining sugar, then add the cinnamon, ginger, nutmeg, cloves, and salt. Add the pumpkin purée, mix, then add the half-and-half.

4 Put the pie plate with the crust on a rimmed baking sheet. Pour the pumpkin mixture into the crust all the way to the top (you might have some left over). Transfer the whole baking sheet to the oven (in case of spillover) and bake for 30 to 40 minutes, until the mixture shakes like Jell-O but is still quite moist in the center. Cool on a rack until it no longer jiggles, then slice into wedges and serve, or refrigerate for a day or two.

If the mixture doesn't clump, add more butter a little at a time, process, and try again.

MOISTENING THE CRUMBS They should clump together when you squeeze them without being too greasy.

PARBAKING THE CRUST Also known as *blind baking*, meaning there's no filling yet. Don't let it get too dark.

Tips

▶ Parbaking the crust is essential for most pies made with graham cracker crust. The filling is so wet (and the crust so porous) that if you don't bake the crust first it will turn soggy. Also the timing works pretty well. In the time it takes for the crust to prebake, you can mix the filling and start to warm it on the stove.

▶ Since pumpkin pie is a Thanksgiving staple, you should be able to find canned pumpkin purée at any supermarket. Make sure to buy the unsweetened and unspiced variety if you have an option (you'll add your own).

Variations

▶ **Ice Cream Pie:** Dessert in a hurry. Skip the pumpkin custard ingredients. After you make the crust, take a half gallon of ice cream (or frozen yogurt or sorbet) out of the freezer to soften. When the crust is completely cooled, spread the ice cream into the shell. When the pie is half filled, add a sprinkle of nuts, a drizzle of fudge, or some chopped fresh fruit if you like and add the remaining ice cream on top. Cover with plastic and freeze until set.

Learn More
▶ Melting Butter (page 70), Dairy—and Not (page 42)

FILLING THE PIE Once you pour the filling into the crust, smooth out the top and let it settle into the crust. Add a little more if you need to.

JIGGLING IN THE CENTER The filling should still be a little liquid. It's better too soft than over-baked, curdled, and dry. It will get firmer as it cools.

Basic Piecrust

You can practice pastry skill by hand (tricky but fun) or machine (easy and foolproof).

CUT IN THE BUTTER In the food processor: Chop 16 tablespoons (2 sticks) very cold butter into ¼-inch bits. Put 2¼ cups all-purpose flour, 1 teaspoon salt, and 2 teaspoons sugar in the machine and pulse once or twice to combine. Add the butter and pulse until the butter and flour are just barely blended and the mixture resembles cornmeal.

To cut by hand: Combine the dry ingredients and bits of butter in a large bowl, hold a knife in each hand, and run the knives back and forth through the mixture. Or pinch bits of flour and butter between all of your your fingers, and crumble them back into the bowl until you've worked the dough into a cornmeal texture.

FORM THE DOUGH Transfer the mixture to a large bowl and add 6 tablespoons ice water. Use actual ice water—not just cold water. It helps keep the dough cold and the butter firm, which are crucial

for a tender, flaky crust. Mix with your hands until you can just form the dough into a ball, adding another tablespoon or two of ice water if necessary (or a little more flour if you add too much water).

FORM 2 DISKS Divide the dough in half with a knife. Gently pat and shape each half into a thick disk between your hands, using your thumbs to maintain a round shape. Again, it's important not to overheat, overwork, or knead the dough; squeeze

it with enough pressure just to hold it together. Wrap the disks in plastic wrap and freeze for 10 minutes or refrigerate for at least 30 minutes before rolling. If you're making a single-crust pie, freeze one disk for another time.

DUST WITH FLOUR Always start with a clean work surface. Pick up a large pinch of flour and, using a quick motion, sprinkle it first on the board and then on the top of the dough. The idea is to put a thin layer on the surface—enough to eliminate friction but not enough to dry the dough. If the dough starts to stick to the surface during rolling, loosen it with a spatula and dust a little more flour underneath. If it starts to stick to the rolling pin, dust the top or rub your hands with flour and run them over the rolling pin.

ROLL THE DOUGH Using firm, steady, but not overly hard pressure on the pin, start from the center and roll the dough outward into a circle. Avoid rolling back and forth; keep the strokes working outward from the center. If the dough feels hard, let it rest for a few minutes. If the dough is sticky, add a little flour; if it's really sticky, return it the fridge or freezer for a few minutes. As you roll, add flour and rotate and turn the dough with a spatula as needed to form an even circle.

PATCH HOLES To repair tears, pinch off a ragged edge of dough, adding a drop of water while you press the patch into place. Continue rolling to work it gently into the crust. Don't worry if you can see where it was; no one but you will ever know.

If you're really having trouble with sticking, try rolling the dough between 2 pieces of parchment paper or plastic wrap.

FIT THE DOUGH INTO THE PIE PLATE When the dough circle is about 2 inches larger than the pie plate and less than ⅛ inch thick, it's ready. Roll the dough up halfway onto the pin so it's easy to move, then center it over the pie plate and unroll it into place. Press the dough into the contours of the dish—without squishing or stretching. Trim the excess dough to about ½ inch all around. (If you're making a single-crust pie, tuck it under itself so the dough is thicker on the rim than it is inside.) Put the pie plate in the fridge. For the top of the pie, roll the second disk into a circle on a flat baking sheet (dusted with flour) and put that in the fridge too.

Apple Pie

A bit of a project, but now that you're a cook, how can you not try it?

TIME   **About 2 hours**
MAKES   **One 9-inch pie (about 8 servings)**

1 recipe Basic Piecrust (page 452), rolled and chilled

½ cup packed brown sugar

½ teaspoon ground cinnamon

⅛ teaspoon freshly grated nutmeg

Pinch salt

5 or 6 apples (about 2 pounds; anything but Red Delicious)

1 tablespoon fresh lemon juice

1½ tablespoons cornstarch, optional

2 tablespoons butter, softened

Milk as needed

Granulated sugar as needed

1   Make the crusts to the point where they're rolled (with the bottom crust fitted into a pie plate) and resting in the fridge. Heat the oven to 425°F.

2   Toss together the brown sugar, cinnamon, nutmeg, and salt in a large bowl. Peel, quarter, and core the apples and cut them into ½- to ¾-inch-thick slices. Toss the apples and lemon juice with the sugar-spice mixture; stir in the cornstarch if you're using it. Remove the crusts from the fridge.

3   Put the apples into the bottom crust, making the pile a little higher in the center than at the sides. Dot the top with the butter. Roll the top crust halfway onto a rolling pin so it's easy to move, center it over the pie, and unroll it over the top. Trim off the overhanging dough, then crimp the top and bottom crust together with the tines of a fork to seal and decorate the crust.

4   Put the pie on a rimmed baking sheet and brush the top lightly with milk; sprinkle with a little granulated sugar. Cut several 2-inch-long slits in the top with a paring knife so steam can escape. Bake for 20 minutes, then reduce the heat to 350°F and bake for another 40 to 50 minutes, until the crust is golden brown and flaky. Cool on a rack, cut into wedges, and serve warm or at room temperature. To store, cover loosely with foil and eat within a day or two.

Always make sure a flat side is face down on the cutting board for stability.

PEELING APPLES Treat them like potatoes.

QUARTERING AN APPLE Cut downward through the core (keeping your fingers out of the way). Then cut each half in half.

REMOVING THE CORE This takes a little practice, but the idea is to work the knife toward you; your thumb helps stabilize the apple and guide the knife.

Tips

▶ To choose an apple for pie, pick what you like to eat. As a general rule, crisp apples soften but keep their shape during baking; mealy ones break down and get saucy.

▶ You don't need to peel the apples. If the skin is thin, unwaxed, and not bitter—or if you just happen to like it—don't bother. But just so you know: Chances are they'll at least partially separate from the flesh during baking.

▶ Cornstarch thickens the juices that release from the apples as they cook. If you like a thicker, more syrupy filling, use the cornstarch; if you like a runnier pie, leave it out.

Variations

▶ **Blackberry Pie:** Use 3 pints blackberries instead of the sliced apples. Skip the cinnamon and nutmeg.

▶ **Peach Pie:** Use peaches instead of apples and skip the cinnamon and nutmeg if you like.

▶ **Cherry Pie:** Use 3 pints pitted sweet cherries (frozen are fine, which makes this a nice wintertime treat; thaw them out in a colander while you make the crust). Skip the spices.

Learn More

▶ Bread-Baking Basics (page 394), Chocolate, Butter, Sugar (page 422)

TRANSFERRING THE TOP CRUST
A rolling pin is the best way. Lay the top crust on so that it is smooth (not puckered) all the way across and covers the entire pie, with some overhang.

CRIMPING THE PIE SHUT There are more decorative ways to seal the deal, but simply pressing down with the tines of a fork all the way around is foolproof.

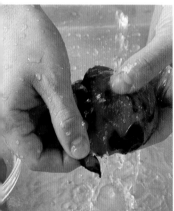 

Making Menus

Do Your Own Thing

When it comes to assembling a meal, I'm not a stickler for the usual conventions. Eat what you like, I always say. This approach can be a boon for beginners—who have enough to worry about anyway—which is why the recipes in this book focus on single dishes and not menus or anything other than basic serving suggestions.

But that said, a little guidance in the menu department can be helpful, especially when you're entertaining and cooking big-deal meals. The combinations here give you some ideas to get started.

Whether we think about it or not, nutrition is the core of eating, so you should pay at least some attention to assembling so-called balanced meals that include a variety of foods. But you don't have to be a dietician to eat well. As long as you keep an eye on mixing flavors, textures, and colors—brown included—and start with mostly fresh, minimally processed ingredients, you'll get what you need and enjoy what you eat.

One key point I can't mention enough: It's okay to serve dishes warm or at room temperature. For more about this, putting together menus in general, and entertaining, see pages 38 and 77.

Weekend Breakfast
Focus on one dish. Maybe add meat on the side. Cut up some fruit.
- Baked Eggs with Onions and Cheese (page 62)
- Breakfast Meats (page 43)

Blowout Brunch
If you make the banana bread, cut up the pineapple, and prep the peppers and onions for the sausage the night before, you can sleep in and pull everything else together mid-morning.
- Cut pineapple (page 431)
- Baked Eggs with Onions and Cheese (page 62)
- Sausage and Peppers (page 288)
- Grilled or Broiled Tomatoes (page 226)
- Banana Bread (page 398)

Lunch at Home
You can't go wrong with "something" and salad. (Or just a big bowl of salad or soup for that matter.)
- Pasta with Broccoli and Sausage (page 182)
- Chopped Salad (page 116)
- A loaf of good bread (page 382) or . . .
- Miso Soup (page 144)
- Tossed Green Salad with Asian Flavors (page 111)
- Plain soba or udon noodles (page 190)

Lunch for a Crowd
For new cooks especially, a lunch party can be a lot less stressful than having a bunch of people over for a fancy dinner—but no less impressive. All of these dishes—even the slaw—can be made up to a day or two ahead and reheated as necessary. Then serve this meal sit-down or buffet-style.
- Herb Dip (page 78)
- Cauliflower Gratin with Blue Cheese (page 246)
- Roasted Peppers (page 98)
- Chickpeas, Provençal-Style (page 254)
- Chicken Stew with Softened Garlic (page 322)
- Butter Cookies (page 426)

Picnic for Two
All you need for a good picnic is a cooler. If you're not going far, you don't even need that. I like to keep it casual, but nice, so bring real plates, glasses, forks, napkins, and a tablecloth or blanket for the table or ground. Leftovers are the way to go for a small impromptu picnic. If you don't feel like cooking up this entire menu, substitute what's handy and enjoy what you've got.
- Grilled or Broiled Chicken with Herbs—served cold (page 320)
- Mediterranean Potato Salad (page 130)
- Oatmeal Chocolate Chip Cookies (page 424)

Lunch at the Office
Bring leftovers. Nothing better than that.

Everyday Dinner

Doesn't have to be much fancier or involved than lunch. Maybe add dessert.

- Chicken Cutlets with Quick Pan Sauce (page 312)
- Rosemary-Roasted Potatoes (page 224)
- Steamed Asparagus (page 220)
- Peach (or Other Fruit) Crisp (page 432)

Everyday Vegetarian Dinner

A lot of people try to skip meat at least one night a week. It's easy, really.

- Spanish-Style Lentils with Spinach (page 256)
- Boiled Rice (page 196)
- Maple-Glazed Carrots (page 228)
- Raspberry Sorbet (page 442)

Indoor Barbecue

Nothing like filling your house with summertime smells in the dead of winter. Invite some people over and make it a party.

- Quick Pickle Spears (page 88)
- Spicy Coleslaw (page 120; make a double recipe)
- Smoky Red Bean Soup (page 150)
- Barbecued Spare Ribs in the Oven (page 296)
- Corn Bread (page 396)
- Coconut Layer Cake (page 448)

Pasta Party

Salad isn't my favorite way to eat pasta since the texture can be sort of chewy when cold. But some pasta dishes are excellent served at room temperature, so this menu is great for entertaining. Here's the strategy: Bake the cookies up to several days in advance. Assemble the lasagna and prep all the vegetables up to a day ahead and keep everything in the fridge. Take the lasagne out about an hour before guests are supposed to arrive; cook the mushrooms then pop the pan in the oven. While the lasagna bakes, prepare the other pastas and toss the salad. Then serve the lasagne hot, as the centerpiece, with everything else as "sides."

- Caesar Salad (page 118; double or triple the recipe as needed)
- Meaty Lasagne (page 188)
- Whole Wheat Pasta with Pesto (page 184)
- Pasta with Broccoli (page 183)
- Pan-Cooked (Sautéed) Mushrooms (page 230)
- Hazelnut Biscotti (page 428)

Family Fish Fry

Perfect for Saturday night—or any night really. The Asian flavors make this meal fancy enough for company, too.

- Crisp Sesame Fish Fillets (page 352)
- Stir-Fried Cabbage with Ginger (page 222)
- Boiled Rice (page 196)
- Stovetop Pudding (page 436)

Restaurant-Style Dinner Party

You have some options, starting with the most complicated: Serve in courses, plated individually. Serve family style. Or set out a buffet.

- Bruschetta (pages 90–93)
- Tossed Green Salad (page 110)
- Roast Pork with Herb Rub (page 292)
- Polenta with Mushrooms (page 212)
- Green Beans with Crisp Shallots (page 238)
- Chocolate Mousse (page 440)

Cocktail Party

A buffet of predominantly make-ahead food is by far the easiest approach, and the number of dishes is flexible. Let the serving size help you estimate how many people you can feed: Double, triple, or quadruple recipes if you need to, then add the serving quantities for all the dishes together so you get a total that is slightly more than the number of guests. (For example, if you're inviting 20 people, figure a total of 30 servings.) No need to make enough of each thing to serve everyone. If you're feeling ambitious (and like to stay busy), do something that keeps you in the kitchen so folks circulate everywhere.

- Sweet-Hot Nuts (page 73)
- Antipasto, Your Way (page 76)
- Deviled Eggs (page 94)
- Stuffed Mushrooms (page 100)
- Roasted Salmon with Butter (page 356)
- Roasted Chicken Wings with Spicy Soy Glaze (page 319)
- Sweet Potato Fritters (page 104)
- Brownies (page 420)

List of Lessons

Need to find out how to do something? Use the reverse lookup here and on the following two pages.

Preparation

Techniques

Index

Muffin tin, 10, *11*
Mushroom(s)
-barley soup, 165
in beef kabobs, grilled or
broiled, 272–273, *273*
cleaning/trimming, 101
in crudités, 75
dried, soaking, *212*
grilled or broiled, 227
in hot and sour soup, 166–
167, *167*
omelet filling, 59
pasta with or without sausage and, 183
polenta with, *212–213*,
212–213
pork chops with, skillet,
291
in quesadillas, 97
salad, shaved, 129
sautéed, *230–231*, 230–
231
sautéed, Asian style, 231
in scrambled eggs, 53
stems, removing/chop-
ping, *100*
stuffed, *100–101*, 100–101
stuffed, with nutty bread
crumbs, 101
tomato sauce with fresh
mushrooms, 180, *181*
turkey thighs braised with
fresh and dried mush-
rooms, 343
varieties of, *231*
in vegetable stock, full-
flavored, *152–153*,
152–153
Mussels, *360*, 360
steamed, *370–371*, 370–
371
steamed, curry-coconut,
371
steamed, French style, 371
steamed, tomato-basil,
371
testing, *370*

Mustard greens, 217, *287*
in pork stir-fry with greens,
286, 286–287

N

Nachos platter, 76
Napa cabbage, 108
coleslaw, spicy, *120–121*,
120–121
in noodles, Thai style,
with shrimp, *194–195*,
194–195
salad, warm, with bacon,
133
New England–style anadama
bread, 411
Niçoise salade, traditional,
131
No-knead bread, *408–409*,
408–409
No-knead bread, whole
wheat, 409
Noodles, Asian
basics, 190–191, *191*
cold, with cashew sauce,
193
cold, with peanut sauce,
192–193, 192–193
cold, with sesame sauce,
193
fried, *191*, 191
pad Thai, almost, 195
as pantry staple, 2
with shrimp, Thai style,
194–195, *195*
soup, cup of, *191*, 191
stir-fry with, *191*, 191, 271
North African-style lentils
with carrots, 257
Nut(s). *See also specific nuts*
for biscotti, 429
bread crumbs, nutty,
mushrooms stuffed
with, 101
brownies, nutty, 421
as bruschetta topping, 92
chopping, *19*, 19
-cranberry muffins, 401

in granola and muesli, *46–
47*, 46–47
honey-roasted, 73
as pantry staple, 4
pesto with whole wheat
pasta, 185
in popcorn, 71
roasted, *72–73*, 72–73
roasted herbed, 73
salad, tossed, with fruit,
cheese and, 111
sweet-hot, 73
toasted, 73
Nut oil, 112

O

Oatmeal, hot, *44–45*, 44–45
Oatmeal cookies
chocolate chip, *424–425*,
424–425
peanut butter, 425
raisin, 425
Oats, *207. See also* Oatmeal
cookies
in granola and muesli, *46–
47*, 46–47
oatmeal, hot, *44–45*,
44–45
Oil(s). *See also* Olive oil
basics, 112
deep frying in, *37*, 37, *104*
flavoring, *362*
pantry staples, 2
pasta with garlic and, *174–
175*, 174–175
sautéing in, *28*, 28
testing, *261, 278*
Olive(s)
in antipasto platter, 76, *77*
as bruschetta topping,
92, 93
in chicken, braised, Mediterranean style, 324–
325, *325*
compound butter, 237
as fridge staple, 4
Greek salad, tossed, 111
in nachos platter, 76

in Niçoise salade, tradi-
tional, 131
pasta with, 175
pitting, *431*
in potato salad, Mediterranean, 130–131, *131*
puttanesca sauce, 180
in quesadillas, 97
salmon roasted with
thyme and, 357
in vinaigrette, 115
Olive oil, 2, 112
dip, warm, cooked vegeta-
bles with, 75
dip, warm, crudités with,
74–75, 74–75
pasta with garlic and, *174–
175*, 174–175
Omelet, cheese, *58–59*,
58–59
Onion(s)
in beef kabobs, grilled or
broiled, *272*, 272–273
caramelized, *232–233*,
232–233
caramelized, bruschetta
topping, 92
chopping, *19*, 19
cooking methods, 217
creamed, 233
eggs, baked, with cheese
and, *62–63*, 62–63
as pantry staple, 4
pickled, 89
in pork chops with apples,
skillet, 290–291, *291*
and potato soup, creamy,
163
Orange
chicken, braised, with
chile and, 325
cream smoothie, 49
Orecchiette with broccoli and
sausage, 182–183, *183*
Oregano
pork stew with white wine
and, 295

Rosemary
  potatoes, -roasted, 224–225, *225*
  pot roast with tomato sauce, 281
  tomato sauce with, fresh or dried, 180
  white bean spread with lemon and, 87
Ruler, 8, *9*
Russet potatoes, 225, *235*
Rutabagas, cooking methods, 235, 241, 243, 245
  with olive oil dip, warm, 75

S

Saffron
  in chicken and rice, *326–327*, 326–327
  in risotto with butter and Parmesan, *202–203*, 202–203
Sage, tomato sauce with, fresh or dried, 180
Salad(s), 106-133. *See also* Coleslaw
  black bean, Southwestern, 123
  BLT, 133
  bread, Lebanese (Fattoush), 127
  bread, tomato, mozzarella and, *126–127*, 126–127
  Caesar, *118–119*, 118–119
  celery, shaved, 129
  chicken, *336–337*, 336–337
  chickpea, curried, *122–123*, 122–123
  chickpea, curried, with greens, 123
  chickpea, curried, with rice or grains, 123
  chopped, *116–117*, 116–117
  fennel, shaved, *128–129*, 128–129
  Niçoise, traditional salade, 131

potato, American style, 131
potato, Mediterranean, *130–131*, 130–131
spinach, warm, with bacon, *132–133*, 132–133
tabbouleh, *124–125*, 124–125
tabbouleh, couscous, 125
tossed, with fruit, cheese, and nuts, 111
tossed Greek, 111
tossed green, *110–111*, 110–111
tossed green, with Asian flavors, 111
tossed green, poached eggs on, 57
turkey, *336–337*, 336–337
vegetable, shaved, 129
Salad dressing
  Asian flavors, tossed green salad with, 111
  bacon, warm, *132–133*, 132–133
  blue cheese, 318, *319*
  Caesar, *118–119*, 119
  coconut milk in, *122*
  oil and vinegar for, 112–113
  vinaigrette in a jar, *114–115*, 114–115
  vinaigrette, simple, *110*
Salade Niçoise, traditional, 131
Salad greens
  basics, *108–109*, 108–109
  dressing, *111*
Salad spinner, 8, *9*
Salami
  in antipasto platter, 76, *77*
  as bruschetta topping, 92
Salmon, *347*
  burgers, grilled or broiled, 373
  cakes, 103
  roasted, with butter, *356–357*, 356–357
  roasted, herb-, 357

roasted with olives and thyme, 357
Salsa
  bruschetta topping, 92
  fresh
    apple, 82
    citrus, 82
    cucumber, 82
    jícama, 82, *83*
    peach, 82
    pepper, 82
    pineapple, 82, *83*
    plum, 82
    radish, 82
    tomatillo (green), *82–83*, 82
    tomato, *80–81*, 80–81
  in nachos platter, 76
  in scrambled eggs, 53
Salt, 2, 12, *395*
Salty ingredients, 12
Sandwich(es)
  cheese, grilled, *388–389*, 388–389
  cheese, grilled, big-batch, 389
  cutting bread for, *382*
  fillings, 382
  sausage and peppers for, *288*, 288–289
Sandwich bread, honey-wheat, 411
Sandwich cookies, jam, 427
Sandwich loaf, simple, *410–411*, 410–411
Sardines, in chopped salad, 117
Sauce(s). *See also* Salsa; Tomato sauce
  balsamic, chicken cutlets with, 313
  barbecue, *296*, 296
  barbecue, Asian style, 297
  blue cheese, 318, *319*
  cashew, cold noodles with, 193
  pan, quick, chicken cutlets with, *312–313*, 313

pan, seared scallops with, *366–367*, 366–367
pasta water in, 173, *174*
peanut, cold noodles with, *192–193*, 192–193
pesto, whole wheat pasta with, *184–185*, 184–185
sesame, cold noodles with, 193
tartar, panfried trout with, 358–359, *359*
thickness, testing, *193*
Sauerkraut, pork chops with, skillet, 291
Sausage(s), 284
  breakfast, browning, 43
  as bruschetta topping, 92
  in calzone, 416
  in cheese omelet, 59
  doneness, *288*
  and grapes, 289
  lentil soup, meaty, 147
  in lentils with spinach, Spanish-style, *256–257*, 256–257
  in minestrone, hearty, 143
  paella with chicken and, 204–205, *205*
  pasta with broccoli and, 182–183, *183*
  pasta with vegetables and, 183
  and peppers, *288*, 288–289
  with spinach salad, warm, 133
  varieties of, *289*, 289
Sautéed mushrooms, *230–231*, 230–231
Sautéing technique, 28, *28*
Scallions
  in crudités, 75
  in miso soup, *144–145*, 144–145
  in nachos platter, 76
  preparing, *295*
  in scrambled eggs, 53
  tabbouleh, 124–125, *125*

cabbage with ginger, *222–223*, 222–223
cabbage, Mediterranean style, 223
cabbage, Thai style, 223
chicken with broccoli, *310–311*, 310–311
chicken with vegetables, 311
fried rice, *200–201*, 200–201
with noodles, *191*, 191, 271
pork, with greens, *286*, 286–287
shrimp with celery, *364–365*, 364–365
shrimp with vegetables, 365
Thai-style noodles with shrimp, 194-195, *194-195*
Stir-frying technique, *29*, 29
Stock
bones and trimmings for, 156
chicken, 154–155, 156
chicken, more flavorful, 155
fish, 156
meat, 156
as pantry staple, 4
from roasted ingredients, *157*
seasonings for, 156
shrimp, quick, *364*
turkey, 156
vegetable, full-flavored, *152–153*, 152–153
Stockpot, 6, *7*
Storage containers, *2, 3*
Stovetop pudding, *436–437*, 436–437
Straciatella (egg drop soup), 159
with greens, 159
Strainer, 8, *9*
Strawberry-vanilla smoothie, 49

Stuffed mushrooms, *100–101*, 100–101
Stuffed mushrooms with nutty bread crumbs, 101
Stuffing in a pan, *340*, 340
Sugar, *423*, 423
as pantry staple, 4
"Sweating" vegetables, *28*, *162*
Sweeter corn bread, 397
Sweet-hot nuts, 73
Sweet potato(es)
cooking methods, 219, 235, 243, 247, 249
fritters, *104–105*, 104–105
garlicky, *240–241*, 240–241
garlicky, with bacon, 241
grating, *240*
mashed, 235
with olive oil dip, warm, 75
pancakes, 249

T

Tabbouleh, *124–125*, 124–125
couscous, 125
Tacos
beef, *392–393*, 392–393
fillings and garnishes for, 393
seafood, 393
shaping shells, *392*
Tahini
in hummus with pita, *86–87*, 86–87
sesame sauce, cold noodles with, 193
Tandoori-style grilled or broiled split chicken, 335
Tangy deviled eggs, 95
Tartar sauce, panfried trout with, 358–359, *359*
Tatsoi, 217
Teriyaki-style chicken, grilled or broiled, 321
Thai style
cabbage, stir-fried, 223

noodles with shrimp, *194–195*, 194–195
shrimp burgers, grilled or broiled, 373
Thanksgiving dinner
gravy, *341*, 341
stuffing in a pan, *340*, 340
timing of, 341
turkey, roast, *338–339*, 338–339
Thermometers, 8, *9, 274*
Thyme
salmon roasted with olives and, 357
in tomato sauce with fresh or dried herbs, 180, *181*
Toast(s), 385
bread salad, tomato, mozzarella and, *126–127*, 126–127
bruschetta, *90*, 90–91, *91*
bruschetta toppings, 92, *93*
crostini, 91
croutons, *384–385*, 384–385
croutons, garlicky, 385
croutons, seasoned, 385
eggs in the hole, 55
French toast, *64–65*, 64–65
poached eggs on, 57
Toasted bread crumbs, 387
Toasting
bread, *90, 126, 384*
grains, *164, 198, 208*
nuts, 73
spices, 13, *13*
Tofu
hot and sour soup, 166–167, *167*
miso soup, *144–145*, 144–145
pad Thai, almost, 195
types of, 4
Tomatillo salsa (green), *82–83*, 82

Tomato(es). *See also* Cherry tomatoes; Tomato sauce
-basil steamed mussels or clams, 371
beans with, quick skillet, *252–253*, 252–253
BLT Salad, 133
broiled, *34, 226–227*, 226–227
bruschetta topping, 92, *93*
canned, 2
chicken, braised, Mediterranean style, *31, 324–325*, 324–325
coring and cutting, *80–81*
with eggs, baked, 63
gazpacho, *138–139*, 138–139
green, 245
grilled, *226–227*, 226–227
in guacamole, 85
in minestrone, *142–143*, 142–143
mozzarella, and bread salad, 126–127, *127*
omelet filling, 59
paella, vegetarian, with lots of, 205
ratatouille, steamed fish with, *354–355*, 354–355
salsa, fresh, *80–81*, 80–81
shrimp, garlic, with cilantro and, 363
slicing, *226*
soup, 140–141, *141*
soup, cream of, 141
soup, hearty, 141
soup, spiced, 141
in tabbouleh, 124–125, *125*
Tomato paste, cooking, *140*
Tomato sauce
bruschetta topping, 92
cheesy, 180, *181*
for freezer, 179
fresh, 180
with herbs, fresh or dried, 180, *181*

Converting Measurements

Essential Conversions

Volume to Volume

3 teaspoons	1 tablespoon
4 tablespoons	¼ cup
5 tablespoons plus 1 teaspoon	⅓ cup
4 ounces	½ cup
8 ounces	1 cup
1 cup	½ pint
2 pints	1 quart
4 quarts	1 gallon

Volume to Weight

¼ cup liquid or fat	2 ounces
½ cup liquid or fat	4 ounces
1 cup liquid or fat	8 ounces
2 cups liquid or fat	1 pound
1 cup sugar	7 ounces
1 cup flour	5 ounces

Metric Approximations

Measurements

¼ teaspoon	1.25 milliliters
½ teaspoon	2.5 milliliters
1 teaspoon	5 milliliters
1 tablespoon	15 milliliters
1 fluid ounce	30 milliliters
¼ cup	60 milliliters
⅓ cup	80 milliliters
½ cup	120 milliliters
1 cup	240 milliliters
1 pint (2 cups)	480 milliliters
1 quart (4 cups)	960 milliliters (0.96 liters)
1 gallon (4 quarts)	3.84 liters
1 ounce (weight)	28 grams
¼ pound (4 ounces)	114 grams
1 pound (16 ounces)	454 grams
2.2 pounds	1 kilogram (1,000 grams)
1 inch	2.5 centimeters

Oven Temperatures

Description	°Fahrenheit	°Celsius
Cool	200	90
Very slow	250	120
Slow	300–325	150–160
Moderately slow	325–350	160–180
Moderate	350–375	180–190
Moderately hot	375–400	190–200
Hot	400–450	200–230
Very hot	450–500	230–260